I0821410

ON DISTANT SERVICE

On Distant Service

THE LIFE OF THE FIRST U.S. FOREIGN SERVICE OFFICER TO BE ASSASSINATED

Susan M. Stein

Potomac Books
An imprint of the University of Nebraska Press

Library of Congress Cataloging-in-Publication Data
Names: Stein, Susan M. (Susan Margaret), 1942– author.
Title: On distant service: the life of the first U.S. foreign service officer to be assassinated / Susan M. Stein.
Description: [Lincoln, Nebraska]: Potomac Books, an imprint of the University of Nebraska Press, [2020] | Includes bibliographical references and index.
Identifiers: LCCN 2019041038
ISBN 9781640121942 (hardback)
ISBN 9781640123526 (epub)
ISBN 9781640123533 (mobi)
ISBN 9781640123540 (pdf)
Subjects: LCSH: Imbrie, Robert Whitney, 1884–1924. | Imbrie, Robert Whitney, 1884–1924—Assassination. | United States. Foreign Service—Biography. | Diplomats—United States—Biography. | Diplomatic and consular service—United States—History—20th century. | United States—Foreign relations—20th century.
Classification: LCC E748.I84 S74 2020 |
DDC 327.2092 [B]—dc23
LC record available at https://lccn.loc.gov/2019041038

Set in Arno Pro by Mikala R. Kolander.

To Hap

CONTENTS

ILLUSTRATIONS

ACKNOWLEDGMENTS

Above all, loving gratitude goes to my husband, Charles H. Stein. This book is dedicated to him, to Hap. And heartfelt thanks to the rest of the Stein family—Ed, Jane, Margaret, Paul, Amy, John, Maggie, and Michael—for giving Robert Imbrie a place at the family table.

My warm appreciation also goes to the many others who helped with this project, in particular Owen Gleeson, Agnes Hindemith, Marty Hosking, Chas Kestermeier SJ, Jim Lawrence, Kris Lawson, Dominic Longo, Mohammed Gholi Majd, Lt. Col. Tom McCann (Ret.), John P. Nelson, Jane O'Brien, Tom Pesek, Todd Peppers, Lee Smith, and Lt. Col. John Nagl (Ret.), whose support came at a crucial moment. Thank you, too, to Thomas Bailey, Katherine Joslin, and Michael Occleshaw for their careful reading and encouragement.

My gratitude also extends to Madalyn Chapman, web content creator; Don Doll SJ and Carol McCabe, Magis Productions, Creighton University; Dustin Hurt, senior graphic consultant; Marianne Meyer, AFS Foundation, Zurich, Switzerland; Kevin Morrow, Ab Initio Archives Research, Washington DC; Tamara Smith (Mrs. Robert I. Smith), widow of Robert Imbrie's namesake; Elizabeth Curtiss Smith and Robert I. Smith Jr., children of Robert Imbrie's namesake; the staffs at the Creighton University Reinert Library; Dr. C. C. and Mable L. Criss Library, University of Nebraska at Omaha; and Omaha Public Library, especially its Interlibrary Loan specialists; and, of special note, Elizabeth Gray and David A. Langbart of the National Archives and Records Administration. Finally, I am happily indebted to the team at the University of Nebraska Press, Potomac Books, including Tom Swanson, who championed my book, Abigail Stryker, Ann Baker, Sara Springsteen, Annie Shahan, and Tish Fobben, as well as copyeditor Jane Curran, cartographer Erin Greb, and all who helped convert my manuscript into a book.

I continue to ask for help: if there are errors in the book or materials regarding Robert Imbrie that would further advance his story, please contact me through my publisher or www.robertimbrie.com. I hope someone has his diary, despite his wife's directive to have it destroyed upon her death.

INTRODUCTION

January 11, 2012: A motorcycle weaves through Teheran's early morning traffic and pulls up sharply alongside a Peugeot 405.[1] A snap is heard as a magnetic bomb is attached to the car and the motorcycle speeds off, disappearing into the congestion. Moments later the bomb detonates, blowing apart the car. A nuclear scientist, Mostafa Ahmadi Roshan, is killed, one of five Iranian nuclear scientists murdered in separate incidents in Iran between 2010 and 2012. Iran blames Great Britain, the United States, France, Germany, and Israel for the murders.

That July Abdollah Ganji, the hardline managing director of *Javan Daily*, a publication dedicated to the Islamic Revolution, asked why in the face of these murders the talks were not suspended and reparations demanded. He wrote that "Iranians remember very well" two justified attacks on foreign embassies.[2] The first occurred in 1829 when Iranians stormed the Russian embassy in Teheran to rescue two Islamic women, killing the ambassador and thirty-four embassy employees. The second was in 1924 "in protest to the insulting behavior of a vice consul in the American embassy [whom the Iranian] people sent . . . to hell in Sheykh Hadi Street in Tehran." Harkening to these attacks, Abdollah Ganji lauded a recent storming of the British embassy with protestors chanting, "Death to England," "Death to America," "Death to Israel." Tolerance, he concluded, was "a naïve concept."

In Abdollah Ganji's invective, who was the American vice consul sent to hell? What prompted the assault? Who killed him?

What was America's response? Who in America knows of this incident that Iranians "remember very well"?

The first American foreign service officer to lose his life while serving his country was William Palfrey, lost at sea on the way to his post in 1780.[3] The first U.S. foreign service officer to die a violent death was Harris E. Fudger, consul at Santa Marta, Colombia, stabbed to death in an apparent robbery in 1826. The first to die a violent death for political reasons was Robert Whitney Imbrie, murdered in Teheran on July 18, 1924.

Of the first sixty deaths of Americans in the foreign service, only three men were murdered.[4] The others died from diseases, including typhoid, yellow fever, and cholera or from other causes such as earthquakes. In the early years of diplomacy the murder of foreign service officers was highly unusual, and from the point of precedent, any foreign service officer would have known the slim odds of a politically motivated death and felt safe.

I came upon Robert Imbrie's story in exploring another subject, no doubt a common redirection for researchers. Specifically I was looking into the life of Boake Carter, an early radio commentator and author, whose given name may have come from his father's posting in Baku, the capital of oil-rich Azerbaijan. Oil and the vast sweep of land then called the Near East led me to Imbrie, so that I approached his history from its conclusion, again probably a common occurrence for researchers.

The story of Robert Imbrie holds the elements of any good story—adventure, danger, suspense, conflict, romance, tragedy, a strong protagonist, and enduring significance. Unfortunately, Imbrie's story has been almost totally neglected. What exists spotlights his death. The primary documentation consists of government records, Imbrie's war memoir and travel writing, some letters, photographs, and newspaper and magazine articles. Little has been written about him in academic circles—a few articles, passing references, a chapter in one book, and a master's thesis. In some sources Imbrie is not named but referred to only as "an American vice-consul." The secondary sources concern his death, but understanding his death requires knowing who he was, how he came to his end, and how it shaped U.S. foreign policy in the Middle East.

There is another reason for attending to Robert Imbrie.

On September 11, 2012, eighty-nine years after Imbrie's death, the attack on the American mission in Benghazi, Libya, resulted in the death of Ambassador J. Christopher Stevens and three other Americans.[5] Both Imbrie's and Stevens's attacks raised questions about the reliability of information gathering and the ability to develop and maintain working relationships among nations. In the aftermath of these attacks, conflicting accounts immediately emerged. In broad strokes the attacks were seen as either spontaneous, led by religious extremists, or as planned in order to destroy an incipient democracy. In Imbrie's case postwar Persia was torn between a clericalism antithetical to democracy and political parties more interested in gaining power than in sharing it. Both Imbrie and Stevens were in countries whose futures were on the cusp of redefinition.

Both men had warnings about imminent danger. The last cable sent by the U.S. mission under Stevens's name contained concerns about security. The largest threat seemed to be from Al Qaeda, a presumption that distracted attention from the fractured militias that developed following the collapse of Muammar Gaddafi's government. Imbrie, too, arrived in the midst of a struggle for political control of a nation. Following a disastrous war, Persia had three choices for governance: a theocracy, a republic, or a dictatorship. Both men's deaths altered the trajectory of their host country's history. How great that alteration is in Libya is yet to be seen.

As their fateful days drew near, Stevens and Imbrie had warnings of attacks, but warnings that were vague as to the perpetrator and the target. Stevens knew that the American diplomatic mission was vulnerable; Imbrie was confident that his was not.

In Benghazi tension grew as the anniversary of the World Trade Center attack, September 11, neared; however, the day passed quietly in the American mission compound, although there were rumblings of disturbances caused by the airing of an inflammatory video. Nevertheless, by 9:30 p.m. the day's peace seemed assured. Fifteen minutes later the attack came.

In Imbrie's case an attack on a foreigner was expected in early August, so on his fateful day, July 18, Imbrie felt secure; further, he had no reason to believe a foreign service officer would be attacked. Having been to a picnic the night before, Imbrie set out in the late morning of July 18 to visit a bazaar with a companion. Within the hour he was a target on the run. In Libya Stevens could well have surmised his fate if trapped; in Persia Imbrie would not have suspected the brutality that descended on him. Both attacks had a religious element. Stevens's attack was at first attributed to the airing of a sacrilegious video, a theory later discredited; Imbrie came under threat at a recently enshrined fountain. Stevens's attack came in waves, as did Imbrie's. In both cases police failed to thwart the attacks. Stevens had a few guards come to his aid; Imbrie, separated from his companion, was on his own during the ordeal.

When the attack began in Benghazi, seven Americans were at the compound: Ambassador Stevens, information officer Sean Smith, and five American security guards. The attacks came throughout the night and predawn hours. Early on Stevens, Smith, and a guard locked themselves in a safe room in the main building of the compound; tragically it was soon engulfed in fire and smoke. When the battle was over, four Americans were dead—Stevens and Smith, from smoke inhalation, and security officers Tyrone S. Woods and Glen A. Doherty, from enemy fire.

Trying to determine what happened in Libya and what the U.S. response should be has delayed justice. After Benghazi, much attention and blame were dealt to the role that the Department of State and the CIA played in the tragedy rather than to those who killed the Americans. Eighty-five years after Imbrie's death, few Americans know the vice consul's name, much less the circumstances of his death. It is my hope that this book will rectify the neglect of Imbrie's life and sacrifice and provide background for reflecting on how better to address assaults on American foreign officers serving their country from abroad.

Imbrie and Stevens believed in the essential goodness of the common people in the posts where they served. Neither sought to change the culture of a country. Both took offense at perceived slights to Islam. Both had high hopes that the United States could establish good relations with their host country. Both deserve justice.

ON DISTANT SERVICE

ONE

In Search of an Orbit

On February 24, 1897, in Washington DC, winter gave way to promises of spring. The temperature was mild, in the forties, and spirits were high. Preparations were well underway for the March 4 inauguration of William McKinley, the twenty-fifth president of the United States and the last of the Civil War era. The Committee for the Balls, said to be working earnestly, with fidelity and endeavor, expected their net profit to benefit seventeen hospitals and orphanages. In some quarters complaints were being registered that "Hail to the Chief" was feeble and disagreeable, not as stirring as the "Marseillaise" or "Die Wacht An Rhein." Surely the new president deserved something better. As the hustle and bustle of Washington DC paused for dinner, lamplighters made their way down the streets. All lights had to be lit by 6:58, an hour after sunset. They would be extinguished by 5:47 the next morning. The world was changing. Soon a new century would turn the calendar leaf. Despite the efforts for a grand inauguration, the luster of the Gilded Age was dimming and the old order dying.

In one household, the fevered activity attending the presidential festivities was ignored. There, attention was focused on a mortally ill Civil War veteran, Jeremiah Rankin Imbrie, age fifty-seven. For eight weeks he had been cared for at his brother-in-law's home, but to no avail. By the end of the day his only child, Robert Whitney Imbrie, would be an orphan. Young Imbrie had lost his mother, Leila Whitney Imbrie, to tuberculosis six years earlier. During the intervening years, father and son had drawn on their close relationship for strength, and as his health declined, Jeremiah had planned for his boy's future.[1] He owned 373 acres of land in Charles County, Maryland, and three houses in Washington DC, although none of the property was worth much. He had named Leila's sister, Mary Ophelia Fishbaugh, beneficiary of his Civil War pension, and she, together with her husband, Charles, had agreed to take in Robert. They themselves had only one child, Paul, four years older than Robert and already like a brother to his younger cousin. Charles was a coal merchant and an active member of the New York Avenue Presbyterian Church, the church that Lincoln had regularly attended. Jeremiah trusted that the Fishbaughs would care for Robert as their own, and his trust was rewarded.

Young Imbrie's life was privileged, and he earned a good education. The Fishbaughs lived in a stately three-story house with rose-colored stone and rounded arches, at 1701 Q Street NW, not far from DuPont Circle.[2] Imbrie attended the Friends Select School, Central High School, and George Washington University, where he earned his AB in 1902 and his LLB in 1905.[3] Upon his graduation the *Washington Times* noted that he was "a well-known man and popular with a large circle of the student element."[4] He was rugged in build, with long arms and big hands.[5] He stood 5'9" with blue-gray eyes and a high forehead. His hair fell casually from a left part with a hint of youthful insouciance.

In the autumn Imbrie enrolled in Yale's graduate law degree program.[6] He joined a class of fifteen students, a diverse group representing twelve universities, seven states, the District of Columbia, the Philippine Islands, and Japan. Well-liked, Imbrie was chosen to write the class history for the *Yale Shingle*, which he sprinkled with lighthearted asides: "The average age of the class is twenty-five, and the average height 5 feet 8¾ inches."[7] Five of the graduates were about Imbrie's age—he had just turned twenty-three; the rest were older, seeking advanced accreditation. One was already a judge; others were practicing lawyers.

Imbrie relished Yale, perhaps because for the first time he was on his own. His year at Kent Hall was lived exuberantly—water balloons tossed out windows, sashes thrown up for hearty yelling at passersby, comradery shared over drinks, pipes, stogies, and dream sticks (cigarettes), strolls down Chapel Street accompanied by raucous singing, local "femmes" courted, and pride in Yale's football team firmly embedded. The exuberance was balanced with and enhanced by serious work—the demanding mortgages class and examination month left lasting impressions—and like students everywhere and at all times, Imbrie thought standards relaxed when, after he left, a 200-page book replaced the 1,700-page book he had used. When he learned his fraternity, Bones and Gavel, might be subsumed into a national fraternity, he baulked. Again a common student proviso: nothing at the alma mater should change. After graduation Imbrie kept up with his many acquaintances, and when he forgot names, he chided himself, "I'd make a good politician, wouldn't I?" Later, when he had his inherited land in Maryland surveyed and platted, he named one street after Yale.[8]

In the 1906 annual Imbrie drolly described himself as having "in mind a seat on the United States Supreme Bench [but had] so far refused all honors." Single, "he hope[d] to reform." Imbrie's class summary illustrates the ease with which he leavened the factual with the facetious, as he did throughout his career, even when reporting in the midst of war or when evading Soviet agents.

Imbrie's Yale thesis was on admiralty law, a topic he considered "a live and open one."[9] Although the more common topic of study was the rapidly consolidating railroad companies, Imbrie looked to the open seas, signaling his free spirit. His studies prepared him well for his State Department work. He became a careful reader, digesting court decisions, the law's far reach to both coastal and inland states, and material about territorial squabbles spanning two hundred years. His thesis ended with a flourish typical of early twentieth-century prose: "After centuries of struggle, caused by the jealousy of other courts, after persecution lasting for years and striking to the very root of its existence, after overcoming prejudice and tradition, after fighting against and overpowering statutes and judicial law, and after surmounting difficulties unparalleled in the history of any existing court, admiralty has, in what no one will deny was a good fight well fought, conquered and has today come unto its own."[10] In using terms such as "struggle," "persecution," "fighting," "fought," and "conquered," Imbrie revealed his worldview: what was worth having was worth fighting for and defending. Complacency was not in his vocabulary.

Not surprisingly, Imbrie felt footloose after his graduation. He did not accompany the Fishbaughs to their summer cottage in Harper's Ferry,[11] but he headed with a classmate, Felix Harold Schmitt, called Hal, to the rugged West—Colorado, New Mexico, and Arizona. There they hiked, fished, and camped. Imbrie also purchased souvenirs, which became a lifelong practice. One purchase, a Navajo blanket, is still in the possession of Schmitt's descendants.[12] Imbrie's friendship with Schmitt lasted a lifetime, evident in their correspondence and in Schmitt's naming his son after Imbrie, a full seven years after Imbrie's death. For Schmitt the trip bridged school and career; for Imbrie it sparked enduring wanderlust.

At summer's end Schmitt boarded a train for his home in Chicago, and Imbrie headed to New York City without firm plans, but with his "mental gun loose in his holster" to scour opportunities.[13] As a port city, New York was a natural selection for an admiralty attorney. Housing, though, was scarce. Before finding an apartment with "gobs of room," Imbrie climbed enough stairs to make "a spiral passage up Pike's Peak" and exhausted his "ration of cuss words." In a surprisingly modern construct, Imbrie wrote that his search had been "a glorious sport—not." Finding work proved even more difficult.

With no job, Imbrie lacked direction.[14] He spent the autumn preparing for the New York bar examination and, in the spirit of admiralty law, studying navigation at the New York Nautical School, which trained merchant marine cadets.[15] Although Imbrie's name does not appear in its records, it is possible that he was tutored by one of its professors between the end of the school's annual voyage and the first part of the new term. He facetiously commented that he was "thinking about getting a pair of wide bottomed trousers and learning to chew tobacco." He also took classes for a first aid certificate, which he said would allow him to "solder up vertebrae and reorganize the spinal duplex," and he began tinkering with motorcycles over which he claimed to be "plum doty."[16] These dalliances played into his future—rugged ocean and overland trips and activities requiring medical and mechanical skills in remote regions—and disclosed his yearning to be elsewhere, wherever that was. He toyed with visiting the Congo Free State or Nicaragua, but in the summer of 1907 he settled for a more conventional tour of Europe.

Imbrie budgeted $200 to $240 for his four-month trip.[17] Schmitt declined to join him; he had a corporate job. Imbrie went alone. The trip began poorly. On the crossing he was as "sick as the devil." His poor luck continued. In some cities he got horribly lost. In two cities he got into late night brawls. He knew no one and was lonely. He spent a few days with a French girl in Rotterdam but was lonelier than ever when she left. In Venice he met an English girl, but that, too, was a passing flirtation.

Imbrie's itinerary took him from Amsterdam to Cologne, Basel, and Lucerne, then through Italy from Milan to Naples, to Monte Carlo and Marseilles, by boat to Barcelona via Algiers and thence to Paris. With poor language skills, he was "worrying all the time." By August he had visited Ireland and was in England; without a language barrier, he enjoyed four or five weeks of bicycling in the countryside and two weeks in London, although he found Oxford gloomy and dull, with "a beastly lot of regulations," unlike Yale.[18] Despite the setbacks the trip proved valuable for Imbrie, opening doors to places he would revisit time and again. More importantly, although he did not come easily to being alone and never courted solitude, he learned self-sufficiency. He quickly became adept at travel.

Back in New York, Imbrie considered opening a law practice in Nevada or Oklahoma, neither good for admiralty law, one might add, but postponed his decision in favor of deer hunting and visiting the Jamestown Exposition, a celebration of the town's three-hundredth anniversary.[19] The short delay proved rewarding. In October he was offered the job of attorney-in-charge at the Seamen's Branch of the New York Legal Aid Society, earning $1,100 a year.[20] The office was at 1 Broadway, opposite the newly opened Customs House. Nearby were the principal consulates of the world—there were at least forty-five consulates in New York City at the time—and various departments of immigration. The proximity of the consulates and the foreign service officers, immigrants, and sailors from around the world prepared him for the bustling, eclectic world of his future State Department work. Most importantly, he learned the value of listening to the common man. As a consular officer in later years, his reports relied on his ability to rub shoulders in pubs and coffee houses, to sit down with merchants and to engage disaffected people, far from the rarified world of power and prestige that was his home in name.

Imbrie joined the Legal Aid Society in its twentieth anniversary year. In that time it had handled 250,000 cases. Each branch had about fifteen lawyers, who took no outside work during their tenure. The office was open six days a week and charged a retainer fee of ten cents to those who could afford it. The annual expenses of the Legal Aid Society totaled about $28,000.[21]

Imbrie's job meant tackling up to two hundred cases a month, with only two assistants. He wondered if he was up to the challenge. There was no one to ask for advice—he was starting at the top—and he claimed to know "about as much of the Federal Courts as [he] did about the head waters of the Orinoco."[22] Nevertheless, he planned to give it a go. The pay was good, and the job would provide invaluable experience for a nascent dream, opening a law practice.[23] He began thinking of settling down. He even considered "popping the question" to his current flame in December. Nothing came of that. By January he was writing to Schmitt that he was "jolly lonesome," the wedding proposal seemingly an anodyne to loneliness rather than a declaration of love.[24]

To Imbrie, New York was "a tough old town."[25] And it was, especially for sailors. Their prestige was so low that merely wearing their uniform on land invited abuse. They were easy targets for shanghaiing by "crimps" who put off in launches from Staten Island, boarded vessels, and seized unwilling sailors, earning $20 a head from ship captains. In addition, "land sharks" and shipmasters defrauded the sailors of their wages. When the Legal Aid Society was founded, sailors in New York were being defrauded of $500,000 a year.[26] Besides kidnapping and fraud, the annals of the Society reveal other dire deeds, even murder. A polite but harrowing note received at the office read, "If my husband is not on the ship when it docks, please arrest the captain for murder." Fortunately, the sailor arrived, alive.

When Imbrie joined the Seaman's Branch, maritime law was on the verge of great change. In the midst of labor struggles the seaman's lot was the last vestige of condoned slavery in America. One of Imbrie's cases, argued in U.S. District Court, illustrates the disadvantages that seamen faced. In England Thomas Murray had signed on for a voyage of two years or less aboard a British ship, the *Ucayali*. He had sailed from Liverpool and, when he reached New York, fell to arguing with the mate. At the time he was due $43.96 in wages. The captain told him that, according to his contract, if he left the ship in New York, he would be entitled to only five shillings a month. Murray rejected the captain's claim, left the ship, and signed on another. He was marked a deserter, and his wages were paid into the British Board of Trade. Bypassing the British consulate, Murray appealed to the Seamen's Branch for help. When the British consul learned of the case, he moved to have it thrown out. The district judge dismissed the motion, and the case went to trial, in itself a victory for Imbrie and Murray, given the prestige of the British consulate. However, it was a weak case. When Murray claimed that he had not understood the articles that he signed, the judge ruled that Murray was nevertheless responsible for understanding them. Likewise, since the ship and sailor were British, the judge ruled that Murray should have appealed to the British consul before appealing to the U.S. courts. Although the U.S. courts had jurisdiction over some cases, such as extreme cruelty, even when protested by the British consul, Murray's case did not apply.[27] He had not been dismissed nor had he been treated with great cruelty, two conditions for the courts to consider in a case against a consul's objections. Murray and Imbrie lost the case.[28]

Despite the loss the case held merit. Seven years later it would have been won. A central tenet of the U.S. Seamen's Act of 1915 allowed any sailor to depart at any port at the rate of half his earnings to date, a corrective to such cases as Murray's.[29] Before this reform ship owners could force sailors to stay on board by withholding wages or underpaying. After 1915 seamen gained the freedom to walk away from a job with wages earned, a right practically guaranteed at the time to land workers. Likewise, when Murray contested that he did not understand the articles he had signed, the judge noted that *parol* evidence could not change a written contract unless fraud was established, but it is possible, even probable, that Murray did not understand the agreement, given the level of literacy of most seamen and the self-interest of agents rounding them up. Further, in language that would have aided Murray in his case, the Act of 1915 thoroughly spelled out stipulations to foreign vessels.[30] For example, a U.S. customs agent could prevent a ship from departing until it complied with U.S. federal law. Unfortunately, in the *Ucayali* case the conflict between British and American jurisdiction conspired against Murray: "there would seem to be no breach of contract or violation of [Murray's] rights . . . according to the terms of the laws of Great Britain as they must be applied in a case of the present sort," wrote the judge. Imbrie had put up a good fight and, in his words, was learning "the tricks of the [legal] trade," but he was becoming disillusioned.[31]

His summer vacation of 1908, spent in the Adirondacks, magnified the "damned horrid grind" of the Seaman's Branch when he returned.[32] Further, his dream of a law practice was ripening. He cut his year's service short and moved home to Washington DC. By December he had opened an office in Baltimore.[33]

Baltimore had multiple attractions. Imbrie had relatives there, he was close to Washington DC, it was a port city, good for admiralty law and less expensive than New York, and he had begun to think of entering politics.[34] He continued handling cases for the Legal Aid Society, Seaman's Branch.[35] His stationery read Admiralty Proctor.

Over the next few years he dabbled in patent law, the stock market, real estate, and timber projects. He considered corporate law.[36] Nothing went swimmingly. He wrote that "for a burnt match," he would chuck the "whole bally [law] business."[37] He didn't. Not yet.

In the summer of 1910 Imbrie went on another European tour, the finest trip so far, he judged. His companion was Herbert C. Hengstler, who had whetted Imbrie's interest in consular work in 1907 by suggesting a job in Abyssinia and then delayed Imbrie's entry to the Department of State by detailing why it was a poor prospect.[38] Hengstler had graduated from George Washington University with Imbrie while working at the Department of State, first as a stenographer. In 1908, at age thirty-one, he became the first principal of the consular school.[39] When Imbrie sat for the consular exam in 1917, Hengstler was the school's administrator. Imbrie thought him "the best fellow on earth."[40] The trip was a success, but afterward Imbrie felt as he had following his summer in the Adirondacks, "confounded restless." He considered "pulling out for parts unknown"—Canada, the Philippines, or Alaska.[41] He was in the doldrums. Four years after his Yale graduation, he considered himself a success—at failure.

Imbrie also thought he was failing in not marrying. It seemed an expected step for a young man, like a college degree. His cousin Paul had married, and Imbrie had been his best man. But whom should he marry? In 1910 Imbrie courted a young woman from Nashville, Tennessee, a millionaire's daughter. She had several maids. She had her own automobile. She had a chauffeur. To Imbrie, theirs was an impossible alliance: "She is willing to give all this up or so she believes but she doesn't and can't realize what all this would mean and I think it cruel to allow her to do it. How on earth she ever came to care for me is one of those things that 'passeth all understanding,' it's inexplicable."[42] His lament went on. For Imbrie, only a lack of money stood between him and this prospect. His estimated law earnings for that year—$500. The relationship languished.

Despite the disappointments in love and the law, Imbrie had good times. He went to Yale football games and fraternity reunions; he met up with Schmitt, though not as often as both wanted; he made friends in Baltimore. Throughout this period he shared his office with an attorney who became a lifelong friend, Howard McCormick, son of a retired admiral.[43] He became a member of the Baltimore Athletic Club and the Maryland Country Club and began moving in Democratic circles.[44] In objection to the Prohibition movement, he joined the Anti-Amendment League.[45] Later, when Imbrie applied to the State Department in the spring of 1917, he used his Baltimore political contacts as references.

Ultimately, however, Imbrie did not find satisfaction in lawyering. He had earned academic degrees, was economically self-sufficient, and was doing productive work, but he wanted more. The records speak of his being restless, but restlessness can also express a desire for purpose on a larger than local stage. He later told an acquaintance that he wanted "a roving career."[46]

In 1911 Imbrie took another extended trip, as if he were testing the waters for an alternate occupation. He turned his practice over to McCormick and headed to Africa for seven months. Africa was much in the air. Imbrie had had a chance to join Theodore Roosevelt's safari of 1909–10 but had not moved fast enough to seize it.[47] Roosevelt's subsequent book, *African Game Trails*, published in August 1910 and reprinted the same month, was enormously popular.[48]

Another African popularizer that may have influenced Imbrie was Ida Vera Simonton, who in 1906–7 traveled with an expedition headed by a self-taught pseudo-scientist, Richard Garner. When Simonton joined Garner, she was on the run to avoid being subpoenaed in the murder trial of a roué. The African trip was life-changing for her. On her return Simonton became a vigorous opponent of African colonialism and an equally forceful supporter of women's rights, working "at a frenetic pace to gain attention and allies."[49] She gave lectures at schools and social clubs, wrote newspaper articles, and organized public events to promote media attention.

Part of the reason for Simonton's activism lies with her expedition leader, Richard Garner.[50] Twenty-two years her senior, Garner had gone to Africa to learn Simian language. He thought he could talk to the animals. Garner proposed making Simonton the queen of West African clans warring against their French oppressors. He hoped that the resulting publicity would attract funding for his research. Once in Africa, however, Simonton broke away from Garner and his fantastical plan and aligned with a succession of government officials, missionaries, and traders before returning home.

In 1911 Garner planned another safari to West Africa. Imbrie hastily signed on, perhaps recalling his lost opportunity with Roosevelt and doubtless unaware of just how strange his host was.

Not surprisingly Imbrie found the sixty-three-year-old Garner a curious bird. Garner considered Africans naturally inferior to whites, yet he relied on African hunters, traders, and workers for his safety and success. He believed apes ranked just below man on the evolutionary ladder, yet he captured and transported them under horrendous conditions, knowing few could survive an ocean voyage. He doted on his pet chimpanzee, Suzie, yet he sold her to a zoo to support his travels.

Throughout his various careers Garner's every effort was imperiled, beginning in 1862 when he joined the Confederacy at age fourteen. After the war he had tried various professions, eventually settling on an interest in evolution and, in particular, apes. He began publishing essays in the very popular *McClure's Magazine* and in 1892 published *The Speech of Monkeys*, in which he claimed that "animal languages could be deciphered through observation and phonographic recordings."[51] He dreamed of becoming a respected scientist and through his connection with publisher Samuel McClure was able to fund his first trip to Africa.

When that trip failed to prove his claim, Garner became a laughingstock. Not easily defeated, he returned to Gabon on two extended trips, and in 1909 he brought Suzie home with him. With her at his side, he became a media sensation, partially recovering his reputation. He even won over a former critic, William Hornaday, the director of the New York Zoological Society, who had been trying unsuccessfully to get a gorilla for his zoo since 1905. What Hornaday needed was "a real live gorilla of size sufficiently large to compel both admiration and awe," a crowd-pleaser.[52] In 1911 Hornaday hired Garner to return to Africa. Here was Imbrie's opportunity.[53]

How Garner and Imbrie met is conjecture. Imbrie may have attended one of Garner's lectures in Washington DC in early 1911. Regardless of how the two men connected, they became travel companions, and Imbrie's taste for the exotic burgeoned. Garner, a self-promoter, may have also influenced Imbrie to try travel writing. He and Imbrie supposedly coauthored a monograph of their trip, which is now lost, and after the African trip Imbrie considered circumnavigating the globe in six or seven weeks, filing stories for newspapers, with membership in the Royal Geographic Society in London and the National Geographic Society in Washington DC to provide gravitas.[54] To Imbrie, the Garner expedition was the stuff of dime novels, "a sure cure for ennui." Africa was "the land of adventure" and Gabon its "most mysterious and enticing" part.

In 1911 Gabon was part of French Equatorial Africa, and the first challenge for the Garner expedition was acquiring gunpowder. As a white hunter, Imbrie had access to it, but natives of the Congolese territories were legally banned from procuring gunpowder, ammunition, and firearms, all of which were necessary for the expedition, including gunpowder to trade for gorillas.[55] To bypass the decree, Garner secured a letter of introduction from former secretary of state and current senator of New York Elihu Root; he suggested it be sent to Imbrie's office.[56]

When Imbrie sailed from New York on April 12, Schmitt came from Chicago to see him off, marking how extraordinary African travel was. Again, Imbrie was sick for most of the crossing and arrived in Cherbourg "all in."[57] He met Garner in Paris, and on April 25 they sailed for Africa aboard a five-thousand-tonnage passenger ship, *L'Afrique*, headed to Cape Lopez. At about thirteen knots, the liner skirted the Spanish coast and headed south, reaching on April 30 Tenerife in the Canary Islands, which Imbrie found "too remote for the tourist element [and therefore] unconventional and mighty interesting."[58] At Cape Lopez the explorers went by steamer up the Ogooue River to Fernan Vaz Lake and from there to Bongo on foot or by canoe. In a letter to Schmitt Imbrie estimated that they had trekked five hundred miles inland and concluded that "marching in Africa is no recreation for a young ladies school." He claimed it was the hardest work he had ever done or was expected to do. For two months they were without adequate supplies, eating bananas and kank, a root meal steamed in plantain leaves. He contracted a water-borne disease, made more miserable by a muscle strain in his groin. The experience, he wrote, was "quite lively." In writing to Schmitt, Imbrie signed off dramatically: Hengstler at the Department of State would know if he "croaked."

Despite discomfort and danger, Imbrie was delighted to be on African soil. The big game hunting was good. Small game, too. He shot elephants and iguanas, downplaying his prowess, writing that having "two tons of meat charging at you" encourages straight-shooting.[59] Garner wrote that Imbrie "within less than one minute killed 2 running buffalo and as [we] came up from Fernan Vaz he killed 2 hippo in three shots within less than 20 minutes."[60] Given the number of specimens that Theodore Roosevelt killed—512 big animals—this feat may not be an exaggeration.

Meanwhile Garner's goal, trapping a gorilla, eluded him. He bemoaned that gorillas were scarce and in high demand.[61] On July 13 Garner reported they had been marching for fifteen days, without success. He became increasingly discouraged.[62] But his woeful letters seem manipulative, designed to prepare Hornaday for disappointment or, more likely, to magnify his ultimate success, against all odds. In one letter he wrote that he planned "to keep shuffling and cutting until I turn up a Jack if there is one in the deck."[63]

In mid-July the men marched seventeen miles in what Garner called the "most severe task" he had undergone.[64] Afterward they took cold baths, ate, and slept nine hours. Imbrie, he reported, was no more than a "bit foot-sore." And then a week later, hooray! Garner wrote an ecstatic letter that he had secured a "fine, young, female gorilla" about nine or ten months old and weighing about thirty pounds.[65] He estimated the cost of getting her to New York at $140. Unfortunately, their return was delayed a month by a porter's revolt deep in the interior.[66] The wait probably weakened the gorilla. Although Garner achieved his goal, shortly after arriving in New York, the gorilla died.

Meanwhile Imbrie extended his travels for an extra month, stopping in Monrovia, Liberia, to visit the president, Arthur Barclay, and eventually reaching Hamburg and arriving in New York on October 11. To Imbrie Africa had been "more like a dreamland than a reality." Later, during the Great War, Imbrie recounted details of his safari, describing how Garner locked himself in a gorilla cage and how he had claimed to know twenty words of gorilla talk. Imbrie believed it was "all rot," and since the "monkeys knew more than the professor," he had gone off by himself to hunt.[67] He brought back several mementos from his trip. Three items—a chief's ceremonial staff, a rattle, and a paddle—now reside in the Smithsonian.

Back in Baltimore, Imbrie resumed his law practice. In April 1912 he served as best man at Schmitt's wedding to Lilian Wyley, held in a garden with orange blossoms and lilies of the valley; the ladies' gowns were decorated with crystal and gold-embroidered net, their delicate beauty suggesting the fragility of peaceful times.[68] Eastern Europe was on the cusp of war, the Balkan War of 1912–13, a harbinger of the Great War. As Imbrie stood in the garden breathing in the sweet aromas of spring, he would have little guessed that in four years he would be in the mountains of Macedonia as nations struggled to seize rock-strewn inches and feet. Schmitt, whom Imbrie had long cajoled to join him in New York, eventually settled in Manhattan on Park Avenue across from the Waldorf Astoria.

In 1913 Imbrie applied for the position of U.S. attorney under Attorney-General James Clark McReynolds. His application was supported by Congressman John Linthicum.[69] Although the *Baltimore Sun* described Imbrie as "a wide-awake and substantial young man," it noted that he had not handled any "spectacular civil or criminal cases" and had not yet rendered political service in Maryland.[70] His failure to secure the position was probably advantageous, given that McReynolds, later a Supreme Court justice, was a noted racist and anti-Semite.

On April 23, 1913, Imbrie turned thirty. He had spent his twenties, as many young people do, finishing his education, working, traveling, and looking for his niche in the world. War was on the horizon. Imbrie's coat of arms features a plough for its crest; its banner reads, in translation, "It renders fruitful by turning over." When the war came, Imbrie turned aside his old life; a new, more fruitful one lay ahead.

TWO

Merry Hell and More

On August 4, 1914, some four hundred thousand people gathered in New York's Times Square, their cheers ascending at the news that Great Britain had declared war on Germany.[1] Following the assassination of Archduke Franz Ferdinand and his wife, Sophie, on June 28, the world had crept toward war. On July 28 Austria declared war on Serbia; on August 3 Germany declared war on France and invaded Belgium the next day. Now it was Great Britain's turn to act. In New York the mayor, worried at the huge turnout, banned further demonstrations.

It seems strange that Americans would cheer on a war. They were only fifty years removed from the Civil War, and since then the United States had been involved in Indian wars, a war with Spain, and a conflict in the Philippines and had recently deployed troops to Mexico. It had also sent troops to China to relieve a siege in Peking. Did another armed conflict need celebrating? Not as far as President Woodrow Wilson thought. To Wilson, the embroilment in Europe was not America's concern. On August 19 he released his neutrality proclamation. By the end of the Great War, 61 million troops from sixteen warring countries would bear arms, of which 7.8 million would be killed, 19.6 million wounded, and another 7 million counted as missing or as prisoners of war.[2]

The casualties would include over 300,000 Americans in uniform. But to Wilson in 1914, the turmoil in Europe was not America's immediate concern.

Along with many Americans Robert Imbrie watched the developments as more and more countries tumbled into the maw of conflict, with empires drawing troops from their far reaches. As a whole America was firmly isolationist, but in the beginning the newspaper coverage was often breathless, dramatic, and even frivolous as though the war were a game or an economic opportunity. The gorgeous summer of 1914 had produced bumper yields, and it was difficult not to look at foreign markets where farmers were trading pitchforks for rifles.[3] France and Great Britain needed help, but in the minds of most Americans, not at the expense of American lives. By the early winter of 1915 the foreign news accounts had grown increasingly grim.

One way to provide help, even in the face of neutrality, was through humanitarian aid. Early on calls went out for ambulance drivers. When the war began, the French ambulance corps relied on horse-drawn wagons, much as U.S. troops had done during the Civil War. Although motorized vehicles were obviously preferable, they and their drivers were relegated to do battle, not to care for casualties.[4] Quickly the United States provided both automobiles and drivers.

The call for drivers spread widely, and in 1915 it emboldened Imbrie to enlist. With headlines tugging at his heartstrings, he closed his law office forever. The war had gone badly for the Allies in its first year, and in November 1915 the news focused on the Bulgarian and Serbian conflict, the torpedoing of the *Ancona*, which killed twenty-seven Americans, and the Gallipoli Campaign, which began on the same day as the Armenian genocide, a catastrophe extensively reported by Armenian Americans and figuring later in Imbrie's life. Stalemated, the Western Front was ominously silent. As Thanksgiving neared and newspapers filled with appeals to aid war victims, Imbrie registered as a Red Cross volunteer at the Washington DC passport office and went to New

York to interview for the American Ambulance Hospital, headquartered in Paris.[5] Imbrie was older than most volunteers—at thirty-one he was considered the "old man" in his ambulance section—but here was his chance to slough off the persona of merry wanderer. Here all the directionless activities of his twenties coalesced to provide him with the wherewithal for this next venture, including his study of first aid and mechanics and his extensive traveling that had cultivated his ingenuity and independence. His passport photograph shows a furrowed brow and down-turned mouth conveying his seriousness of purpose. On December 15 he sailed for France.[6] He would return home only after seventeen months of service.

For the first six months of the war the French had banned foreign nationals from the war zone for fear of bringing German sympathizers near the trenches. Accordingly the American ambulance drivers were first used solely to ferry the wounded in the rear line. Further, hospitals had been slow to recognize the importance of ambulance services for trench warfare. Whereas in prior conflicts mobile hospitals followed the troops, with trench warfare the wounded needed transport to stationary hospitals out of artillery range. Evacuation was further complicated because trains were not necessarily aligned to points of battle, and the springless, horse-drawn wagons often bogged down, overloaded with wounded or mired in mud or both. In the face of these challenges, the usefulness of automobiles, once demonstrated, created a surge in demand.

Horrific war wounds were another reason the ambulance corps grew. Modern weaponry produced destruction the world had never seen. Fragmentation shells were designed to maim and cripple rather than kill outright, with shrapnel producing three times the casualties of bullets. Machine guns delivered carnage with a single sweep. Gas, both the suffocants and mustard gas, disabled with body-racking effect.

In response to the dire needs, three major American voluntary ambulance groups formed in France. Imbrie served with the most notable, the American Ambulance Field Service (AFS), "the most complete volunteer organization in France."[7] The organization is still in existence, as an intercultural nonprofit fostering peace and understanding. Its founder and director was Abram Piatt Andrew, a forty-one-year-old former assistant secretary of the Treasury, who had lost a Massachusetts congressional election in 1914 and hoped to find a new calling in France. He did.

When Andrew learned that the American drivers were limited to rear action, he gained permission for them to become virtual members of the French Army. They were to receive the same provisions and wages as a French infantryman (five sous a day, or about five cents) and be subject to the same military discipline and regulations. Unlike Red Cross volunteers, who were neutral, Andrew's corps was committed to serving the cause of France. Translated, its motto read "Everyone and all for France." In mid-May 1915, the French prohibition against neutrals in the war zone was lifted, and by summer the AFS was providing essential support to the French Army and growing dramatically, with cars zipping up and down the front. By November, when Imbrie enlisted, the AFS had four sections, each with twenty-five drivers and twenty ambulances. Besides the Americans, each section had four French soldiers, including a lieutenant to liaison with the French command, and three Frenchmen to serve as cooks and mechanics. There were also two large trucks or camions, one to carry spare parts for the Fords and one to serve as a cook wagon. Two ambulance drivers served as section chief and sous chief, volunteer positions that added administrative duties to the ambulance tasks. Given his oft-commended performance in the corps, Imbrie could have served in either capacity, but he seemed to have preferred being only a driver and, as his future choices suggest, avoid bureaucracy when he could.

The drivers provided their own uniforms and other personal equipment and arranged their own traveling expenses to and from Europe, explaining why so many drivers came from privileged backgrounds. The AFS furnished room and board, including when the drivers were in Paris on leave. It paid each man two francs a day to supplement the French wages. It provided the ambulances, trucks, trailers, staff cars, spare parts, tools, and section equipment such as tents. The French Army furnished the gasoline, oil, and tires. In 1917, when the United States entered the war and the corps was turned over to the U.S. Army, the AFS had thirty-four ambulance sections and fourteen camion sections, which delivered supplies to the front, including munitions. There were 1,200 ambulance drivers and nearly a thousand ambulances. Of the 2,437 volunteers in all, 127 Americans died, including 5 youths from Philips Academy in Andover, Massachusetts. This was the world Imbrie entered. Only 32 volunteers, some of those serving in headquarters but not in the field, served longer than Imbrie.

Imbrie's trip to Europe would have mirrored that of other American ambulance drivers.[8] After a week at sea, occupied with bridge games in the smoking room and lifeboat drills, the drivers neared their destination with a mixture of excitement and trepidation. With two tense days awaiting them, French sailors appeared in uniform from below deck, and a French naval officer mounted the bridge to take command. The gun on the stern was uncovered, cleaned, and tested. The ship steamed through the submarine zone and up the Garonne River, arriving at last at Bordeaux. From there the drivers went on to Paris and the AFS headquarters. A few days were spent tumbling through bureaucratic hoops—filling out paperwork, passing a chauffeur's test, picking up a uniform and regulation blanket roll, and packing a kit, including shirts, socks, sweaters, soap, toothpaste and brush, towels, and underwear. American men still wore union suits, difficult to find in Europe, where the men wore two-piece underwear.[9] Imbrie was assigned to Section One, which carried the prestige of being Director Andrew's own section.[10] Section One began by providing transportation of the wounded streaming in from Belgium and had recently been sent to Ypres, a city pivotal to supplying the British forces.[11] There the drivers became the first noncombatants to witness a gas attack when on April 22, 1915, an insidious mist floated over the fields, turning from ethereal blue to putrid yellow and green as it reached the French lines.[12] By early winter after almost a year of work, Section One had earned a reprieve in Beauvais. It was there when Imbrie arrived in France.

After easing the section's Christmas dinner into two ambulances, Imbrie and George Spaulding, a Rhodes Scholar, left Paris and its poplar-lined streets behind and drove into the countryside.[13] It was December 23. Once over the Seine, they encountered few vehicles, only a few wagons and donkey-drawn gigs, and occasionally a large staff car, flying its colors as it roared past. As the afternoon light faded and mist turned to rain, Imbrie's anticipation intensified. It was almost palpable. Dark descended. Finally they reached the ill-lit Beauvais and wound their way through the moonlit streets until luck brought them to a large open space with a row of ambulances. As they shut off their engines, the section's sous chief appeared through the gloom to greet them. They grabbed their kits, stumbled across the muddy road into a building and up the stairs to a straw-strewn room, threw down their gear, ate some chocolate and bread, their only meal since leaving Paris, and settled into their sleeping bags. To the tramp, tramp of a sentry, Imbrie fell asleep.

The next morning Imbrie awoke to the noise of the section preparing to move a short way to accommodations in a former schoolhouse in the town of Maracel. The schoolhouse was what seasoned drivers expected—a cavernous room with few furnishings. Cots with straw mattresses lined the wall. There was a table, a stove, and a few benches. The drivers piled in and shortly their detritus—dirty boots, blankets, automobile lamps, gas cans, and overcoats—cluttered the room.[14]

Imbrie served with a varied lot. Volunteers came and went, some reenlisting when their commitment ended, others going home, some early. In the beginning many of the drivers were Americans trapped in France by the outbreak of war. Among Section One drivers were a cowboy from Buffalo Bill's Rough Riders show, a race car driver, a football player, two jockeys, an Alaskan dogsled driver, a gold prospector, an undertaker, a Harvard professor of classics, a Maine lumberjack, and several big game hunters, with whom Imbrie could reminisce about Africa. Although in the course of the war the AFS recruited increasingly from colleges and universities, lessening the diversity, when Section One disbanded in 1918, it was still remarkably diverse: along with four college-age students and three "schoolboys" were a gold miner, a life guard, a plumber, a white slave investigator, a farmer, a city magistrate, an advertising agent, two engineers, and two bank clerks, among others.[15] Imbrie took pride in the egalitarianism of his section. Some of the volunteers became fast friends. In Maracel Imbrie reconnected with journalist George End, whom he had met aboard ship. Their friendship lasted until Imbrie's death.[16]

A strong camaraderie existed within the sections, reinforced by rituals such as yelling "Is this Moscow?" when they reached a city, any city, before delivering a roaring rendition of "She Wore a Yellow Ribbon." Surely one day the Allies would complete the decisive pincer action that wedged the Germans between the Western and Eastern Fronts, and they would, indeed, reach Moscow. Their hope sprung eternal, bolstered by silliness amid the horrors of the war, a defense against the work that "was at all times unpleasant, exhausting, [and] dangerous."[17] Once, when the drivers shaved their lice-infected hair, they let stand waxed clumps looking like devil horns.[18]

Imbrie's induction to the work of Section One was gradual. It was, after all, Christmas time, even in France in 1915. On Christmas Eve the men decorated the dining hall with greenery, played billiards with three balls, slightly rounder than "the average potato," and sang carols, accompanied by a nearly tuneless piano. On Christmas morning a dozen or so drivers returned to Beauvais in fog and rain for church services, and thanks to Imbrie and Spaulding, that night all in the section enjoyed a traditional Christmas dinner of turkey, cranberry sauce, and mince pie. It was a festive beginning to Imbrie's grim task ahead. The cathedral in Beauvais portended that task: its astronomical clock, which was as large as a small house, featured an angel driving Satan into the fires of hell; for Imbrie, a potent image.

At the evening meal Imbrie met his unit's commanding officer, Lieutenant Marquis Robert de Kersauson de Pennendreff, mercifully called "the Lieut." He spoke excellent English, having lived in the United States for several years, and had fought in the Boer War against the British.[19] Imbrie noted that he was "a man to whom danger was a tonic," with a "smilingly imperturbable front." Imbrie called him the "ideal" leader for a volunteer group, a role model. The Christmas festivity ended the next day with the somber news that a Section Three driver, Richard Hall, had been killed on Christmas Day, his ambulance shelled on a mountain route in Alsace.[20]

At first Imbrie had few concerns for his own safety. His section had been pulled back for car repairs, and his first task was refurbishing Ambulance Number Nine, an adapted Model T Ford, a marvel of simple construction and interchangeable parts.[21] Ambulances were in constant jeopardy from bad road conditions, overuse, and enemy fire, and the AFS relied almost exclusively on the Model T, which had much to recommend it. It had a small, lightweight chassis, making it relatively inexpensive to buy and ship. It allowed for ease in switching out parts. It provided a relatively soft ride and literally death-defying speed. It could get up to fifty-five miles per hour and had a cruising speed of thirty, although later its speed was restricted by the cruder grade of gas turned out to meet increased demands. Unlike heavier vehicles, this "mechanical flea" could dart over muddy and shell-pitted roads, be lifted by as few as three men, and benefited from a tight-turning radius, essential in the chaos of battle. The Model T also had what seems an odd advantage: it carried only a few wounded at a time. Larger cars had to wait for a full load, meaning the wounded had to wait as well. Finally, it used only one driver, with the passenger seat occupied by an evacuee if need be, although driving alone had its disadvantages: no friendly voice to quell nerves or keep the driver awake, and no one to help shift a car out of mud or ditches.

The chassis on the Model T was mounted with a long, boxy body that extended beyond the rear axle. The right side housed a depot of four cans of gas, a can of oil, and a can of kerosene. On the left was a locker for tools, tubes, pump, bucket, and emergency rations of biscuits and chocolate. On either side of the driver's seat were stored spark plugs, chains, rope, and permits, including an authorization to commandeer gasoline. On the running board was a tin of water. Two swinging doors provided access to the back, where its two benches could accommodate four people or be folded back to the wall to admit three stretchers that were strapped to the floor when not in use. When in use, the third stretcher slid into rails overhead. With the back seats, stretchers, space in front, running boards, and fenders all in use, a Ford ambulance could carry as many as ten wounded. The drivers carried few medical supplies to keep the car as light as possible.

When Imbrie inherited Number Nine, it had been in the field for eight months. The Fords, while easier to maintain than most cars, required regular upkeep. It might seem strange that a Baltimore attorney could refurbish a car, but from the beginning of the automobile age, drivers tinkered with cars, regardless of class and privilege, mechanics being scarce. By doing so, they developed skills, showed off their ingenuity, and became amateur experts.[22] Squad members were also quick to tutor each other, and Imbrie had studied motorcycle mechanics.

During his first few weeks in the AFS, Imbrie took apart the engine, ground the valves, replaced a spring lead, and tightened bolts and nuts. He painted and relettered his car. He installed a new carpenter's box and a canvas windshield. Glass, easily shattered in wartime, was too dangerous to use. Ford chassis and spare parts were available from the French Ford assembly plant in Paris, and during the war, as the need for vehicles soared, hundreds of Ford chassis and parts were shipped from America for assembly in France. The Ford ambulance, much admired and sometimes derided, was trumpeted in a variation of Rudyard Kipling's poem "Gunga Din," concluding,

Yes, Tin, Tin, Tin!
You exasperating puzzle, Hunka Tin.
I've abused you and I've flayed you,
But, by Henry Ford that made you,
You are better than the Big Uns,
Hunka Tin.[23]

In the following months Imbrie would camp and decamp, settle in and pack up, as the section was called forward, relocated, and recalled for *repos*. He craved action and abhorred boredom, enjoying the antics derived from living under trying circumstances, like tossing a well-aimed boot at a chess board after players ignored lights out. He took his turn at mess and sentry duty. He was unpretentious. All of these traits stood him in good stead in serving the French government, and later in serving his own government. He was courageous. Shortly after his arrival, he wondered how he would fare when he was in the thick of battle, but when he finally made his first runs, he was too immersed in the intensity of the moment to dwell on his own situation. He was able to put self aside.

At the end of January, after a month of rain and fog and trips to Beauvais to while the time, Imbrie's section received its new orders. In a flurry of activity the convoy set out on a long journey to replace a French ambulance section in Julzy, rattling out of town across a wooden bridge, a stand-in for a stone bridge blown up in 1914. When darkness fell, they drove for an hour without headlights, as they were nearing the front, and, parking on a former soccer field, tromped to an evil-smelling barn for the night. Imbrie fell asleep to what he thought was the rumble of thunder; instead, he was hearing the sound of battle.

Before continuing their journey, the drivers aligned their ambulances along the road as the Tirailleurs d'Afrique marched by, an impressive corps of twelve thousand men from northern Africa, each company carrying a yellow flag with the Islamic crescent, and the whole group led by a band. The column, with all its gear of war, its cook battery and pack trains, took four and a half hours to pass. Then the *ambulanciers* drove on to the ruins of Choisy au Bac, a badly shot-up town about four miles from the line.[24] There they stopped for lunch, heating their coffee pot with a blowtorch, before heading to Soissons over a road cluttered with convoy and munitions transport. The going was slow. After much delay, on January 27, they reached Julzy and on February 1 replaced the French ambulance section. Throughout the area were scattered field hospitals—at Villers-Cotterets, which the Americans called "Veal Cutlets," at Pierrefonds, which had a railhead as well as a hospital, and at Compiégne, which Imbrie would recall for its wind-swept streets and dark, icy nights.

The section's mode of operation was to transport the wounded, or *blessés*, to a hospital as rapidly as possible, preferably no more than a forty-five-minute drive from the front, an excruciatingly long time by today's standards. *Blessés* were first treated at an aid station and then carried or led through a communication trench to a *poste de secours* (a central dressing station), ideally less than half a mile away, where physicians gave preliminary treatment, and from there to a *poste de triage* (a mobile hospital) where they were separated into three types depending on the wound, and finally to an evacuation hospital beyond the range of guns. If necessary, they might then be sent further back to an urban hospital. The wounded were carried to evacuation points by *brancardiers* (stretcher-bearers), men who were generally unfit for combat, some because of age, but who stalwartly carried the wounded through swampy mud across open stretches of the front lines in such severe conditions that a thousand-yard trip could take an hour.[25] The AFS drivers had enormous respect for the *brancardiers*.

The Americans introduced a small but significant change to the mode of ambulance operation. Before their arrival, drivers came up to the *poste de secours* only when called, but the Americans had the drivers wait at the post for the wounded rather than having the wounded wait for the drivers, a procedure so preferable it makes one wonder that it was ever done otherwise but is perhaps explained by the earlier use of carts and horses.

At Vic-sur-Aisne, where Imbrie was assigned, the picket post was about half a mile from the front. Three cars serviced a twenty-four-hour shift, only about 550 yards from the German line. In addition to the three routes to the front and the station at Vic-sur-Aisne, the squad was on call for the entire countryside. The drivers had off one day a week, usually spent working on cars. When the fighting was particularly ferocious, there was no time off, day or night, heightening the dangers for drivers and wounded alike. In the records for one section, in a twenty-day period, eighteen cars carried 2,046 wounded, totaling 18,915 miles of driving.[26] This in the midst of battle.

Connecting the battlefields to Vic-sur-Aisne was one single-span iron bridge, an object of persistent enemy fire. Night driving was ghastly. With the headlights off, drivers had to rely on moonlit markers, at times the carcasses of white horses.

When Imbrie arrived, the village had been under attack for months, although its stone buildings, camouflaged with brush, were still habitable. Having watched the panorama of war for six weeks, Imbrie was now in the thick of it. At last he could test his mettle. On a frigid February 10, at about eight in the morning, whistling shells signaled the bombardment of Roche, a nearby village. At noon the range shortened. Shells began to drop on Vic-sur-Aisne. As Imbrie came out of the mess from lunch, he heard a deafening screech followed by a thud. A cloud of smoke rose about a hundred yards away. In a seemingly impossible reaction, one man dropped flat on his face, with no attempt to block his fall. Imbrie heard another shell come crashing in as though a pile of lumber had fallen. Then two more shells exploded even nearer, and another hit in back of the mess, killing a *brancardier*. Imbrie raced for his car and headed to Roche to lend a hand. He evacuated three *blessés* to Atichy. In the early evening he was back in Vic-sur-Aisne. The village was still under fire. Imbrie crawled into his sleeping bag for warmth but was hardly settled when he was called out again, this time for Vingre. The road was a sea of mud. As a German observation balloon drifted toward him until it was directly overhead, Imbrie gunned the Ford, with mud spraying over the windbreak, virtually blinding him. He pulled up to a *poste*, a dug-out in a hill and, amid the distinctive popping of hand grenades, loaded up two men, one hit in the chest, another in the leg. The light was fading, and as he drove past overgrown fields, he now and then saw a soldier's head jut up from a dugout like a prairie dog's. He headed to Compiégne, where he delivered the chest wound to surgery and then unloaded the leg wound. Back at his station by seven, he shoveled down a quick dinner and headed out again. It was now dark. He drove as fast as he could, recalling the squad's motto, "Save first"—not "Safety first." The wounded man waiting for him was delirious, his hands tied to prevent him from tearing his bandages. Imbrie loaded him in and headed again to Compiégne. They arrived near midnight and, numb with cold, rolled through the silent streets. Imbrie dropped off his charge and returned to Vic-sur-Aisne. At last the shelling had stopped. His twenty-four-hour shift was over. In the dawn, as he drove down the city streets, a light snow drifted over the buildings and cars. He had survived his baptism of fire.

Imbrie later wrote that in all that day and night of being fired upon, he could never fully comprehend the awful destruction that the shelling caused, and that even after months of ambulance duty, no one ever got used to it. The ambulance trips never became routine. Each carried the newly wounded. Imbrie worried over each bloody load, whose pain was sharpened by jolts on the pitted roads, and over his own helplessness to ease their journey. Yet he persevered.

On February 12 the line near Vingre came under attack, a minor skirmish, except to the men involved. As night fell, the German big guns lengthened their range to harry the transport behind the line. The entire squad was called up. Imbrie had already been on duty for fourteen hours. He had had only two hours' sleep in the last forty and had driven almost two hundred miles. Nevertheless, he sped off with headlights doused to pick up the wounded, delivered them to Compiégne, eased into his bedroll at 4:30, and rolled out again at 6:30 to work on his car in a cold rain.

At dawn on February 21 the Battle of Verdun began to the south. The longest battle of the war, it spanned ten months. In the Franco-Prussian War of 1870–71, Verdun had fallen after a ten-week siege. The French were determined not to let it fall again. In turn, the Germans, although anticipating the French commitment to Verdun, moved forward in their plans, confident of success. They were wrong. Despite at least half a million casualties, both French and German, Verdun held. Imbrie would transfer there in June as the Germans sent waves of phosgene gas across the battlefields.

While a massive number of French troops were being rushed to Verdun, Imbrie's work at Vic-sur-Aisne continued, with the weather turning increasingly cold as he transported what he termed the "bloody backwash of wounded." One night in a blinding snow he picked up a man with a lung wound. Lung wounds demanded quick attention, but four miles from the *poste* Imbrie's engine began to miss. With snow stinging his eyes, he quickly changed the spark plugs, a common remedy for malcontent Fords,[27] and drove on, the car still stuttering and the evacuee's moans sounding like a whistling wind. In the dark and unable to turn on his headlights due to the enemy's proximity, Imbrie lost his way. When he got far enough away from the front to use his lantern, he again pulled over to work on the car, his fingers stiffening with cold. Finally he got the car running well enough to complete the journey, distracted only when he heard a voice call out of the dark for a password (which was lugubriously "France"). He reached the hospital a little after midnight. His passenger was still alive.[28]

A brief reprieve came in the driving when *ambulancier* Bill Woolverton received a medal, the Croix de Guerre, for stopping his car in the midst of a bombardment to pick up several wounded.[29] He used the award ceremony to host a supper, called a "burst," with white tablecloths and china and food catered from Paris. Vic White, an accomplished artist in the section, illustrated the menu card, which all the men signed.[30] Since "Wolvy" was a Yale man, he placed a bunch of violets at each Yalie's plate, including Imbrie's. For that one night, instead of boiled beef and army bread, the men ate fish, ham, salad, and sweets. "Bursts" were rare.

On March 4 Section One set out for new headquarters. It was one of the coldest days of the year, with tree branches encased in ice. Snow keened under the tires. Feet, hands, and ears stung. On March 10 the convoy arrived at Mericourt in the dark, about 350 yards from the Somme River and less than five miles from the front. Imbrie's home for several months, Mericourt marked the juncture for the British and French armies, the former to the north, the latter to the south. Both shared tracks and roads, creating a tangled skein of congestion.[31]

At about this time the AFS was formally incorporated into the French ambulance corps. The Americans were now subject to the rules and regulations of all enlisted men, although they were not compelled to serve for the duration. Their enlistment was for six months with the option of three-month extensions. Their induction served as a warning of the intensified fight to come.

Although Mericourt's outlying chateaus, cottages, orchards, and farmyards were sheltered by woods, the village, as the center of an important salient on the British line, had been under bombardment since August 1915. Imbrie described Mericourt as a "merry hell." The squad camped in two rat-infested cottages.

The section went into action the day it arrived. It served at least eight *postes*, several so close to the line they could only be approached in the dark with the driver turning the engine off and pushing the car for the final stretch. On his first trip Imbrie was told not to go too far forward, but no one said what "too far" meant. He made the assumption that if he went "too far," it would be "too late." As he neared the line, he pushed the Ford up two small hills, wondering what would greet him at each crest. Near the top of the third hill, something made him look back. He saw a soldier semaphoring at him. As Imbrie slid the car back down the hill, the soldier scrambled toward him with unnerving news: the third crest would have brought him in full view of the Germans.

It was now pitch dark. Imbrie transferred the *blessés* from a dugout to the Ford. For a time, he hurried the car along without incident, but then he slid off the road and into what he thought was a mound of snow. It was a pile of rocks. With no apparent damage, he maneuvered the car back onto the road and, without further incident, brought his passengers to the hospital, returned to base, and went to bed. The first run the next day, however, disclosed the real damage to his car. As Imbrie drove quickly up an incline, it shot off to the side, roared down the hill, hit a boulder, and flipped on its top. He turned off the car to avoid an explosion but could not free himself. Luckily some soldiers passing by extricated him and helped right old Number Nine, whose steering mechanism had become detached in the previous night's collision. He reattached it and resumed his run.

On that trip Imbrie was headed for twenty-four-hour duty at the town of Cappy, just inside the British lines. Like so many other villages and towns in 1916, it was a forlorn little place, and on gray days with sleet pouring down, it was forsaken indeed. The previous month an elaborate defense system had been set up so that an invader, after crossing the Somme and its marshland, would first meet wire entanglements and then machine-gun fire from fortified buildings.[32] As Imbrie drove into the town, he felt its aura of tension, its eerie silence intermittently broken by screaming shells. The villagers lived in reinforced cellars and caves, wistful defense against the shells.

The dressing station was in the sandbagged town hall. There the wounded were trundled in on two-wheel carts, each holding a single stretcher. A shallow, straw-filled trough ringed the central room, awaiting the wounded. To the left a wing housed an operating room, and to the right were the quarters for personnel, but both wings were frequently hit, including five times when Imbrie was in the building. Eventually a new shelter was built in back of the town hall with tunnels seven-feet high and large enough to hold forty patients. Its winding passageways deflected flying shrapnel and provided alternate escape routes. As bad as Cappy was, at least Imbrie did not have to sleep with the wounded as he did later at Cerisy, where the groans and delirium and the smell of blood and anesthetic kept him awake. Twice while Imbrie was at Cerisy, his "roommates" died. Often he would slip out to sleep in his car.

One day as Imbrie exited the town hall, he heard a piano playing "The Star-Spangled Banner." He stood at attention and when the last strands died away, a corporal came out of a nearby house and invited Imbrie in. It was the house of the gravediggers, and amid the stacks of crosses marked "Mort pour la patrie" were a piano and some friendly, good-natured men. Before Imbrie left, the pianist played "The Marseillaise." Imbrie was deeply moved.

At this period of ambulance service Section One was attached to the Third Colonials, whom Imbrie described as "a reckless, hard-fighting bunch." He spoke of their courage, kindness, cordiality, and devotion to duty. They embodied the ideal Imbrie admired, but he was not starry-eyed. One night, after sleeping in his car, he went off for breakfast, only to see two bodies in the stretcher-bearers' room that doubled as mess, with one man's jaw shot off, and the other half eaten by rats. Another day when he was in Cappy to attend the funeral of the doctor in charge, two shells exploded behind his car just as he was about to leave.

Imbrie had been in France a little over three months when he was assigned to take a load of wounded to Amiens, forty miles distant, a city quite different from the villages near the front. Driving down its clean streets in his mud-spattered Ford, he felt out of place, and he found the transition between the war zone and such a peaceful place "stupefying." He described the town as "modern," with up-to-date shops and tearooms and trams driven solely by women, another reminder of the war's cost. Because Amiens served as an administrative headquarters for the British, its streets were filled with "swanking" spit-and-polish officers, including Scots in kilts. Imbrie's feeling of displacement intensified shortly afterward in Paris.

Three months at the front entitled Imbrie to six days' leave. He and George End drove to Paris in a badly damaged ambulance that looked, as Imbrie drolly noted, as if "it had been through the wars." The ambulance was destined for New York as a display at the Allied Bazaar, a million-dollar fundraiser for the war effort. On April 15 the men headed south to Beauvais, stopping at a café they had once frequented and transforming the waitresses to giggling school girls. By evening they were in Paris, the City of Lights, except in 1916. Still, it was Paris. They drove to the headquarters of the AFS located on an eighteenth-century estate on loan for the war's duration.[33] Its winding paths, vast lawns, trees, and gardens covered five acres. Its natural springs had enthralled Rousseau, Balzac, Voltaire, and Benjamin Franklin.[34] Although, or perhaps because, its barracks housed 300 men and its restaurant accommodated 150 at a sitting, Imbrie and End headed for a more peaceful spot, most likely the Henry at 11 Rue Volney, the semi-official hotel of Section One. Before the war it had been a gaming house for the rich, but now aviators, ambulance drivers, and army officers mingled with the well-groomed, insouciant men still playing dice. Overseeing all was Henry, a short, trim man with a florid face and gray mustache, who fancied a frock coat and squinted his eyes into little slits as he appraised his clientele. For those who met Henry's approval, his hotel was a welcome relief from the front. Its rooms provided thick draperies, clean white pillows and sheets, warm, clean bath water, and a telephone for ordering breakfast in bed—grapefruit, boiled eggs, and white bread with sweet butter—and cigarettes, imported Pell Mell being the preference during *repos*, although Imbrie preferred Fatimas and Blue Boar pipe tobacco, which his dear Aunt Mary had unsuccessfully tried shipping—it was considered contraband.[35] Near the hotel was the Chinese Umbrella, a café frequented by Americans, and, even better, a little café across the way.[36] Imbrie had once again fallen in love. He spent his repos with Lucette. He wrote to Schmitt, "I sometimes wonder what kind of a pluperfect damn fool I am. The last pretty girl I meet makes me forget the others and has me draped across the ropes groggy in about the third round. Heaven help me if I ever consider matrimony."[37] Their relationship seemed more than casual. Two years later, when he was in Petrograd, he wrote that he was "half crazy with apprehension" about Lucette during the bombing of Paris.[38] After the war, when he was about to embark on another "great adventure," he mused that he would feel easier, "if it were not for Lucette," but he had become "a confirmed fatalist."[39] Perhaps she had died during the bombing; perhaps she had found someone else. Her name disappears from the record.

While Imbrie was on repos in Paris, the war was never far away. Occasionally he found himself giving pause as if he were missing something and then realize he was listening for the rumble of guns. He wrote that he didn't realize until he "got back of the lines what a strain we really live under [and] I didn't feel the strain till I experienced the tranquility which absolute safety brings."[40]

Imbrie's thirty-third birthday, April 23, 1916, fell on Easter Sunday, and just after midnight on the feast day, Imbrie and End arrived back at their quarters, having driven through a cold sleet. Flares lit the night sky, and all around was the boom of guns. Paris was a memory. They were "home."[41] Christ's Resurrection, in which "death is swallowed up in victory," according to St. Paul, must have seemed fantastical on the slaughter fields of 1916. Hope seemed to lie only in more killing. Imbrie stayed on.

In May Imbrie was partnered with William Yorke Stevenson, who had arrived in France in March and was now serving as sous chief.[42] He would be named section chief in mid-June after his predecessor, Benjamin R. Woodworth, was killed.[43] May was one of Imbrie's worst months at the front, but he described it as merely "hectic." Three shells hit a building where he was waiting to load *blessés*, one shell landing about fourteen feet from him—he paced it out afterward. He was covered with dust, but unhurt.[44] One night eighteen shells dropped on the town, and four hit the hospital where Imbrie and Stevenson were sheltered. Stevenson was asleep; Imbrie was reading the newspaper. One shell destroyed the empty mortuary room. Another sent shrapnel into Stevenson's car, the first time a section car had taken a direct hit. Almost immediately the two men were called out to make runs. They ferried *blessés* throughout the night, until 9:00 the next morning.[45] Another night Imbrie made one of his more nerve-racking runs. The shell-pocked road was bordered by a canal on one side and batteries on the other. Imbrie was exposed to machine gun fire the whole way. As he wrote, there was not a thing between him and the guns "but thin air and Providence."[46] On his return trip he plowed into a tree that had fallen across the road he had just traversed. A difference of minutes, and he would have been crushed. "A fellow lives ages at such a time," he remarked. The extent of the horror of war was reinforced when he saw soldiers' bodies shunted into the sides of trenches, affixed with basketwork and mud.[47] At least the *blessés* were spared that ignominy.

By May Imbrie had driven his ambulance over 4,300 miles under terrible conditions. It was in terrible shape. A new Ford replaced the original Number Nine, and with it came distinct advantages—electric rather than carbide headlights, a steel shield in front of the driver's seat, and an improved locker system. The electric lights were particularly important as carbide headlights dimmed and brightened when the engine's speed changed, rapidly burning out at high rpms.[48]

Having been at Mericourt three months, the section moved back at the end of May about an hour's drive to Bayonvillers. The squad pitched its tents in a park that they christened the Country Club, but the site was far from serene. The build-up for the Battle of the Somme was reaching fever pitch. Armament and construction material, including enormous quantities of barbed wire and trench flooring, came pouring in. Airfields were laid out, hangers were painted to look like barns, siege guns were camouflaged with brush. Tent hospitals and mobile soup kitchens sprang up, antiaircraft guns appeared, oxygen tanks to combat gassing arrived, as did telegraph and telephone wagons, searchlights, artillery, trucks loaded with shells, and tractors for moving big guns, horse-drawn wagons piled high with bread, and mule trains. For Imbrie and for almost everyone, the question about this monumental offensive was not "what" or "where" but "when."

Since March the British body count at the Somme had been increasing monthly, from 485 to 692 to 836, according to burials, although likely the toll was much higher.[49] Then on one single day, June 4, there were 100 casualties.[50] It was an ominous accounting, but no one imagined the horrible devastation once the offensive began in earnest. Imbrie was growing restless. He considered leaving the ambulance service and joining the British army as a lieutenant.[51] He pined for action. After a mild May, June came in wet, cold, and raw. The ubiquitous mud made for heavy going. Bayonvillers teemed with troops. Day by day, almost hour by hour, troops threaded through the town—Colonials, Chasseurs, Zouaves, and Senegalese. When Imbrie was in Africa, his headman in Congo had been Senegalese, and Imbrie enjoyed hailing the African soldiers in their language and watching their faces transform with dazzling smiles.

In the park more and more tents sprang up; campfires flickered in the dark. It was soon overrun with troops, including a transport convoy whose horses by the hundreds plunged and pulled at restraining ropes. When the rains ceased, the fields filled with crimson poppies, yellow daisies, and blue cornflowers, recalling for Stevenson a maudlin line from the *Rubáíyát* of Omar Khayyam: "I sometimes think that never blows so red/ The rose as where some buried Caesar bled."[52]

Once when there was a lull, Imbrie and Stevenson made a run to their former headquarters, rat-infested Mericourt, to deliver a car and to lunch with an English captain, who to their amusement and delight gave them tea and toast served with napkins and china.[53] The trip was a cheerful break from the buildup, which was to end on June 20. Imbrie, as the only lawyer in the squad, began receiving visitors, men wanting to write their wills.[54]

Amid the congestion of the buildup Imbrie continued to make his runs to the *postes* near the front, and when he wasn't on the road, he tinkered with his new car, improving it with straps, hooks, and a stronger rear suspension spring. The weather turned warm and dry; dust replaced the mud. Daylight savings time went into effect. In mid-June Imbrie's squad was moved to a more advanced position, although Imbrie continued to make his runs from nearby Cappy. On June 20 he made runs all day, the final one ending at six the next morning.

And then, after all the buildup and tension, and without warning, the American section was replaced by a French section. Imbrie was as stunned as if a 210 had landed near his Ford. His section chief sent a formal objection to Paris. Imbrie made another run, and on his way back to Cappy he picked up three *blessés* near a canal bridge and drove them to the hospital. In the morning Imbrie learned that the protest had failed. The squad felt bitter about missing out on what promised to be history's greatest offensive, but they needn't have. They missed the Battle of the Somme, but not the Battle of Verdun, for that was where they headed. By then the region had been embattled for almost four months, and one incentive for action at the Somme was to relieve pressure on Verdun by forcing the Germans to relocate troops.[55] Imbrie's squad was going to a long-suffering battlefield, and although they would not be at Verdun at battle's end in December, they were there until the worst was over.

When Section One prepared to pull out, they traded rumors of where they were going, and as word spread, men began pummeling their horns and yelling "Yea, Verdun!" as if heading to a summer resort. The convoy lined up in numerical order, but as they cruised down the road, a race broke out as cars jockeyed for the lead—according to Imbrie, like the chariot race from *Ben-Hur*. With them were their mascots, including a sheep named Mrs. Caesar, a rooster, two cats, a fox, and numerous dogs, including the section's beloved terrier, Vic. Mrs. Caesar hated riding in an ambulance, but the dogs loved it, especially Vic, with so many new things to see and smell. The trip covered 250 miles, passing through smashed-up villages, and with section cars sometimes overturning as drivers fell asleep at the wheel, something Imbrie barely avoided doing.[56]

That summer in Verdun was far from bucolic. By June 23 twenty million shells had been fired, pulverizing the landscape. By the end of June two hundred thousand men had been killed or wounded on each side.[57] On July 11 the Germans initiated one more offensive, before relapsing into a defense, and in October, after Imbrie had left, the French moved to seize their lost ground. By the end they had regained much of the ground lost at the start of the battle. The French had prevailed, at a terrific cost.

But that was in the future. On June 24, after skirting Paris and driving through the stricken battlefield of the Marne, a trip in which only one ambulance broke down, the squad reached Bar-le-Duc, fifty miles from Verdun. Bar-le-Duc's houses were sandbagged, and some bore placards advertising cellars safe from bombs. At a crossroads a sign with large black letters pointed to Verdun, quite unnecessarily, for even in Bar-le-Duc Imbrie could hear the heavy growling of big guns. The drivers inched closer to the front to the village of Veil. It was, as Imbrie wrote, as "dark as in the inside of a cow." Too exhausted to pitch tents, they curled up for the night in their cars, but shortly all were called out, with instructions to wear helmets and gas masks. The drivers loathed the cumbersome masks, which virtually blinded them for nighttime driving.[58]

Bar-le-Duc and Verdun were connected by a single road, commandeered as a supply route for trucks, twelve thousand of which were being brought up when Imbrie arrived, forcing the infantry to march through the fields.[59] Newly named the "Sacred Way," the road was clogged with traffic even at night. With divisions rotating in and out ever more rapidly, ninety thousand French soldiers passed along it every week, in addition to support traffic. At the height of the battle, it carried fifty thousand tons of ammunition and supplies.[60] In transporting their wounded, the *ambulanciers* had to contend with trucks, which were supposed to average twelve miles per hour and maintain intervals of sixty feet between them. This distance allowed the ambulances to duck in and out between the trucks, while dodging oncoming vehicles.

When Imbrie's squad reached one of the field hospitals, hundreds of gassed soldiers were waiting treatment. Under a red half moon the drivers loaded up the ambulances, drove to the evacuation hospital at Bar-le-Duc, arriving in the early morning, entrusted their loads to the orderlies, and returned to Veil. The next night was a repeat, with the squad called out at 2:30, this time to report to Dugny, a village about three miles south of Verdun where even more gas victims as well as wounded were waiting. Along the way Imbrie had a blow-out and lost contact with the squad. Unsure of where he was or how close to the line, he inched his way to Dugny, by himself, in the dark, a hair-raising trip. The drivers completed their evacuations at two in the afternoon and ate their first meal of the day.

On June 28 the section moved up to Dugny. Between it and Verdun rose a hill pocked by shell holes, some of its craters big enough to swallow five ambulances. Between the hill and Dugny lay a railroad, which the Germans bombed every afternoon. Imbrie estimated that within a few kilometers of the front were concentrated five thousand pieces of artillery. The noise was "prodigious." The squad sought safe quarters in a barn shared with horses and *blessés*. They slept on platforms above the horses. The office was housed under a platform, and the workshop was in a hall. As Imbrie noted, what with the pounding in the workshop, the comings and goings to the office, the horses stomping and snorting, the wounded coughing and moaning, the guns roaring, and traffic rumbling, a boiler factory would have been more peaceful. He often slept in his blood-spattered car.

The squad's principle *poste* was in Cabaret, which was in "continuous performance." In all there were six *postes*. Imbrie's charge was to shuttle the wounded from the cratered line to Dugny. The wounded came in so fast that the schedule of having one car arrive at intervals of ninety minutes was shortened to every sixty minutes, then to forty-five, then to a half hour, at which point the schedule was discarded and the men drove continuous round trips. The only relief came by dividing the squad into groups of five to allow a full night's sleep every third night.

Imbrie's first run made him break out in a sweat. His ambulance rocked from the shockwaves of heavy bombardment, and he gripped the steering wheel until his hands ached. And this was the safer of the two routes. On his next run he took the alternate route, where the Germans were firing 155s, and a piece of shrapnel passed through his car.

On his second day Imbrie was called to Fort Fillat, an outlying defensive point, said to be at the crest of a hill. As he approached, all he could see were jagged tree stumps and debris—empty shells and abandoned trucks and wagons. No road was visible. He got out of his Ford and started searching for some indication of a road. Within moments a shell barreled in, throwing him with such force that he went down face first without breaking his fall, just as he had seen happen in Roche on his first day of heavy bombardment. In years to come he tried to repeat the fall; he never could. Reeling from the impact, he scrambled over to his car and clambered in. He turned around, and as he edged his way down, a head popped up over a crumbling wall—Fort Fillat, reduced to a subterranean passage.

Night drives were even more treacherous. One night Imbrie followed another ambulance through Verdun and into the countryside. Their way was lit by incessant firing, an "almost unbroken line of flame." The fighting was so furious at Verdun and the drivers so taxed that the progress of the battle was lost to Imbrie, even when he reviewed his diary. Ground would be won or lost, soldiers would report victory or defeat, but no clear narrative of the battle emerged. Once as he headed to Cabaret and rounded a spot called "Dead Man's Corner," an ambulance driver passing him on a return trip called out, "Be careful! They're shelling the road ahead." He wondered what that meant—should he cautiously advance or quickly turn around? Later, he mused, "If we wanted to be careful we should have been careful not to leave America!"

Drivers gave varied and often contradictory orders to each other. Another time Imbrie's drive to a *poste* was clear sailing, but on his return a freshly killed horse lay in the middle of the road. "Now that's the kind of thing that causes one to stop and reflect," he wrote, "but I didn't. I jammed down both levers and did my reflecting at forty miles an hour!"[61]

Ambulance sections were supposed to serve only ten days at a stretch, but Imbrie's first tour at Verdun lasted two weeks. On July 11 the Germans mounted their last offensive, during which the squad earned a citation for "passing through a sheet of poisonous gas again and again, without respite, under a sustained fire, for thirty-two hours, bringing the men prostrated by gas to the ambulances."[62]

The next day the squad was relieved, but even before they pulled out, they had new evidence of how lucky they had been. Their replacement squad lost two men, one gassed and the other killed by a shell. Up to that point at Verdun no one in Imbrie's group had been killed or injured, although they had lost six cars. On July 26 the drivers were cited for their work and the Croix de Guerre awarded. In all, at the height of this battle, 120 American ambulances were in service.[63]

From Verdun Section One drove to a villa near Triaucourt owned by the brother of President Raymond Poincaré. Peace and relative silence descended on them. They had beautiful weather, in contrast to the alternating rain and searing sun of Verdun. They took long walks in the country. They played soccer, a game unfamiliar to the Americans, and baseball, which intrigued the French. They had a dog show, with each man adopting a stray. New volunteers were tutored in slang terms, nicknames, and favorite songs, as if they were joining a fraternity.

Imbrie joined in the fun and the pranks, including early morning "evacuation," in which late risers were deposited outdoors while still asleep, but try as he did to enjoy this break, inaction troubled Imbrie, and he took to growling with Stevenson about what a "hell of a life" they were leading. George End, weakened from dysentery, went home when his time expired in July. Imbrie thought maybe he would, too. His commitment was over in August—he was "fed up"—but by August 1 he had reenlisted for another three months. Stevenson found Imbrie rather sheepish about his disgruntlement: "He loves [what he is doing] . . . and he could no more leave this than fly."[64]

During the second week of August the section moved to a village on the edge of the Argonne where wild boar roamed through thick forests. Imbrie and his commanding officer went hunting, unsuccessfully, but enjoyed each other's tales of Africa. In August, too, Imbrie was allowed a quick trip to Paris. When he returned, he found his section had shifted back to Verdun, cheerful news to Imbrie.

The squad was installed in the Chateau Billemont, which was badly shelled but serviceable. Although the weather was rainy and most of the window glass was missing, the rooms, with the shutters closed, stayed dry. Showering was done in the courtyard fountain with its eighteen-inch deep basin. Ironically, the men had little time for sleeping, showering, or bathing. Their new *poste,* Caserne Marceau, was under constant shelling—they were less than a kilometer from the German trenches—and the work was more hazardous than at any previous *poste*. Even their own troops made the trips daunting. They had to drive past a railroad spur mounted with a battery that used a foot-long shell, and as the drivers passed, the concussion from the detonation rattled their heads. Thousands of wounded poured though this one *poste* from the attacks and counterattacks at the town of Fleury.

As before, the squad's schedule quickly proved useless. Worse, during this period the nights were especially dark. Imbrie commented that he had to drive by feel rather than by sight. Cars sometimes met head on and were knocked out of commission. Other times the drivers fell asleep and careened into a wall or ditch. Regardless, the drivers carried on, even when their cars were hit by shrapnel. One *ambulancier,* driving at night, grazed the engine of an ammunition train. His only damage was torn mud flaps.[65] Another driver vividly described the shelling at Verdun, the flashing and the fireworks on the hillsides, the deafening noise at the *poste*, and the perpetual whiz of passing shells: "In daylight one could see a shell as it flew past. . . . Some shells are so big and travel so slowly . . . that they are visible not merely as they leave the mouth of the gun but as they pass overhead."[66]

The squad's second tour at Verdun ended on September 9, with Imbrie making the last run. As at the Somme, they were replaced by a French section. Two days after the handover the new section lost four drivers, two killed and two injured, and at the *poste* three stretcher-bearers were killed. Again the squad escaped relatively unscathed and received another commendation. In all Imbrie received the following French medals for his wartime service—the Croix de Guerre, the White Rose Croix de Guerre, the Ambulance Medal, Field Service Medal, and Medal of Recognition for serving six months or more at the front.[67]

Before leaving Verdun, a few drivers, including Imbrie, visited the prized city. They had been through it numerous times, but always in their car or on duty. Now they wanted to explore the cause of so much suffering, this "deserted, stricken city," this French Pompeii.[68] They toured the citadel on the hill whose two towers stood "four-square to the world" and, descending, wound their way down a side street to a corner café, entered through a broken wall, and sat at a dust-covered table. How deceptively cozy the café seemed with its paneled walls and high-backed banquettes. Neatly arrayed drinking glasses lined the shelves behind the bar, as if waiting the war's end.

The men moved on, weaving in and out of buildings for brief looks. In one house a china chanticleer mutely greeted them from its perch on a mantel. Further down the street they entered a hardware store, its floor littered with bolts, screws, and tinware. At a hotel office, room keys hung in orderly fashion. Imbrie knocked the dust off the open register and signed his name. Marble-topped tables were overturned, and upholstered chairs were rotting. In the upper floors bed linen was scattered, broken glass crunched underfoot, and plaster dust coated everything. For three hours the men meandered without encountering a single soul, not even a dog or a cat. As they left the city gate, though, they heard a crash and, looking back, saw a cloud of dust rising as if the Germans had been watching their every step and were signaling the end of the tour.

Back at squad quarters Imbrie joined the men lounging in the grass, smoking their pipes, talking, and waiting for the regimental chaplain to arrive. Suddenly the screech of a shell broke the calm. Talk ceased, pipes froze in midair, and then came the explosion, about a hundred yards down the road. Eleven seconds later came a second shell, closer. The chateau was being hit with 130s. Still no one moved. Then the chaplain's car came roaring through the gate, a shell hitting fifty yards behind it, and for ten minutes the bombing continued. When it ceased, the men rose from their grassy spots and gathered under a tree with bowed heads as the chaplain began the service, "*Le bon Dieu,* our protector in times of peril, our strength in moments of trial."

The next morning as the squad drove away from the Chateau Billemont, the thunder of guns grew ever fainter. They passed through Dugny, stayed at Triaucourt for three days, and moved west into the Argonne. There they quartered at a village between Verdun and Reims, far enough back of the line that without newspapers they would not have known there was a war. Yet, it was unpleasant. Their barracks "leaked like a five dollar raincoat." Cold set in, with wind and rain. As winter approached, Imbrie and two friends relocated to a one-room house with a leaky stove and resident rats. They stuffed the windows with rugs, scrounged a table and bench, and resigned themselves to a winter lived in their very own "Fagin's Den."

Then, quite unexpectedly, came a call from Inspector General Andrew for three volunteers for the Eastern Front. The section sous chief came to the hut, looked at Imbrie, and grinned. "How would you like to go to the Orient?" he asked. The "Orient" referred to Greece, Serbia, Macedonia, and Albania.

"When do we start?" Imbrie rejoined as smoke chuffed down the leaky pipe and into the room. But then Imbrie paused. He had two considerations. The commitment was a long one, seven months, and he would have to leave Section One behind. He had made good friends; there was not a man in the squad he did not like. Trying to decide, he approached two other drivers, Giles Franklyn and Bob Bowman, and when they agreed to sign on with him, he made his decision. The next day the three prepared to transfer to Section Eight and the Army of the Orient.[69]

The commitment indicates Imbrie's dread of ennui. After leaving Verdun a second time, Section One stayed back for four months. Even though ambulances continued operating, it was usually only one per day, and no amount of journaling, card playing, and hiking would alleviate the boredom for Imbrie. To him, the *poilus* needed and deserved the rest; he did not.

Before the three men left, a Section Four driver, Edward Kelly, newly arrived that week, was killed exploring an area that had been quiet for days.[70] Afterward Bowman chose to stay in France, and the good-natured Frank Baylies volunteered for the Balkans. On September 28 Imbrie and his companions hitched a ride to Paris with their commanding officer. Stevenson hated to see Imbrie go, calling Imbrie's parting "a great loss" to the squad.[71] A year later, on September 30, among the rolling fields and heavy woods of the Vosges at Aillianville, not far from the home of Jeanne d'Arc, the American Field Service was taken over by the U.S. Army.[72]

THREE

All There Is of Terrible

Twenty-six ambulance drivers stood by their dunnage, talking softly in the hush of wartime Paris.[1] It was close to midnight. Stretching into the blackness was their train holding forty-two ambulances. When the commander of the Automobile Service of the French Army came down the line, the men snapped to attention. He gave a short address of gratitude, saluted, and dismissed them to board the passenger coaches. Then as tin whistles blew, the train lurched slowly off, its wheels grinding and creaking. Somewhere a bell tolled midnight.

The first stage of Imbrie's journey, to Marseilles, took two days. The city had been spared the horrors of war and was free of the melancholy of Paris, so near to the fighting. It bustled with wartime activity. Its streets streamed with electric lights. Sailors crowded the cafés. The nights were hectic. It was not the sleepy port Imbrie had visited in 1907. The early October weather was warm, and the ambulance drivers lolled on the beach, went swimming, and ate at an excellent restaurant, La Réserve. Then their holiday ended.[2] They collected their belongings and trooped to the dock, headed to Salonica.

Their transport was a converted German tramp steamer, flying the flag of Portugal, the SS *Madeira,* manned by Portuguese sailors and officers under a French captain. As Imbrie ascended one gangplank, mules picked their way up another. Cattle, penned on the main deck, bellowed. Chains clanked, winches creaked, and steam hissed as orders were shouted in multiple languages. The decks were piled high with life rafts, hay, and cargo.

As Imbrie looked over the rail, eight hundred Indochinese—French Colonial troops called Annamites—came aboard and disappeared into the hold. To Imbrie their high-pitched voices sounded like the twang of a banjo and their laughter like flute notes being tossed aside. That night high winds kept the ship in port. It was Imbrie's first and last night in the hold, for him a hellish experience. Tier upon tier of iron shelves served as bunks. The smell was vile—Imbrie described it as "a sort of gaseous Gorgonzola"—and there was no fresh air. The next morning the squad moved to the deck and for the rest of the trip slept in the lea of the life boats.

What one driver sardonically described as the "comedy" of the trip began almost immediately.[3] As their ship passed the Chateau d'If, a Greek ship moved in, signals were confused, and both boats bore down on each other, with the Greek boat clearing the *Madeira*'s bow by inches. Confidence in the *Madeira*'s captain plummeted.

Because a submarine had sunk a French transport a week earlier, the *Madeira* zigzagged its plodding way, extending the usual four-day trip to eight days, with all hands called into service to watch for enemy ships, the *ambulanciers* on four-hour shifts at the bow, on deck below the bridge, amidships on the same deck, on the bridge, and at the stern. Their weapons were a few rifles and one pistol. Slowly they sailed along the French coast to Toulon, then on to Corsica, Sardinia, and the African coast near Bizerta.

On October 25 an Indochinese, Mohammet San Chu, died of spinal meningitis, and a formal burial at sea followed. Three hundred of his fellow soldiers gathered on deck, and the *Madeira*'s captain and commander, in full dress and with side arms, descended the companionway stairs and advanced to where the casket rested on the port quarter. The engines slowed and stopped.

The commander read the burial service, and as officers saluted and three hundred men presented arms, the casket slid into the sea to the plaintive sound of a bugle. That night three more men died and again honors were accorded, but thereafter bodies were unceremoniously heaved overboard in the night. The disease tore through the ranks of the Annamites. One *ambulancier* claimed that the captain, who liked to drink, was attending an Annamite wake for the whole trip.[4]

Unease spread among the 1,500 passengers and crew. Quarantine was impossible. Water for bathing gave out, filth collected on the deck, cinder-laden smoke belched from the stacks, and the sun beat down fiercely. The great fear of submarines continued. The German and Austrian U-Boats were known to score regular successes. Only at night did the fear seem to dissipate. With no lights permitted, not even the glow of a cigarette, the debris disappeared from sight, a cool breeze sprang up, and under the stars someone would start singing, perhaps "Just a Song at Twilight," as Imbrie, Frank Baylies, and Giles Franklyn drifted off to sleep, wrapped in blankets beside the small boats. At times Imbrie's thoughts might have cast back to his navigation class at the Nautical School in New York. It must have seemed very long ago.

From Tunis the *Madeira* swung north into the Ionian Sea between Italy and Greece, alert for enemy destroyers based in Trieste and prowling for prey. The ship then skirted the southern tip of Greece and headed north, into the Aegean Sea. At last, on the ninth day of their tortuous voyage the men awoke to see Mount Olympus, its snowy cap tinged crimson against the blue sky. Beneath lay the white minarets and red roofs of Salonika. Flying a yellow quarantine flag, the *Madeira* glided past the torpedo net guarding the outer harbor with its dozens of battleships and merchantmen. Riding at anchor was the four-funneled hospital ship, *La France*, and close to shore bobbed a bevy of wooden boats. The *Madeira* passed the length of the harbor as if reviewing troops and dropped anchor. Presently health inspectors came aboard, signal flags were broken out, and shortly three launches arrived to transport about fifty ailing Indochinese. On board an anxious night passed, but the next day the yellow flag was lowered, the ship warped alongside the quay, and at noon the much relieved *ambulanciers* disembarked.

Imbrie's arrival in Salonika came amid a grueling campaign. Bulgarian forces were embedded north of Salonika, about ten miles within the Greek border. In October 1915 they had driven the Serbian army from its homeland, but in mid-August 1916, when Romania entered the war on the side of the Allies, Serbia had seen an opportunity to regain its territory, sparking a three-month battle.[5] When the Bulgarian troops stalled, the Allies pressed on, pushing up the Kajmakcalan Mountain ridge and, after eighteen days of fighting with bayonets and mortars, through the forests and up the rock face in bitter winds, forced a Bulgarian retreat.[6]

It was during the ensuing pause that Imbrie arrived in Salonika. There was no grand welcome. No one had even heard of their coming. There was no place to lodge, and given the shortages, they were only begrudgingly fed. Worse, they had arrived on what amounted to a plague ship, so their camp, north of the city where the plains merged into foothills, was quarantined for several days. The first night they slept on rock-hard ground. The next day their eight-man tents arrived, but so did the rain. Once liberated from the quarantine but with little to do until their ambulances arrived on another ship, they wandered about the city. Imbrie found it fascinating, this "stamping ground of history." Fought over for hundreds of years, it was a polyglot city with Turks, Serbs, Romanians, Greeks, Cretans, Czechs, Senegalese, Moroccans, Russians, Annamites, Albanians, and Spanish Jews, all in a city of 150,000, not counting refugees, troops, and prisoners of war from four nations, guarded by troops from six nations.

The population in their varied native dress intrigued Imbrie—the Macedonian mountaineer in his kilt and pom-pom shoes, the black-hatted Greek priest, the old men in white turbans and flowing robes, the ragged lepers, the befezzed Turk. Even the cacophony captivated Imbrie—honking horns, braying burros, chanting muezzins, crying vendors. The smells and tastes jockeyed for dominance—frying fish, sticky sweet Turkish coffee, honey as thick as putty. Lorries sped along roads that caravans had once traversed carrying wares from the Bosporus to the Adriatic. Trams swayed under the seven-hundred-year-old Arch of Galerius. The crenulated White Tower of Suleiman the Magnificent reflected the lights of a cinema where a Charlie Chaplin movie was playing. Imbrie was enthralled by the wares at the bazaars—the flintlock pistols, sheepskin coats, cigarette holders, amber beads, and filigree silver work. At sunset an orange glow pricked every spar and rope on the ships in port, and at night the great street paralleling the waterfront for miles filled with soldiers heading to restaurants, dance halls, theaters, and cafés. Imbrie asked some soldiers what it was like in the north. "It is all that there is of terrible," said a *poilu*. A Tommy told him, "It's 'ell, that's wot it is, 'ell." But other Tommies belted out rousing renditions of "Keep the Home Fires Burning," tempering the gloom.

November brought cold, torrential rains churning up yellow mud, and then on November 11, in the thick black of night, a staff car hit *ambulancier* Edward Sortwell. He never regained consciousness and died the next morning. Sortwell, whose cot was next to Imbrie's, had attended Harvard, leaving when his father died and funds dried up to be a manufacturer's representative in Calcutta.[7] In August 1916 he had enlisted. He was tall, with a thick mustache, a pronounced widow's peak, and a winning smile. The morning of his burial, with full military honors, the squad paid their respects and then with low spirits learned that their vehicles had arrived and were ready for discharge. The next day in the rain they set to work with crowbars, freeing the Fords from wooden crates, reassembling them, gassing them up, and driving them to camp.

Finally the drivers were ready to do their job. Their convoy pulled out of Salonika and headed north to Monastir. The 160-mile front was divided into five sectors among the Allies, with the French operating in the sector furthest west, in the environs of Lake Prespa and Monastir. Imbrie's first trip north typified the driving challenges of this campaign, made much more difficult than that in France because of the topography. Across the Vardar River the barren fields gave way to near-barren hills, and the drivers began their steady climb as snow-topped mountains came into view, rising to a height of six thousand feet or more. The drivers wound their way up a steep, trench-like road, almost a gully, their cars groaning. Imbrie wrote that at one point it looked as though someone had tired of road building and had "leaned the unfinished product against the mountainside." Periodically the drivers had to push their overheated cars up the steep grade with a bone-chilling wind whipping up a rain. On this first day of driving, darkness fell as the last car topped a rise. Using their headlights, they inched along the trail, flanked on one side by a towering cliff and on the other by a black chasm. At one point Imbrie rounded a sharp curve and almost shot off into space.[8] By the time they stopped at a town for the night, they had been at the wheel for sixteen hours but had covered only ninety-three miles. With the kitchen wagon stalled miles behind, the drivers lined up the cars, nose to the road, wrapped their greatcoats around them, and went to sleep.

The climb into the mountains showed how different the fight in the Balkans was from the trench warfare in France. Here the soil was shallow with little vegetation. Instead of trenches, the troops dug slits in the rock, shallow individual dugouts where a man could lie down with earth piled in front to form a barricade, quite different from the eight-foot-deep trench Imbrie had explored in Cappy.[9]

On his first morning in the mountains Imbrie awoke to Russian troops tramping by, one man crying "as though his heart would break," a fitting serenade for a village clinging to the hillside above whose barrenness were abandoned breastworks, like crowns of thorns, where Serbs and Bulgarians had fought. To the north of the village was a barbed-wire corral holding several hundred Bulgarian prisoners.

Imbrie could hear the boom of heavy guns coming from the

northwest and, when the wind was right, the crackle of gunfire. The sound was punctuated by the slap of villagers' clogs, banging like shutters in the wind. Not even word that the French had taken Monastir raised spirits. With several cars lagging behind and others with broken axles, the squad could not advance. Finally, three days later, the kitchen wagon appeared, bringing a welcome hot meal.

On November 24 the squad headed northeast toward the Serbian frontier. It passed hundreds of German, Bulgarian, and Turkish prisoners working on the nearly impassable road. Dead horses, overturned trucks, and abandoned wagons clogged the route. On a muddy plain French, British, Italian, and Russian troops were encamped, including several aviator groups. At midday outside the village of Sakulévo, with its shelled houses, the drivers set up in a shell-scarred clearing from which the road bent east and then northwest before entering a long valley at the far end of which lay the much-contested Monastir. For Imbrie the landscape evoked lines from a Robert Service poem, "The Land God Forgot": "The lonely sunsets flare forlorn/ Down valleys dreadly desolate, / The lordly mountains soar in scorn."[10]

The squad was about eighteen miles from the front, which meant they would operate as a taxi service, taking the injured from a nearby dressing station to the *hôpital d'évacuation*, a back-of-the-line task Imbrie had found tedious in France. However, with Macedonia's fearful roads the operation was different. Imbrie entered the fray with determination, laying on his horn to signal the *ambulancier*'s right to cut through the traffic—the shell-laden camions, pack trains, carts, lines of stolid Russians and prisoners of war, and huge lorries with crews of Tommies singing out a friendly, "Are we downhearted yet?" as Imbrie passed. Wooden crosses speared the fields. A single run of three wounded could take from 7:30 in the morning until 2:00 in the afternoon.

As the days grew ever colder and the snow foot crept down the mountains, the squad's tents bred a thick sheath of ice. At night the drivers drained their radiators and wrapped themselves in sheepskin coats and extra blankets. Cranking the engine to start the car was an arduous task, the motors recalcitrant in the cold. With frostbite threatening, the men greased their feet with fat from the field kitchen.[11]

Respite came when drivers were rotated to Florina, two at a time for five days, to serve a large field hospital. Florina had been the scene of heavy fighting and had at one time been in Bulgarian hands. Now its fifteen thousand inhabitants were hosting a throng of refugees. The city's main thoroughfare was shielded with a vine-covered canopy, and along it were Turkish cafés, yogurt shops, and booths selling hammered copper and carved wooden saddles. Given the fighting in the hills overlooking Florina, the town's apparent normalcy emanated an air of unreality, making Imbrie feel like a character in a play, as if in turning a corner he would encounter an audience.

From Florina Imbrie made his first run to Monastir, to transport two corporals. It was a cold, gray day, the clouds hanging low over the snowy mountains. Past Florina the flat fields were riven with deep trenches that the Bulgarians had occupied two weeks earlier, now half-filled with water. For the first time in the war Imbrie saw piles of enemy shells and shell cases abandoned in the haste of retreat. The Fords drove on past the ruined villages of Negocani and Kenali. The sound of guns grew. Two months had passed since Imbrie had been under fire, and he was curious about how he would react. Outside the city the road improved remarkably, but then five hundred yards ahead a geyser of earth spouted into the air. Shrapnel whirled and whirred, muted only by another burst. Under fire, Imbrie felt a sinking sensation he described as being "gone." A crash resounded as if two trains had collided, and earthen debris—dirt, stones, rocks, and snake-like tree roots—uplifted by the blast of a 155mm shell rained down on the car. Without pause, Imbrie shot past Monastir's outlying buildings and slowed only when he reached the city center and the welcome burst of Allied shells sounding overhead.

Imbrie dropped off his passengers in a little square and, while he waited for instructions, chatted with an Algerian Zouave who told him that the town was in full view of the enemy up on the hill. Imbrie found the revelation "disconcerting" and easily complied when a new passenger, a doctor, darted to the car, calling out, "*Allez vite*." Imbrie drove as though "all hell and a policeman" were after him and reached Florina without mishap. That evening he recuperated in a cozy café populated by old men silently smoking giant hookahs. He ordered coffee and sat in meditative silence. He had survived his baptism of fire in the Orient with honor.

As the days went by, matériel for an offensive accumulated in Florina. Gray skies with low-slung clouds intermittently gave way to rain and sleet, and the river rose, threatening its banks. Across the river camped ten thousand Russians whose singing floated tenderly on the night air. On rare sunny mornings the mountain tops glowed a rosy orange. Then on December 17 Imbrie's squad was called up for frontline work. They set off behind a long line of troops, burros, hay-filled carts, and trucks with ammunition, making Imbrie think he was part of "one of those incomprehensible revolutions" in the Balkans.

The squad had been told to decamp at 3:00 a.m. in order to be in Monastir before dawn, fifteen miles distant. They were to extinguish headlights three miles from the city and maintain hundred-yard intervals so if shelled, only one car would be disabled. Without headlights, only a faint, gray light from the east revealed the car in front. Just as the first glow of dawn fell on Monastir's minarets, they pulled into the city. The caravan wound its way through a maze of streets to a narrow, debris-strewn lane. As Imbrie got out of his car next to a shattered house, two shells crashed into another street, greeting the morning like a raucous rooster.

After weeks of living in tents, the squad, assigned to a compound with two houses of five rooms each, finally had dry quarters. They were elated, even though there was no heat or window glass. They parked the cars out of sight of the enemy in another street and stored their gasoline and oil in a root cellar. A mosque in a nearby square served as a dressing station for the wounded coming from the front lines before being shuttled to the field hospitals.

About forty thousand inhabitants still lived in the city, down from a prewar sixty thousand. Behind the city clustered hills, and beyond the hills reared mountains now occupied by enemy troops. At night snipers penned everyone indoors. During the day the city was raked by shells, leaving wounded and dying in the streets, including women, children, and the elderly. Spies were led out daily to be shot.

One afternoon, a few days before Christmas, Imbrie and a friend called Doc set out to shop for gifts even though, as Doc said, "A chap is liable to start out full of peace and good will and come back full of shrapnel and shell splinters." The day nearly bore out his observation. It was a fine, sunny day, the first in a long time. Some ill-supplied stores were still in business—with inflationary prices—and the bazaar still operated. Imbrie and Doc enjoyed a hot milk at a booth and ate at a bakery where the proprietor used a twelve-foot wooden paddle to pull cakes from his oven. They walked past a bread line of three hundred people, mostly women. Then, on this idyllic day, when they were about fifty yards beyond the bread line, they heard a too-familiar screech. They flattened themselves against a wall, small protection against the incoming 155mm shell. Behind them the whole street rose in the air. They ran toward the crowd of screaming, terror-stricken people. The breadline had been obliterated. Three more shells came in, knocking Doc off his feet, and when a lull in the shelling came, the two men raced to their quarters. Imbrie and Doc survived; many others had not.

Another excursion before Christmas had a much happier ending. Imbrie was making a run before dawn, to evade gunfire, and as he entered the village of Negocani with his wounded, about ten miles southeast of Monastir, he saw a man flashing a torch at him. Imbrie braked and looked over the shrapnel hood. It was George End. There he was as he had been on the Aisne, on the

Somme, and at Verdun, his dark eyes sparkling from under his black wavy hair. He had rejoined the AFS in November and had made the long trip from New York to France, to Salonika, and then by train to Florina before hitching a ride on an Italian truck to Negocani, all the while intent on joining up with the squad as Sortwell's replacement. Imbrie leapt out of the ambulance, and the two men pounded each other on the back, shouting in glee while the wounded exclaimed in wonder at the two men's antics. In high spirits Imbrie completed his delivery and came back for End, who, along with news from Paris, had Christmas packages and the football scores: Yale had beaten both Harvard and Princeton.

On Christmas Eve the men hung coarse woolen stockings for each other to fill, a very different observance from the previous year when they had attended mass in Beauvais and feasted on turkey in Maracel. Shelling greeted the Christmas dawn but stopped in midmorning, seemingly a Christmas truce. Imbrie and some other drivers went to the Turkish bath, a house with bowls of water to sluice over their bodies, and then to a yogurt shop. Heading back to quarters, they heard the dreaded distant whistle winding up to a screech. They wedged themselves against a wall marred with an ominous hole. Then more shells fell, and they started edging along the walls toward the city center. When the firing finally ceased, they estimated that 150 shells had come in over a period of an hour and twenty-five minutes, aimed at obliterating a 75mm field gun two hundred yards from their compound. When they got to their quarters, the yard was carpeted with shrapnel, but no one had been hit. During dinner the firing began again, and intermittent bursts of a machine gun routed the quiet of night. End had brought two plum puddings from Paris, but nothing lifted their spirits, and they gave a half-hearted toast "To the folks back there" and retired for the night.

Between Christmas and New Year's, the shelling worsened, the enemy intent on welcoming the new year with a victory. Monastir crumbled around the squad. The baker with his twelve-foot paddle was killed. An artisan who was making silver pieces for Imbrie was killed. On December 29 five squad cars were partially demolished, including Imbrie's, its sides blown in, but that wasn't the worst. A little girl of seven, who often talked to the men as they greased their cars, was blown to pieces in their courtyard. The men had to remove fragments of her body from their cars and the square. Part of her head had landed on one of the ambulances, and Lovering Hill, second-in-command, found a piece of her on his steering wheel. Imbrie wrote that "In all the war I have seen no more horrible sight. . . . The scene was appalling." It was almost more than the men could bear.

A welcome distraction came for Imbrie the next day when he and Cornelius Winant were assigned to a division serving southern Albania.[12] In Florina they loaded up on gas and oil for the two-hundred-mile trip in Imbrie's Ford and set off behind a staff car carrying the commander of the Albanian Division and several other officers.

The road was steeply graded, and the kneaded soil a quagmire. When the cars foundered, the officers commandeered soldiers to free them, and by stops and starts they reached the top of the frozen divide, Pisaderi Pass, at noon. There they put chains on the tires and, with snow falling, started down a trail, hugging a wall to avoid the drop-off. In the evening they came through a pocket in the mountains, crossed a gorge, and called it a day. They had driven thirty miles. Wrapped in blankets, they slept in the cars, and as snow shrouded their windshields, the Year of Battles, 1916, ended.

The next day's journey of twenty miles took eight hours. The cars passed through a narrow valley, repeatedly crisscrossed a small river with no bridges, threatening the carburetors with flooding, and gradually climbed through a forested area and into a region of towering cliffs and stone-strewn ground. Finally they emerged from the mountains into a valley. At noon they reached the town of Beclista. The *ambulanciers* bid farewell to the officers and continued on their way, each armed with a carbine against the prospect of mounted bandits who supported the Austrians. Imbrie also had his army revolver. He checked his ammunition—120 rounds.

At four in the afternoon the car, unmolested, reached Coritza, 110 miles from the sea and 95 miles from a railroad. Despite the isolation, it was a bustling town. The streets were well surfaced; there were even stone-slab sidewalks. The populace of ten thousand was diverse and colorfully dressed. Burros were everywhere. As the news quickly spread that Americans had arrived, townspeople poured into the street, crowding around them, issuing invitations to tea. Imbrie found to his surprise that some of the shopkeepers had lived in America. One had run a lunch counter in Washington DC. Another had worked at a barbershop that Imbrie frequented while at Yale. Possibly the man had cut Imbrie's hair. Amid the crowd was a former brigand chief, big and powerful, his bandolier laden with knives and revolvers. He was raising an army to support the French.

Imbrie and Winant stayed in Coritza for two weeks, sleeping at an inn with two "almost-beds" and eating with the French noncommissioned officers assigned to the hospital. Evenings they whiled away in a cozy café with old Turks and soldiers of many lands, their rifles resting across their knees. One, a Zouave, regaled Imbrie with his stories of Peru and Persia, of ballistics and violent deaths. How eerie that Imbrie was entertained by tales of violence in Persia, given his own fate. At night wolves came to the edge of town, scouting for dogs or donkeys. In the town center was an ancient square-walled tower from which the French surveyed the landscape. Unlike the battlefronts of France, the region had no sharply defined line or trenches—the terrain prevented artillery from being brought up—and the fighting largely consisted of cavalry skirmishes between the Chasseurs d'Afrique and the bandits, or *comitadje*. Further east, however, in the border mountains where the Monastir line began, the Zouaves were entrenched. It was from that region that Imbrie's calls came, occasionally providing Imbrie, after a drive of hairpin turns, with a magnificent view of Lake Prespa, a vista Imbrie found more beautiful than any in Switzerland.

Late one afternoon Imbrie and Winant were called to a village nestled in the foothills to the east. Dusk was coming on when they neared their objective; the road was a muddy slough. They abandoned their car and walked the last stretch. There they found three Indochinese, all badly hit, in a stone courtyard halfway up a mountainside and over a mile from the ambulance. By then it was night. For the next six hours, with the help of *brancardiers,* Imbrie and Winant carried the men down the path, with the snow falling, the mud like cursed souls gripping their boots, their sweat steaming into the night air. It was so dark that Imbrie at one end of a stretcher could not see the *brancardier* in front of him. When the wounded were finally stowed, he and Winant set off. Three wounded meant slotting one above the other two, near the roof, where the jostling was more pronounced. Imbrie was well aware of the men's agony, but the best he could do was traverse the mountain road as rapidly as possible. At 2:00 a.m. they delivered their wards to the field hospital and, with the snow falling more heavily and in fear of becoming snowbound, pushed on for Coritza. At 3:30 a.m. they passed the town sentry and pulled into their compound.

Imbrie had expected to be in Coritza five days, but weeks passed, and no relief came. With almost continuous rain and snow, the pass was blocked and the meandering rivulet swollen. Finally, on January 15, as he and Winant crouched in the dark, warming themselves over a brazier, they heard the hoot of a horn. At the wheel of a lightweight touring car was the squad's lieutenant and two *ambulanciers,* sent to bring them home. Leaving the ambulance behind—it was too heavy to negotiate the pass until spring thaw—they headed back to Monastir, stopping on their way in Biclista, where the chief medical officer treated them to some especially good pinard.[13]

While Imbrie was away in Albania, his squad's cars had suffered such severe shell fire that headquarters had moved nine miles south, beyond mid-caliber range, to Negocani, which was in the center of a valley at the crossroads of Macedonia and Serbia. A third of its houses had been leveled in fighting. Imbrie's billet was a two-story building, its windows without panes. Upstairs a hall connected two rooms. Ten men were assigned to each room and four, including Imbrie, to the connecting hall. The snow sifted in through the windows, the roof leaked, and the wind whistled through every crack. Imbrie erected a pup tent over his bedding. The poor living conditions may have led to his becoming seriously ill. The drivers' meals were mostly of macaroni and hardtack, which Imbrie thought could break a tooth. If toasted, it generated mealworms. The men mixed almost everything with yogurt, including the macaroni. They never felt full. They also lacked ready wood for fuel, the hills having been deforested by previous campaigns, and they took to tearing down heavily damaged houses.

Meantime, the squad continued to serve the Monastir sector. Two cars at a time were placed at Monastir on twenty-four-hour service, subject to special call. From four to eight cars, according to need, left one hour before daylight each morning to evacuate the dressing station and head to either the field hospital at Negocani or to the evacuation hospital at Florina. The weather was punishing. At times Imbrie's hands were too cold to hold a pen and write in his journal. Two weeks passed without sun, what Imbrie called "iron days." Cold at times impeded sleep, when the temperature lingered at ten degrees below zero Fahrenheit. Toward the end of January, the drivers took over an additional segment of the line, southeast of Monastir, collecting *blessés* from the village of Scleveka, about fifteen miles away. Scleveka was the highest point reached by wheeled transport, some ten miles back from the line. From there supplies were carried into the mountains on mule back, the wounded coming out by the same punishing transport. To reach Scleveka Imbrie drove through the town of Brode, where two bridges crossed the River Tcherna. Beyond was a pass through which poured French, Serbian, and Italian troops, the last Imbrie noted as having particularly big, powerful cars. With the merging of the river, bridges, and pass, the congestion became terrific. It frequently took Imbrie as much as three hours to cover ten miles. At one point the way was divided by two graves lying squarely in the middle of the road, the traffic of war bypassing them on either side, saluting the dead with this slight arc.

During these early months of 1917 Imbrie's squad performed the work of three sections, the one back of Monastir, the Brode division, and the division in Albania. On one day Imbrie recorded four harrowing trips. Another day his wiring shorted out just as he reached the most bombarded section of Monastir. There he worked on his car in plain view of the enemy, which was steadfastly reducing the city to rubble. By then only about twenty thousand civilians remained, all suffering from terrible deprivation. The drivers' efforts during these particularly trying tasks were acknowledged. Imbrie and four other Americans were cited for valor, "for [their] devotion and courage in dangerous service" in Monastir.[14]

On February 16 Imbrie picked up four little girls, one with a head wound, who sat in front and chatted with him in quaint French all the way to the hospital. When he dropped them off and returned to quarters, he was unable to stand. He had not kept food down for three days. He was seriously ill, suffering from jaundice and typhoid fever. The doctor recommended a diet of milk, but as Imbrie wrote, "As there was no milk, matters were further simplified." The doctor thought he should be evacuated to Salonika and shipped home. He refused. He also resisted being sent to a field hospital—he had seen the dark side of too many of them. Refusing to leave the front before his commitment was up, he stayed in Negocani, in his hall billet, inside his pup tent, watching snow sift through the cracks. February turned to March. Word spread of a planned offensive on Hill 1248 overlooking Monastir. With each day artillery fire grew more intense, and sometimes as Imbrie lay in his bedroll, it reached the density of a drum roll.

A full month after he fell ill, Imbrie returned to duty. His squad had departed for Monastir on March 15, and three days later he cranked up his car to join them. An offensive was underway with bombardment followed by infantry attack. As Imbrie approached Monastir, he encountered a steady stream of wounded plodding along the road. The ambulances had been overwhelmed. Some badly wounded were being transported on mules, a stretcher on each side, a horrendous ordeal for the injured. Amazingly, the stone bridge a half mile from Monastir was still intact. From there on, the terrain was littered with freshly killed horses. Given the carnage and the recently released gas shells, Imbrie was not surprised to find the city greatly reduced: it had perhaps a thousand inhabitants left. The squad's old quarters had been shelled, but a new one had been solidly constructed, although not impervious. One day a gas shell sailed through a small window in a back room.[15] It did not explode, but if it had, it would have taken the lives of four drivers. Imbrie reached the cantonment at dusk. The night before, the enemy had shelled the city with gas, killing 344 civilians. Imbrie spread out his bag, set his gas mask close by, and, despite the steady crash of shells, went to sleep. For several weeks Imbrie lived the horror of Monastir—the burning houses, rotting carcasses of gassed horses, machine gun fire from low-flying enemy airplanes, blackened and bloodied *blessés,* and debris everywhere. Normally the ambulances ran only in the safety of darkness, but the volume of wounded had them rolling continuously, day and night.

As March waned, the squad's headquarters was ordered back to Negocani. Imbrie loaded his ambulance with wounded and started to Florina. Planes were targeting a supply area out of range of artillery, tearing apart men, animals, and matériel, but with a full car, Imbrie could not pick up the newly injured. This was the first of many air raids that penetrated as far back of the line as twenty-five miles, driving the transport camps from the open plain to the shelter of the mountains. Four months after Monastir had fallen to the Allies, it was still under fire. Hill 1248 north of the city had changed hands seven times.

With spring, the snow receded slowly up the mountain; puny shrubs leafed out, millions of frogs tuned up. Behind the line peasants started their planting. Mosquitoes and flies reappeared; quinine and pith helmets were issued. At night the squad no longer drained their car radiators to prevent freezing. In this unromantic way, spring inched its way through the Balkans.

Walking became a popular recreation. Of special interest was the village of Kenali, which lay about two and a half miles across the valley from Negocani. There on November 14, 1916, the Bulgarians had made a ferocious stand before falling back on Monastir. The heat of that battle had blighted the earth, and there were no signs of spring. Not a blade of grass grew. Opposite Kenali were monasteries, half-wrecked, deserted, and forlorn in what truly seemed a godless land.

As spring advanced, low-lying Negocani became unhealthy, and on April 12 the squad moved nearer Monastir, to a camp in the hills, choosing an area where Bulgarian and German soldiers had dug platforms into the slopes. The squad covered these excavations with tents to produce cliff dwellings, and there they lay in off hours in relative security. With their door flaps pulled back, they watched cloud shadows scud across the valley, the blue, pink, and gray sunsets, the haze and mist, and the storms. They listened to the muttering and crackling of guns and watched planes cut in as men below, seemingly the size of mites, ran crazily about the valley floor. At night the silvery stars vied with the orange of bursting rockets. Scrambling one ridge over, they could look down on Monastir and watch enemy transport as it wound its way along the road from the city of Prelip. Some nights brought raging winds filled with grit and sand. Another time a snowstorm raged for three days. The men, confident winter was over, had left their sheepskins and woolens in Negocani. A year later Imbrie recalled his pup tent days from the comfort of a palace apartment in St. Petersburg.[16]

Imbrie spent much of April in Monastir service, often making runs with Giles Franklyn. In one late spring snowstorm they drove to a *poste* known as Grande Roche, which could only be approached at night. Past Monastir, the route was raked by enemy fire. Imbrie doused the headlights. Franklyn got out and walked with his back against the radiator, in the dark and snow, directing

Imbrie. Even then they had to halt periodically to determine their position. Occasionally a flare went up, pinning them in light. That night they made not one, but three trips. For Imbrie, it was one of the longest nights of the war. Finally, in a gray dawn, with their third load, they passed once more through Monastir, its bazaars deserted and its streets obliterated. Unbeknownst to them, it was their last trip to Monastir. America had entered the war. On the night of April 2, President Wilson had outlined the case against Germany, the first president to address Congress in person since John Adams in 1800, signifying the momentous occasion. A week later Congress declared war.

America's entry into the war had been rumored since November; now it was real. Up in the hills the drivers waited to be relieved. On April 23 Imbrie wrote that the last day of his enlistment had arrived, "notable only [in] that it brought [the] last snow." It was his thirty-fourth birthday.

Imbrie was not out of danger yet. The next day as the drivers worked on their cars to the sound of anti-aircraft guns firing away, a German plane swooped overhead. The drivers ran for cover. Three bombs dropped, and shrapnel winged across the hillside, but the squad's luck held. None of them was hurt, but they also knew that a fraction of a second could have dealt a different hand. Three days later a courier came to say six of them could leave that night: their French replacements had landed in Salonika. The drivers drew straws. Imbrie drew a short one. He left after a last celebratory mess with the squad. Frank Baylies went with him. At Florina a freight train huffed at the station as Imbrie heaved his dunnage into a boxcar and jumped aboard, headed to Salonika.[17]

Four days later, after numerous hot baths, Imbrie sailed on the *Le Duc d'Aumale,* convoyed by three destroyers, a cruiser, and a dirigible, but warned of two U-boats approaching, the ship detoured to a safe harbor filled with a score of ships, other transport, and freighters also with their convoys. There Imbrie spent three days, and not one to waste an opportunity, he spent the delay swimming, sailing, and burro riding, horses being scarce.

Two days after again setting out, the *Le Duc d'Aumale* reached Italy. Imbrie went on to Rome, stayed two days, revisited Turin, and two weeks after leaving his hillside camp near Monastir, was back in Paris, reporting to the French Army headquarters. With him was the rifle he had carried in Albania and shrapnel from his days with Number Nine in Verdun. He was well decorated and held the rank of major.[18] On May 18 the U.S. Selective Service Act designated June 5 as the day of registration for all American men ages twenty-one to thirty. Despite his age, Imbrie tried to enlist but was rejected due to his recent illness. On his draft card he listed no nearest of kin, and on the line asking whether he claimed draft exemption, he wrote an emphatic "No!" Later he helped organize Paris Post number 1 of the American Legion,[19] but now it was time to discover how he could serve his country-at-war. He sailed for home.

Although the dangers of sea voyages paled in comparison to those of Verdun and Monastir, ocean crossings in the spring of 1917 carried their own threats: mines and torpedoes. One ambulance driver described his voyage, which would be much like Imbrie's. He wrote that it began in almost palpable tension before easing into calm and even enjoyment, a gradual sloughing off of the terrors of the war. His ship's departure from Liverpool was delayed for three days due to a newly laid nest of mines. When the boat at last slipped its moorings in the early morning dark, it hugged the English and Scottish coast until well north of Belfast. In early afternoon patrol boats signaled last-minute directions for its route with flags and exaggerated arm waving. After another tense day the boat passed safely out of the danger zone. Gradually the passengers' nerves matched the calm of the sea, and shuffleboard sticks appeared for hard-fought but harmless contests. Most amazing to an ex-ambulance driver was the bounty of food—pancakes, sugar, sweet potatoes, squash, corn, beer, and ice cream, twice a day. It was not only restorative; it was heavenly.[20]

Back in Washington DC, Imbrie set to work, not by reopening his law practice but by transposing his diary into a memoir,

Behind the Wheel of a War Ambulance, providing a view of the war that journalists had neglected or been unable to cover. One can imagine Imbrie typing away in the Fishbaugh home in late spring and early summer, breezes fluttering the summer curtains, the porch dark and cool under the Romanesque arches, so very different from his accommodations in France and the Balkans. He would have, like the poet William Wordsworth, recollected in tranquility, but the noise of war must have intruded at times, distant echoes calling forth shadowy figures, as he wrote about them. The book, based on the diary he had faithfully kept, was published in November 1918, in time for the holiday trade, as one reviewer put it. Another reviewer noted the influence of Imbrie's age in the reportage, that it was "more a grown man's account, [than some others] . . . especially good in descriptions of Verdun and French peasant life. Some touches are gruesome but on the whole it is humorous and cheerful, convincing the reader that 'the Americans have received far more than they have given.'"[21] An early twentieth-century reviewer described it as a "humane" treatment of life, giving a "full and vivid impression" of Imbrie's experience and written in a straightforward style with a "good eye for color, and for the significance of events."[22] A recent writer noted that other young writers such as e. e. cummings, Dashiell Hammett, John Dos Passos, and Ernest Hemingway also wrote war memoirs, but Imbrie's 1918 book "remains the most vivid and humorous account."[23] In writing his memoir Imbrie distanced himself from the romanticism of some drivers' recollections, prefacing his book with his characteristic wry humor: "Lest those who have read the bombastic accounts of American journals be misled: the men of the American Ambulance have not conducted the Great War nor been its sole participants."[24] One reviewer caught Imbrie's personality: "Those who know Bob Imbrie—and who in Washington doesn't—can imagine the spirit of abounding youth and adventure he has breathed into his tale. . . . Bob Imbrie is a born adventurer; and ever since he grew up he has had a way of breaking away from conventional ties at frequent intervals and slipping off to the far corners of the earth in search of excitement." Although many of the books written by ambulance drivers were in the form of letters and diaries, Imbrie's was a narrative. It is worth reading today.[25]

Imbrie's memoir was an important document in covering the Great War. Will Irwin, a journalist who visited Verdun when Imbrie was there, thought prewar American foreign correspondence was in its nadir.[26] At the time most newspapers and magazines believed Americans were not interested in the war. Few publications sent their best reporters abroad, relying mostly on inexperienced young men assigned to color stories or on freelancers whose reliability could be questioned.[27] There were exceptions, such as Richard Harding Davis, regarded as the first modern war correspondent, as well as Will Irwin himself.[28]

As war correspondents in the true meaning of the word, journalists were compromised.[29] During the Great War reporters were carefully shepherded through battle zones and, easily censored, they self-censored, afraid of endangering men's lives. Memoirs such as Imbrie's supplemented the journalist's reportage. Whereas journalists were witnesses of the war, rather than participants, the ambulance drivers were both. They were immersed in the action but distanced by their assignment. This dichotomy shaped Imbrie's book. He was a witness, but beyond war-office censorship. Despite the horrors he witnessed, he was not cynical. He did not display the disillusion that surfaced in writers later, which derived largely from postwar suffering, not from the war itself. Ernest Hemingway's *A Farewell to Arms*, published eleven years after the end of the war, the year Imbrie died, echoes the disillusion of the 1920s, not the earnestness of the war years.[30] Although Hemingway's novel is set during the war, it does not have the tone of writing contemporaneous with the war.[31]

In *Behind the Wheel* Imbrie reveals himself in his admiration for his commanding officers, the troops, and the stretcher-bearers. He admired the "Lieut" in France who fought against the British in the Boer War, "purely for the love of adventure," and garnered a thousand-pound price on his head for his efforts, and one wonders if, when Imbrie himself came to have a price on his head, he felt a bond with this man. Similarly, Imbrie felt honored to be assigned to the Third Colonials of the French Army. He found the men reckless and hard fighting, cordial to the *ambulanciers*, courteous, kind, cheerful, and courageous. The *poilu* he extolled, as did most writers, almost rhapsodizing about the "rough, cheery philosopher whose kindly bonhomie makes him the most lovable of comrades." This adulation speaks to Imbrie's ease in moving among all social levels as well as the value he placed on physical and mental toughness.

One aspect of Imbrie's memoir calls for explanation: he downplayed the suffering of the ambulance drivers, understandably in the face of troop suffering, but he also might have wanted to minimize his own good fortune in surviving intact when others did not, and he seemed sensitive to their suffering. One such driver was Philip Sidney Rice, who courageously detailed his own physical and mental deterioration in his memoir. Rice joined Section One later than Imbrie so when he arrived at Verdun, he was not seasoned to the demands of what he called "the slaughterhouse of the world."[32] At first he was able to sleep anywhere at any time, but later he rarely slept, frequently shooting awake in the midst of horrific nightmares. He lost weight so that his face became pinched to the bone; he feared he would turn coward; his feet trembled so that he could barely keep them on the car pedals. He resorted to barbiturates. When the section pulled back for *repos*, his section chief drove him to Paris for a rest, but still he refused to return home and soon rejoined his section, staying not only until the Americans took over the Ambulance Service, but until his replacement arrived a few days after Thanksgiving. He received the Croix de Guerre on November 15, 1917. He had gone through all this suffering, despite a weak heart that kept him out of the army. Perhaps his bravest effort, though, was in detailing his mental sufferings for future generations.

Imbrie's ability to survive in France and the Balkans attests to his strength and luck, but he would not have wanted accolades at the expense of others' trials. Some men in the AFS were sent home for fighting, feigning sickness, disrespecting officers, and taking unapproved leaves. Some were active alcoholics. Some were injured. One man broke an arm cranking his Ford; another developed appendicitis.[33] Imbrie detailed none of this in his book. He excluded what would have shamed or diminished the AFS and presented the drivers as steadfastly carrying on in the face of the awful suffering of civilians and soldiers. They suffered, but the divide was deep between *ambulanciers* and the other victims of war.

By the end of the war Imbrie had demonstrated the ability to endure appalling conditions, engage in rigorous physical labor, commit himself to a larger cause, acquire and exhibit a plethora of mental and physical skills, and display compassion, initiative, and resourcefulness. He rarely spoke of his feelings, but they were there. He choked up when he heard "The Star-Spangled Banner" being played on a rickety piano in a stricken village, and he sickened when he saw how a bomb had shredded a little girl.

These war experiences left some of the drivers returning home feeling alienated, removed from the concerns of daily living. As the literary critic Malcom Cowley said of his experience as an *ambulancier*, "I have been drawn out of my fixed orbit."[34] So had Imbrie. In his memoir he quoted a poem about an adventurer, both spiritual and worldly. In its original wording the poem begins: "We are the fools who could not rest/ In the dull earth we left behind/ But burned with passion for the West." Imbrie gamely changed "West" to "East." Although relishing the motif of an adventurer east of the Americas, he also describes himself as having "a reposeful nature."[35] This self-assessment qualifies his professed enthusiasm for engagement. He had traveled the world seemingly without purpose for years, while running a law practice. He seemed to be a bit of a dabbler, at times a tourist, at times a crusader. The war gave him focus fed by an inner calm. This was the veteran selected as the lone U.S. representative in St. Petersburg, the man who could face down the Russian secret service but who also knew when flight trumped fight.

FOUR

Imbrie, Acting

At 3:00 o'clock on the morning of April 5, 1918, U.S. vice consul Robert Imbrie swung down from the train and edged through a throng of passengers with caps pulled low and mufflers knotted above their chins. Despite the crowd, the station was ominously silent. No welcoming shouts pierced the noise of hissing steam.[1]

Imbrie headed toward the exit, intent on his assignment, to reopen the U.S. consulate in Petrograd that had closed in late February. Since then the American legation had been holed up in Vologda, 372 miles east, first living in train cars and later in a twenty-room clubhouse, rented by the enterprising ambassador, David Francis. Although Vologda was well located with rail lines connecting it to both Moscow and Petrograd, and news came in with each train, Francis needed someone on site. Too much was happening too quickly in the former capital of Imperial Russia, and he ordered Imbrie back to Petrograd. The United States was at war with Germany, Russia had made peace with Germany a month earlier, and the provisional government had been overthrown by the Bolsheviks, whom the United States regarded as anarchists. Imbrie's consular status was a thin veneer for information gathering.

At the train station Red Guards were funneling passengers into lines to search for contraband, in particular food. During the previous year, even while the Allied embassies were still open, deprivation was rife at every level of Russian society. The diplomatic corps had watched as meat, sugar, buckwheat, and potatoes gradually disappeared. The cost of fish, fowl, milk, and cheese had soared.[2] Despite promises by the Russian government, flour and butter no longer reached the legations. An American military attaché's wife had rhapsodized at receiving eggs as "a gift that is beyond my power to return in kind or value."[3] The diplomatic colonies had hired servants to queue for food, kerosene, candles, tobacco, and other household goods. One hostess claimed that food at any price was cheap.[4] The food shortages were chronic.

As Imbrie squeezed into the jostling line, waiting to present his pass, he eyed the Red Guards rifling through the passengers' luggage, parcels, and coats. Then, as the line began moving, a peasant sprang loose and ran. A guard spun around, pulled his revolver, and, firing from the hip, killed him. Imbrie moved forward, his pass in his hand. The guard waved him on, and Imbrie emerged from the dimly lit station into nighttime Petrograd.

No trams were working. He flagged down a horse-drawn cart and climbed in, settling back for the twenty-minute drive to the Hotel l'Europe on Nevsky Prospect, but the image of the peasant's last moments stayed with him, an image of desperation and danger. Contraband was a small price for a life.

Ostensibly Imbrie was in Petrograd to fulfill normal consular duties, but nothing was normal in Petrograd in April 1918. Five months earlier the ambassador's top adviser had written of the "constant, wearing calls upon [the] Embassy. . . . Commissions, visits, commerce publicity, railroads, extraditions, land values, military preparations, naval statistics, finance, passports, prisoner relief, moving picture propaganda, capacity of printing presses, house furnishing and repairing, lost passports, censorship, mail inspection, wharf and port capacity and dues, relief ships, strikes, coal mining operations, couriers for mails, ocean cables, etc. etc.

etc."[5] In the coming months, Imbrie would handle most of these duties and more.

Reaching the hotel, Imbrie generously tipped the driver, a hallmark of Americans in Russia, and crossed the threshold of what once had been a luxurious accommodation but had become a refuge for those caught in the turmoil of revolution. It was filled with Bolshevik spies. After a good night's sleep—the train ride had lasted three days—Imbrie would reopen the consular office and find an apartment, away from prying eyes.

The Great War had altered the consular service, involving it more deeply in information gathering. Its commercial interests, including help in developing business relations between American firms and foreign countries, were extensive and provided an opening for clandestine activities. During the first full year of the war, trade between Russia and the United States had almost doubled. Between 1916 and 1917, it had risen from $310 million to almost $560 million.[6] Dreams of postwar investments enfolded visions of Russian water power, mining, and railroads. Every Allied country wanted Russia to form the "right" alliances, which meant not with Germany. In Moscow, U.S. consul general Maddin Summers thought Russia "the greatest of all markets" and strove to capitalize on this perception.[7] Early on he asked for more consuls in Russia.[8] Then, with the Russian revolutions of 1917, economic opportunity yielded to a greater need. Newspapers were heavily censored; reliable information was scarce. Summers intensified a long-term practice of supplementing consular reports with those from businessmen and aid workers, expanding reporting on political and economic conditions and, increasingly, on military developments. By late 1917 the consuls and quasi-official agents were reporting from across Russia. Still, Summers needed more help. In late October of that year Imbrie arrived in Petrograd to help fill the need.[9]

Imbrie spent his first four months in Petrograd, learning the consular business well enough that in April, with the American staff having retreated to Vologda, he was assigned as the sole State

Department official in a city of a little over a million. He quickly found an apartment on the Palace Quay and got to work. The pace was frenetic. The embassy, located in a fashionable district of Petrograd at 34 Furstatskaya Street, had only a skeleton staff of three Russian workers. Its furnishings were draped in sheets.[10] Its gated courtyard, offices, and living quarters echoed only the occasional footfall. Formerly a festive venue, the embassy was now forsaken.

Besides overseeing the embassy, which warehoused official documents, Imbrie oversaw the American consulate's offices situated on the third floor of the Singer Building at 18 Nevsky Prospect. It was the nearest thing to a skyscraper in the city whose code banned any building being taller than the Winter Palace, the official residence of Russian monarchs.[11] When revolution broke out on November 7, 1917, the consular staff, including Imbrie, had gathered at the Singer Building. There they had watched as a cordon of soldiers supporting the provisional government lined the bridge over the Catherine Canal.[12] The embassy staff, expecting a pitched battle, had ordered the consulate evacuated, but Imbrie had baulked. They would carry on with their duties, even though they felt they were living "above several tons of dynamite with a live fuse attached." In September when Consul Roger Tredwell arrived in Petrograd, the staff had greeted him wryly: "We have been promised no revolution for to-day, but these never come off according to schedule." Then the day of revolution came, a definitive day in Russian history.

That day had ticked away peaceably in the consulate, and in the evening the staff had attended a ballet at the Mariinsky Theater, but on leaving the theater, they found the atmosphere in the streets sharply altered. No street lamps illuminated the gently falling snow. The lights had been cut. As the men wended their way home in the darkness, in an eerie quietude, a shot boomed from the cruiser *Aurora* moored in the Neva River across from the Winter Palace, and a flash of light filled the night sky. Shadowy figures streamed toward the river. The Bolshevik revolution had begun in earnest.

Caught on the street between the theater and their apartments, the Americans had no idea how extensive the fighting was. Now and again they were halted by patrols and then waved on. Armored cars zipped down streets and then scuttled away, like beetles, with gun barrels bristling out the windows, but no one shot at them. In fact, for the next few days Tredwell found the prevailing spirit almost "fraternal."[13] But after that, tolerance and restraint give way to terror when, in Tredwell's eyes, the army devolved into a gang of thugs. With this introduction to Russia, Imbrie must have thought, at least briefly, of the Russian troops he had encountered in the Balkans, and in particular of one big fellow in a long line of infantry, sobbing as "though his heart would break."[14]

Throughout November and December, the situation had continued to deteriorate. In January Ambassador Francis learned that his life was threatened due to the U.S. incarceration of certain socialists, including Emma Goldman. He gathered Tredwell and four others to guard the embassy through the night, most likely including Imbrie, given his wartime experience. The night passed peaceably. In February, with Russia about to sign a treaty with Germany, the U.S. embassy and consulate closed. The staffs left Petrograd. Now, in April, Imbrie was back. He was there for twenty-two weeks before the Bolsheviks ordered his arrest.

When Imbrie had arrived in November 1917, the temperatures had been brutal, as much as 24 degrees below zero. In April it was still cold. Nevertheless, spring brought promise. With the polluting factories at a virtual standstill, the skies were a startling crystal blue. Soon the trees would leaf out, and a sparkling Neva would flow free of ice. Soon the lengthening days would render White Nights, bringing light to the darkness. Candles could be extinguished; the unreliable electricity spurned. But now, in April, people were still scurrying from one street corner brazier to the next to snatch a bit of warmth. In spring one hoped to saunter, look around, pause and admire, stop to talk to strangers, or even flirt, but in April 1918 fear chilled the air as much as the temperatures. People kept their heads down and avoided eye contact. They tried to stay inside as much as possible.

In his first few days back in Petrograd, Imbrie rented an apartment overlooking the Neva, with a canopied bed and tapestry-lined drawing room. He began plowing through a backlog of mail.[15] Then on April 8 Consul Summers made Imbrie's assignment from short-term to ongoing.[16] Imbrie turned to issuing reports based on contacts or his own observation, signing them "Imbrie, Acting," a signature that characterized his entire life, a man on the move. The reports ranged widely in topic, including food shipments, the condition and control of railroads, the conditions in Petrograd, petroleum supplies, the situation in Finland and Lithuania, and the state and movement of the Red Army. There was even a report on shoes, which may seem insignificant, but shoes had become outrageously expensive, and an army needs leather: the Bolsheviks hoped to import a million pairs, signaling their military intentions.[17]

Although Imbrie was the only U.S. representative permanently assigned to Petrograd, other American officials filtered in and out of the city. They show the varied backgrounds of consular officers collectively working for American interests. In the first month Vice Consul Ralph B. Dennis came to help Imbrie with correspondence. Dennis empathized with the Russian peasant and, in particular, with Russians who had emigrated to the United States and then returned home, unable to fulfill their dreams. Too often in American cities they had been ostracized, these men with whiskers whose names ended in "ski" and "vitch" and were unable to assimilate, unwanted, and suspected of being socialists. In 1916 Dennis had traveled throughout Europe as a bank representative and, when the war broke out, found his new calling with the YMCA working with Russian soldiers. After Russia withdrew from the war, Summers recruited him for consular work. Like other staff members, he was strongly anti-Bolshevik.[18]

Vice Consul William Lancaster Jenkins, a Pennsylvania Quaker, also helped Imbrie. Tall, with receding black hair, Jenkins had served in Trebizond and Tiflis before coming to Moscow. In fleeing Trebizond, he had lost all his personal belongings, which perhaps heightened his antipathy to the Bolsheviks.[19]

U.S. military attachés were also active in Petrograd, consigned to moving military supplies out of reach of the Germans. Between May and August the Americans, French, and British helped remove about 80 to 90 percent—over 170,000 tons—of matérial from Petrograd and surrounding industrial areas.[20] Among the attachés, two worked closely with Imbrie, Lieutenants Peter Bukowski and Earl Packer. Both had been working in Petrograd, at the consulate and embassy, respectively, when America declared war on Germany.[21] Imbrie also befriended a military attaché from the British embassy, Captain Francis Cromie, who was deep into espionage work, having been in Russia since 1915. Uniting these friendships was a mutual revulsion for Bolshevism and compassion for the Russian people.

As Imbrie's duties increased, so did his exposure to danger. He needed to know about German troops in Finland and North Russia, their movement and supplies, and the resistance by Russian naval and military forces to Bolshevik authority.[22] He also sought information on civilian anti-Bolshevik activities. In sum he needed a network of agents. He chiefly engaged ex-military officers, two of whom had been professional spies under the tsar. Others were common soldiers, valuable because of their ease in passing through enemy lines. Women, some in Bolshevik employ, also joined. In building his network, Imbrie established "checking trips," sending new agents out for information and comparing their reports to what was already known. He gave them colored charts to help in memorizing German insignias, ranks, regimental corps, and divisional and departmental marks. His reporting expanded to include German personnel, equipment, probable lines of advance, and the condition of railroads and transport roads leading to the front. When Allied troops landed and formed a front in the north, agents began reporting on the Bolshevik troop movements there. By June Imbrie was receiving a steady stream of information, including details on German activity as far away as Lithuania.

Although Imbrie took precautions, he was most likely under Bolshevik surveillance as early as his first week back in Petrograd. While on the train to Petrograd, he had questioned a porter about an American, Lewis Simmel, who claimed he had been robbed several weeks earlier. The porter remembered the man and contradicted his story. The U.S. military mission had entrusted Simmel with an envelope containing 3,000 rubles for delivery to Moscow. When Simmel reached Moscow, he claimed to have been forcibly removed from the train and robbed, and thus the story held until Imbrie reached Petrograd. Imbrie summoned Simmel to the consulate on the pretense of visaing his passport. German-born Simmel, who had spent almost two years in Russia as a salesman, had drooping eyes and a hangdog look. When he presented himself at the consulate, Imbrie confronted him about his theft. Simmel protested his innocence, but when Imbrie related the porter's testimony, he confessed. At first Simmel claimed that he did not have the funds to reimburse the American mission, but under pressure he returned the entire amount and in front of a witness signed a confession.[23] Simmel then began helping Imbrie gather information. It seemed that Imbrie had won the day; however, the British suspected Simmel of being a Bolshevik agent.[24] If Simmel were a Bolshevik agent, Imbrie was probably a marked man from this time on.

Regardless, Imbrie would have eventually fallen under suspicion from being the lone U.S. consul in Petrograd and from his frequent visits to Bolshevik offices, sometimes on behalf of arrested Americans. The Bolshevik intelligence bureau, informally called the Cheka, knew who he was.[25] Once when Ralph Wilner, an Austrian-born American, was arrested on charges of speculation, Imbrie spent six hours tracking him to the former Smolney Institute, then housing the city government. Cannons guarded the entrance to the enormous Palladium-style building. Pale electric lights flickered in its cavernous hallways. Mud covered the marble floors, once polished to a high sheen. The smell of cabbage soup permeated the air; typewriters clacked incessantly like cricket clickers. Imbrie pushed his way past lounging soldiers and peasants and the men and women issuing from the warren of offices.[26] He did not know what treatment he would receive, much less Wilner's condition. Wilner had been traveling for several years as a manufacturer's representative, working for a variety of firms, including tool, hardware, cabinet, and lubricant companies. He generally stayed at the luxurious Hotel l'Europe. He was not used to the deprivation and indignity of a prison cell. With persistence, Imbrie located him in what he termed a dungeon, conducted an interview, and, convinced of Wilner's innocence and satisfied as to his well-being, set off to confront Moisei Uritsky, the head of the Cheka in Petrograd.

The Cheka was housed at number 4 Gorokhovaya Street, not far from Imbrie's office. Uritsky, a lawyer by education, was a small man who favored pince-nez glasses. Determined to be direct rather than diplomatic and using Bukowski as his translator, Imbrie was bold and blunt. He demanded Wilner's release immediately, and Uritsky soon consented, perhaps because the Americans were helping move supplies out of German reach. Imbrie then pressed his advantage, demanding a written apology addressed to Ambassador Francis. Surprisingly, the apology was delivered, written by Minister of Foreign Affairs Leon Trotsky.[27]

In July, when Imbrie learned of the arrest of two more Americans, he and Bukowski returned to Uritsky. One American was a corporate representative with a contract to deliver condensed milk to the Russian government, but because the United States refused to recognize the Bolshevik government, he had been arrested on charges of fraud. Imbrie must have been furious. At the time the infant mortality rate was estimated at 50 percent. The American Red Cross had shipped as much as 450,000 cans of condensed milk between February and April but had had to abandon its program in May. The need for milk was critical. Again, Imbrie was successful in gaining an American's freedom.

After one of his visits to Uritsky, Imbrie himself barely made it out of Cheka headquarters. As he and Bukowski approached the exit, a soldier thrust a bayonet at Imbrie and ordered him back. Through some error the two men had only one exit permit. "Let me pass," Imbrie remonstrated. "I'm the American Consul." The soldier stood firm. As Imbrie let loose with some choice words, an English-speaking commissar stepped out of his office and told Imbrie that if he felt that way, he should tell Uritsky so himself. "That's just what I'm going to do," Imbrie snapped, spinning around and bounding up the stairs. The startled commissar, his bluff called, chased after Imbrie, waving the requisite permit. Imbrie retraced his steps, and as the guard muttered an apology, he and Bukowski sailed out the door.

The above confrontation makes for a good story, an adventure story with a lone figure riding into town and thwarting evil, and it was later recounted as such in the *New York Times*, but the breadth and villainy of the Cheka should not be underestimated. The Cheka had no affiliation with the police, courts, or the commissioner of justice. When the Treaty of Brest-Litovsk freed two million prisoners of war, the Cheka began filling the empty camps with political prisoners. In June Trotsky had Czech war prisoners placed in just such a camp, and in August Vladimir Lenin, the head of the Soviet government, called for political enemies in Pena to be similarly placed. These concentration camps were central to what became known as the Red Terror, the Bolsheviks' savage suppression of the counterrevolution following an attempt on Lenin's life.[28]

Imbrie knew the dangers of the Cheka, even when he expressed them ironically. Once when he made a list of new Bolshevik officials, he put an asterisk next to the commissar of justice and wrote, "A useless post. There is no justice in Soviet Russia. . . . [N]ext to taking moving pictures of a glacier, the position of Commissar of Justice in Russia is the world's greatest sinecure."[29]

Besides helping Americans in legal trouble, Imbrie helped those without basic provisions. One time when he learned of some fifteen destitute Americans, he obtained relief funds from the American Red Cross in Petrograd and secured their safe exit from Russia, despite repeated delays due to fighting along the railways and poor telecommunications. Imbrie worked closely with other humanitarian organizations as well. An orphanage originally run by Americans who had since left the country fell into a pitiable state with little food; Imbrie sent the children to Viatka, putting them in the care of the Salvation Army and gathering food for their journey.[30]

At all times Imbrie was in danger. At one point, when he thought the Germans were within two hours of Petrograd, he made plans to leave by airplane. "If they come in I go up," he wrote.[31] Another time he sent punning doggerel to the consulate in Moscow, "Spring is coming. So are the Germans. Trees are leaving [leafing]. So am I."[32] He was back in a few days.

As the Germans advanced, eventually coming to within fifteen miles of Petrograd, Imbrie's agents made increasingly shorter journeys, allowing for more accurate and timely information, but Imbrie also began receiving threatening letters, and these increased throughout the summer.[33] Imbrie had hoped to disguise his intelligence work by having only his chief agent, Lt. Michael Perts, know its extent.[34] Perts was a former tsarist officer assigned to the U.S. military mission, and his service and dedication to Imbrie and the United States came at a heavy cost and reveal how thorough the Cheka was in its intelligence work. To save his life, Perts eventually had to flee from Russia. The Bolsheviks retaliated by executing two of his brothers. Another brother, John, escaped, fleeing to Finland, and after the war both brothers worked alongside Earl Packer at the U.S. legation in Riga. Both became U.S. citizens. Improbably John Perts became a Capitol Hill caricaturist in Washington DC.

Imbrie's network produced both helpful and misleading information. One incident involved Imbrie acquiring documents purportedly implicating the Bolsheviks as paid German agents. Earlier, in February, a set of similar documents had come to the attention of Ambassador Francis, which Francis used to justify U.S. military intervention in Russia. At that time Francis contacted Edgar Sisson, a representative of the United States Committee on Public Information (ComPub), a propaganda agency active in Russia, and told him of the stolen files. Sisson already had copies of such documents, dating from early in the war and from the previous summer. He headed for the United States with the cache. Unbeknownst to him and Francis, the documents were fraudulent, although it was years before they were thoroughly debunked.[35]

Even after Sisson's departure the document saga continued. In the second week of April Imbrie met an American, George Ackerman, who claimed to have forty-three documents of interest, purportedly proving a Bolshevik-German alliance as well as the workings of the German spy system. After Imbrie had an expert examine the documents, Ambassador Francis approved their purchase, and Imbrie completed an exchange for half the asking price.[36] He then made copies of the documents, sending one set to Francis, another to Summers, and a third set under seal to the Norwegian embassy for safekeeping. But Ackerman's documents, too, were fraudulent. The easy acceptance of documents seems blameworthy but can be understood in context: the horror of anarchy and its violence, the rejection of Bolshevik legitimacy, and a willingness to believe in a Bolshevik-German connivance all promoted a suspension of disbelief.

A second incident also involved the so-called Sisson papers and Imbrie. Through his agents Imbrie obtained a copy of a telegram sent from Petrograd by a reporter for the *Chicago Daily News*, Lewis Edgar Browne. The telegram was, in Imbrie's words, "flagrantly indiscreet." It read in part: "Please cable me urgently . . . what disposition Sisson made or intended making of certain material he collected regarding Soviet-German affiliation. This confidential."[37] When questioned by Summers in Moscow, Browne did not divulge his sources. Subsequently, on Imbrie's recommendation, he was forbidden to use the wire service and in mid-May left for the United States.[38]

Imbrie had been back in Petrograd for only a month when tragedy hit the American mission. On May 3, in Moscow, Summers went home, feeling ill. He had been under enormous pressure since the Bolshevik revolution in November, he was worried about the well-being of his Russian-born wife and his son, and although he seemed in fine health, he had a serious health concern—he had had a brain tumor removed the previous summer. He was extremely fatigued.[39] That evening, at the age of forty-one, he died of a brain hemorrhage. Ambassador Francis, who was also battling serious health problems, came from Vologda to attend Summers's funeral.[40] With Summers's death, DeWitt Clinton Poole became acting consul.

By May only about fifteen American civilians remained in Petrograd.[41] As representatives of American firms left the country, Bolsheviks confiscated the abandoned property almost daily, and Imbrie had his hands full protecting property, demanding the return of property, and taking inventory of property that might be seized. In early May the American Red Cross turned its relief effort over to Imbrie, thereby centralizing all U.S. relief work through the consulate. On May 14 the last representative of ComPub left, adding to Imbrie's increasingly long job description the tasks of furnishing propaganda against German intrigue and preparing dispatches for the Russian press. He had excerpts from Wilson's speeches translated into German and printed as posters, ready for when the Germans reached Petrograd, a daily expectation. By then Imbrie's reports were so numerous that he established a regular courier service to Vologda and Moscow.

On May 29 the Bolsheviks announced that they were appropriating the American-owned Singer Building for nonpayment of taxes. The Bolsheviks had been systematically working their way down Nevsky Prospect, seizing one building after another. Now the Singer was in their sights. To thwart them Imbrie contrived to raise the U.S. flag and claim the building as official American property. Imbrie telegraphed Vologda for approval and awaited the answer. The return message read: "No precedent," a statement of fact but not permission denied.[42] Imbrie tossed the message aside, borrowed a flag from the ComPub office, had Bukowski run it up, and dispatched a second telegram, "Precedent established. Imbrie, Acting."[43] The flag-raising incident was captured in a cartoon, most likely by John Perts, later published in the *New York Times*. As Consul Poole noted, Imbrie was "a live wire."[44] In the face of danger he exuded bravado, but he was not foolhardy. "I'm never looking for trouble," he told a friend, "but if it comes, I'll welcome it with open arms."[45] The Singer Building remained inviolate, and Francis gave the flag raising tacit approval.

In June Ambassador Francis made another trip south, this time to Petrograd. The trip was for personal as well as professional reasons. On his way to Russia in 1916, Francis had met a Madame Matilda de Cramm on board the ship. In Petrograd she had set up residence two blocks from the American embassy and had become a frequent visitor, serving as Francis's French tutor. Among the diplomatic staff and at the State Department suspicion grew that she was a German agent. Further, her relationship with Francis, who was married, seemed indiscreet. Francis insisted the relationship was platonic, and when he moved the embassy to Vologda, she did not accompany him. Nevertheless, he kept in contact with her. In May, when he learned that the Cheka had described her as his mistress, he was livid. He wrote to Imbrie: "If anyone charges that I have improper relations with Matilda De Cramm he is a liar."[46]

Defying the rumors and drawn by circumstances, Francis returned to Petrograd in early June. According to reports, the Bolsheviks were about to fall.[47] Here, the ambassador thought, was an opportunity for democracy. He moved back into the American embassy. Amid the desolation of closed shops and deserted streets, he visited Matilda de Cramm and probably brought her food. He warned her to destroy his letters as she was surely being watched. He could be compromised; she could be imprisoned. Francis also met with counterrevolutionaries and with industrialists favoring a constitutional monarchy, but those visits sank his hopes. In a vast understatement he reported that the Bolsheviks had "irreparably injured democracy in Russia for a generation."[48] After four days Francis returned to Vologda, where he stepped up his anti-Bolshevik efforts, authorizing widespread espionage and covert activities across western Russia with an emphasis on military and revolutionary matters. Francis committed the U.S. Treasury to fund these anti-Bolshevik activities, engaging the government in intelligence efforts against a former ally.[49] It is doubtful he ever saw Matilda de Cramm again.

In June Imbrie learned that the property of yet another American was to be confiscated. To protect it, he went to the owner's estate about thirty miles from the city, near Strelina, claimed it as his official residence, and registered his passport with the local authorities. Occasionally on weekends, he and a "stunning girl" made it their weekend retreat.[50] Until the time he left Russia, the villa remained untouched.[51]

Back in Petrograd, Imbrie resumed his work. From the third floor of the Singer Building, he could look down on peasants and former nobles intermingling on the corner of Nevsky Prospect, once a broad, commercial boulevard, now the outdoor market for ragged entrepreneurs selling newspapers and saccharine-sweetened cakes. Trucks carrying flour drove past, headed to barracks where it was mixed with sand and baked into dense black bread.[52] The city's life was becoming ever more desperate. The ruble, once valued at 51 cents against the U.S. dollar, was worth 10 cents. Tobacco sold at $35 a pound, horse meat at $1.10 a pound, an egg for 35 cents. Sugar sold at $6 a pound and flour at $3.[53]

Although Imbrie's living accommodations were enviable, he also faced shortages of supplies, including food. He was also in constant danger from both Bolsheviks and Germans. He oversaw millions of tons of supplies delivered by the United States and the Allies before the revolution, and he had agents' reports hidden throughout his office and apartment.[54]

On Independence Day, as Francis hosted a reception in Vologda with his Victrola scratching out dance music in the garden,[55] the

Fifth All-Russian Congress of Soviets opened at the Moscow Opera House. The weather was hot and sultry.[56] With the delegates split, the Left Socialist Revolutionaries began denouncing the Bolsheviks, shouting, "Away with the German butchers!"[57] Two days later the German ambassador, Wilhelm von Mirbach, was assassinated in Petrograd by leftists seeking to sever the Bolshevik-German alliance. When the Left Socialist Revolutionaries barricaded themselves in their headquarters near the U.S. consulate, the Bolsheviks brought up field artillery and, in Imbrie's words, "blew the Social Revolutionary headquarters to pieces."[58] Intermittent fighting continued for the next several days. The foreign legations feared they would be held hostage under the ruse of protection. Francis stepped up his appeal to Washington for armed intervention, and on July 17 President Wilson finally agreed to send U.S. troops. Francis was ecstatic. He wrote to Imbrie that "Soviet rule in Russia is about finished."[59] Ironically, on that very night of July 16–17, the deposed tsar, Nicholas II, and his wife and five children were murdered by Soviet troops.

Then Francis encountered a further setback. Only 4,500 U.S. troops were deployed to North Russia, not the 10,000 he recommended.[60] Neither Francis nor Secretary of State Robert Lansing could sway Gen. John J. Pershing, commander of the American Expeditionary Forces, who opposed intervention as unwinnable and a distraction from the demands of the Western Front. On the other hand Pershing, and most of the Allies, failed to consider the Bolsheviks' long-term threat to world peace. The Allied and U.S. troops in North Russia, numbering fewer than ten thousand men combined, were assigned to an area larger than the Western Front, facing an army growing ever stronger. By the end of 1918 the Red Army numbered a million men.[61]

On July 23 Francis received a telegram from Georgi Chicherin, the Soviet commissar for foreign affairs: "Danger approaching. Tomorrow can be too late."[62] Francis was prepared for this eventuality. He had had train cars at the ready for weeks. The diplomatic community hastily packed its belongings and with 140 people in the entourage left Vologda for Archangel, about seven hundred miles northeast of Moscow, just below the Arctic Circle.[63] Three American staff members stayed behind.

Meanwhile in Petrograd an American, identified to history as Madame L., was in a Cheka prison. Imbrie went with Bukowski, his translator, to negotiate her release. This time Uritsky was obdurate, saying that the Americans must first remove their troops in northwest Russia. Imbrie stayed his course. "Tell him I am not the Secretary of State or the President," Imbrie retorted, rapping his cane on Uritsky's desk. "If he wants our troops removed, tell him to write a note to Washington. But I want Madame L. released now." Uritsky relented, and Imbrie hurried her off to the safety of the embassy to live under its protection. She was just one of many people whom Imbrie hid.[64] Unfortunately, when Imbrie had to flee Petrograd, she was rearrested.[65] Her fate is unknown.

By the summer of 1918 the once picturesque city of Petrograd had turned into an unsanitary displaced persons camp with contaminated water and food. Predictably cholera was rapidly spreading, about 1,500 new cases daily, and Imbrie estimated that without clean water and proper medicine, the death rate among cases could rise to 80 percent.[66] One of Imbrie's colleagues, not quite sardonically, recommended, as a substitute for water, "champagne . . . or even a pinch of red or white wine," and when one of his consular colleagues sent Imbrie some tobacco, Imbrie thanked him, writing that "I shall cut up some thousand rouble bills and mix them with the tobacco, thus making it go further and cost less."[67] His sense of humor did not fail him in Petrograd. He sent one letter identifying himself as "Manager of the Committee on Public Information and Inspector of Icebergs, Somewhere in Russia."[68]

During the summer communication became increasingly difficult. On July 11 direct communication between the Americans in the north and in Moscow was cut. Imbrie became their liaison. He also handled the transmission of communiqués by the French, who had been banned from wiring coded messages.[69] In mid-July when cables were cut with Washington, passports could no longer be processed. Imbrie had to turn away clamoring, desperate Russians. When the last direct line for the Americans was cut, Imbrie's telegrams and dispatches had to be transmitted through the Norwegian legation. By July 31 matters had become so fraught that Imbrie lowered the American flag at the consulate and raised the Norwegian flag. He considered destroying the codes.[70] He had been in Petrograd as Francis's emissary for three months. His time was running out.

On August 2 Imbrie received a telegram from Poole announcing a break in de facto relations with the Bolshevik government. It seemed that war between the United States and Russia was imminent. Earlier that day in a fiery speech Lenin had harangued a crowd in Moscow: "The enemies of the Soviet Union have gone to war with us, gone to war against the Soviet government, against the workers' and peasants' government. . . . They have declared war on the Soviets and on the workers and peasants. . . . America, too, is now fighting together with the British and French. . . . The last decisive battle is near. There can be no compromise with the bourgeoisie. Either them or us. . . . As we declare war on the rich, we say, 'Peace to the cottages!'"

Although the Soviet foreign minister rapidly issued a correction, saying that war had not been declared but only that Russia was prepared to defend itself, dispatches with Lenin's supposed declaration of war went to the State Department, and both Petrograd and Moscow shuttered their consulates for a short while. On August 22 and 23 American newspapers from coast to coast ran headlines that America was at war with Russia. The *New York Times* ran the story on page three, suggesting that the threat was not taken seriously by the State Department, but smaller newspapers gave it prominent bold-banner, page 1 display.[71] By then the American consuls were deep into other concerns.

The day following Lenin's speech in response to the Allied troop landings in North Russia, the Bolsheviks interned a large number of British and French residents in Moscow, including the consular staffs. They also arrested the last three American officials in

Vologda. The American mission in Moscow was spared, thanks to a warning sent by a British agent. His warning was not completely altruistic: he had hidden British money in the U.S. consulate.

Then, through his network, Imbrie learned of a directive for his own arrest. In response he picked up a visa at the Norwegian embassy, borrowed a car, and went again to Strelina, this time for four days, continuing his consular work by telephone and messenger. J. Butler Wright, counselor of the embassy in Russia, commended him for his "untiring efforts to get things through to the Department."[72] He had also received commendations from the ambassador, the consul general, and two military missions.[73] As soon as he secured a guarantee of immunity, he returned to Petrograd and, without waiting for departmental approval, destroyed the diplomatic code.[74]

Imbrie also began destroying the remaining U.S. matériel stored in and around the city so it would not fall into Bolshevik or German hands. On August 13 he attended a conference of representatives of the British, French, Danish, and Swedish governments who hoped to gain the release of their imprisoned citizens. A protest was composed, which Imbrie did not sign as no American was currently imprisoned. On August 25 Allied representatives met in Moscow. According to the Bolsheviks, they discussed a plan to use Latvian troops to overthrow the Bolshevik government. Poole denied any American knowledge of the plot, but since July, at least, the Americans had been in touch with agents plotting a revolt. How involved the American foreign officers were or if they were involved at all is unknown. What is known is that Poole allowed American, French, and British agents to meet in his office.[75]

Following the August 13 meeting, Imbrie advised the remaining Americans in Petrograd to leave Russia, especially as neutral ministers were offering safe conduct through the German lines into Finland.[76] Imbrie gathered food for their ten-day journey, arranged for inoculations against cholera, and procured health certificates necessary for entry into Sweden. Lieutenants Packer and Bukowski retreated to the U.S. mission in Archangel. Imbrie obtained blank visas from the Swedish consulate for the Americans and left them with Uritsky to be stamped. They were never returned.[77]

On August 17 Uritsky was assassinated, gunned down by a revolutionary in a rival political party. He was buried in the Field of Mars, its sulfuric yellow dust billowing in the summer sky. The reprisal for his murder was swift and brutal. The Cheka ordered summary executions and detained members of the Russian bourgeoisie as hostages. "A veritable slaughter is going on," Poole wrote from Moscow.[78] He reported that in Petrograd seven thousand people had been arrested and five hundred shot. Then another event intensified the slaughter. On August 30 an attempt was made on Lenin's life. As Lenin was leaving a factory after a speaking engagement, a Socialist Revolutionary, Fanny Kaplan, approached him and fired her revolver. The retribution was swift, brutal, and this time unrelenting. The Red Terror had begun.

Imbrie had only hours left. He issued the remaining American nationals Certificates of Citizenship under the consular seal and prepared to evacuate. He gave 100,000 rubles to Perts to continue the espionage work and consigned the embassy and consular records to the Norwegians for safekeeping. He packed up the remaining money, the consular seal, and a small bundle of papers containing copies of the ambassador's correspondence.[79] These papers, later stored in the State Department along with another set brought out of Russia by Norwegian diplomats, were thought for years to be the sole surviving records from Petrograd from this period. Only with the establishment of diplomatic relations in 1933 and though the intrepid efforts of Vice Consul Angus Ward were more records found, now stored in the National Archives.[80]

Imbrie made a last offer to stay, which Poole rejected.[81] On August 28 a special train from Moscow with almost a hundred American officials and nationals had reached Petrograd. Some had helped Imbrie in the spring and summer, including Vice Consuls Dennis and Jenkins. Consul Poole remained in Moscow. In

Petrograd the train languished, waiting permission to continue its journey. Dennis took the opportunity to scrounge some food for the trip, buying four and a half pounds of cheese for $12.25 and a pint of strained honey for $4.00. The delay proved a stroke of luck for Imbrie.

On the night of August 30 the Norwegian legation telephoned Imbrie that unless he left immediately, it could not guarantee his safety.[82] The train was his best chance for escape. The next afternoon the Norwegians picked him up in a car flying their flag and headed to the depot. They almost didn't reach it. As the car approached the British embassy, Imbrie saw it was under attack. In the battle the senior British official, Captain Francis Cromie, Imbrie's friend, was shot and killed.[83]

Cromie had been assigned to the British embassy in December 1917, shortly after Imbrie's arrival. He had been posted to the Baltic Fleet in 1915, but after the Treaty of Brest-Livosk, which required that all British submarines in Russian ports be turned over to the Germans, Cromie had sent his men home and scuttled his boats. He had then joined the British legation in Petrograd as naval attaché. He spoke Russian and, like Imbrie, was reputedly a witty conversationalist, at ease among people of all walks of life. Cromie's activities included handling money for British commercial interests since the Petrograd banks were closed, gathering intelligence information, and engaging in interventionist activity. This last activity was his undoing. When he came under suspicion, he moved to a safe house and, when that was raided, to the British embassy.

In early August two men came to the embassy, posing as counterrevolutionaries. Cromie arranged a meeting with them and other counterrevolutionaries at the Hotel de France. Only one of the plotters turned up. A second meeting was scheduled for August 31. By then Cromie was working out the details of an attack on the Bolsheviks by a combined force of Allies and counterrevolutionaries.

On the afternoon of August 31, as Imbrie was being picked up by the Norwegians, Cromie met with the two plotters in a room on the second floor of the embassy. Elsewhere in the building were other embassy staff members and servants, about thirty-three people in all. While the plotters—in reality Cheka agents—stalled, supposedly waiting for a third man to join them, Bolshevik troops pulled up in front of the embassy and charged inside. Cromie rushed into the hall, his revolver drawn. Gunfire was exchanged, and Cromie was killed.

With Bolsheviks storming the British embassy, Imbrie's car was flagged down. Soldiers quickly surrounded it. Remonstrating, the Norwegian consul proffered Imbrie's false papers. Meanwhile Imbrie could see the British staff being lined up outside the building. After Imbrie's papers passed muster, the car rolled slowly by as the British staff was marched off to Cheka headquarters. Without further delay Imbrie reached the railroad station and boarded the train.[84] The train belched steam from its smoke stack and ground forward, pulling away from the city. For two days, it lurched toward the border, thirty-five miles from Petrograd. There the Americans grabbed their belongings and walked two hundred yards to a country bridge where they presented their credentials. They passed into Finland, safely out of Russia, where, as one man wrote, "things had been getting a little thick." From Finland most headed to Sweden and to home.

The Allied diplomatic corps still in Moscow were not as lucky as Imbrie but were luckier than Cromie. On September 1 the British embassy workers were arrested.[85] British consul R. H. Bruce Lockhart was taken to Lubyenka Prison on September 4, where he was held for a month, his release most likely contingent on Lenin's recovery from the attempted assassination.[86] Daily he paced the prison grounds, stopping to visit the chapel of Our Lady of Unexpected Joy and waiting for release.[87] It came joyfully in October in a prisoner exchange.

In addition to the British arrests were French arrests, although the chief of the French secret service, Colonel Henri de Vertement, escaped the roundup by climbing out an apartment window and running across rooftops.[88] One American agent was also arrested, Xenophon Kalamatiano, a businessman with extensive contacts throughout the former Imperial Empire. Although condemned to death, his sentence was reprieved in exchange for famine relief in August 1921.

Consul Poole learned of his own imminent arrest on September 14 and set out for the border, crossing it six days later, crumpling in exhaustion as he stepped onto safe ground, ten minutes before his arrest order reached the border guards.[89] Meanwhile Imbrie was gloriously free and headed back to the United States. In 1918 he had had adventures that made his game hunting and globe-trotting seem to him like "a Sunday school picnic"; he had witnessed atrocities that staggered him, even after spending seventeen months at the front in France and Macedonia; he had lived amid "absolute anarchy"; but he concluded that he had also "rather enjoy[ed] the show."[90] He was a marked man, but his luck was holding.

FIVE

Living with Banquo's Ghost

On November 11, 1918, at 11:00 a.m., Germany formally surrendered. Eyes turned to Paris and the peace talks, not to Russia, although its civil war, which continued until 1922, shaped the twentieth century. If Russia had been invited to the peace talks, history might have followed a different trajectory, but it was not. Instead, the Allies rebuked the Bolsheviks for repudiating Russia's outstanding war debts and for signing the Brest-Litovsk treaty with Germany. Further, neither the Allies nor the United States recognized the Bolshevik government as legitimate. While others looked to Paris, ignoring Moscow, Imbrie was in Washington DC, hoping to continue his reconnaissance work.

The preferred observation post for northwest Russia was Viborg, Finland. Situated on the Gulf of Finland, Viborg was about thirty-five miles from the Russian border and eighty miles from Petrograd. It was a city of about seventy-five thousand people, with peninsulas and islands tethered by bridges. Its quays, alleyways, streets, and boulevards wove past medieval structures, gardens, and parks, under the great eye of a thirteenth-century fortification built to deter the Muscovites, a daily reminder of the new threat, the Bolsheviks. Because Viborg was a port town, it had a polyglot atmosphere exaggerated by war, like Salonika. It was, according to one memoirist, a "hornet's nest" of conspirators and spies.[1]

In a relatively short time, given the State Department's heavy workload after the war, Imbrie's appointment to Finland came through, and he arrived in Viborg on February 25, 1919, as vice consul in charge.[2] He stayed until June 1920. He would have already been somewhat familiar with the city. While he was in Petrograd, his agents had informed on conditions in Viborg, and the train from Petrograd's Finland Station stopped there. Once at his new post, he presented his credentials to the city's mayor and, with reciprocal dinners, developed a cordial relationship. The city was crowded with émigrés, and for three weeks he stayed in a hotel until he could secure two rooms in the business district, at $47 a month, a decided decline from his accommodations in Petrograd. His nearest State Department colleague in Finland was Consul William Thornwell Haynes in Helsingfors (today's Helsinki). As in Petrograd, he was largely his own man.

Imbrie had similar assignments to those in Russia: fulfill normal consular duties, such as visaing passports, assisting with humanitarian efforts, and continuing his information gathering. He immediately began establishing a network of agents.[3] Being close to the border, he could meet the agents the day they crossed into Finland, but he also knew the border was carefully watched and executions were summary. Southeast of Viborg in the Gulf of Finland lay the island fortress of Kronstadt, the headquarters of the Russian Baltic fleet, with its sweeping searchlights and strategically placed mines off the Russian shore. Weather also dictated passage between Russia and Finland. As long as the Gulf of Finland was frozen, agents leaving Finland could cross on the ice and head for a point near Peterhof, southwest of Petrograd. When the thaw came and the gulf was patrolled by the Russian navy, Imbrie arranged for a boat to leave from the Finnish side of Lake Ladoga, cross the border in midlake, and touch shore about twenty-two miles east of Petrograd. Imbrie himself had hoped to use these routes, but the border scrutiny was so intense that no

Russian would accompany him to Petrograd. He had to rely on his agents for information.

Imbrie knew Bolsheviks and Germans might infiltrate his network, and the Finnish authorities, not wanting to rankle Russia, had to be courted to turn a blind eye to his activities. Most of the agents in Imbrie's previous network had been executed, perhaps due to information seized during raids, but with the help of two former agents, Imbrie rebuilt his operation so the State Department and Office of Naval Intelligence soon had a "regular flow of information about conditions in Petrograd and about the morale and movement of Soviet military and naval forces."[4] Because Imbrie used a system of cutouts, only three of his agents knew his identity.[5] Eventually his network formed a diverse and well-positioned cadre: a clerk at the Smolny Institute, a member of the Bolshevik General Staff, a clerk attached to the Commission Against Counter Revolution, an engineer at the Poutilovksy Locomotive and Machine Works, a commissary attached to the staff of the Finnish Front, a clerk in the Bolshevik Bureau of Statistics, two officers in the Semenovsky Regiment, a commissary in Moscow, and various ex-officers in the north or on the Estonian front. Imbrie also developed a network working out of Reval, Estonia, with only one agent knowing his identity. Three from that network went in and out of Viborg, Reval, Petrograd, and Moscow.

Although agents provided Imbrie with abundant material, he also gathered information as part of the daily routine of being a vice consul. Finland, a Grand Duchy of Russia prior to the Bolshevik revolution, had declared its sovereignty in December 1918, but its situation was fluid and tenuous. To protect its sovereignty and perhaps even gain more territory, it supported the anti-Bolshevik White Army of Northwest Russia. Estonia, too, supported the White Army, knowing the Bolsheviks wanted the country as a link to Germany by way of the Baltic Sea.[6] Despite being in Finland, Imbrie was in the midst of the Russian civil war as the Whites launched their offensive from the west. His dispatches from March to December of 1919 detail this offensive as hopes rose and fell with the spring to winter temperatures.[7]

During the first weeks of March Imbrie met with the financial and military leaders of the Whites, whose paramount concern was food, although this changed over the course of the campaign.[8] At first they believed their supplies sufficient for a ten-day campaign and, after their proposed victory, for the Petrograd populace for ten days. Thereafter, more food shipments would be needed. The State Department was willing to consider food relief as a commercial venture, but not as charity. It seems hard-hearted, but the dispatches regarding food relief have to be read in light of several factors—the high-priced food surplus in America, increases in postwar shipping, the effort to contain Bolshevism through food relief, and the food needs of all liberated countries in Europe.[9] More to the point, the State Department was skeptical that a White victory could be achieved in a mere ten days and urged Imbrie to be cautious in his dealings and guard against false hopes.[10]

Imbrie also met with the commander of the Finnish forces supporting the Whites.[11] The Finns had a large standing army and a larger voluntary reserve force as well as a considerable navy; however, by July 1919 the economic situation in Finland was dire. The Finnish mark had suffered a 40 percent decrease in value in four months, the cost of living was accelerating, work was scarce, and wages were low. Partly due to supporting the Russian Whites, government expenses had soared, ironically giving the populace even more reason for discontent, a fruitful ground for sowing the seed of Bolshevism, as Imbrie put it.[12] The meetings with military leaders generated a rumor, perhaps the work of Bolsheviks, that Imbrie had also conferred with the German consul. The British cabled the rumor to the American embassy in London, which dismissed it. Nevertheless, Imbrie responded with vigor: "[The] Bare fact that the German Consul is still alive disproves the fib."[13]

Imbrie's negative view of Bolshevism held fast, as it did for the State Department. To Imbrie it was a failed social experiment. Based on his agents and other sources—refugees, border guards, messengers, Russian newspapers, and a captured Bolshevik courier—and his own interviews, Imbrie sent an overview of northwest Russia to the State Department in March: "The Bolshevick [*sic*] government is essentially a government of and by force. It owes its continued existence to the Red Army."[14] He wrote that not more than 12 percent of the population of Soviet Russia favored Bolshevism, commerce and production were at a standstill, the railroads were in a deplorable state, all educational institutions had closed, disease was ravaging the populace, and justice was nonexistent. Only soldiers found privilege, leading to the disaffection of workers and peasants. Imbrie concluded that the regeneration of Russia would never come from the inside: "Matters [can] only grow worse. There is no power of self-healing. The remedy must be an external one," either military or humanitarian, or both. He reported that the conditions in Petrograd were dire: inflation was skyrocketing, and the ruble was virtually worthless. Red troops were receiving a ration of seven herrings a day; Bolshevik clerical employees, five herrings; and the remainder of the population, nothing—"they were on their own."[15] Although Imbrie's reports were sometimes unwittingly based on exaggerated or fabricated source material, designed by his informants to manufacture Allied support, much was authentic, and in their antipathy to Bolshevism, the reports supported the State Department position. More importantly, they led to a massive, urgent relief plan.

At the beginning of the Paris peace talks, there was not a single report, recommendation, or study about the potential impact of Bolshevism upon the world.[16] Yet to Herbert Hoover, chairman of the American Relief Administration (ARA), it was "Banquo's ghost sitting at every Council table."[17] Unlike so many other officials at the peace talks, he knew Russia demanded and needed the world's attention. He called upon the power of American capitalism as the best weapon to confront communism wherever it spread. Although he was sympathetic to the causes of Bolshevism—especially the poverty of the downtrodden—and recognized the social injustices under the tsar, he knew little had been done to combat the famine in Russia in the winter of 1918–19.[18]

When Imbrie's report on northwest Russia reached the American delegation in Paris by way of the State Department, it helped force the question of how long the Allies could ignore the situation both from a humanitarian point of view and as a counter to Bolshevism. Imbrie's report helped harness attention and enact the far-reaching and fast-moving food plans that eventually averted starvation for millions of people.[19] By June 1919 the food supply had arrived in Finland, sufficient to last until September. Although Hoover deserves accolades in providing food relief, Imbrie's role in this massive effort has been virtually ignored. Imbrie deserves due credit. When the famine worsened in 1921, the ARA provided food to Russia directly, feeding eleven million people. Unfortunately, when the Communist leadership conspired to sell relief food to gain gold for militarism and industrialization, the ARA was forced to withdraw.[20]

In the midst of the relief effort Imbrie learned that a colleague from his Petrograd days, who had been missing since September 1918, had been found.[21] That month Roger Tredwell had left Moscow for Turkestan to investigate the political situation and assess the German purchase of cotton.[22] Eventually he was tracked to the city of Tashkent, where he was under house arrest.[23] After months of negotiations and diplomatic protests, he was released. He then had a long and dangerous train ride from Central Asia through at-war Russia to Finland. Imbrie was waiting for him as he crossed the border on April 27, 1919, for what Tredwell described as a "spectacular" reunion.

In the coming months Tredwell spoke of his experiences in Central Asia, painting the Bolsheviks in dark colors. In addressing the Russian Economic League in New York, he noted that the Bolsheviks had published a list of two thousand people executed in Tashkent, including a Swedish Red Cross aid worker. He recalled seeing four laborers arrested in a café and later shot without trial, and he knew of a village bombing, causing the deaths of twelve thousand people.[24] Although Tredwell himself had been generally well treated, he had had harrowing experiences, including five hours when he was imprisoned with the intimation of a quick execution. The arresting commander was known to have executed twelve men in one night.[25]

Tredwell's experience reinforced the State Department's view of Bolshevism and the importance of the Russian White Army defeating the Red Army, which Imbrie was tracking. An offensive began in mid-May under Gen. Nicolai Yudenitch, commander of the northwest White forces. It met with immediate success, and by the end of May the army had reached Gatchina, tantalizingly close to Petrograd. Imbrie planned to return to the city as soon as it fell, but the advance faltered. With the Whites stalled, the Bolsheviks had time to bring up reserves and began pushing back, retaking what they had lost by midsummer. Time was running out for a victory before winter. Food, forage, and fuel were in short supply in the battle zone, while thousands of tons of food stored in Viborg and Reval waited distribution. Imbrie concluded that if the Whites did not take Petrograd, "hundreds of thousands, if not millions of lives [would] be sacrificed to starvation and terrorism."[26] When the American Food Administration office in Viborg closed, Imbrie took charge of about seven thousand tons of stores valued at $3 million, over which he was to keep a "watchful and benevolent eye," and waited.[27]

In late July the White Army's needs increased exponentially. General Yudenitch asked Imbrie to appeal to the American government on his behalf for "every sort of military supply and munitions, [including] artillery, both field and heavy, airplanes, machine guns, small arms, transport cars, field telephones and telegraph instruments, horses, intrenching tools, 1,500 meters of pontoon bridging, as well as clothing, shoes and personal equipment, and the supplies and equipment sufficient for an army of 100,000 men and later for double that number."[28] The exhaustive list reveals fatal weaknesses in the Whites' campaign. It was ill-prepared, and the United States could not provide the White army with military supplies, partly due to geographic distance. The State Department recommended appealing to the Allies.

As Yudenitch mobilized for the last offensive of 1919, Imbrie doubted he would succeed. He had watched false hopes inflate during the previous campaign. He went to Reval to check on the status of the food stores.[29] At first the Whites defied the odds. The army stormed through mud and marsh, reaching Gatchina on October 14.[30] Petrograd looked open for the taking, two years to the month after the Russian Revolution of 1917, but Imbrie believed that if it were not taken within a week, Yudenitch would fail.[31] He watched euphoria balloon again: the empire would be restored, crushing the Bolshevik experiment. Rumors circulated that the city had indeed fallen. The acting secretary of state telegrammed Imbrie to "proceed [to Petrograd] as soon as you safely can and cable . . . a report upon general conditions . . . a part at least of [which] will be given to the press here."[32] To move supplies eastward, Imbrie received permission to draw up to $10,000 on the Russian embassy in Washington DC.[33] More promising news arrived. The railroad between Petrograd and Moscow had been cut and the Kronstadt Fort in the Gulf of Finland taken. Neither report proved true.[34] As fighting reached the outskirts of Petrograd, eyes focused on the waning calendar. Then more bad news. The railroad line from Viborg to Petrograd had been destroyed as well as the railroad bridge from Reval. Stores would have to reach the fallen city by water. Worse, Petrograd had a population much larger than previously thought, despite the daily death tolls and emigration, with an equal number—750,000—in the environs.[35] Food had to reach Petrograd before the freeze, predicted between December 1 and 15.

Then the balloon burst. Leon Trotsky, the commissar of army and navy affairs, arrived in Petrograd to take charge of the Bolshevik military operations. Imbrie's next report was of a Red offensive and reinforcements—the Red Army defending the city was now reported at one hundred thousand troops. On October 21 the counterattack began.[36] By early November Yudenitch was in retreat. The State Department recommended the food stores in Viborg be used for his troops, but there was no way to transport them.[37] The end had come to the White Army of the North. Yudenitch went on to live in exile, and Estonia signed a peace treaty with the Bolsheviks in what was called "a dance with the devil's grandmother."[38]

In the east, the White Army led by Gen. Alexander Kolchák had also launched a spring offensive, but by mid-June it, too, was in retreat, also never to recover. In January 1920 Kolchák resigned his command; he was executed by the Bolsheviks in February.[39] In the south, Gen. Anton Deníkin, commanding the third branch of the White Army, had pushed into Ukraine, conquering most of it by the end of June 1919. Deníkin then devised a three-pronged attack with the goal of capturing Moscow. At first his campaign was successful, but as the front expanded, his army thinned out, fatally weakening it, although it fought on through the fall of 1920. Deníkin, too, eventually went into exile. His army was the last hope for the Whites and a reason Imbrie went to Turkey in late 1920.

For Imbrie, the fall of Yudenitch was followed by alarming personal news. The Bolsheviks had tried him in absentia and delivered a death sentence. After he had left Petrograd in 1918, rumors circulated that the Bolsheviks had sacked the U.S. embassy. In July and September of 1919 Imbrie reported on these raids, but how much information had fallen into Bolshevik hands no one knew.[40] Finally, in late 1919, Imbrie's cover was blown when a British operation collapsed in Petrograd.[41] Earlier, in the spring of 1918, Sidney Reilly, a British agent, purportedly the inspiration for Ian Fleming's James Bond, had fled Russia to avoid arrest.[42] The British had replaced him with Paul Dukes, a thirty-year-old concert pianist with no training in espionage. Among his agents were Ilja Romanovitch Kurtz, supposedly the son of the Romanovs' chief of intelligence, and his fourteen-year-old daughter. Kurtz gathered information for the Allies under the ruse of visiting friends at the Hotel Astoria, where the Cheka and Smolny staff were quartered. Also in the network, working for both the Americans and the British, was a former tsarist officer who had defected from the Red Army, Rodinoff. His code names were "Fixer" and "Nicolaeff." The agents were paid with funds that Imbrie had left behind in August 1918. Zinaida Mackenzie-Kennedy, a U.S. embassy employee, began collecting information from Rodinoff in December.

Before Ambassador Francis had left Petrograd, Third Secretary Norman Armour told Mackenzie-Kennedy to keep away from politics—it was useless to take such a risk, he had said—and to stay close to the embassy for protection. But he also told her to "do quietly whatever there was to be done." She followed some of his advice. When Kurtz offered to introduce her to Dukes, she declined and banned Rodinoff from the embassy. When Imbrie, however, sent her notes from Finland, wondering about Rodinoff's whereabouts, Mackenzie-Kennedy kept tabs on him by meeting him at her place. After the U.S. embassy in Petrograd was sacked, she sent Imbrie a note through a Finnish courier. Shortly after, Rodinoff told her that Imbrie wanted a fuller report, which he would deliver. She fell into his trap. Later she learned that Rodinoff had handed this report to the Cheka. She also wrote a report that Dukes promised to deliver to the U.S. embassy in London but that for unknown reasons never arrived.

Dukes had a grandiose plot to overthrow the Bolshevik government. Red officers in the Eighth Army would open a front to the White Army, British ships would bombard forts in the Gulf of Finland, saboteurs would blow up Petrograd's bridges, including railway bridges, and Lenin, Trotsky, and Grigory Zinoviev, who at the time was in charge of Petrograd's defense, were to be poisoned. Zinoviev's secretary was one of the conspirators. Mackenzie-Kennedy thought the plot would have succeeded, except for a small incident.

On Monday, November 10, 1919, Kurtz's daughter went shopping. On her person was a concealed revolver, which was a gift from Dukes, and cartridges. As she wended her way past the stalls, soldiers suddenly swept through the market, rounding up buyers and sellers. In the chaos of screaming, pushing, and shoving, she was shunted aside because of her age, but then two cartridges fell from her pocket. If only she had scurried away at this point, but perhaps she was trapped by the crowd. Or perhaps her next movement was instinctive, done without thought of consequence. Regrettably she stooped to retrieve the cartridges, was seized in the act, and arrested. Her father's arrest followed quickly and his house searched. Seized documents led to other arrests. Agents who came to the house were arrested, and with confessions more arrests occurred. Among those seized was Rodinoff; he in turn fingered Mackenzie-Kennedy. In January 1920 Rodinoff was executed. Kurtz and his daughter were spared by agreeing to work with Soviet intelligence, although Mackenzie-Kennedy surmised they would be shot when their usefulness ended. Mackenzie-Kennedy herself was released from prison in late 1920, saved most likely because her husband, Chessborough J. H. McKenzie-Kennedy, had worked before the war with Igor Sikorsky, the famed Russian aeronautical engineer.[43] She reached London in early 1921.

Dukes, too, survived the dragnet and was knighted for his bravery.[44] Later, when he came to the United States on a speaking tour, the War Department and the Department of Justice tracked him as a known British agent. Contributing to the investigation were J. Edgar Hoover of the Justice Department and Maj. Sherman Miles, the director of military intelligence, who in 1924 went to Teheran to investigate Imbrie's murder. They found Dukes harmless.

The trials in Petrograd that followed the collapse of Dukes's network resulted in Imbrie's own trial. On November 29 the State Department received a telegram that the Bolsheviks had sentenced him to death.[45] This sentence stalked him in Finland, Turkey, and Persia.

At the start of January 1920 Imbrie reported losing two couriers to Finnish border shootings.[46] By then he had lost a total of fourteen men. To stem further loss, he sought Finnish cooperation in operating his agents. It took a month to get it. Meanwhile Consul Haynes in Helsingfors asked the State Department to post Imbrie to Reval. Felix Cole of the Division of Russian Affairs demurred, writing to Acting Chief of the Consular Bureau Hengstler that "Haynes has always been a shade Bolshevoid. . . . I more than suspect that he doesn't care for Imbrie and his work anyway and doesn't care whether it flourishes or not."[47] The State Department told Haynes to secure two passes for new agents. Haynes complained that the men Imbrie had chosen were suspect and asked them to find alternates. As Imbrie and Hengstler surmised, no completely reliable person ever volunteered for such hazardous duty, but Imbrie complied, allowing Haynes to save face.[48]

By then Imbrie had been in Finland for a year, keeping watch on the ever-changing scene in Russia. With the exception of Vladivostok, which was under Japanese control, no State Department official was in Russian territory. To keep informed, the U.S. government relied on its foreign service in Stockholm, Riga, Helsingfors, Viborg, and as far afield as Warsaw, Constantinople, and Harbin, Manchuria. All were important sources of information, but Viborg stood out for its proximity to Petrograd and Moscow and for its frequent reports.[49] Imbrie's efforts drew praise. He was awarded the Order of the White Rose, second class by the Finnish president and The Order of Vladimir, fourth class by the White Russian government, headquartered in Paris, both of which he had to return as such awards were against not only State Department policy but also the U.S. Constitution.[50]

Imbrie also received commendations for his relief work from the Russian and American Red Cross, the Methodist Foreign Mission, and the YWCA. These commendations came from the people with whom he worked closely on food relief. Dr. Hermann Zeidler, director of the Russian Red Cross, recalled the "real brotherly help" that Imbrie provided.[51] George Simons of the Methodist European Relief wrote that Imbrie's involvement in humanitarian work "greatly endeared" him to the Russians of Viborg as well as the American relief workers.[52]

Imbrie also worked with the American Red Cross. Its workers had entered Russia in 1917 at Vladivostok to aid the Russian Red Cross. In the northwest they had delivered supplies to Murmansk and provided hospitality centers for the Allied Expeditionary Forces.[53] They also had had offices in Petrograd. One amazing Red Cross effort was helping to reunite eight hundred children with their families in Petrograd when they became trapped behind enemy lines. The children, who had been at a summer camp in the Ural Mountains, were taken east by Red Cross workers in what became a round-the-world voyage, ending at the Finnish border where they were finally reunited with their families, the last arriving in January 1921.[54]

Maj. Robinson Smith and Lt. Hugo R. Norbeck headed the American Red Cross work in Finland from November 1919 until May 1920. Headquartered in Viborg, they, too, thought highly of Imbrie. Smith noted that he relied on Imbrie at every stage, writing that Imbrie gave of himself "ungrudgingly." One time Imbrie was accused of feeding military refugees, but Smith noted that Imbrie always consulted Washington about "doubtful points." According to Smith, Imbrie's interest was solely in building bridges between nations.[55]

When Smith returned to the United States, his American replacements "completely destroyed the good feeling that Mr. Imbrie and [he had] built up between the two countries, since, although speaking no Russian, they tried to take over the distribution [of relief supplies] themselves [while letting] the Russian Red Cross foot the bill. In other words, they made a mess of it."[56] Smith said that the men were drinking and carousing, and the Russian refugee women felt unsafe in their presence. It must have pained Smith to write this accusatory letter, and he tempered it by noting the strain of relief work. He concluded, "Mr. Imbrie . . . has done more than any man living to save the world from bolshevism." While over the top, the compliment conveys genuine respect for Imbrie's work: "Whatever Imbrie did, he did to uphold the interests of his country."

Before Smith left Finland, he was feted at a farewell dinner on May 7, 1920, during which he described the approach he and

Imbrie took in providing relief. He later sent his remarks to the State Department in testimony to Imbrie:

> The problem was not one of feeding only; it was also one of moral support. It was a means of letting these refugees know that they were not entirely forgotten, that they still had a friend in the world. . . . [W]hereas we have had critics, they have been over-night critics who like ghosts scattered with the first streak of truthful day. . . . You cannot . . . try to run the affairs of another country for your own selfish ends, without in the end incurring the ill-will of that country. As Americans we believe in fair play. The first question we ask of any man or of any country, Is he or it playing the game? And we despise the man or country that does not play the game.[57]

Smith's good will and dedication provide insight into Imbrie's work, running an espionage ring on the one hand and relief work on the other, all while tending to consular work.

The director general of the Russian Red Cross, at that time headquartered in Paris, wrote that "the Russian Red Cross benefited from the goodness of Mr. Imbrie on multiple occasions who, in his role as United States Consul in Viborg in 1919–20, rendered invaluable service to the cause of Russian refugees in Finland. As testimony of our esteem for his service we conferred on him the Distinguished Award of Merit."[58]

Imbrie was likewise well thought of by the American YWCA workers, called secretaries, and the arrival in Viborg of one secretary in particular must have brightened Imbrie's spirits after the military disasters of 1919. She became a good friend. She may have been more, but there is no known evidence. In 1917 the Provisional Government in Petrograd had invited the YWCA to help Russian women, recently granted full civil rights, negotiate their new position in society. When the workers opened a school in Petrograd, its classes in gymnastics, French, Russian, hygiene, and stenography quickly filled. After the Allied diplomatic missions moved north in February 1918, the American consulates helped the YWCA workers evacuate, the last leaving in September 1918.

Despite the exodus, YWCA women in America continued to answer the call for additional secretaries in Russia. One aspirant was a blue-eyed, sandy blonde, Ebertha Roelofs.[59] Imbrie's age, she left teaching when the war broke out to become a war work secretary. After the armistice she and Gladys Cline, another secretary, were assigned to Petrograd. They sailed on the *Frederick VIII*, arriving in Christiana, Norway, with high hopes for their Russian adventure, but by the time they arrived, Petrograd had been closed off. They had a long delay, staying in Christiana, Stockholm, and Helsingfors until finally receiving permission to go to Viborg. They arrived on January 8, 1920, as close to Petrograd as they ever got, two and a half hours away by train, when trains were running well and the border was open. Across the bay they could see Kronstadt, barring their entrance to the city of their dreams. Imbrie welcomed their help. He had worked with YWCA secretaries in Petrograd, helping them provide relief to soldiers' and officers' families.

Reconciled to their new posting, Roelofs and Cline joined Imbrie, Red Cross officials, and the Methodist Relief women in setting up a center for refugees escaping across the frozen bay. On weekends "the American Colony," or the "Baltic Club" as they called themselves, went on outings, often going to Rauha, not far from Viborg, to sled, ski, and hike through the snowy forest. The American colony, quite small—Roelofs joked about a quorum of four—took trips to islands and locks and made the Hotel Andrea their gathering spot. Roelofs teasingly annotated a photograph of Imbrie cross-country skiing, commenting that he was feigning enthusiasm for the sport. When they met for church services, Imbrie read the Bible lessons. Roelofs referred to him as their leader. She thought him a "live wire," a phase Consul Poole also used for Imbrie. Despite living in a city labeled by one relief worker as unequaled in "abject wretchedness," with families living in hovels the size of packing boxes, the American colony supported and energized each other.[60]

When Roelofs and Cline arrived in Viborg, they devised an

open kitchen for refugees with Russian women as assistants. The food came from American stores. The cost of a meal was set at five marks, but no one was turned away. Roelofs and Cline found a facility by happenstance when a ninety-year-old Russian doyen invited them to teach a Bible class in her home. Twenty young refugees attended, more interested in learning about the lives of American women than about religion. They were particularly taken by the idea of physical exercise. After a few failed explanations, Roelofs opened a window, jumped up on the dining room table, and gave a vigorous demonstration.[61] The audience was delighted, and the doyen warmed to the Americans. With Cline, Roelofs was able to open the kitchen and secure two rooms for evening classes.

As the head of the YWCA work in Viborg, Roelofs frequently sought Imbrie's aid and advice. She reported that his efforts "took heroism. . . . Not only did he help [the refugees] materially, but also in keeping up their morale. . . . They were broken-hearted when he left in June."[62] She agreed with Smith that the Red Cross replacements did not have the same "sympathetic understanding of the Russian character and there seemed no one left to plead their case." She, like Smith and Imbrie, believed that material aid could form the basis of America's "friendship of the future Russia." Although Roelofs's affection for Imbrie comes through in her correspondence, there is no way to know if there was more to it than that. The conditions and hard work certainly conspired against it. Roelofs spent part of March 1920 at a sanatorium in Rauha, exhausted, and when she left Finland, she went to a Swiss sanatorium overlooking Lake Geneva to rest before returning home.[63]

In March 1920 Imbrie requested a sixty-day leave to start by October and wrote that if he weren't granted leave, he would resign.[64] He was confident that his network in Finland could proceed seamlessly.[65] It is impossible to know what motivated the request. Disappointment in Yudenitch's failure? His death sentence? The prospect of a bleak, inactive winter? Or the desire to go where the action was, in Southern Russia? Whatever the cause, his request was granted, although he later moved his exit date to July on a claim of ill health and actually left in June.[66] The reason for leaving earlier may have been the signing of the Treaty of Versailles on June 28. With the work on the treaty concluded, the State Department would be shuffling its personnel. In Washington Imbrie could plead his case to continue his Russian work. He had received the Interallied Russian Cross, the Russian Medal, and the Order of Nobility for his service.[67] For Imbrie the next logical posting was the Crimea, where the White Army was still active.

SIX

Roaming the Black Sea

In 1920 in a Parisian suburb on a glorious August day, the Allies signed the Treaty of Sevres with Turkey. But in Constantinople black flags hung in the streets, newspapers carried black borders, and cars came to a five-minute stop at noon.[1] The treaty contained stipulations that incensed the Turks, including placing the Dardanelles and the Bosporus under international control, reducing the size of the Turkish army, and giving parts of Anatolia and Thrace to Greece. The show of protest in Constantinople was no mere gesture. Never ratified by the Turkish parliament, the treaty made war with Greece inevitable and necessitated the Lausanne Peace Conference of 1922–23. Imbrie's next stops were Turkey and Switzerland.

In July 1920, as a late addition to a ship's manifest, Imbrie, having said farewells in Viborg and London, sailed from England, heading to Washington DC and to home.[2] His uncle, Charles Fishbaugh, advanced in years, had died in April, but his small family was at the house on Q Street to greet him—his aunt Mary, cousin Paul, and Paul's wife, Isabelle. Imbrie spent the next five months writing reports and recharging. The country was in an economic downturn that had begun in January and extended for eighteen months, part of the downturn stemming from the

Great War with its cycle of fear-driven lending and spending. It was an unsettling time in America as industrial production and stock prices plunged and unemployment grew. The immediate postwar exuberance was over.

That autumn in Washington DC, a year after the war had ended, Armistice Day celebrations spanned three days, but America was once again turning inward. In the *Washington Times,* William Hearst lambasted former secretary of state Elihu Root with his "cold, corporation blue eyes" for espousing the Versailles Treaty and the League of Nations. Warren G. Harding, a Republican, had been elected president in 1919 in an unprecedented landslide, with 60 percent of the popular vote.[3] In his nomination speech Harding declared that America's present need was "not submergence into internationality, but sustainment in triumphant nationality." It was the "Age of Wonderful Nonsense," espousing American exceptionalism.[4]

On September 27 Roger Tredwell, detailed to the State Department after serving at the Paris Peace Conference, recommended that a consular officer be assigned to the Crimea to gather political and military information.[5] Four days later Wilbur Carr, director of the Consular Service, assigned Imbrie to Constantinople as vice consul and clerk.

Turkey was in the throes of building a nation, which did not emerge from a peaceful plain like an autumn harvest, but out of a broiling, heaving fen bordered by countries in a similar state of flux. Within its fluid borders were peoples seeking self-determination, some with great grievances like the Armenians, who had suffered campaigns of extermination spanning decades. Into this maelstrom Western countries threw their might. Britain, France, Italy, and Greece all laid claims to segments of the former Ottoman Empire. In addition, foreign corporations, including those from the United States, sought their own kind of mandates, termed concessions.

After a brief plunge into the Great War in 1917–18, the U.S. government had resurrected its Open Door policy, which espoused equal opportunity and transparency in commercial and economic matters but did little or nothing to help define the geopolitics of the postwar world. In the early 1920s the State Department rarely had the president's ear and, in lieu of firm directives, conducted its business with startling independence.

Imbrie interpreted his new posting as an extension of his Finland assignment, which in turn had extended his Petrograd assignment. What might at the time have seemed an anti-Bolshevik obsession by the State Department must now be viewed in light of the devastating transformation of Russia into a brutal autocracy governing over 293 million people across eight million square miles. Russia's far reaches, not only across territories but across time, were being determined as Imbrie left the United States.

Although assigned to Constantinople, Imbrie was to move immediately to Sebastopol to report to Admiral Newton A. McCully, United States special agent assigned to track the White Army's efforts to defeat the Bolsheviks. McCully knew that Imbrie had been working independently in Viborg as a "political intelligence officer for Russian affairs. His work [had been] performed to the entire satisfaction of the Department."[6] Now Imbrie's job was to obtain for McCully "information of a definite character," and if McCully were recalled, Imbrie was to assume his official duties until a naval replacement arrived, a prize posting for an admiralty attorney and a former French Army major. Unfortunately Imbrie never met McCully. He never assumed those duties. It was a frustration beyond measure for Imbrie.

On December 6 Imbrie was in Constantinople, not Sebastopol, and going no farther. The White Russian Army had disintegrated, and McCully had been recalled.[7] In November the White Army retreat had produced mobs of soldiers and civilians fleeing south to Novorossiysk on the Black Sea with the Red Army bearing down on them. Thousands of refugees had crowded the harbor, jockeying for transport on British, French, Greek, and American ships. This sorry scene was reenacted at Sebastopol after Gen. Pytor Wrangel made his last stand, so that when Imbrie arrived, Constantinople, experiencing an intensely cold winter, teemed with refugees.[8] Overseeing the city were fifty thousand Allied troops, of which thirty thousand were British.[9] Britannia was posed to rule.

With the fall of Wrangel's army, Imbrie transferred from McCully's staff to that of the broad-shouldered, barrel-chested Admiral Mark L. Bristol, United States high commissioner for Turkey.[10] Bristol's abiding interest was promoting commerce in the Near East. He was ferocious in this objective even when humanitarian demands deserved preferential attention. Imbrie's new assignment included information gathering and consular duties, especially in regard to commerce, Bristol's bailiwick.

Although many American industries were competing for mastery in the Near East, in Imbrie's story one stands out among all others, oil. Imbrie was not immediately involved in its intrigues, but he came to be, both in Turkey and later in Persia. During the war oil had assumed enormous importance with the use and development of automobiles, tanks, and airplanes, as well as the conversion of much of the world's navies from coal to petroleum. American refineries had supplied 80 percent of Allied demands for petroleum products,[11] but if there were another war, and many thought there would be, that rate could not be sustained. Further, European countries wanted independence from American oil. In addition, the United States, Britain, and France were concerned about Russian oil exploration once Russia's civil war ended.

Because the United States had neither gone to war with Turkey nor joined the League of Nations, it held a weak hand at the Paris Peace Conference in pressing for oil leases in the former Ottoman Empire. Britain was especially interested in the oil fields of Mosul, north of Baghdad, which at present was disputed territory. The Turks considered the oil concessions their "greatest undeveloped wealth . . . open to American companies . . . and not pledged to other companies."[12] They would hold this card high and let the Western powers leap for it.

One official on Bristol's staff, First Secretary Allen Dulles, was favorable to Standard Oil, which had an installation on the Asiatic side of the Bosporus, a visual advertisement for its power and reach.[13] Dulles's uncle was Robert Lansing, secretary of state when Imbrie joined the State Department. Dulles had spent the war years attached to embassies in Vienna and Bern and served at the Paris Peace Conference as a statistician.[14] He was ten years younger than Imbrie, newly married, yet to get his law degree, and a bon vivant. Imbrie was less well connected, but more seasoned, better educated, and more captivated by international affairs, and he had been to war. However, Dulles's connections offset his youth. After he left Turkey in March 1922, he was named chief of the State Department's Division of Near Eastern Affairs.[15] His new assignment covered five million square miles of territory, including Turkey.[16] Imbrie's last assignments came from this division.

It may seem odd in Imbrie's story that certain names appear and reappear as they do, in this case Dulles's, but the staff of the Department of State was small in those days. The senior staff of the State Department in Washington DC amounted to no more than fifty officers of the rank of second secretary or higher.[17] At times the State Department roster reads like a repertory company's.

Imbrie's consul general in Constantinople was Gabriel Bie Ravndal, who had held that position from 1910 until America entered the war and returned to it in 1919. The failure of the U.S. government to clarify the respective authority of naval, consular, and diplomatic missions in Turkey strained relationships between Bristol and Ravndal, although the turmoil in Turkey accounts for some of the friction.[18]

Constantinople, divided by the Bosporus between Europe and Asia, was also divided by economic and political realities. For some it was an exotic city. For others, a vast refugee camp. For still others, an experiment in modernity. It was undoubtedly expensive. Dulles thought Constantinople more expensive than London and Paris and "almost as bad as New York."[19] So did Imbrie, who found his salary deplorably low for Turkey, as he routinely reminded the State Department.[20]

The American embassy was housed in the elegant Palazzo Corpi on the city's European side, in the quarter known as the Pera. Its rosewood door and window frames had come from Piedmonte and its marble floorings and facade from Carrara. Frescoes covered the walls of the reception area, and a grand stairway dominated the entrance.[21] The Pera was a beehive of activity, abuzz with the daily workings of legations, shops, hotels, and cafés.

Away from the Palazzo Corpi was a vast underbelly to the city. The minarets, towers, mosques, domes, and palaces, which awed shipboard passengers, revealed on closer look a city in extremis. Penning in the city was a flotilla of huge battleships, cruisers, destroyers, and gunboats bearing American, British, French, Italian, and Greek flags. Above the harbor, the hillsides were scarred from four major fires in eight years that had incinerated as much as a fourth of the city.[22] Below the scarred landscape roiled waves of refugees—Jews, Georgians, Armenians, Azerbaijanis, Greeks, and Russians. In November 1920, some 120 ships had steamed into the straits, bringing nearly 146,000 White Russians.[23] In addition, 54 Russian ships had arrived at Buyukdere Bay, farther up the Bosporus, carrying thousands more refugees. Most of the refugees were destitute, the men, even the aristocrats, scrambling for work as skilled and manual laborers, the women taking in washing, cooking, and sewing, running laundries, and waitressing. Often the women were prostituted. Refugees filled the streets, peddling their belongings for pennies on the dollar, including furs and diamonds. Still others crept away to hovels, sick, starving, and dying.

The relief effort was enormous. Unlike in Finland and Petrograd, Imbrie was not integral to this work because the city was not under siege. Well-oiled organizations were already in place, such as the American Red Cross, the YMCA, and the Near East Relief (NER), which had been founded in 1915 in response to Armenian appeals. In addition, the embassies had joined the humanitarian efforts in multiple ways, some arduous such as hospital work, others less stressful such as fund-raisers—concerts, tea dances, balls, parties, and receptions.

When McCully left Turkey, Bristol wrote to Secretary of State

Charles Hughes that he wanted to retain Imbrie to work with the refugees and to gather information, chiefly in Constantinople, although he might be posted to the Crimea or other places in the Black Sea region where there was no consulate. He also thought Imbrie could help with negotiations between Armenia and Turkey and with reopening trade with Russia, although Bristol was skeptical about any success in that arena, given that the Soviets were seizing cargo without, in his words, "going through the formality of payment."[24] Imbrie did not think he would be of much use with refugee work—the United States had expressed little interest in relocating refugees. The Immigration Quota Act of 1921, signed in March by President Harding, limited the number of émigrés from Russian or Soviet soil to the ludicrously low number of between two thousand and three thousand. Among the reasons given for the severe quota was a fear of Bolshevism, the postwar recession, high unemployment, and the worrisome effect of immigration on American culture.[25]

Used to greater autonomy and perhaps sensing Bristol's authoritarianism, Imbrie had no great desire to stay in Constantinople. He asked to be moved to Bessarabia, with funding to employ agents. An alternative was to work on Russian affairs in London.[26] Bristol disagreed. While Bessarabia would enable Imbrie to report on events in South Russia, Bristol wanted Imbrie in Constantinople where Bolshevik representatives were arriving to renew trade relations. He asked the State Department to increase Imbrie's $3,000 salary and $1,500 expense account with a salary of $4,500 and a generous $2,400 for his translator. Bristol wanted Imbrie to stay. Perhaps he thought Imbrie would do so if he were paid more, but that was never what motivated Imbrie, although he did want a fair wage. Bristol also hoped to have McCully's funds redirected to him, especially to counter Russian intelligence.[27] The State Department turned down Bristol's requests. On December 28 Imbrie's proposal for Bessarabia was also rejected, primarily because of the diplomatic situation: Bessarabia was occupied by American-friendly Romanian troops sent to quell Bolshevik agitation; quaintly, placing an American spy on friendly territory was deemed hostile.[28]

After two months in Constantinople Imbrie sent a long telegram to Tredwell at the State Department to get things moving. He wrote:

> After touching four continents, five countries and six cities in search of a modicum of Justice, I reached here to find, as usual, there aint [*sic*] no Justice. . . . I expected to find orders from the Department awaiting me here. After a week it dawned upon me that the matter of my having arrived in Constantinople had probably slipped the President's mind and so, as you have probably noted, I let out a telegraphic bleat to be taken out of here and assigned to Bessarabia, for the establishment of an information service. During three weeks, which time was I supposed [*sic*] occupied by the Department in endeavouring to find out what was Bessarabia and where it was, I waited with such amount of patience as I could muster for the Department's answer. With usual perspicacity they did the easiest thing and denied my request. . . . Say, what in hell is the matter with you all there? Has the absence of proper stimulants affected the place?[29] Now, Roger, bend forward while I give you an earful of the dope. I've been here two months and damned if I can see that I have accomplished a thing. My hardest job is to find a job. I have no fund for an information [service], even if such a thing would be practicable of operation here. So I just pot around the Russian Embassy once a day, click my heels a few dozen times, say a few assorted "distrachis" and "stho novavo?," occasionally go out to see General Wrangel, write a few memoranda for the Admiral and—that's all.[30] The Admiral, let me tell you is one of the finest chaps and best sportsmen I have ever met. Why the other night when I was arrested by the British Military Police for refusing to let them search me, on the ground that no Britisher had any right to search an American, the Admiral actually commended me for my stand. I digress. What I want to make plain is this: I am of very little, if any use here. But I could be of use in Bessarabia, either in Akkerman, Bendery or Kishniev, from

either of which points I could operate a service into Soviet Russia. If the Department really wants to have the dope on what's going on in Russia, there's no better place from which to operate. I already have the ideal man with me for this work. . . . Now can't this thing be put across? I know, if it can, you are the one who can manage it. So break Pop Lee and Herbert away from the dances long enough for an executive session on this proposition and "let's go."[31] An alternative proposition, I might be sent to Constanza.[32] The Admiral thinks we should have someone there for consular work and I suppose I might get away with it, if I am given a clerk for accounts and allowed to retain this Russian assistant of mine.[33]

Imbrie concluded by saying he had been too distressed by his situation to correspond much but hoped to have an answer by mid-March.

In his letter Imbrie referred to a Russian assistant. Shortly after he arrived, by chance on a street in Constantinople, he met Michael (Max) Moukhanoff, whom he had known in Petrograd.[34] Moukhanoff had grown up in privilege on a country estate in Kazan, Russia, and had served in the tsar's army. He had returned to Petrograd shortly before the provisional government was overthrown by the Bolsheviks and joined the British Mission as a translator. As Bolshevik power grew, Max looked for an escape route. Amid the tumult he proposed to a Russian-American socialite, Helen de Smirnoff, called Nelka, whom he had known since he was seven years old. He was then twenty-one; she was forty. Nelka had served as a nurse in Russia after the Russo-Japanese War and during the Great War. On visits home she often stayed in Washington DC at her aunt Martha Wadsworth's grand mansion on DuPont Circle, about three miles from Imbrie's Q Street address.[35]

When Max first proposed, Nelka turned him down because of their age difference, but she later accepted. The two were married on September 9, 1918, and on Christmas Day fled the country, arriving in the United States in February 1919. Stirred by reports of the White Army's fighting in the Crimea, they decided to join the cause. They left for Constantinople in late 1920. Shortly after, Imbrie encountered Max as he was out walking, recognizing him from his days at the British embassy in Petrograd. He offered him a job. Max was with Imbrie for the next eight months as his translator and travel companion while Nelka aided French relief efforts. With Max at his side, Imbrie took several trips in early 1921 for a sweeping view of the areas under siege by multiple forces fighting for multiple causes. Bristol helped with transportation.

One reconnaissance trip was to the west, another to the east. On February 26 Imbrie and Max joined Red Cross workers aboard the USS *Smith Thompson 212*, a destroyer. The next morning the destroyer left its berth in weather that was poor, cold, and gray.[36] At twenty knots they sailed through the Sea of Marmora to Gallipoli. There beyond the hills in a shallow valley was a forest of white crosses, the cemetery of those fallen in battle in 1915–16. Imbrie made a brief visit to the refugee camps, greeted by cheering Russians, and the next day sailed past the hulks of British ships sunk by Turkish and German gunfire in the Gallipoli campaign, masts and spars protruding from the water at grotesque angles. Turkish forts overlooked the bay on both sides as the *Smith Thompson* passed into the Aegean.

At the Isle of Lemnos was another refugee camp, using equipment the British had left behind in 1916. This camp was unfortunately perched atop a barren plateau sluiced with a cold wind. Fresh water was scarce. The tour of inspection lasted only a few hours before the ship left for Salonika, sailing all night at fifteen knots and arriving in the morning. As the morning mists cleared, Imbrie saw a familiar sight, Mt. Olympus, with the morning sunlight turning its snowcap pink. A light breeze wafted across the bay. Fishermen were getting underway for the day's haul. But Imbrie was in for a jolt. Four months after he had left Salonika in 1917, a fire had gutted a third of the city, including much of the waterfront.[37] On land Imbrie explored what was left of old haunts and, after spending a night and another day in the city, boarded the *Smith Thompson* for Smyrna. By morning the wind had picked up, and overcoats were donned, but they had no sooner anchored at Smyrna than they were redirected to Varna, Bulgaria, where a destroyer was kept at all times to handle radio messages to Central and Western Europe. The *Smith Thompson* upped anchor and sailed first to Constantinople, reaching the city the next morning, on March 6. Although this reconnaissance trip was over for Imbrie, he quickly sailed again, this time to the east and to war.

The Red Army had been closing one Black Sea port after another to Allied and American ships as it extended its dominance. One American sailor thought the Black Sea should be called "Bolsheviki Lake." On March 8 the *Smith Thompson* sailed for Varna with Imbrie aboard.[38] The ship stayed there for nine days, and when its relief arrived, it sailed for Batum, Georgia, 625 miles across the Black Sea, skirting the mine fields. In good times Batum was a tropical jewel framed by snowcapped mountains with orange trees and palm trees growing luxuriantly in its valleys to the south. The countryside teamed with game, but this was not a good time for Batum.[39]

About six hours out of Batum, the USS *J. D. Edwards* radioed for the *Smith Thompson* to meet it outside the outer edge of a mine field, an unusual request. Another directive came several hours later, also unusual, so that when the *Smith Thompson* was four or five miles north of the mine field, it sighted the *J. D. Edwards* standing out to sea and signaling for it to come near, which it did, hoving to about five hundred yards off. The captain of the *J. D. Edwards* came aboard with news: the Bolsheviks had reached Batum. The *Edwards*'s decks were crowded with refugees. Initially Turkish troops had moved into the city to protect the Georgians, but when the Bolsheviks arrived, the Georgians had switched sides and were now fighting the Turks. The city had not fallen, but the situation was dire.

The two ships parted ways, with the *Smith Thompson* continuing on toward Batum. At 8:30 p.m., it spotted a schooner sending up distress signals. Its engines had broken, and in the dead calm it was drifting back to Batum, from which it had sailed three days earlier. Forty White Russians were aboard. The *Smith Thomson* put over a boat, passed a line to the schooner, and towed it to Trebizond. During the night the destroyer's surgeon was called over to deliver a baby.

From Trebizond, the *Smith Thompson* set out once again for Batum. Although the ship violated the navy's prohibition of having a U.S. man-of-war in a Bolshevik port, the return meant Imbrie was an eyewitness to the city's fall. The destroyer steamed around the outlying mine field and backed into port, ready for a quick getaway. All hands came on deck to peer through binoculars at the Bolshevik cavalry of about two thousand filling the city streets. Into the early evening, artillery fire sounded; late into the night came sounds of a pitched battle. From a hillside echoed a big-gun report, answered by a machine gun. Missiles began dropping close to the ship. The *Smith Thompson* decided to leave. It headed to Samsun and, after ten days there, arrived back in Constantinople on March 29. Combining both trips, Imbrie had been gone for the better part of a month.

The next month, spent in the city with little to do, Imbrie must have felt like Coleridge's Ancient Mariner, "as idle as a painted ship upon a painted ocean." He wrote to Alexander Barton, a steamship representative, who with his wife, Helen, had befriended Imbrie in Constantinople before returning to the States:

> I [have] missed your belligerent presence very much and the office did not seem quite natural after you left. There have been no great or epoch-stirring events here. The sun has continued to rise behind the mosques and to set behind thither mosques; the mud is just as thick when it rains and the dust just as irritating when it doesnt [*sic*]; there are just as many street cries and I think, perhaps, a few more smells; the same crowd continues to sit around the club and to settle all world problems, agreeing, as of yore that prohibition—in the abstract, as a theory—is a fine thing. In short life in Constantinople continues the even tenor of its way.

I have managed to get in a couple of trips, one to Isle of Lemnos, Gallipoli, Salonika, through Thrace and southern Bulgaria, the other to eastern Bulgaria, Samsoun, Trebizon [*sic*] and Batum. It was my good fortune to be at the latter place at the time of its capture. I still study the map of Asia Minor and periodically marshal my arguments before the Admiral in an endavor [*sic*] to obtain his sanction for going into Angora. As we go to press, I seem as about as near getting there as when you were here. Still I have not abandoned all hope. For the rest, I hike to the Russian Embassy every day or so, have deep and weighty sessions with their various committees, councils, soviets, delegations and boards. Also, from time to time, I receive delegations, admirals, generals, senators, dukes, princes, and potentates who call to inform me and the American people at large that there is "no justice."

But I am getting pretty fed up; its [*sic*] not a he-man job and unless I get considerable more field work than I have had thus far, I shall get out of the Service by July first. I am on the spoor of a couple of jobs in London and hope I wont [*sic*] have my usual luck of finding the game bagged when I arrive. You don't happen to know any firm, corporation, individual, association, partnership, joint stock company or organization that would be willing to profit by my service for the purely nominal salary of about $5000 per year, do you? If so don't stop to write, wire or say it with flowers.

I entirely agree that we should keep in liaison, with two such minds and such energy in combination, the Lord only knows what might be made to eventuate.

Imbrie signed off with greetings to Barton's wife and gave his mailing address as in care of C. J. Petherick, U.S. Despatch Agent in London.[40]

For Imbrie life in Constantinople was too placid. He had spent seventeen months in war zones in France and the Balkans, ten months in Russia in the midst of a revolution, and sixteen months in Finland during a civil war. In heading to Turkey Imbrie had anticipated serving in a war zone. Instead he saw time a-wasting while geopolitical pressure was building. In Petrograd he had been able to set up a network of operatives and gather information. In Viborg he had cast a wider net, covering several countries. His assignment in Turkey required starting anew. He did not feel this posting used him well, although Bristol complemented him on his work with anti-Bolshevik groups.

When a new assignment in the region was not forthcoming and Max and Nelka returned to the States, Imbrie, too, decided to go home. While the Bolsheviks were spreading south, east, and west, like hot lava, Bristol was dealing with Ottoman officials in Constantinople to promote trade. Hoping to be put to better purpose, Imbrie wrote to the State Department vaguely claiming family matters as his reason for departing. By July 1921 he had left.

Despite the reference to family matters, Imbrie seemed in no hurry. He stopped off in Bucharest, spent four days in Budapest, and moved on to Vienna and Brussels, before finally arriving in London. Imbrie was in England from July 30 to September 20, including as much as a month in London, perhaps using the opportunity to meet with members of the U.S. Russian Affairs office there.[41] Imbrie proposed returning to Estonia or Russia, although he was blacklisted in both countries. His last stop was Paris, where he met with former American Field Service drivers, including George End, who by then was married, working in Paris, and had had a son, whose middle name was Whitney.[42]

Finally, sailing from Boulogne-Sur-Mer, Imbrie arrived in the United States on September 30, 1921.[43] Once home, he arranged for a package to be sent by diplomatic pouch from London, probably his sword collection, now housed in the Smithsonian.[44]

Imbrie may have thought he was finished with Turkey. He wasn't. He may even have helped eventuate his return by making presentations on Russian refugees in Turkey. One luncheon talk was sponsored by Princess Julia Cantacuzene, granddaughter of Ulysses S. Grant, and attended by Mrs. Robert Lansing, wife of the former secretary of state.[45] Imbrie was not done with Turkey, and sometime before leaving Constantinople he had set his eye on Angora, now the country's capital and renamed Ankara, in the country's central Anatolia region.

The Turkish National Movement, which had formed in opposition to Ottoman rule, had established its seat of government in Angora, for a fresh start, away from Constantinople. Allied representatives were there but no American, and in early November the U.S. State Department decided to send a "good man," although not in an official capacity. The French and British had previously sent intelligence agents independent of their high commissioners, who were still dealing with the Ottoman faction, thereby limiting the usefulness of agents and undermining the authority of the commissioners.[46] The State Department wanted its agent to be more transparent and capitalize on America's clean slate: the United States had no history of invasion, colonization, or oppression in the Near East. This was its great advantage.

On February 9, 1922, Imbrie was assigned to Angora and, in a freewheeling phrase, to other "such places."[47] Communication from the interior would be difficult, given the town's isolation and lack of modern communication systems. It was decided that reports would go to either Bristol in Constantinople or the State Department via Aleppo or Beirut with copies to Bristol. If those avenues failed, Imbrie was to report to Bristol in person. Imbrie seemed pleased with the assignment. He wrote to Barton that his assignment "embrace[d] a pretty thorough casing of Asia Minor as far east as the Persian border."[48]

Angora was the place to be. The Bolsheviks had been courting the Nationalists since 1919 and, though poor, had supplied the Turks with money, arms, and ammunition in its quest for independence. In late January 1922, Semyon Ivanovich Aralov, one of the founders of the Cheka,[49] had arrived in Angora as ambassador to the new government of Turkey, commandeering the largest and best house.[50] The nationalist leader, Mustapha Kemal, however, did not believe in Bolshevism and its "Workers of the World" sloganeering. He wanted Turkey for the Turks, but he also wanted friendly relations with Russia, and it was unclear how much pressure Russia would put on the new country. America needed an observer in Angora.

After a ten-month absence from Turkey, Imbrie left the United States on March 9, 1922, but as fate or Bristol would have it, he again got no farther than Constantinople. Despite the State Department's explicit instructions for Imbrie to go to Angora, he was stonewalled, it seems because Bristol still favored the Ottoman Turks. Then on May 6 a story appeared in the *Times* (London) condemning the Turkish genocide of the Armenian people.[51] The accusation seemed incontrovertible and led to Imbrie finally reaching Angora.

In February 1920, during Imbrie's first tour in Turkey, the State Department had received a report that five thousand Armenians had been massacred in Cilicia. Bristol had dismissed it, cabling the department that there was no massacre. Bristol continued to receive reports of atrocities from outlying regions, including those from captains of his own ships. Despite these reports and others, Bristol maintained a position of neutrality, even when one report detailed the massacre of eight thousand Armenians. A year earlier he had presented his view of Armenians in a letter: "I am sure that the mass of people at home believe the Armenians are Christians in action and morals, and that they are able to govern themselves. You and I, and others that know them, know that this is not the case. . . . The Near East is a cesspool that should be drained and cleaned out without any halfway measures."[52] When the *Times* story resulted in a rancorous debate in the British House of Commons, it spurred renewed interest in the United States about Armenia. Letters on behalf of Armenians poured into the Near Eastern Affairs Division of the State Department. In a two-week period 1,500 letters were received.[53] When the British proposed an investigation, Dulles knew the United States had to cooperate.

Near East Relief workers appealed for investigators to proceed to the interior at once, perhaps to Trebizond on the south shore of the Black Sea.[54] Secretary of State Hughes agreed to the investigation, but he also wanted to address Turkish countercharges.[55] He summed up his position, which seems to devalue justice: "The important thing is that there should be peace in the Near East."[56] As Allied and American investigators moved inland, Bristol could not keep Imbrie in Constantinople. With the Nationalists exposed to charges of genocide, Bristol needed a representative at their capital. Imbrie's Turkish contacts in Constantinople had told him that Bristol had been blocking his entry to Angora, but Bristol blamed the Ottoman Foreign Office. With the Nationalists on the ascendency, Bristol changed camps largely to further American commercial interests. At last Imbrie was on his way inland to do the reconnaissance he so enjoyed.

Imbrie left Constantinople aboard the USS *Williams*. He arrived in Ineboli on the Black Sea on June 20 and headed inland. At every stop on the way to Angora he met with local officials, from Ineboli to Kastamoni, across the Ilgas Mountains to Tshangry, and onto Kaliijack. He arrived in Angora on June 24, 1922.[57] One journalist compared reaching Angora to going into the heart of Africa.[58]

Angora, ringed with low mountains, rested on two hills cut by the gorge of a malarial river. Imbrie described it as a "series of wall-connected towers [with] houses sprawl[ing] in slipshod fashion down the hill to the swampy plain below." Amid the minarets, battlements, walls, and towers was a modest building, the home of the Grand National Assembly of Turkey, the fulcrum for the city's transformation into a national capital. The streets were debris-strewn. There was neither sewage system nor sidewalks. There were no street lights, and the nights were "as dark as the inside of a camel."[59] Always there was mud or wind-blown dust. Imbrie dryly noted that "unless one is interested in international politics or in watching the governmental machinery of an infant nation, there is little in Angora to hold the attention."

Angora was a boomtown, lacking lodging. A half mile from the city proper, near a rail spur, Imbrie moved into a boxcar. He carefully detailed his expenses: steamer from Constantinople, $160; overland by camel, horse, "or whatever" to Angora, $125; six weeks reconnoitering in Asia Minor, $200.[60]

Despite the fleas, the scarcity of coal and wood, the constant screeching of wooden cartwheels, and the malarial swamp, Imbrie relished his assignment. His new translator was Reschad Bey, who spoke English, German, and French as well as Turkish.[61] Near the boxcar lived Raouf Bey, future prime minister of Turkey, who became Imbrie's frequent and informal visitor.[62] Also at the railroad station was the office of the future president of Turkey, Mustapha Kemal.

Tall and fair with blue-gray eyes, Mustapha Kemal was a man of great energy.[63] His rise to prominence had begun in his youth, but the Gallipoli Campaign had made his name. In January 1915, the Allies had developed a plan to cut the Ottoman Empire off from Germany and on April 25 attempted to establish beachheads at three points, including Anzac Cove. There Mustafa Kemal's Nineteenth Division was ordered up and in fierce fighting held the important hill of Conk Bayiri. This first engagement was followed by months of attacks and counterattacks, until the last British troops withdrew from Gallipoli in early 1916, its invasion a disaster.

After Gallipoli, Mustafa Kemal continued to advance through the ranks until he was in charge of the longest line held by the Ottoman armed forces, but when Bulgaria sued for peace, leaving Constantinople open to attack, Turkey capitulated. In November 1918 Mustafa Kemal returned to the capital. Although he had fought the British in his homeland and in Syria, he began to court them as the most powerful of the occupiers, with the goal of protecting the remnants of Ottoman land.

Mustafa Kemal spent six months in Constantinople, meeting with fellow officers and emerging as their leader. With the Greek's provocative landing in Smyrna, Mustafa Kemal went to Samsun, arriving on May 19, today a national holiday in Turkey, marking the beginning of the country's War of Independence. In effect, he was the commissioner for the whole of Anatolia from Angora eastward. He set about organizing a resistance, and war ensued with all its brutality, confirming in Westerners' eyes their image of the "Terrible Turk." As difficult as it was, while in Angora Imbrie tried bridging this image to that of the new Turk, a citizen of a modern, democratic, capitalist country. He also met his future wife.

1. Robert W. Imbrie graduated from Yale Law School, drolly claiming in the class notes an interest in being a Supreme Court judge but having so far "refused all political honors." Single, he "hoped to reform." *The Shingle,* Yale Law School, 1906.

2. After graduation from Yale Law School, Felix Harold Schmitt and Imbrie maintained a lifelong correspondence. Schmitt named a son after Imbrie, seven years after Imbrie's death. *The Shingle,* Yale Law School, 1906.

3. Theodore Roosevelt, pictured here in 1901, cultivated an image of manliness, energy, and optimism that influenced young men of the era. His presidency (1901–9) spanned Imbrie's college years. The Perry Pictures, Library of Congress, LC-DIG-ppmsca-36063.

4. In 1907 Imbrie detailed his adventures in Europe with touches of self-deprecation. Courtesy Robert Imbrie Smith.

5. In 1910 Imbrie accompanied zoologist Richard L. Garner to West Africa. Garner believed he could learn to speak to apes and sometimes lived in a cage to observe them in their natural habitat. Imbrie found him strange. Smithsonian Institution Archives, Accession 90-105, Science Service Records, Image #SIA2008-1819.

6. Many American Field Service (AFS) ambulance drivers came from privileged backgrounds, providing their own transportation, uniforms, and kit. Serving with Imbrie was George Spaulding Jr., a Rhodes Scholar from the University of Arizona who became a financial adviser and patron of the arts. Luther College Archives, Decorah, Iowa.

7. Richard Neville Hall was the first AFS driver killed by enemy fire. His ambulance was so flattened that although other AFS drivers passed by during the night, the wreckage was not discovered until daylight. Rauner Special Collections Library, Dartmouth College Library.

8. In October 1916 Imbrie (*front row, far left*) joined the newly formed AFS Section Eight supporting the French Army of the Orient in the Balkans. Lovering Hill (*top row, far right*) commanded the section. Bain News Service, Library of Congress.

9. In Viborg, Finland, in 1920 YWCA worker Ebertha Roelofs and Imbrie, as U.S. vice consul, provided aid to Russian refugees. Ebertha Roelofs HS #93408, Alumni Association of the University of Michigan Individual Photographs circa 1880–1960s, University of Michigan Alumni Association, Box 145, Bentley Historical Library, University of Michigan.

10. Imbrie made five reconnaissance journeys throughout Turkey in the early 1920s. Imbrie hoped to encourage the country's move toward democracy. "Crossing Asia Minor," *National Geographic* magazine, October 1924.

11. Imbrie's travels at times left him stranded. Once he missed a train connection, and after being told that "tomorrow was another day," he agreed there would be another day but perhaps not a train. He borrowed a car. Underword & Underword Collection, Library of Congress.

12. Katherine Gillespie, a Near East Relief worker caring for war orphans, married Imbrie in Constantinople on December 26, 1922. "Murdered Consul and Wife," *Daily Messenger* (Canandiagua NY), July 22, 1924, 1. Reproduction by the New York State Library.

13. Journalist Louise Bryant, pictured here in Russian attire, supported the Bolshevik uprising of 1917. Later she traveled to Ankara to interview Mustapha Kemal, the president of the new Turkey, hoping Imbrie would provide an introduction. Linda Lear Center for Special Collections and Archives, Connecticut College.

14. (*opposite top*) Some critics posthumously blamed Imbrie for inciting a mob by photographing women, but friends defended him as respectful of native customs. As a photojournalist he often photographed women, as he did in this picture in Anatolia. "Crossing Asia Minor," *National Geographic* magazine, October 1924.

15. (*opposite bottom*) On a rainy September 24, 1924, Imbrie's remains were taken from the USS *Trenton* to the New York Avenue Presbyterian Church, where President Lincoln had worshipped. President Calvin Coolidge attended Imbrie's funeral and internment. National Photo Company Collection, Library of Congress.

16. Katherine Imbrie pursued justice as she saw it, appealing to the U.S. government for what she regarded as proper recompense from Persia, later Iran, for her husband's murder. Pacific & Atlantic Photos, Inc. New York World-Telegram and the Sun Newspaper Photograph Collection, Library of Congress.

17. The obverse side of Imbrie's marker at Arlington Cemetery designates his rank as major in the French Army; Imbrie also held the rank of major in the U.S. Army Reserves. Katherine is buried with him. Photograph by Jane Nelson.

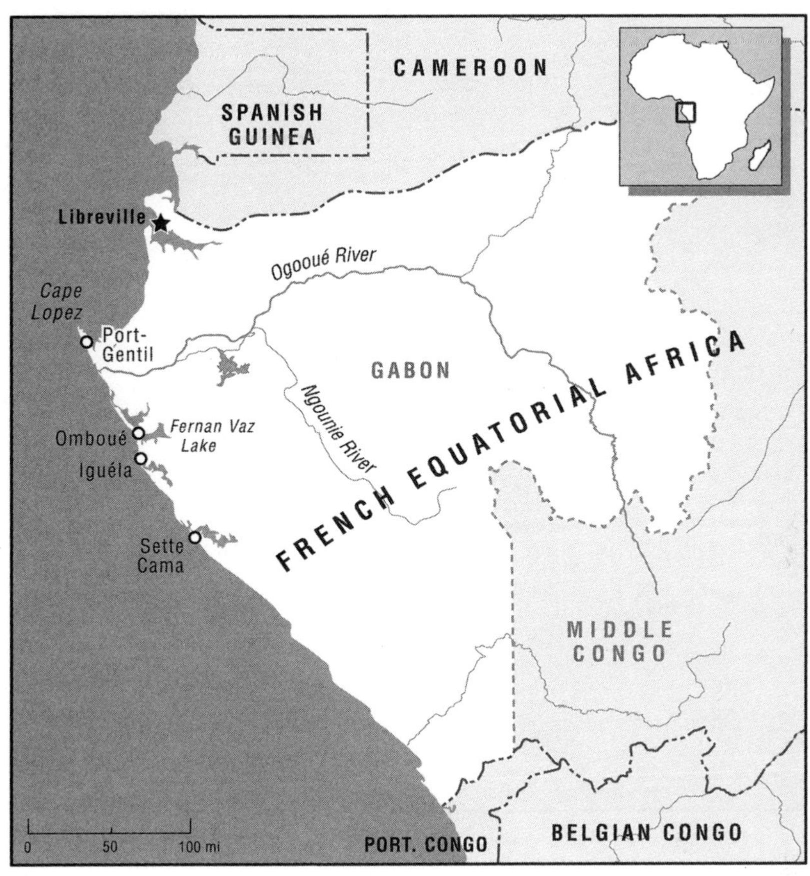

18. Gabon. In 1911 Imbrie accompanied zoologist Richard Garner on an expedition to French-controlled Gabon, hiking through the grasslands, rainforests, and flat plains, canoeing through lagoons and rivers, and visiting small trading posts in search of a gorilla for the Bronx Zoo. Gabon's capital, Libreville, had eight thousand residents.

19. France. Imbrie spent ten months as a volunteer ambulance driver in France, beginning at the Aisne front and ending at the Battle of Verdun. Imbrie considered his service "insignificant" compared to that of a soldier.

20. Macedonian Front. From October 1916 to April 1917, Imbrie served as an ambulance driver with the Allied Army of the Orient facing Bulgarian forces in the treacherous and often frigid mountains of Macedonia and Albania. The gateway to the front was Salonika.

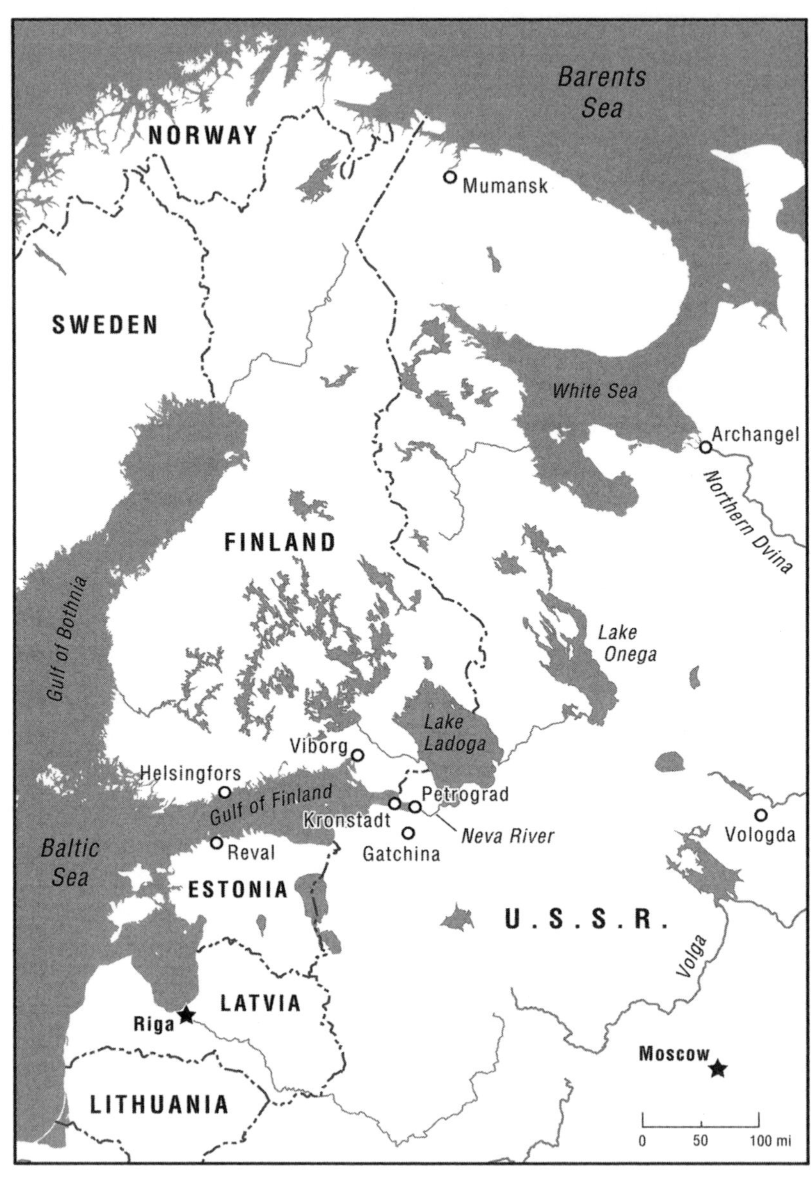

21. Russia. As a U.S. vice consul, Imbrie served in St. Petersburg, Russia, and Viborg, Finland, from late 1917 until June 1920, gathering information throughout the region during the Russian Revolution and the Russian Civil War.

22. Turkey. Imbrie traveled widely across Asia Minor and along the shores of the Black Sea during the Turkish War of Independence. He became the first U.S. foreign service officer assigned to Ankara, the capital of the new republic.

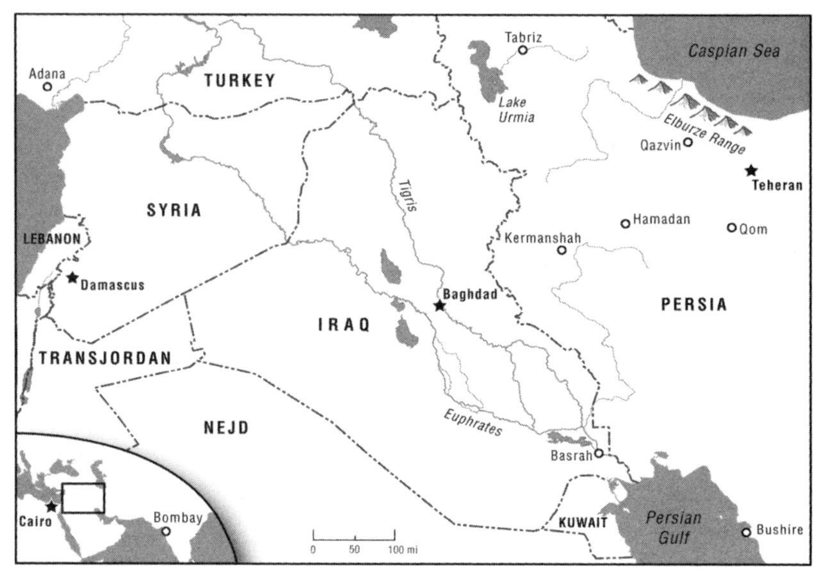

23. Persia. Assigned to Tabriz, Persia, as vice consul in 1924, Imbrie detoured to Teheran to provide a temporary replacement for the current consul. After his death his body was transported from Teheran to Bushire near where the USS *Trenton* waited to carry him home.

SEVEN

Netting Oil

Much of Imbrie's tenure in Angora was successful professionally and personally. He used the city as a jumping off point for reconnoitering. He helped advance U.S. commerce. And he married. But it ended with a $40,000 price on his head, in gold, and a Turkish guard to protect him.

According to protocol, Imbrie presented his credentials upon arrival and extended the offer of American friendship to government officials. Some he found promising as U.S. partners. Minister of Religion Vehbi Effendi, who spoke Arabic and Persian, seemed broad-minded; Minister of Sanitation Riza Nour Bey, a physician, was anti-Bolshevik and pro-American with great ability and a pleasing personality; Minister of Justice Rifat Bey, an attorney, was also pro-American with a pleasing personality. Others Imbrie found less promising. He thought Minister of Public Affairs Feizy Bey and Minster Ismail Seffa lacked great ability or influence. The very important minster of foreign affairs Ismet Pasha, a major general, lacked a broad understanding of international affairs but was passionate about Turkey's place in the world. Imbrie filed his first report on his first impressions.[1]

Dulles did not find Imbrie sufficiently circumspect in the report. He reacted within hours of receiving it, addressing Undersecretary of State William Phillips and demonstrating the Western opinion of the Turks that Imbrie would have to combat:

> The Turks are a remarkably clever people and when they put themselves out to be agreeable there is no nationality that can be more pleasant or congenial. They are adept at showing people what they want them to see and in giving the impression of injured innocence. I am not sure that Imbrie is right in assuring the Turks of the friendly feeling borne by the American people for the Turkish people. I have yet to find any real evidence of such a feeling and I am rather inclined to believe that it would be better if Imbrie left with them the impression that the American people were disturbed by the reports of Turkish deportations and atrocities and that they were looking for a change of attitude on the part of the Turk toward the Christians. It is significant that practically every American who has gone to Angora has come away as a staunch supporter of the Turks. It is in fact very hard to reconcile the undeniable ability and democracy of the Angora authorities with the stories of atrocities which Missionaries bring us from other parts of Anatolia: where the Turk is under observation he is generally on his good behaviour.[2]

Firmly aligned with Bristol in promoting commerce, Dulles seems to have interpreted Imbrie's expression of friendship between Turkey and the United States as more than it was, but his caveat illustrates the dilemma the State Department faced—how to address the atrocities and at the same time promote commercial ventures. While this may seem an easy choice, it wasn't. The former demanded immediate attention, but the latter promised a desirable long-range effect, a stable democratic nation that would, it was hoped, preclude such atrocities.

The signature commercial venture of Imbrie's stay in Angora pitted a quixotic retired naval officer against powerful corporations such as Standard Oil and Royal Dutch Shell.[3] Although the so-called Chester concession eventually won approval from the Angora government, it was used by both the Turks and the Americans as a ploy for gaining greater goals. In itself it was inconsequential. The conniving placed Imbrie in the awkward position of first shepherding the project and then abandoning it as illusory, a waste of time when he preferred intelligence work, showing why Imbrie much preferred chasing Bolsheviks than dealing with corporate America.

In 1920 retired rear-admiral Colby M. Chester, seventy-six years old, had resurrected a dream from the prewar years. During his naval career he had assessed the areas he sailed for commercial opportunity. He had also watched as ships converted from coal to petroleum. Gradually he envisioned a vast commercial empire and began securing rights to land in Turkey, Syria, and Mesopotamia.[4] His efforts foundered with the Great War, but with peace he resurrected his plan to build 2,500 miles of rail and exploit the subsoil resources within twenty miles on both sides of the track, including the very desirable area of Mosul.[5] His claim was fraught with difficulties: it included areas under military occupation, was ill-funded, and faced competing claims. His one solace was that both Turkey and the United States wanted an American company in the region to offset British claims, and unlike Standard Oil, his company already had a claim dating to the prewar era. In this way the Chester concession took on undue importance.

Giving added urgency to the Chester and other American commercial endeavors was a fall in American exports to Turkey. In 1919–20 America had enjoyed the lion's share of trade for various reasons—postwar Europe's inability to meet the demand, the availability of American shipping in the region, and the amount of necessities being shipped to Turkey by American philanthropic organizations—but a rapid decline began in 1921 as Europe became more competitive.[6] With the decline, U.S. foreign officers and American businessmen needed to be more aggressive, helping to explain Bristol's sense of urgency in commercial dealings.

In early 1922 Chester approached the Division of Near Eastern Affairs, headed by Dulles, for help in resurrecting his claims.[7] That spring the Ottoman-American Development Company incorporated, a phoenix arising from Chester's prewar American Exploration Company. One of its directors was Kermit Roosevelt, son of Theodore Roosevelt.[8] With improved backing, at least on paper, Chester gained enough credibility that by the time Imbrie left for Angora, his concession was a player in the oil game. For the United States, the concession would mean getting a strong foothold in the region. For the Turks, an American company could be used as leverage in negotiating with the Allies, which is how it played out.

In the middle of September Arthur Chester, son of Admiral Chester, arrived in Anatolia to reopen negotiations.[9] He accomplished nothing. With him was Maj. K. E. Clayton-Kennedy, who held no passport, offering Imbrie his business cards instead.[10] He claimed to be a Canadian citizen and a British subject. When the younger Chester vouched for him, Imbrie told him that associating with Clayton-Kennedy was "a tactical mistake," given the current Turkish attitude to the British. Imbrie must also have been suspicious of him but reluctant to come across too strongly to Chester. In early October Clayton-Kennedy left Angora for Constantinople to seek additional funding, $30,000 to use for "further negotiations." When the Nationalist government asked Imbrie to vouch for Clayton-Kennedy, he declined: Clayton-Kennedy was not an American citizen. The Nationalists then told Imbrie that they had proof that Clayton-Kennedy was a British spy. In early November Clayton-Kennedy reentered Anatolia, getting as far as Ismet, where he was arrested and a week later deported. About the same time Chester left Angora. His two months in Anatolia had been ill-spent and made his father's project appear backed by British interests. Although there is no hard evidence that Clayton-Kennedy was a spy, he was an opportunist. He returned to the United States, hoping to buy out the Chesters, without success, and moved on to Europe to seek other opportunities.[11] Chester's concession moved ahead without him and sometimes without Imbrie, who made at least five reconnaissance trips during this period. Although the Chester concession eventually took Imbrie to the peace conference in Lausanne, it was not all-consuming.

Imbrie was often absent from Angora gathering information. In those times he was happiest, virtually on his own to explore and assess.

Only one extended record of Imbrie's travels through Turkey exists. This detailed account appeared in the *National Geographic* magazine of October 1924, a month after his funeral, but the travel piece masked his consular work. Nowhere in the article is there a hint of what he gathered regarding military movement and commercial opportunities. Tracking the trip, however, lends insight into his work.[12]

The trip likely occurred in August 1922, a fateful month in Turkey's history. The Turkish-Greek war was in its final weeks. In 1919, seeing opportunity in the dismembered Ottoman Empire, the Greeks had seized the port city of Smyrna and eastern Thrace. Ostensibly to protect Greeks and other minorities living in the region, they had pushed inland in 1920 and 1921. When Imbrie left Turkey in the summer of 1921, the Greeks were on the offensive; when he returned in 1922, the Turkish Nationalists had turned the tide. Mustapha Kemal was about to launch a massive offensive.

Imbrie's trip was before the battles that earned the Turks their definitive victory, capped by the tragic burning of Smyrna in September, which drove multitudes to the harbor, with too few ships to effect a rescue operation. In the aftermath of this horror, the final stipulations for the Greek withdrawal were concluded.[13] Turkey would claim its sovereignty but at a terrible cost to its reputation.

As the Greek and Turkish troops clashed in the west, Imbrie skirted the zone of conflict and headed east. With two unnamed companions, most likely a translator and a guard, he started in Mersina on the Mediterranean coast and crossed overland, north through Angora to the Black Sea. His *National Geographic* article conveyed none of the tragic backdrop for this journey. The article remains upbeat, delighting in everything, including marauding bandits, immersing armchair adventurers in the writer's adventurous persona. Imbrie was not dismissing the suffering in Turkey; he was separating his two passions (photojournalism and consular work) and two kinds of writing (travelogue and news story). His account was not meant to be political or polemical. But there was another reason for Imbrie's approach, a desire to humanize the Turk to Westerners. In contrast, events covered in newspapers fed the image of the Terrible Turk. Nevertheless, today's reader must filter the article through a scrim of Armenian and Greek deportation and persecution. Mersina, his first stop, had suffered a tidal wave of refugees in 1920–21 as Armenians fled to port cities. In December 1921 Bristol, hoping to stem the tide, had ordered a stop to aid in the city.[14] When Imbrie arrived, the mass evacuations had decreased throughout the region. Mersina's mayor invited Imbrie to his home, plied him with syrupy black coffee, and loaned him his car, the only automobile in town.

The next stop was Adana, which like Mersina had been inundated with refugees in 1920–21, its fields and vineyards destroyed, the city and refugee camps shelled. Adana had long been a producer of cotton and sugar. The hope in 1922 was for an economic recovery.[15] There the men spent the night on the flat-topped roof of a khan (inn), with pack animals and oxen housed beneath, insuring an early morning wake-up call.

Imbrie and his companions next boarded a train north to Konia, winding their way through the central plateau of Asia Minor with its gnarled hills, sluggish streams, and arid land flecked with cottonwoods. In Imbrie's lovely description, they passed from the land of tilling to the land of grazing, from cotton to wool.[16]

After an excruciatingly slow thirty-six hours, the train reached Konia, long known for its strategic location on trade routes and at the time connected by rail with Adana through the Taurus Mountains and with the Bosporus through Angora. Seven years earlier it had been overwhelmed with thousands of Armenians refugees. As many as forty-five thousand lay in the fields and ditches, a story whose ending told of acute hardship, staggering cruelty, and unmarked graves.[17] When Mustapha Kemal planned his August offensive against the Greeks, he strictly censored Konia's post office.[18] Like Adana, Konia had vast potential for development.

At Konia Imbrie and friends traded train travel for horses and a pack animal. They had brought their own saddles, finding them more comfortable than Turkish saddles. They had water bottles and colored goggles and were armed. Imbrie's rifle was slung over his back. They donned wool kalpaks, a conical Turkish headgear of lambswool, the better to blend in but uncomfortable in searing heat and torrential rains. Thus equipped, the men moved along a flat landscape under a glaring sun, the saddles creaking, and the horses' gait monotonous and mesmerizing.

After several days of crossing this barren landscape, they reached the new capital of Turkey, Angora, where Imbrie had been living since June. They did not pause long. It, too, in 1915 had deported Armenians, as many as twenty-seven thousand. Many had been massacred after leaving the city. A Russian Armenian reported in September 1915 that Ankara was a "dead town."[19] After a night's rest, the men set out again, taking an eighty-mile detour through wadis and rocky gorges to avoid brigands. Three days' ride brought them to Kirshehr. In 1919 the Greeks had toyed with the idea of taking Kirshehr. Now Imbrie found five hundred Turkish soldiers camped around a bonfire. The presence of soldiers suggested that they were part of a Nationalist rear action unit. They invited the travelers to join them in dancing, wrestling, and playing spoon castanets and hautbois, but after a time Imbrie opted for sleep. He had a long way to go before reaching the Black Sea.

The next day Imbrie rode into one of the world's oldest towns, Kaisariye, known in ancient times as Caesarea, guarded by Mt. Argaeus, the highest mountain in Anatolia. Mule and camel caravans, flocks of sheep and goats, and cavalcades of horsemen filled its streets. Imbrie took time to scout the bazaar where one merchant, asked about the town's specialty, answered, "Before Allah, everything."

Two days out of Kaisariye, the landscape gave way to small streams, cottonwoods, and increased traffic, including horsemen in capes with long daggers and carbines. Upon reaching the town of Shehr Kishla, Imbrie and his companions were in the geographic center of Asia Minor. There the mayor greeted them, warning of dangers ahead and offering the safety of his khan. Imbrie declined. The dangers, however, were real, and Imbrie noted that on one of his journeys both the party ahead of his and the party behind had been wiped out "to a man."

Two days later, under a burning noonday sun, the travelers reached Sivas, a stronghold for the Nationalists early in the civil war. For centuries caravans from Baghdad to Constantinople had passed through this region. In the summer of 1915 twenty-five thousand Armenians had been deported, many never heard from again.[20]

Imbrie was now on the last leg of his journey. From Sivas to the Black Sea, two hundred miles away, the riders descended a thousand feet and then rode through wooded country into an open valley and into Turkey's famed tobacco district. After crossing a ridge at twenty-seven thousand feet, the men found themselves gazing down on Samsoun, well known for its tobacco trade. Following the burning of Smyrna in the autumn of 1922, a few months after Imbrie's trip, it would be inundated with tens of thousands of Greek refugees scheduled for deportation.[21]

Although Imbrie did not participate in the official investigations of Turkish atrocities, his trip gave him a clearer notion of what had been happening to minorities in Turkey in the past seven years as Turkey sought to forge a republic without ethnic or religious diversity.

Imbrie gained a deep understanding of Turkey from such journeys, but he also had a new source of information, Katherine Helene Gillespie. Five feet five inches tall, with brown eyes, her brown hair pulled back, a slight scar on her left cheek, and pertly perched, wire-rimmed glasses, Gillespie had served in Turkey with Near East Relief since 1919.

Gillespie was a self-made woman. She had grown up in New Bedford, Massachusetts, the daughter of Irish immigrants. In the 1870s and 1880s the north end of the city, once farmland, had given way to industrialization as cotton mills, tenements, and boarding houses took over the meadows and woods. At their peak the mills employed forty-one thousand workers. The working conditions were abysmal. Ten-hour days were the norm. Hot and dusty, with cotton bits and remnants filling both air and lungs and covering the floor, the typical mill space was three hundred feet long with high windows and high ceilings that echoed the clanking power looms running day and night. The noise was deafening; the work monotonous, grinding, and dangerous. Most of the workers were women, wearing long sleeves and long skirts, their hair piled high, daily facing the threatening grasps and bites of gears, levers, and machine belts.[22]

Gillespie began work in a knit-stocking factory at age fifteen. At the time neither of her parents was employed; her father was once a foreman, and her mother, once a mill worker. It is possible that her mother was disabled from mill work and her father was caring for her. With the prospect of a grim life of hive work, Gillespie left New Bedford as soon as she could, but her leaving was prescient, too. Competition for mill work, especially from the South, doomed New Bedford. In 1916 city fathers bragged of their "strong, right-living, prosperous community . . . a modern city [with] nothing lacking," but by 1928 its mill industry was gasping for breath, and by the 1930s it had passed into history, like New Bedford's earlier boom industry, whaling.

Seeking better prospects, Gillespie headed to Boston and, improbable for a mill worker, found a job as a jewelry buyer, or so her passport reads. By the time she joined the Near East Relief (NER) in Turkey, she was claiming New Rochelle, New York, as her home, and on her 1919 passport she listed her father's birthplace as Chelsea, Massachusetts, not Ireland. Although remade, she did not abandon her family and, given the conditions of her last will and testament, it seems likely she provided for them during her lifetime, especially for the family of her brother John, who died young, leaving a widow and six children. But there is no evidence that she ever returned to New Bedford. It is tempting to think that in meeting and marrying the far more privileged Robert Imbrie, she was achieving the crown of her life's goals, a kind of Cinderella story, but that would be a mistake. By the time she married, she had earned her new identity. She was intrepid, a trait Imbrie admired. When he died, she was able to draw on this spirit in the pursuit of justice.

When American newspapers published appeals on behalf of the suffering Armenians, Greeks, Syrians, and Jews of the Near East, vividly depicting the plight of over four hundred thousand orphans in Turkey, Gillespie may have recalled the millworkers' lives, especially those of children ages ten and eleven, prompting her to apply to the NER. Soon she was part of its vast humanitarian effort. She spent two years working with orphans largely in Trebizond, although she was in Constantinople from December 1920 to February 1921, serving as a liaison between the American embassy and the NER and working in its refugee handcraft shop. During that winter she went to Kars, east of Trebizond, to help move seven thousand orphans northeast to the NER's largest orphanage complex, in Alexandropol, the "Orphan City," formerly the site of a Russian military installation. The NER had converted the military complex of 170 buildings, including 40 two-story barracks, into dormitories for children escaping the wars. In 1922 it housed thirty-one thousand children.

Gillespie returned to the United States in November 1921 but was back in Turkey by April 1922.[23] Her return to the Caucasus by May 6 coincided with the atrocities report in the *Times* (London). In Angora, in the midst of war, Katherine and Robert met and, after a whirlwind romance, took most of their friends by surprise when they married in Constantinople at the Catholic Basilica of Santa Esprit on December 26, 1922.[24] After Imbrie's years of dalliances—the rich young woman from Nashville, Lucette in Paris, the stunning woman in Russia, and all those others who had him hanging from the ropes, as he had said—Imbrie felt that he had no time to dally. In an undated and unpublished short story, "The Lure of Little Voices," Imbrie described an adventurer who realized he had met the love of his life, but who delayed proposing, only to lose her to another man. In Turkey Imbrie chose a different ending for himself and married Katherine. At the time she was the intermediary for the NER and the new Nationalist government. Bristol congratulated Imbrie on his marriage: "I have known your wife for some time so I know personally your good fortune."[25] Even Wilbur Carr in distant Washington DC was familiar with her work. Imbrie seems to have chosen a wife whose interests meshed with his. With his marriage Imbrie reflected on his former life of "whims, risks, and fancies." Now he no longer came first. He was responsible for another person. Seemingly for the first time in his life he felt apprehensive.[26]

Before the newlyweds left Constantinople, Bristol gave Imbrie open-ended directions, emphasizing commerce: "We are looking toward the future and while anxious to have full information at the present time still it is more important to build up a good place for ourselves. In case of any unforeseen events . . . stay at Angora as long as possible."[27] The latter part of the message breathed danger.

The Imbries boarded the train to Angora on January 5 but were stopped in Izmir by soldiers checking for military passes. They had none. After another American was turned back, Imbrie vigorously asserted his right to proceed, and the soldier stood down. A day later yet another American was turned back. In turn, he demanded to know if he was in a "civilized country or Africa."

The Imbries set up house in the boxcar. Their marriage and their unusual housing arrangement found mention in *Time* magazine.[28] Imbrie named it "the best home in Angora," a sly comment on Angora's housing, but it had some rare amenities for the time and place—a library, electric servant bells, a telephone, running water, a shower, and a gramophone.[29] Their servants included an Albanian orderly, a Turkish interpreter, and an Egyptian cook, who spoke English "small, small." Mustapha Kemal's wife occasionally visited them, admiring their ingenuity in setting up house, jokingly offering to exchange her villa for the boxcar.[30] The small American colony found welcome there; nights were often passed playing bridge.

Unfortunately for Imbrie, he was not free of Bristol, who was circumventing the consul general. On August 24 Bristol complained to Secretary of State Charles Hughes that he had not heard from Imbrie for two months.[31] He complained again in September. On October 3 Secretary of State Hughes contacted Bristol: "Telegraph whereabouts wellbeing Imbrie."[32] In a snit Bristol demanded Imbrie's removal from Angora, Hughes countermanded Bristol, most likely due to Imbrie's work with the Chester concession, and Bristol backed down. He wrote Hughes that Imbrie was somewhere in Anatolia, and he would order Imbrie to return to Angora by way of Constantinople. How he was to execute the order was unexplained. On October 30 Bristol telegraphed Hughes that Imbrie had returned to Angora on October 25. There is no indication that the two met in the interim.

The communication problem was not all, or any, of Imbrie's fault. Trustworthy couriers were scarce, and dispatches from Turkey took between six and ten weeks to reach Washington. The telegraph office serving both official and private communication was near Mustapha Kemal's office, hardly suitable for confidential reports. There was no mail service. Further, Imbrie was traveling through remote places as the account of his trip from Mersina to Samsoun illustrates. At one point Hughes insisted the Turks provide better communications between Washington and Angora, or Imbrie would be withdrawn.[33]

When Imbrie did report, Bristol sometimes took exception to what he wrote, complaining that Imbrie was too lenient with the Turks. Bristol advised him to be firm and offer no commitments. To be effective with the Turks, Bristol counseled, a person needed to speak plainly. But even as Bristol was chiding Imbrie, he needed him. Bristol was frustrated with the Turks, particularly on commercial matters and what he regarded as the unfair taxation of American products, such as a retroactive tax on American flour languishing in warehouses. When Bristol failed in negotiating the matter with Adnan Bey, the Nationalist representative in Constantinople, and Adnan Bey suggested that Imbrie address it in Angora, Bristol relented and sent Imbrie a dispatch to handle the matter.[34]

In February Bristol's temporary replacement sent Consul Maynard Barnes to Angora to present a letter to the prime minister. Imbrie thought a special envoy to the Nationalists would be used to pit Americans against each other. Instead he and Barnes rehearsed a conversation between the prime minister and Imbrie, based on the letter. Although Barnes had planned to accompany Imbrie to the meeting, Imbrie went without him, and Barnes only met with the prime minister later. It is likely that Imbrie thought Barnes's presence would weaken his standing in Angora. Barnes did not seem to object to the change in plans. In his report he praised the Nationalists' great desire for and progress toward peace. Bristol was unimpressed. In a staff meeting he stated that Imbrie was too conciliatory with the Turks, and in general his reports were unhelpful. He concluded that Imbrie might not be up to the posting.[35] Yet in the coming weeks he continued to rely on Imbrie. In late April Imbrie visited Constantinople despite the dangers of traveling through a war zone with confidential papers secreted on his person.[36] He returned again in May with Katherine, and Bristol hosted them at a dinner party.[37]

Meanwhile Imbrie had growing concerns about the viability of the Chester concession. Not even the deposit, an insignificant amount for such a large project, had been paid, although it had been promised in December. For months there had been nothing but talk. Nonetheless the project, which had received so much news coverage in Anatolia, could not be easily dismissed without damaging American prestige.[38] Bristol agreed with Imbrie. He held that America's prestige depended on the concession for "years to come throughout the Near East," but he, too, had misgivings about its financial backing.[39] While the concession was being debated at the peace conference in Lausanne, Bristol counseled Imbrie to pose as a Chester "know nothing" in Angora.[40]

Despite the weakness of the Chester concession, an agreement between the Ottoman-American Development Company and

Turkish representatives was finally signed on April 29.[41] It seems not to have been done in good faith by the Turks. They were playing a card before final terms were agreed upon at the peace conference. One or both of the Chesters were also suspect. They overstated their ability to meet the terms of the agreement, logistically and financially. Nevertheless, Imbrie reported that "every peasant in the country has heard of, and is waiting for 'the American railroads.'"[42] Despite the ultimate failure of the concession, Admiral Chester later praised Imbrie's "valuable assistance."[43] He wrote to the State Department, "Mr. Imbries [*sic*] stirling [*sic*] integrity and great ability for carrying on diplomatic work made him greatly respected by all Turks who knew him. His intimate association with the Grand Vizier and acting President of Parliament during the time the case was pending in legislative body gave him the means of working for American interests to great advantage and he used his power well. Next to Hon. John Ridgely Carter, former American Ambassador at Constantinople, Mr. Imbrie did more to secure the success of this enterprise than any other official."[44] His mention of Carter slighted Bristol. The State Department chose not to respond to Chester because, strictly speaking, no American official had participated in the negotiations on behalf of Chester, as the American delegates repeatedly assured the Allies at the Lausanne Conference, although Imbrie certainly did what consuls often do—open doors.

With the Chester concession apparently concluded, Imbrie asked for thirty days' leave. He may have been concerned that the contract, which threatened Russian designs in the region, would prompt them to target him once again. In November 1922 Raouf Bey informed Imbrie that the Russian ambassador had ordered Bolshevik operatives to kill him. Turkish officials had quickly arrested some of the gunmen and assigned guards to protect him. On the surface Imbrie appeared low key about this incident, so much so that when he left Turkey, Consul Maynard Barnes believed he had just learned of the threat. Nevertheless, Imbrie seemed to think a temporary leave was advised, if only to clear the air.[45]

Using understatement, Bristol wrote to the secretary of state that Imbrie's replacement, Maxwell Blake, would find Angora's living conditions "somewhat unusual from every point of view [and that it] is difficult to arrange for the installation of a delegate at that post."[46] Blake lasted five months. During that short stay he had growing admiration for Imbrie and became a stalwart supporter of his work. He left Angora in frustration at the high cost of living and the poor housing conditions.[47]

When Imbrie asked for a leave, he was not asking for a new posting. He expected to return to Turkey. However, between late April and June when he went to Lausanne, two events altered his plans. One could say they paved the way to his death. First, though, Lausanne.

The Peace Conference at Lausanne had initially convened on November, 21, 1922, to address the punitive Treaty of Sevres. Since 1920 relations between Britain and Turkey had become increasingly fraught, and a military showdown seemed imminent by late summer 1922. As a precondition for the conference, an armistice was reached on October 11. The U.S. delegates, attending only as observers to protect American interests, were Bristol, Joseph Grew, ambassador to Switzerland, and Richard Child, ambassador to Rome and head of the American delegation. A former editor at *Collier's Weekly* and a political appointee, Child was enthralled by the new fascism in Italy and ambitious to make a name for himself.[48]

The first phase of the conference was overly contentious, the delegates casting each other in cartoonish light. Grew described the British delegate, Lord Curzon, as sneering and scolding, treating the Turkish representative, Ismet Pasha, like "an office boy."[49] In turn, Ismet used his deafness to great and selective effect, turning Curzon into "an angry bull." The Greek representative, Eleftherios Venizelos, acted the firebrand, reportedly bellowing and waving his arms.[50] The Russian delegate, Georgii Chicherin, was described by another delegate as a "golden, but mangy cocker spaniel."[51] Grew mused that some of his colleagues reminded him of characters in *Alice in Wonderland*.[52]

After two months, on February 4, 1923, with Curzon and Ismet deadlocked over questions regarding foreign economic influence in Turkey, the peace conference broke apart. Grew faulted Curzon for acting like a viceroy as if Ismet were "one of his natives."[53] Child left for Rome, suspicious that Bristol would negotiate with Ismet on his own. Bristol, annoyed by Child's insinuations, left for a vacation in Venice. Grew stayed on. A second phase of the conference was inevitable.[54]

The next phase opened on April 23, Imbrie's fortieth and second-to-last birthday. There was a change in personnel. Child did not return, nor did Curzon. Sir Horace Rumbold, high commissioner in Constantinople, represented Britain. Grew represented the United States. Both had known each other in Cairo and Berlin—Grew had helped Rumbold pack and seal the British archives at the outbreak of war in 1914—but in Lausanne Rumbold treated Grew coldly probably due to his friction with Bristol.[55] Rumbold thought Bristol of "limited intelligence and outlook."[56] In turn, Bristol thought the Britisher high-handed and anti-Turk, exuding a sense of superiority. Their differing attitudes toward the Turkish treatment of Armenians and Greeks is certainly one reason for their mutual dislike.

Even before the conference officially reopened, the Chester concession was bandied about, with the Italian representative encouraging the French not to bring it up, and Ismet insisting that it was a matter for the Turkish courts, not the conference. As Grew recalled, "The corridors buzzed with the Chester Concession."[57] In truth, the real issue was the meaning and application of America's Open Door policy, which demanded equal opportunity among nations for commercial ventures. On June 5 Ismet told Grew that the Allies were taking direct aim at the Chester concession by trying to force him to confirm prewar, imperialist concessions. Grew encouraged Ismet to stand firm, although he suspected that the Turks were using the concession as leverage.

Before Imbrie left for Lausanne to meet with Grew about the concession, he tangled with two American journalists. One appealed to the State Department's sympathy for beleaguered Armenians; the other evoked its hard line against Soviet Russia. One reporter was given undue consideration; the other was dismissed out of hand for her Bolshevik past.

William T. Ellis, an independent journalist, claimed that when he first called on Imbrie in Angora, Imbrie reportedly said, "I hope you are not one of those Americans who think the Turks are always massacring the Christians."[58] According to Ellis, Imbrie supposedly went into a

> tirade against Armenians and Greeks, expressing the wish that they all had been exterminated. . . . At the same time Mr. Imbrie made a comprehensive and intense attack upon the Near East Relief and its workers and work, and upon the American missionaries. It seems that his wife, who was formerly a Near East Relief employee, has some sort of a feud with the organization. . . . Naturally the Angora government highly approves of him. [Imbrie] says that Raouf Bey, the premier, who speaks English, spends two or three hours a day in Mr. Imbrie's [railroad] car. It appears unfortunate that from an American official the Turkish prime minister should be hearing continually, as is apparently the case, criticisms of the major American enterprises in this country; of the American workers here; and of the Christian people who however great their faults have suffered sorely, and are the special concern of the American people. . . . Doesn't it seem to you, Mr. Secretary, that a man of more mature years, ripe discretion and tested conservatism; [*sic*] who speaks Turkish but thinks American [*sic*] should represent us in this remote capital, where the American delegate and the young man employed by Standard Oil and the representative of the Chester project, are the only resident American citizens?[59]

Ellis's letter jumped the track in its accusations. Ellis accused Imbrie of undermining American commercial interests in conversation with the Turkish premier but gives no indication of how he knew the content of daily conversations between the two men. He accused both Imbries of denigrating the NER, yet years after Imbrie's death Katherine continued to represent and support the organization. More telling is the accusation of Imbrie's lacking compassion and empathy for the downtrodden. His work, extending from his tenure with the Legal Aid Society and his wartime volunteerism to his stays in Russia and Finland, amply display both. Finally, one of his close associates in Turkey championed the Armenian cause, Lewis K. Davis.

In 1919 Davis, a major in the Army Tank Corps, was ordered from France to Armenia to serve as a technical adviser. Davis advocated for Armenia in several U.S. publications, including the *New York Evening Post* and the *Literary Digest*. He described the Armenians as "diligent, shrewd, industrious, and passionately eager to develop their country themselves." He advanced a $50 million plan involving the NER to modernize Armenian farming practices and lead to Armenian self-sufficiency. According to Davis, only the United States had the wherewithal and ability to save Armenia. Davis was also aware of the country's mineral resources. While in the vicinity of Alexandropol, he had discovered coal deposits and put refugees to work opening up a vein to provide coal for heating orphanages.[60] Surely Davis would not have befriended Imbrie if the two had a fundamental disagreement about the Armenian tragedy.

The State Department tepidly supported Imbrie. In an office memo Secretary of State Hughes suggested that perhaps Imbrie had been away from America for too long, although he had been gone only a little over a year. Carr postponed discussion of the accusations until Imbrie arrived in Washington. Dulles wanted more input from Bristol, although Bristol was not reliable in judging Imbrie on an Armenian matter, given their rocky relationship and given Bristol's own suspicious and even dismissive attitude to the reports of atrocities.

It is inconceivable that Imbrie would have minimized the Armenian tragedy. For years the U.S. consulates had been monitoring and reporting on the Armenian slaughter. Bolstering the consular reports were those from diplomats, missionaries, philanthropic organizations, and businessmen. There was ample evidence of genocide. Imbrie had traveled widely through the affected regions, and his wife was one of the workers protecting the Armenians. They were housing two Armenian orphans in their boxcar.

Nevertheless there was concern at the State Department that Imbrie, in supporting the Nationalists, may have slighted the Armenian cause. In the United States it was a political as well as humanitarian issue. Imbrie's position was a delicate one. Although he knew of atrocities, he supported the new Turkey as it faced the future and stripped away at its stereotypes of the "Terrible Turk." Unlike Bolshevik Russia, Imbrie found Turkey embracing republicanism and allying with America. That did not mean he abandoned the Armenians, but perhaps he overstated his position to Ellis. Imbrie would need to explain himself.

Significantly, despite State Department concerns over the allegations against him, Imbrie was sent to Lausanne, leaving on June 23, the same day that Blake wrote a strong defense of Imbrie to Carr and revealed the reason for guards being assigned to him: "I feel [Imbrie] has been made something of a victim because of somebody's whim. This removal from Angora was a mistake. He was well liked and doing his best under difficult conditions and in justice to him this I want you to know. Imbrie has risked everything for this Government. It is you alone that I want to tell that the [Turks] at Angora were offered $40,000 (gold) for permission to blow him up. This I have learned from a most confidential source and it is only today that I have told Imbrie."[61] Blake's rhetorical flourishes—"this I want you to know"—reveals his depth of feeling, but Blake was naive in thinking Imbrie did not know he was a marked man, although Imbrie may not have known that Turks had been offered a bribe to aid in an assassination. After Imbrie's death, Bristol said he had never heard directly from Imbrie about the death threats although he "did remember that Imbrie said something about Raouf Bey having [stationed] guards around his [railroad] car. But [he] did not attach much importance to [it] at the time." He said that he knew Imbrie did not like the Bolsheviks and was "very bitter" against them.[62]

On June 25 Consul General Ravndal also wrote on behalf of Imbrie:

> My distinct impression is that he succeeded in gaining the confidence and good will of the Angora leaders in an unusual measure, and that he filled a most difficult post with real credit to himself and to his country. He did not report as often and as much in detail as he undoubtedly would have done had he enjoyed the privilege of exemption from Turkish censorship. It is only with the last 2–3 weeks that it has been possible to send cipher messages between Constantinople and Angora. However, [Imbrie] quite frequently came from Angora to Constantinople to report in person.[63]

"Frequently" takes on added meaning when one considers the state of rail transportation. One American diplomat facetiously recalled that the train trip to Constantinople could render "a person all but bursting into tears upon his arrival." The bridges were in deplorable condition, "positively dangerous," and some sections of rails were made of "small bits of the original rail in some cases no longer than three or four feet laboriously pieced together after the Great War."[64] Yet Imbrie braved these conditions to deliver reports.

Ravndal recommended that Imbrie be returned to Angora or, if not, perhaps be sent to Addis Abba in Ethiopia or to Kabul since Afghanistan had by then acquired full national independence "and is desirous of joining the sisterhood of civilized nations." Imbrie might even be sent to Asia or to Rhodesia or, if not there, to the Soviet state of Bokhara in Central Asia, where it was "reported that Bolshevik rule [was] tottering if not overthrown."[65] In June Hughes responded tepidly to Ellis regarding his accusations, not defending Imbrie but stating only that there was a new representative in Angora.

Unfortunately Ellis was not the only American journalist to attack Imbrie. Another attack came from Louise Bryant, who had greatly distressed American officials in Petrograd during the Russian Revolution for her outspoken support of the Bolsheviks.[66] Her attack was virtually ignored by the State Department, but

Bristol gave it some countenance instead of defending his vice consul. Her complaint reveals details of Imbrie's job in Angora and how frustrating it could be. In 1923 Bryant was a reporter for the Newspaper Feature Syndicate.

On June 26, three days after Imbrie had left Constantinople for Lausanne, Bryant met with Bristol to tell him "something disagreeable" about her recent trip to Angora. In presenting her credentials, she related how in 1920, intent on seeing her dying husband, journalist John Reed, in Moscow, she had applied to the State Department for a passport, only to be turned down. Defiant, she had boarded a ship disguised as a boy. She also told Bristol that she was a good friend of Enver Pasha, Mustapha Kemal's "natural enemy." And finally, although she knew a great deal about the Nationalists' plans, she had not published any of it to endear herself to the Turks. In this way she led up to her charge that Imbrie was spreading a rumor in Angora that she was a "dangerous woman," making the Turks wary of her and thereby impeding her news gathering. She thought Imbrie had been unfair, especially as she was a woman and by herself.

Instead of defending Imbrie or merely being noncommittal, Bristol needlessly told her that Imbrie had reported seeing her "from a distance and that was all [he] wanted to see of her." Bristol excused this cut by saying Imbrie had witnessed Bolshevik atrocities and "naturally had strong feelings against them." Anyway, now that Imbrie had left Turkey "for good," there was nothing more to be said. Bristol complimented her as someone who could take care of herself and advised that any remarks made about her by Turks should be given their "proper weight." He cautioned her that her friend Enver Pasha was persona non grata in Angora and then excused himself for another appointment.[67] In passing, Admiral Bristol might have wondered about her boast to have boarded a ship illegally when her visa was denied.

Bryant was not appeased. Two weeks later she wrote an accusatory letter to Secretary of State Hughes:

> I am a rather lonely spectator of those impulses and formulas which men find to save the world and upon which wars are made and histories written. . . . I have been in England, Ireland, Germany, France, and the French African provinces, Italy, Sicily, and now I am in Turkey. Shortly after I arrived in Turkey I asked permission to go to Angora and, after some weeks, I obtained it. I had only been there a short time when a man who had been acting as American Observer, in the consular service, Mr. Robert Imbrie, came back to Angora from Constantinople. I was working very hard, under difficult circumstances for a woman, to get a clear view of this new government which is now directed by Mustafa Kemal like an army . . . and which is putting a new spirit into Turkey, more like that which dominates other modern nations, whose ultimate goal is a democracy like the United States. Mr. Imbrie, from the moment of his arrival, waged a bitter, personal campaign against me, going from official to official to say that I am a dangerous individual and waxing more intense as he met their incredulity. He even became so undignified as an American official as to descend to the most extravagant lies. He said, for example, that it was I who led the Communist parades in Petrograd in 1917. Of course I did not lead them because there were no parades and I am not a Communist! You will understand Mr. Imbrie better if you look up his record. He was one of the Wilson spies who put so much useless discord into American life, piling up in your own department so many false accusations against every citizen who dared an independent opinion. You will easily realize, in a remote spot like Angora . . . Mr. Imbrie was quickly making my position extremely dangerous. It is all the more amazing when you consider that I have never in my life seen or spoken to Mr. Imbrie.[68]

Bryant's diatribe is full of contradictions and misstatements. She presents Mustapha Kemal as dictatorial yet democratic; she condemns information gathering as spying; she accuses Imbrie of biased reporting on his own countrymen; she claims there were no parades in Russia although there were many. She denies she and Imbrie ever met, although it is very possible they had.

According to Ambassador Francis, her husband had visited the embassy in Petrograd a few times and the consulate often. Most likely Bryant was with her husband on several of these occasions. His passport for reentry into America was visaed at the consulate. It is likely Bryant's was as well. Perhaps Imbrie remembered her.

Continuing her letter to Hughes, Bryant stated that two ministers in the Angora government whom she knew in Moscow in 1920 vouched for her and told her that Imbrie had made charges against other correspondents and that any American traveling in Angora must have Imbrie's permission to go about their business. She claimed that Bristol was "highly indignant" at her ill-treatment, although he appeared not to be in his account of their meeting. She concluded with the expectation that Hughes would deal with Imbrie. Although Hughes knew Imbrie was strongly anti-Bolshevik, he had no reason to suppose Imbrie behaved improperly toward Bryant despite her earlier support of Bolshevism. Hughes also would certainly have known that she was in a romantic relationship with William Bullitt.

Bullitt, as a twenty-eight-year-old from a wealthy Philadelphia family, had served at the Paris Peace Conference in the Russian division, delivering daily briefings. He had been sent to Russia in March 1919 to explore the conditions for an end to hostilities and met Imbrie in Viborg when Imbrie was hoping to go to Petrograd himself. Imbrie provided him with safe conduct to the border. Upon arrival Bullitt reported that the "frightful" famine conditions in Petrograd had been "ridiculously exaggerated," but a few days later he had changed his mind, reporting, "Everyone . . . is pitifully undernourished."[69]

After visiting Petrograd and Moscow, Bullitt had returned with an agreement that verified Secretary of State Lansing's assessment of him: he was too soft on the Reds. Wilson never responded to the report, and the disgruntled Bullitt resigned his appointment in May. In September he appeared before the Senate Foreign Relations Committee and embarrassed Lansing in his testimony by unnecessarily divulging a private conversation, contributing to the secretary's resignation in February 1920. Bullitt met Bryant the following year, and by 1923 they were living together in Constantinople in a decrepit seventeenth-century mansion on the Asiatic shore of the Bosphorus. Her office was in the popular Tokatlian Hotel, where Ernest Hemingway had filed his dispatches in 1922 for the *Toronto Star*.[70] On Sundays Bryant and Bullitt hosted lunches prepared by a Basque chef and an Albanian barman. In his biography of Bullitt, Alexander Etkin describes Bullitt as the prototype of F. Scott Fitzgerald's Great Gatsby and Bryant as Zelda Fitzgerald.

Hughes must have questioned how uninformed Bryant thought he was about her political activities. She was a known socialist even before her first trip to Russia. Her passport of 1917 contains a particularly disagreeable portrait and appended to it is a Bureau of Citizenship memorandum, noting that the applicant is a socialist, "which accounts for her wild hair and open mouth." Her 1922 passport photograph is stylish, even lovely. There is no comment on it.

Bryant's protestation that she "was a lonely spectator" who had been "working under difficult circumstances for a woman" conflicted with her avowed feminist position, making her seem manipulative and calculating. One can almost picture the back of her hand pressed against her forehead. Given the number of war widows and young women who could expect never to marry after the Great War's slaughter, her aggrieved persona seems callow.

Her attack on Imbrie seems to stem from her experiences in Russia, rather than in Angora. She doubtless blamed the U.S. government for John Reed's death. In March 1920 he was arrested in Finland for diamond smuggling. He was tried, convicted, and held in solitary confinement for four months but avoided being extradited to the United States on charges of treason. At last, with his health compromised, he was allowed to leave Finland and entered Russia, journeyed to Baku, Azerbaijan, where he contracted typhus, and died in Moscow on October 17, 1920, at age thirty-two.

Bryant was with him when he died, and she stayed on in Russia for a time. In her letter about Imbrie, she referred to "two ministers in the Angora government." In February 1921 in Moscow Bryant met Enver Pasha and Ali Fuat (Cebesoy) Pasha. For six months she and Enver Pasha, who helped bring Turkey into the Great War, frequently ate at the same table at the Sugar Palace and attended the theater together. She often visited the Turkish embassy. They might have been lovers.[71] In 1923, when she was in Turkey, Ali Fuat was deputy speaker of the National Assembly. He would have known of her friendship with Enver Pasha, Mustapha Kemal's rival. Her inability to see Mustafa Kemal in Angora likely came from her association with Enver Pasha, who once told Bryant that Mustafa Kemal had no warmth and no friends. She herself concluded that "All fear him."[72] She had cozied up to Enver Pasha in Russia; her choice may have trailed her.

Bryant spent seven months in Turkey; of those, ten days were in Angora. Her Turkish Journal, as she named it, begins in April 1923 in Constantinople.[73] In June, shortly before Imbrie left Turkey, she traveled to Angora. She had interviewed Lenin and more recently Benito Mussolini, who had come to power in March 1922, and now she hoped to interview another rising leader, Mustafa Kemal. She expected to see him on her first full day in Angora. Instead he sent her a message that he wanted her to rest and he would see her the next day. He was putting her off.

Among her hosts in Angora were Raouf Bey and Fethi Bey, the minister of the interior. Bryant scoffed at Raouf Bey's boast that he had gotten the Chester project through the National Assembly in record time, six hours, but could not arrange a meeting between her and Mustapha Kemal. She did not consider that he might be reluctant to introduce her to his president, perhaps because of her former association with Enver Pasha, which he could have easily learned about from Ali Fuat.

During each day of her stay, Bryant had a regimen of outings and interviews, her interests spanning the political and the social. Bryant noted the Imbries were "the center of much admiration in Angora social circles" but at the time were away from the city.[74]

By Thursday she had still not seen Mustafa Kemal, although she heard that a Greek had tried to assassinate him on his way to a wedding, which she dismissed as yet another excuse for his not seeing her. On Saturday she wrote, "The Imbries have arrived. It is curious how the Turks have been fooled by such a cheap spy." She called at the Imbrie home in a sour mood. She was running out of time and fed up with being in Angora, which she regarded as a backwater town. She had sent a letter to Mustafa Kemal's wife asking for help in securing an interview, but nothing had come of it. Aware that she was being put off, she approached the Imbrie boxcar and later made note of her first impression: "Mrs. Imbrie came to the door—a regular missionary type—false teeth and a crooked smile." The two women did not hit it off.

According to Bryant, the women debated about whether Imbrie was the U.S. consul in Angora, or ever would be. In her notes Bryant tried to portray herself as sophisticated and knowledgeable, while casting Katherine as petty in contending that Imbrie was serving as the delegate of the high commissioner and not as vice consul. Katherine's explanation may have been too fine a point for Bryant, which Bryant refused to concede. Of Katherine, Bryant concluded, "What an idiot!" Katherine invited her to visit that afternoon with Maxwell Blake. She reported spending about two hours with this "amusing, old man," as she called him, as he told stories and drank whiskey. He was forty-six years old; she was thirty-eight. She recorded none of the stories or anything he had to say, if he said anything, about the situation in Turkey. It is unfortunate for Bryant that she was unable to win over Katherine, who spoke some Turkish and seemed well liked by Turkish women,[75] including Mustapha Kemal's wife.

The next day Bryant learned she would not get her wished-for interview. During what she called her "dismal" farewell meal, she wrote that her host repeated lies Imbrie had said about John Reed, making her cry. Bryant's mention of weeping seems disingenuous.

After Bryant left Angora, she did not return to the topic of Imbrie in the scattered notes that concluded her diary, nor is it clear what the "lies" were. Although she did not meet Mustafa Kemal, she had had an active week and visited with many dignitaries. No doors seemed to have been closed to her except the president's, yet she made a damning, sweeping conclusion about the Turks—that the only thing they knew how to do well is fight and they had no art and culture—thus denigrating her Turkish friendships of long standing. If accepted as serious, Bryant's complaint could have added some weight to Ellis's accusations, but at the top of Bryant's letter to the secretary of state is scrawled, "no answer required."[76]

When Imbrie bid farewell to Bristol, the admiral told him he was sorry he was leaving and wanted to congratulate him on his work. In his opinion Imbrie had done everything he could, given his experience and knowledge, but he did not have the rank and experience to accomplish more. What Bristol meant by "experience" is unclear. Bristol did not regard any failures as a reflection on Imbrie personally but simply a "question of fact." The assessment sounds tepid, almost a damning by faint praise, but given his association with Imbrie and recognizing that the comment came from a naval officer whose service had begun in 1887, it seems somewhat conciliatory.[77] In turn, Imbrie diplomatically stated how pleased he had been to work under him.[78] Both men avoided choking on their words.

The Imbries' stop in Switzerland came at a crucial time for the Lausanne Conference. Imbrie left Constantinople on June 23 and arrived in Lausanne on June 26.[79] A week earlier Ismet had gone to Grew to say the Allies were pressuring him over the prewar concessions, specifically aimed at discrediting the newly won Chester concession. Grew told him to stand fast. Grew was championing the Open Door policy of which this concession was an example. For his part Ismet was championing the right of the new Turkish government to start with a fresh slate. The State Department had decided not to forward the details of the oil negotiations to Grew to avoid compromising its neutrality,[80] but Imbrie's presence suggests that he was helpful to Grew. At least five telegrams between Washington and Lausanne had been exchanged regarding the company's affairs, and no doubt Imbrie was sent to aid in clarifications.[81]

Grew was convinced that the Allies would not go to war over prewar concessions. He was right. On July 17 the Allies capitulated, signing the only treaty concluding the Great War in which a vanquished state was treated equitably. As with the Russian famine relief, Imbrie's shadow assistance deserves some credit. Grew then moved on to negotiating the Treaty of Amity and Commerce between the United States and Turkey, which he and Ismet signed on August 6. Four months later, on December 18, Turkey annulled the Chester concession. Both sides had used it for their own advantage. The loser in the negotiation was Admiral Chester. When the concession was signed, he noted that for years the United States had been trying to get into Asia by the back door, but now the front door was open. After the annulment the front door remained open.[82] Although Chester had failed in his quest, his quixotic effort had a long-term, positive impact on U.S.-Turkish relations.

The Imbries left Lausanne on July 14 and arrived in the United States a month later.[83] The first order of business was countering the calumny of Ellis. Dulles arranged a meeting between Imbrie and Under Secretary of State William Phillips. He wrote, "I should be glad if you saw fit to see him for a moment. He is rather disturbed over what he believes—and I think with justice—are unjust attacks against him on the part of Ellis. He has done faithful service under difficult circumstances, and a word from you that this service is appreciated would go a long way to recompense him . . . and might do away with the impression that undue emphasis was placed upon one unfavorable report."[84] Dulles refers to "one unfavorable report." He does not allude to Bryant's complaint, and one wonders if Imbrie ever knew of it.

On August 21 Imbrie reported to the Near East Office and followed up with a letter. He wrote, "With reference to Mr. Ellis' statement that I am pro-Turkish in my attitude, I submit on my record that I am Pro-American and nothing more." Imbrie noted that Ellis came with "preconceived and erroneous ideas . . . about which he showed no disposition to alter in conformity with the facts." He stated that that "there was too much wholesale condemnation of the Turks . . . and too little inclination to verify the facts before making sweeping assertions."[85]

Ellis had been in Angora for only forty-eight hours and had been piqued at not meeting the Nationalist leaders. Imbrie met Ellis only once, when he requested immediate interviews with Mustafa Kemal and Raouf Bey. Imbrie had explained to Ellis that there was a cabinet meeting that day, a Saturday, and it was unlikely he could get an appointment before Monday, but Ellis had insisted, saying he had to leave on Monday. Imbrie offered to have someone accompany Ellis to Raouf Bey's house, but they found, as Imbrie had predicted, that he was not at home. Ellis left on Monday as scheduled without returning to Imbrie.

Imbrie said that he believed Ellis was angry at not getting the interviews and that he had "by no means indulged in a diatribe against the minorities or Near East Relief." He thought it "improbable" that he had spoken as Ellis charged—"I hope you are not one of those Americans who think the Turks are always massacring the Christians"—although he conceded that he might have made the statement as a warning against bias. Imbrie seemed concerned that Ellis's accusations could be ruinous. He offered four names that Hughes could contact about their own negative experiences with Ellis.[86] He also suggested the department contact five other journalists as to how he had treated them in Angora.[87]

The referrals included Consul Frank C. Lee, whom Imbrie called "Pop," Diplomatic Secretary Richard Southgate, who had served in Turkey with Imbrie, Assistant Chief of the Division of Near Eastern Affairs Harry G. Dwight, and Commander Halsey Powell. All these men were influential, but Powell's name stands out as someone Imbrie befriended outside the State Department. Powell was athletic, almost six feet tall, with blue eyes under thick eyebrows, and a jutting jaw. He and Imbrie were the same age. Powell's first command, in 1909, was the destroyer USS *Dupont,* and when Imbrie and he met in Washington DC, he had just detached from a destroyer. In June 1921 he had achieved his permanent rank as commander and begun serving in the Office of Naval Intelligence. In the fall of 1922, before Imbrie returned to Turkey, Powell was assigned to Berlin as naval attaché, scouting industries and technical inventions in Germany and Scandinavia. He was adamant that he was not a spy, regarding himself as an information gatherer, doing everything "aboveboard." By his own assessment Powell saw things in black and white and was forthright to the point of tactlessness.[88] When Imbrie met him, neither man would have guessed at Powell's illustrious career. During World War II he served as commander of the South Pacific Area and Force, and in August 1945 he steamed into Tokyo Bay as commander of the Third Fleet aboard the USS *Missouri* for the signing of the Japanese surrender. Imbrie and Powell seemed to have hit it off in a short time, and Powell's character sheds light on Imbrie's.

The State Department consoled Imbrie saying that "few officers in the field . . . had not had complaints lodged against them. The only thing to do was to grin and bear it," but the department also concluded that Imbrie had "a somewhat decided manner of speech," which may have stirred Ellis's ire. Ellis perhaps "expected too much" of Imbrie, and it must be added that "[Ellis] appear[ed] to have a particular facility for getting into difficulties during his foreign trips [and] at Constantinople he expected one of Bristol's destroyers to be put at his entire disposal and that it would make such stops as he desired, with wide deviations from the prescribed routes."[89]

The "difficulties" alluded to include Ellis's earlier behavior in Egypt in June 1919. Ellis and his son had arrived dressed in American army uniforms and, when told to remove all insignia, did so but then sent a cablegram of protest to the secretary of war. They then began filing stories, submitting one set of articles to the Cairo censors and sending another version in disguised envelopes from Suez, thereby creating a breach of faith between the two governments. The two men also made themselves conspicuous at Nationalist rallies. At one the elder Ellis received an enthusiastic ovation. After receiving a letter of complaint from the British high commissioner, the State Department modified Ellis's passport, eliminating India and Turkey from his itinerary. Subsequently the British authorities allowed him to proceed to Constantinople and on to Angora.[90]

Unfortunately Bristol backed Ellis. He wrote that "having seen a good deal of Mr. Ellis during his sojourn in Turkey, I have no reason to question the accuracy of his statements."[91] His testament is baffling, especially in light of similar attacks Bristol himself endured. Like Imbrie, he faced censure and even demands for his removal. These were based on three charges—that he was pro-Turk, that he was unsympathetic to the Christian minorities, and that he was more interested in commerce than humanitarian aid. A member of the United States delegation in Lausanne thought Bristol was "very pro-Turk."[92] What was clear was that Imbrie would no longer work under Bristol. When he requested funding to ship his personal effects home, the State Department gave approval, noting that he would probably not return.[93]

In the midst of the propaganda that depicted the Turk as "the other" and the Armenian as the victim, Imbrie had tried to humanize the Turk and resist the stereotype. Imbrie was up against a long history of prejudice against the Turks. When the Lausanne Treaty of Amity and Commerce was presented to the U.S. Senate, it was defeated amid a storm of public opposition, which cast the treaty as condoning the Armenian genocide. Stereotypes of Turks were marshaled. The Turk was ignorant, barbaric, fanatical, and bloodthirsty. Henry Morgenthau, U.S. ambassador to the Ottoman Empire from 1913 to 1916, described Turks as bullies and cowards: "[The Turk] is as brave as a lion when things are going his way, but cringing, abject, and servile when reverses are overwhelming him."[94] In his protestation against prejudice, Imbrie walked into a firestorm. Ironically, in his next posting, that ambassador would be derided for too strongly supporting the Armenian cause.

Although Imbrie's name was cleared to the satisfaction of his superiors, Katherine felt her husband was not vindicated until 1938, when Ellis wrote a series of articles for the *Washington Sunday Star* lamenting the "tragic process" of Greek and Armenian deportations: "Before and during the war I was a severe critic of Turkey and the Turks; now I find them a nation in the van of the march toward peace and progress . . . it was to the sound of the Wilson slogans that prostate Turkey revived, after the war, and went into battle for the independence which it is now enjoying and employing as an instrument of peace in the whole Near East."[95] With this mea culpa, Ellis distanced himself from his accusations and mollified Katherine. Unknown to Katherine was that Ellis had much earlier written to the State Department supporting Imbrie. In June 1925, after visiting with the physician who attended Imbrie after a mob attack, Ellis wrote to the State Department that he had learned of "antecedent circumstances" to Imbrie's death that questioned the conduct of both the American minister in Teheran and Imbrie's predecessor there. He encouraged the State Department to interview the physician.[96] No one seems to have followed through.

Meanwhile, after Imbrie dealt with Ellis's accusations, he was given leave with pay from September 25 to October 24 and leave without pay from October 25 to December 31, 1923.[97] He secured an appointment as major in the U.S. Army Reserve Corps, and at the end of October he suggested he be appointed to Tabriz, Persia, a fateful request.[98] In an expression of confidence the State Department on January 2 informed Imbrie of his new posting, Tabriz, with a temporary assignment to Teheran while its consul was in the United States.[99] Imbrie would be leaving war behind for the first time since December 1915; nevertheless he wrote out a new will before he and Katherine boarded ship on March 3, bound for Persia.[100] Two weeks later Douglas Fairbanks's movie *The Thief of Bagdad* premiered, a tale with winged horses, flying carpets, and giant spiders, flamboyantly coloring America's flawed conception of the Near and Middle East. Fostered by popular plays and movies, interest in the region was growing and may have contributed to the intense interest throughout the United States and the world in what happened to Imbrie in Persia.

EIGHT

Before the Last Picnic

In late 1829 Alexander Griboyedov, a Russian envoy, arrived in Teheran seeking to repatriate Russian defectors who had joined the Persian army.[1] Mirza Yakub, a Christian eunuch who had converted to Islam and was in the shah's entourage, sought asylum at the Russian embassy, bringing with him two women from the harem. As rumors spread that the women were being held against their will, a mob, incited by mullahs, swarmed to the embassy. When Griboyedov refused to turn over the supposed hostages, the mob attacked the compound, and Mirza Yakub was killed. The mob ebbed, but then flowed back, this time with mercenaries. The embassy walls were quickly scaled, and the slaughter of the Russian staff began, spilling over to the stables of the British embassy housing Russian grooms. All but one Russian died, including Griboyedov.

During the melee, the shah took refuge in his citadel, allowing his capital to descend into chaos for four days. When peace returned, both Russia and Persia were vexed about how to respond. The Russians, who were fighting the Turks, did not want war with Persia, yet the Persians feared retribution. In the end Russia settled for punishment for the murderers and contrition, which came in the form of an abject apology and gifts to the tsar, including an enormous diamond looted from India in 1739.[2] The murderers were hunted down, executed, and in some cases mutilated. Peace reigned again. The contemporary accounts attributed the slaughter to Griboyedov's unfamiliarity with Persian customs (although he had lived in Persia and spoke the language), a fear of what Mirza Yakub might disclose if allowed to emigrate, a British conspiracy (for which no documentary support exists), an attempt to overthrow the shah, and Islamic fundamentalism.[3] The death of Griboyedov points to how rare attacks were on emissaries, with ninety-five years intervening between it and the murder of Imbrie.

Imbrie's posting in Turkey had taken him as far as the Persian border. In 1924 he crossed that border. His destination, Tabriz, reputedly the site of the Garden of Eden, lay 150 miles south of Mt. Ararat, tucked into the northwest corner of Persia, close enough to Russia and Turkey to have absorbed the revolutionary ideas pervading each country. Nearby was Lake Urmia, the largest lake in the Near East, salty and shallow, with flocks of flamingoes and migrating waterfowl, covering more than two thousand square miles.

Tabriz was not a remote outpost. It was the site of a revolution in 1906 that forced the shah to accept a constitution and form a parliament. Unfortunately, when his autocratic son succeeded him in 1907, parliament was disbanded and members of the opposition were executed. Undeterred, the constitutionalists in Tabriz regrouped, and in 1908 the shah's troops laid siege.

Among its residents was a young graduate of Princeton University, Howard Baskerville, a Presbyterian missionary born in North Platte, Nebraska. Caught up in the constitutionalists' fervor, he began consulting the *Encyclopedia Britannica* at the U.S. consulate on how to make grenades. Furious at the breech of protocol, U.S. consul William F. Doty called him to task, reminding him that missionaries were forbidden from involving themselves in local politics. Undeterred, Baskerville resigned his post and threw himself into the struggle for liberty. On April 19, after a ten-month siege and with the city low on supplies, Baskerville agreed to head a sortie seeking food. The next day, in the dim light of dawn, as he and a handful of men slipped through a break in the city walls, a sniper fired, killing Baskerville. Shortly thereafter the siege was broken, not by the shah's forces, but by Russian and British officials seeking to protect and remove their citizens.[4] Fourteen years later Imbrie was posted to Tabriz. It is doubtful that either Griboyedov's or Baskerville's murder would have worried Imbrie. The first was long ago, and the second was prompted by a missionary who could be dismissed as a renegade or a naive idealist. Furthermore, Imbrie was a U.S. official.

Once the crossroads of ancient trade routes, Tabriz now lay in the zone of petroleum exploration. About 350 miles away were the oil fields of Baku, Azerbaijan, which had been a revolutionary hotbed in 1905.[5] There Lenin's paper, *Iskra,* had been printed and future Bolshevik leaders developed, including Iosif Djugashvili, later known as Joseph Stalin. In the fury of the 1905 Russian Revolution, two-thirds of Baku's oil fields had been destroyed, and its export business had collapsed.[6] With Russia in need of oil, Britain and Russia looked to their mutual interests in Persia. Both countries wanted control over Persia, Britain to use it as a buffer between Russia and India, Russia to secure a naval presence in the Persian Gulf. In 1907 the two powers reached an agreement, without Persian input, whereby northern Persia would be under Russian influence and the southern two-thirds of the country under British influence. Between them lay a narrow zone, considered the Persian sphere of influence.[7] In the ensuing years oil exploration in the north remained undeveloped. After the Bolsheviks abrogated all tsarist concessions in Persia and after they sought peace with Germany, the British viewed the earlier agreement as void.[8] When Imbrie arrived, the north was once again up for the taking.

In terms of Imbrie's story, three oil companies are important: Anglo-Persian Oil Company (APOC), Standard Oil of New Jersey, and Sinclair Consolidated Oil. APOC was well established in the region, dating to an agreement, covering almost fifty thousand square miles, made in 1901 between the shah and a Britisher, William Knox D'Arcy, who had accrued a fortune from Australian gold mining.[9] When mounting expenditures threatened the concession's solvency, D'Arcy sought financing from a British oil company in return for access to his admiralty contracts. Anglo-Persian Oil Company emerged from this union, eventually being named British Petroleum, today's BP. The British government infused the company with money and acquired controlling interest, thereby muddying the relationship, responsibilities, and roles of free enterprise and government. When APOC went public, the government was partial owner of a private business.[10] In postwar Persia the company controlled all of the oil-rich territories except the five northern provinces. It was the only oil producer in Persia.[11]

Standard Oil was also interested in Persia. In May 1911 the U.S. judiciary had found Standard Oil in violation of the Sherman Anti-Trust Act and ordered it disbanded. The largest of the emerging entities was a holding company, Standard Oil of New Jersey.[12] In August 1920 Standard Oil of New Jersey began jockeying for a position in Persia.[13] It hoped to combine efforts with APOC, which controlled the pipelines through southern Persia, necessary for reaching marine terminals. The unsatisfactory alternative, transporting oil to Black Sea outlets, meant dealing with the Bolsheviks.

A second American company, Sinclair Consolidated Oil, founded by Harry Sinclair, had by World War I become the largest independent oil producer in America's heartland.[14] In 1922 the U.S. Interior Department signed contracts with Sinclair for the lease of an oil field in Wyoming named for its shape, Teapot Dome. This field and two others had been set aside earlier by the government as naval oil reserves.[15] A debate ensued over using the reserves for commercial development. After Warren Harding's election in 1920, his newly appointed secretary of the interior, Albert B. Fall, took control of the naval oil reserves from the Navy Department. He then leased Teapot Dome to Harry Sinclair, assuring Sinclair of a guaranteed market, the U.S. Navy. A separate lease for a second government oil reserve was signed with another oil entrepreneur, Edward Doheny of Pan American, a larger crude producer than any of the Standard Oil successor companies.[16] Rumors soon began circulating about the contracts, prompting an investigation that infected Harding's administration and may have hastened the president's death. Both Albert Fall and Harry Sinclair went to prison. When Imbrie arrived in Persia, however, Sinclair was the favored corporation of the Persian government. Imbrie was immediately brought into the conflict, which pitted a powerful British corporation against competing American companies.

In the years following the Great War, and despite wartime solidarity, a hostile rift had opened between Great Britain and the United States. Bitter wrangling at the Paris peace talks, an American sense of being underappreciated for aiding the Allies, the prospective growth of the U.S. Navy, and the world's financial leadership slipping from London to New York—all contributed to this division and to petroleum competition in Persia.[17] Statistics convey the cause for British alarm as an island nation. In 1920 the United States produced 443,402,000 barrels of oil, ranking first in the world; Russia was third with a mere 25,429,600 barrels, and Persia, fifth at 17,529,201. England, discounting its territories, produced a paltry 2,909 barrels.[18] Together all British companies were turning out less than 5 percent of the world's production, and between 1904 and 1913 Russia's share of world petroleum exports had dropped from 31 percent to 9 percent.[19] But neither was America in the catbird seat. By the end of the war British companies had acquired more than half of the world's estimated future reserves.[20] After the war U.S. industrialists were fretting over how long America could rely on its current domestic oil fields. The most informed estimates calculated thirty years.[21]

U.S. oil industrialists wanted help from their government, although they resisted regulations hamstringing their commercial operations.[22] In July 1919 the State Department recommended that their foreign service officials help American interests in obtaining oil properties abroad and direct field representatives to report on the petroleum industry.[23] This directive had dovetailed with Imbrie's work in Turkey. Although at the time most Americans paid too little attention to Persia and the Middle East, world history was being shaped in remote and virtually ignored regions.

The Imbries left for Persia in March, charting a circuitous route that took them as far as Bombay.[24] Imbrie celebrated his last birthday on this long and winding trip. The couple traveled old ground from London to Constantinople and then headed to Egypt, a jumping-off point to India. From Port Said their ship eased through the Suez Canal and into the Red Sea. The sun beat down on the steel decks, wilting the passengers. Breezes brought a dusting of fine sand but no relief. After refueling at Aden, at the tip of Arabia, they sailed on in the stifling heat, the ladies' gowns transparent from sweat, revealing straps and cami-knickers. Passengers played quoits, drank pink gin, languidly practiced the new dance—the tango—and none-too-soon reached Bombay. There reporters, photographers, and Buddhist monks in saffron robes crowded the dock as passengers disembarked, greeted with wreaths of white and yellow frangipani.[25] After a week in the subcontinent meeting with U.S. foreign service officers, the Imbries retraced their route to Egypt and set out on the last leg of their journey, from Egypt to Teheran by way of Baghdad. Their trip had taken them to the heart of the British Raj.

Their trip from Egypt to Teheran invites elaboration, not only to suggest how remote the Persian capital seemed to Westerners, but to provide contrast between their entrance, buoyed with expectation, with Katherine's mournful exit in August following her husband's death.

Although Robert Imbrie's notes on the journey were destroyed, American novelist Mary Roberts Rinehart detailed their route, which she traced with relish in 1925. Her account illustrates the dangers travelers faced. She set out from Cairo the day after she learned that Bedouins had attacked a convoy along the route.[26] Blithely she dismissed any concern because, as she pointed out, a Pullman train had just been robbed outside of Chicago, and people still rode Pullmans. From Cairo she took a ferry across the Suez Canal and a train for Haifa. There she hired a Panhard car, which she hoped was bulletproof, and stuffed her two suitcases inside along with a fur coat that Field Marshal Viscount Henry Allenby, high commissioner of Egypt, had insisted she needed for the desert nights. With several other passengers and a chauffeur she set off, climbing the hills away from Haifa, leaving behind its refugee camp of thirty-thousand Armenians. When she stopped for coffee and looked down at the blue Mediterranean, she bolstered her courage by recalling that "Major Imbrie had gone in by this route safely enough; it was in Teheran he had been killed."[27] Her casual mention of Imbrie, without further explanation, in a book printed two years after his death, suggests the renown of his story.

Rinehart and the Imbries used the old caravan route to cross the desert to Baghdad, a three-day trip by automobile, one that took camel caravans a month or more. When Rinehart's group reached Damascus, it joined up with a small truck and another passenger car carrying a guard with a rifle. The trio then drove off into the Syrian desert, stretching five hundred miles eastward. When they reached the Wadi Haroun, a treacherous creek, they were about ten miles from the site of a recent ambush by brigands who had fired on the car of a French vice consul, murdering his wife. The contents of stolen dispatch bags littered the landscape, the attack unprofitable, the death meaningless.

Galvanized by this story, Rinehart's convoy soldiered on to Baghdad the next day. There Rinehart, like the Imbries, reported to the American consulate overlooking the Tigris River. As Rinehart wrote, "So great was the heat in summer the [consulate's] executive offices are moved into the basement, but the business of America must be looked after, her occasional tourist speeded on their way. What thought do we ever give these people, serving us in exile?"[28] Again, she turned to Imbrie: "Just beyond us, in Teheran in Persia, our Consul there, Major Imbrie, was recently murdered, but it required his death to let most of us know he was there. In the heat and in cold, often under impossible health conditions and in hostile surroundings, these remote agents of our government live and frequently die, not only unhonored and unsung, but unknown."[29] She laid it on a little thick. They certainly did not "frequently die," but her empathy is generally well deserved by the consular services of all nations.

At this point the Rinehart and Imbrie journeys diverge. The Imbries' trip from Baghdad to Teheran is reconstructed from an account by a British secret agent in 1925.[30] With a crank of the starter handle and grinding of gears, the Imbries set out for Kermanshah, trailing fumes of gasoline and camel dung, their speed slowed to thirty-five miles an hour due to rising dust. At the border of Iraq and Persia they would have switched from driving on the left of the road, as was done in British Iraq, to the right, hoping that oncoming drivers honored the custom. One never knew.

Past the border the road began to rise, rounding the treeless, boulder-strewn spurs of the Zagros Mountains. The car ground its way upward in low gear to the Paitak Pass, gateway to the great Persian plateau. They had climbed 8,000 feet from the plain, the air growing increasingly chilly. They then began the run downhill to Karind and on to Kermanshah, where they spent a night before pushing on the next day in a steady climb to Hamadan, 6,280 feet above sea level.

From Hamadan the landscape was windswept and dismal, but every few kilometers they passed a tea house, as regular as rest stops on today's interstate highways. Traffic increased, including four-wheeled covered wagons, a design said to have been used by Napoleon's armies for military transport but now laden with merchandise from Russia, largely cotton goods, sugar, and kerosene. They were much like the wagons pulled by eight to ten horses that Imbrie had seen in New Mexico in 1906.[31] The Imbries passed hundreds of these wagons, the drivers, almost all Azerbaijan Tartars, buried in heavy sheepskin kaftans. Also crowding the roads were mules laden with merchandise, including chests of tea from India and bales of cotton from Britain, carried by sea and by river to Baghdad and then to Teheran and points beyond. In the midst of all were camels shuffling along on their flat, padded feet, defying their drivers' urgings to pick up the pace.

In the early evening, after battling bitter head winds, the Imbries arrived at their last way station, Qazvin. The next day they headed east along a road dating to the Romans, but not surprisingly in poor repair. A chilly wind blew straight from the snow-covered crest of the Elburz range, and the number of pack animals increased. Soon Mt. Demavend at 18,600 feet came into sight. And then, finally, the Imbries arrived at Teheran. They drove through the archway of the Qazvin Gate and headed to the American consulate. Three months later when the Imbrie cortege passed through Qazvin, Hamadan, and Kermanshah, Katherine must have felt deep grief, recalling the bright prospects with which she and Robert had traveled this same route just weeks earlier.

A tragic irony is that the initial directives were for the Imbries to go to Teheran only to pick up consular papers before moving on to Tabriz. Imbrie already had a lease for a consular office and residence on Ark Street in the Charandab district, with the annual rent of $871.72, to be shared with the U.S. government. His salary had been set at $3,000, with an additional $1,000 for expenses.[32] However, when Consul Bernard Gotlieb asked for leave, Imbrie was assigned as his temporary replacement in Teheran. He assumed the consul's duties on May 12, and Gotlieb sailed from Beirut on May 30.[33] He never returned to Persia.

When Imbrie arrived in the capital, there were two missions staffed by Americans, one of U.S. State Department appointees and another, the American Financial Mission, headed by Arthur Millspaugh, who had been named treasurer-general of Persia in 1922.[34] Millspaugh's directive was to modernize Persia's business practices. His office was well staffed with Americans as well as with English-speaking Persians, including his secretary, who had attended Ohio State University. His office and residence were on a thirty-acre park with two French-style houses bearing large windows and spacious rooms to combat the heat. The park featured gardens, waterfalls, pools, and fountains and was thickly planted with poplars and sycamores. Despite these attractions, it had no electricity and hence no motorized fans; kerosene lamps provided the lighting. Millspaugh also had a summer home outside the city at Tajrish.

Although Teheran was moving toward modernity, much was left wanting for Europeans and Americans as far as Millspaugh was concerned. He noted the following amenities as virtually nonexistent: opera, theater, polo and informal soccer matches, restaurants, professional sports, yachting, stock exchanges, and "petting parties," which were exactly what they sounded like, a backlash against Victorian mores.[35] There were no public libraries. In the summer the heat was stifling, and beginning at 6:00 a.m. the staff worked in shirtsleeves with window shades pulled down until the temperature reached 95 degrees, at which time they went home to try to cool off.[36] Telephones had been introduced, but connections were made by giving an operator a name, not a number, producing near constant confusion.[37] Newcomers faced a different language, script, calendar, and business practices. The ornate rhetoric of Persian officialdom made American officialese sound off-the-cuff.

When Imbrie arrived, Millspaugh was enduring a "veritable storm" of criticism as he attempted to balance the Persian budget by raising taxes.[38] One proposal was to regularize the opium trade, almost half of which was contraband. The smuggling was highly organized. One transaction in 1923 had been guarded by 150 horsemen.[39] The trade was highly lucrative, and Millspaugh was not a natural diplomat. Often arrogant and tactless, he had difficulty instituting change.[40]

Oil concessions were also at issue for Millspaugh. In 1921 when Standard Oil of New Jersey expressed an interest in Persia's northern oil fields, the Persian government linked the concession to a $10 million loan, a poorly disguised bribe. Standard Oil concluded it would do better by partnering with APOC. Both companies would benefit, APOC because it sought support for a concession open to challenge, Standard Oil because it needed the use of APOC's pipelines in the south. In 1916 a Georgian-born speculator, Akaky Khostaria, had negotiated a concession in northern Persia. A year later the Bolsheviks voided concessions made under the tsar, including this one.[41] Nevertheless, in 1920 APOC bought it, believing or feigning belief in its validity.[42] Against this background, APOC and Standard Oil agreed to a partnership. The Persian government denounced the arrangement, determined to corral British influence.

As Standard Oil fought for a foothold in the oil fields, Sinclair Oil sent a representative in December 1921 to Teheran, Ralph H. Soper, described glowingly by the chancellor of Stanford University as one of the school's ablest graduates in engineering, a man "in whose implicit truthfulness all trust can be placed."[43] In the following months Standard Oil and Sinclair Oil vied for State Department help in the region.[44] Behind the scenes Secretary of State Charles Hughes favored Standard Oil and future president Herbert Hoover favored Sinclair Oil, although both claimed neutrality.[45] Finally, in June 1923, Persia offered both American companies the opportunity for a new concession. By then, however, Standard Oil had joined forces with APOC, orchestrating its own failure in Persia. In a protest against British imperialism, Persia held that the proposed concession could not be assigned or transferred to any non-U.S. company or nation, including APOC.[46] That left Sinclair Oil, which signed the concession on December 20, 1923. While Sinclair Oil waited for the Persian Majlis, or parliament, to ratify it, Imbrie arrived in Persia. Soper found Imbrie "extremely likeable," and the two quickly became friends, even though Sinclair was working with Moscow on oil development projects.[47]

Almost as contextualization for future reporting, Imbrie filed a long commentary on June 11. It reveals his view of the situation in which he found himself. He wrote in part, with a lemony twist of irony, "The climate of Persia is said to be changing. Always favorable to intrigue, its salubrity in this respect was never greater than to-day. And here two great practitioners of the gentle art, the British and the Bolshevik, find venal fields for the playing of their games. That American enterprises are serving as the football does not lessen our interest."[48] Imbrie's attitude toward the

British seems rooted in his experience with the British in Turkey, although he liked England itself and would have welcomed a post in London, a center of intrigue. The message conveys his typical wit.

Imbrie continued:

> Persia has long been regarded by Great Britain as merely an outpost of India. . . . The British policy as to Persia is, undoubtedly, that there shall be an 'open door' but they construe this to mean, as exemplified by countless and continuous acts, that they shall not only occupy all the chairs in the house but they are prepared at any time to raise so much disturbance therein that visitors will be glad to leave. The methods the English have employed to discredit American enterprises here may be taken as indications as to the length to which they are prepared to go in order to prevent further American penetration into Persia. Without exception, representatives of American business and American interests here trace the opposition they have encountered, and their many difficulties to British intrigue. . . . The representative of the Sinclair interests in Teheran [Roger Soper] is firmly of the conviction that the opposition with which he is met is fed with financial nourishment from the Bank of England. . . . That the British do not want a railway in northern Persia is also apparent. The menace of [a] Russian invasion of India . . . is still, as ever, an ideé fixe with Great Britain so that a railway connecting central or southern Persia with Russia and offering a potential road to India cannot be looked upon with favor. The American financial mission in Persia has been subjected to criticism, opposition and vituperative comment ever since its arrival and, while members of this mission admit that they are unable to pin upon the British the proof of having actuated this opposition, the Americans are, nevertheless, convinced that their difficulties are largely of British origin.

Although in this report Imbrie supported the financial mission, Millspaugh's work may have unwittingly contributed to Imbrie's death, as will be seen.

Imbrie was understandably suspicious of Britain's intentions and actions. Britain had troops in practically every part of the country, and it helped fund the country's running expenses. It controlled the country's entrances and exits as well as its telephone and telegraph lines.[49] The lopsided Persian-Anglo agreement of 1919 protected Great Britain from Persian claims against war damages.[50] To some Persians the agreement rendered Persia a British mandate, like Iraq, in all but name.[51]

To its discredit, Britain had made Persia a debtor nation and used bribes to get what it wanted and to feed corruption. In 1922 James Balfour, a member of a British advisory team to Persia, mentioned the bribes in his book *Recent Happenings in Persia*, creating a furor in England and Persia. Although the book was withdrawn in the face of libel proceedings, the exposé confirmed a well-known suspicion: graft was part of the cost of doing business in Persia, and the size of the bribes was proportionate to the expectations of those controlling an oil-rich country.[52]

Although Imbrie noted that the British were in a stronger position in Persia than the Russians, he penned a warning:

> Since Bolshevik interests would be advanced by projected American developments, it may be stated that the Bolsheviks are, with reservations, in favor of these enterprises. . . . The Sinclair people seem to have the confidence of the Bolshevik Government, and certainly if this project is to become an operating and marketing success it must find the outlet for its oil through Bolshevik territory and Bolshevik pipelines. The northern railway project is looked upon with favor by the Bolshevik Government since, when completed, it would connect the Caucasus with Persia, provide an accessible market, and in the event of war, open up an available route for a Russian force to penetrate Persia.[53]

A sticking point to the prospect of an American company working with the Russians remained: the United States had not recognized the legitimacy of the Soviet government.

In concluding his report, Imbrie wrote that American enterprise in Persia could succeed amid the intrigue only with the active support of the American government, which would "emphasize to foreign powers the right of Americans to work unhampered . . . so long as they do not dabble in politics."[54] In other words, the Open Door policy remained a prerequisite for doing business.

However, not dabbling in politics was an impossible caveat, as the bribes attest. A corrupt and immature ruler, Ahmad Shah, headed the Persian government. Only twenty-one years old, he had already amassed a small fortune and cared little about the complexities of governing a country: he was absorbed with personal gain. His Majlis was unstable, a revolving door for ten prime ministers from 1920 to 1923: in the same period Great Britain had had three. His people were suffering. During the Great War more than ten thousand Persian villages had been destroyed, and a hundred thousand Persians had died of starvation.[55] After the war the Spanish flu pandemic caused one million deaths in a country of nine million.[56] The country was suffering from famine and cholera. It was bankrupt. Amid these circumstances, the Persian military found political footing.

In 1919 the British had set out to integrate the Persian Cossacks, Gendarmerie, and smaller provincial security units into a uniform Persian army.[57] The Cossack Division was an infantry and field artillery unit established in 1885 with the help of Tsar Alexander II, initially meant to guard the ruler and foreign legations. The Gendarmerie had been established in 1910 with the help of the Swedish mission, primarily to secure trade routes. Among the Cossacks was an upcoming officer named Reza Khan.[58]

Six feet three inches and proud of his height, Reza Kahn came from the village of Alasht, located on the rugged slopes of the Alborz range near the Caspian Sea. Shortly after his birth in 1877 his father died, and his impoverished mother moved to Teheran to be with family, but she died when he was six, and he was largely neglected. When he was about fifteen, Reza Khan enrolled in the Cossack infantry brigade and in his early years stood guard duty at the American Presbyterian Mission compound, the German legation, and the British and Russian banks.[59] Within ten years he was a sergeant major. He continued to rise through the ranks and consequently became someone to watch as he took part in small campaigns throughout Persia. In 1917 he was assigned to command one of the Cossack regiments, and in 1918 he was promoted to brigadier general. When the British, unable to meet the financial demands of an occupying army, committed to pulling out their troops in the spring of 1921, a power vacuum emerged. Reza Khan took advantage of it.

During this period a parallel scenario was playing out. A Teheran journalist, Sayyid Zia od-Din Tabataba'i, was also emerging as a future leader. Unlike Reza Khan, he was well educated and well traveled. He came from a family of respected religious leaders in Tabriz and in 1920 was a member of a Persian delegation sent to Baku to negotiate commercial treaties.[60] His understanding of international politics brought him to the attention of public officials and foreign legations.[61] He courted favor with the British in particular. In the summer of 1920 he was chosen to be an intermediary between the Imperial Bank and the British legation in a review of drafts and checks drawn by the Persian government, thereby increasing his contacts with top-level officials. The British began to regard him as a possible anti-Bolshevik, pro-British candidate for prime minister.[62] The joint rise of Reza Khan and Sayyid Zia od-Din Tabataba'i culminated in their seizing power in February 1921, with Tabataba'i as prime minister and Reza Khan as minister of war.[63] Tabataba'i stayed in power until May 24, when he was ousted by his coconspirator.[64] Reza Khan was on the path to dictatorship.

Although Imbrie established a cordial relationship with Mustafa Kemal in Turkey, he seemed not to have had a chance to meet Reza Khan. Both Mustafa Kemal and Reza Khan achieved far-reaching reforms in their countries; however, their backgrounds, education, travels, and military experiences contrasted sharply, resulting in diametric differences. Mustafa Kemal had a nation in place when he came to power, albeit one in disarray. In contrast, Reza Khan's Persia was a confederation of tribes with little centralized power. Mustafa Kemal became a president and Reza Khan a shah. Although both men became increasingly autocratic during their rule, Reza Khan became arbitrary. At his death Mustafa Kemal left behind a system that, despite his cult of personality, could assure a transition without the loss of representative government. He is extolled as the father of modern Turkey. Reza Khan was eventually deposed and exiled.[65]

Besides the commercial and political conflict detailed above, a third area of conflict drew Imbrie's attention in Persia: religion. The country was a Muslim country. The religious situation for non-Muslims was tenuous. In the mid-1920s about fifty thousand Jews were scattered across Persia, less than a half percent of the population.[66] For centuries Persian Jews had lived a life of uncertainty and hostility, discrimination and pogroms, but as international trade expanded in the nineteenth century, they took advantage of the new economic opportunities and their influence grew.[67] In the early twentieth century and especially after the Great War, Western powers attended more closely to the Jewish situation in Persia and increased their demands for religious tolerance. The appointment of Rabbi Joseph Saul Kornfeld as U.S. ambassador to Persia in 1921 seems an extension of these demands on behalf of Persian Jews.

Beside the Jews, the Baha'is were also persecuted. Their numbers were far greater, and they were considered heretics by Muslims.[68] Baha'iism had been founded by Sayyid Ali Mohammed, who in 1844 proclaimed himself the "Gate of God," or "Bab." Begun as a reform of Shi'ite Islam, the religion departed radically from orthodox Islam, abolishing the call to prayer and the pilgrimage to Mecca, introducing a new calendar and feasts, discarding the veil for women and proclaiming their emancipation, and disavowing Jihad, or holy war. In the 1890s Baha'i missionaries visited the United States, and when its leader, Abdul Bhah, visited Europe and America in 1911–13 as war clouds gathered, he drew widespread attention by advocating for the oneness of humanity and world peace.

Three days after Imbrie wrote his first assessment of Persia, he wrote another, "Political and Religious Demonstrations in Teheran," noting how religious prejudice was being used for political purpose, although he also noted that American missions, primarily Presbyterian missions, had created "a friendly feeling for all things American." It was largely due to these missions that Americans were "more respected in Persia than the people of any other nation."[69]

Imbrie might have noted that the good feeling toward America was also bolstered by its neutrality during the early part of the Great War, which had sent European armies tramping through the region, disrupting life and bringing famine, disease, and death. Imbrie continued, pointing out that "the [Presbyterian] mission investment in Persia approximates more than $2,000,000. Ten schools are maintained and seven hospitals. Recently ground has been broken in Teheran for an American Mission College." Unfortunately a memoir written in 1915 by an American traveler complicates this sunny assessment of evangelical efforts: "The American missionaries direct a huge and prosperous school in Tihrān. The pupils come from all ranks, and one of the main endeavors of their teachers, is to supplant the oriental attitude of servility or disdain by a sense of healthy self-respect in those from the lower classes, and of considerate equality on the part of the better born."[70] In introducing Western ways, the American missionaries threatened tradition and custom, in particular the power of the mullahs and the upper class. The situation in Persia for the Jews, Baha'is, and Christian missionaries was delicate, but it was made more fragile by the commercial and political upheaval.

Imbrie's July 14 report was prompted by a political incident with religious overtones, the murder on July 3 of a newspaper editor, Mirzadeh Eshghi.[71] He was, according to Imbrie, "a notorious character, a man of evil repute," but political significance was immediately attached to the assassination by the parliamentary minority. Shortly before his death Eshghi had published several articles and poems against government leaders. In his last issue of the newspaper *Twentieth Century*, he castigated Reza Kahn. At the funeral, which Imbrie described as a "tremendous demonstration, excited by the Mullahs . . . Reza Kahn was denounced as a murderer and assassin and the oppressor of the people."[72] The news reportage resulted in editors and writers of twelve opposition newspapers taking asylum in parliament. The demonstrations continued after the funeral. They showed the severe split between the mullahs and Reza Khan, who needed their support to consolidate his power. When anti-Baha'i demonstrations sprang up, rumor claimed that the government was staging them to divert attention from Eshghi's murder. These anti-Baha'i demonstrations also provided a background for Imbrie's murder.[73]

After the Great War strong opposition to Baha'iism in Persia extended beyond religious conflict. At a time of nation building, the faith seemed unpatriotic, if not treasonous. It was anticlerical at a time when clerical power formed a parallel structure to secular power, exercising its own system of law and vying for supreme control. Wallace Smith Murray, second secretary of the American legation in Teheran, estimated that the number of Baha'is in Persia numbered one million and pointed out that one of the more notable Baha'is was the Persian chargé d'affaires in Washington DC, who had been responsible for the American financial mission to Persia in 1911 on which Millspaugh's was patterned.[74]

On July 6 the shops in the bazaar owned by Baha'is were closed as a safety measure. The next night a mob broke into a Baha'i physician's house, and the family escaped injury only by fleeing over the rooftop. Imbrie reported the incident to the chief of police "in most vigorous terms," and given Imbrie's confrontation with the Cheka in Petrograd, one can imagine his firmness. Two American Baha'is were also rumored to be special targets of religious bigotry, Susan Moody, a physician, and Elizabeth H. Stewart, a nurse. At the insistence of Imbrie a guard was sent to their house on the night of July 8, and Moody believed that without Imbrie's help there would have been "a holocaust of bloodshed and looting." Nevertheless, there was a large demonstration.[75]

Two months earlier Moody had heard that a "black hand committee" had advanced 150 tomans to an assassin to kill her and another physician. A balance of 350 tomans was to be paid when the deeds were done. The anti-Baha'i demonstrations continued until July 12, but by July 14 calm had descended, and the city wore a veneer of normalcy.

When Moody wrote to Ambassador Kornfeld after Imbrie's death, commending Imbrie's quick action on her behalf, her letter angered Kornfeld. Without knowledge of Moody's concern and Imbrie's reaction, he had visited Reza Kahn on July 9 to urge him to temper the anti-Baha'i demonstrations, but the prime minster had shrugged off his concern, assuring him that nothing would happen. Kornfeld wrote that if Imbrie had reported the incident, he might not have died. More likely, whatever Kornfeld said would have been ignored. But more on that later.

Upon arrival in Teheran, despite its being a temporary assignment, Imbrie began building a network of contacts, independent of Kornfeld and Murray.[76] Born in Austria, Kornfeld had grown up in Ohio and at the time of his appointment to Persia was the rabbi for Temple Beth Israel in Columbus. He was well known in educational circles and had campaigned for his fellow Ohioan, Warren G. Harding. He was an amateur diplomat much like David Francis in Russia but less suited to his posting as he had no prior government service.

However, Kornfeld's appointment in November 1921 was understandable. The previous year the *Dearborn Independent*, under the aegis of Henry Ford, had published the first in a series of ninety-one anti-Semitic articles. In addition, *The Protocols of the Elders of Zion*, a spurious document purportedly revealing a plot by Jewish bankers to take over the world, had been published in the United States. The hateful publications found a large readership. In January 1921 one hundred prominent citizens, including former presidents Wilson and Taft, signed a response entitled "The Peril of Racial Prejudice," denouncing anti-Semitism as un-American. With this background Kornfeld became the first rabbi named U.S.

ambassador.[77] He arrived in Persia in April 1922. His wife, Josephine, and their three children, ages twenty-one, twelve, and six, arrived shortly after he did.

In contrast to Kornfeld, Murray was better prepared for his role. A modern language teacher before the war, he rose to become a first lieutenant in the American Expeditionary Force and after his discharge joined the foreign service. About the same age as Imbrie, he was a bachelor, although he married a British subject in November 1924.[78] He had joined the U.S. legation in Teheran in April 1922 and later became U.S. ambassador to Iran. In the summer of 1924 Kornfeld and Murray found themselves plunged into a murder investigation neither could have anticipated or been fully prepared to handle.

In setting up his information network, Imbrie invited Persian officials to the consulate or met them at the homes of friends, including two physicians, Dr. Habib, a Persian married to an American, and Dr. Harry Packard, director of the American Hospital. Packard had been in Persia eighteen years and stayed in Teheran that summer to treat patients, despite the heat that drove most Westerners out of the city. He and Imbrie saw a good deal of each other, and Imbrie impressed Packard and his wife, who realized what "a fine man our consul was. It was marvelous how much he did, and how deep an impression he made, in the short time he was in Teheran."[79]

Two days before his death, in preparation for writing a report on Reza Kahn, Imbrie met with Dr. Habib and his brother, who was the kaimakam, or governor, of Tabriz. Imbrie wanted to know whether the recent Baha'i demonstrations were incited in part or wholly by Reza Kahn to divert attention from the Eshghi murder and foster anti-foreign feelings. Dr. Habib's brother was blunt: he said that Reza Kahn's plan was to have two or three foreigners killed, have martial law declared, have his army appropriation bill passed, and close the Majlis, whereupon Reza Kahn would become dictator. Dr. Habib's brother was prophetic, although only one foreigner was killed.

Imbrie also questioned Reza Kahn's secretary, who assured Imbrie that no harm would come to any American, although other nationals might be in danger, corroborating what Imbrie had already heard. But were the warnings based on reliable information, or were they attempts to tarnish Reza Kahn's reputation or curry favor with the Americans, or were they even meant to reassure Imbrie, thus making him more vulnerable? In his journal for July 17, his last entry, Imbrie wrote that he expected a murder, but not before August 1.[80] Although this date is left unexplained in the record, it may have referred to the sacred month of Muharram, which was to begin on August 2–3. During this month fighting was forbidden, although there was often riotous behavior that could be used to mask an assassination.

On the evening of July 17 the Imbries went on a picnic, seemingly an insignificant outing, but in fact their last.[81] It was the evening of a full moon. The Imbries were guests of Dr. and Mrs. Packard. As Mrs. Packard recalled,

> We had such a jolly evening together! And Bob told us about his perilous experiences in Russia & Turkey; we, in turn, told a little about our experiences in Northwest Persia (Urmia) during the war years. And Bob laughed & said, 'It's rather pleasant just for a change, to be, for a while at least, in a quiet, safe place like Teheran.' Bob & my husband, since the first of their acquaintance, had planned a trip thru Kurdistan next year, when we expect to be in Urumia [*sic*] & they in Tabriz. They were as keen as two boys about it,—both felt that the security and conventionality of Teheran would grow tiresome if too greatly prolonged. When we took the Imbries home & said goodnight at the door of the consulate, we were planning another moonlight picnic for the August full moon, and we parted in this merriest mood.[82]

This, then, was the situation before Imbrie was murdered.

NINE

Death on Distant Service

To understand Imbrie's murder, it helps to know the layout of Teheran in 1924.[1] It was a walled city of about 150,000 people, with flat roofs and minarets, built on a plateau, with the Elburz mountain range to the north and east. Overlooking all was the snow-covered, volcanic Mt. Demavénd. The city was built in an irregular octagon with twelve gates. Like Constantinople, it was divided in two. The European quarter lay to the north, with broad streets and electrically lit shops. To the south lay Old Town with its large, covered bazaars and narrow, crooked streets and alleyways, many of them unpaved. The shah's palace stood near the city center, with a citadel and some modern buildings, including the War Office. Throughout the city were mosques. Near the city center was the American Mission Church, the site of Imbrie's first funeral service. The legations lay in the north, the American, British, and French legations very near each other, the Russian embassy set apart.

Teheran was a colorful, vibrant city, with white turbaned mullahs, long-haired dervishes, mounted cavalry officers alongside clanging trams, women in white veils and yellow shoes, and turbaned sayyids, so named as descendants of the prophet Mohammed. The summers were hot and dry, with daily highs averaging in the nineties. Westerners wore pith helmets and "smoked spectacles" (sunglasses). Water was a problem, irregularly and unequally distributed via private canals independent of government control. In April the canals provided forty-two gallons of water per person, but in July only seventeen gallons. Not everyone got their allotment. The gardens of the rich were well watered, leaving the poor parched. When the heat soared, the wealthy citizenry and foreign legations moved about six miles north to summer residences in the foothills. Malaria was a constant threat. Dr. Edward Ryan of the Millspaugh mission died from it in September 1923 at age thirty-nine.

A thoroughfare, the Rue des Légations, led from the north to the Mediàn-I Tupkhaneh, or Square of Cannons, which measured 268 by 120 yards and was enclosed on three sides. On one side were the artillery barracks, on another the police headquarters. To the west of Mediàn-I Tupkhaneh was an even larger square where military reviews were held, and to the north of that square, the Cossack Battery. This was the layout of the sites pertinent to Imbrie's murder.

Accounts of Imbrie's murder vary significantly. Dr. Packard, who tended to Imbrie's wounds, Wallace Murray, and Katherine Imbrie each wrote an account, as did many others, including other American officials, foreign legations, and individuals such as Sinclair's Ralph Soper.[2] The American newspaper accounts leaned heavily on what the State Department fed them. The initial accounts—newspapers throughout the United States followed the story avidly—were simplistic. A *New York Times* headline read "Imbrie Murder Laid to Religious Hate."[3] The State Department also received unsolicited letters in regard to the murder, some unreliable, others valuable. The following narrative of his death draws judiciously from the source material, including witness depositions.[4]

On the morning of Friday, July 18, Imbrie donned a white rajah silk suit, his preferred attire for summer outings, and a sun helmet.

Despite the heat he wore a tie, the one he had worn the previous evening to a picnic.[5] With his yellow camera in hand, he prepared for a photographic expedition.[6] Katherine did not accompany him; she was visiting a sick friend. With him was Meshedi Mehmed, the consulate guard, and Melvin Seymour, a twenty-eight-year-old American roustabout, slightly built, with a scar on the middle of his forehead.[7] Seymour had worked for APOC for two years and been in Teheran since September 1923, confined to the consulate for eighteen months by Consul Gotlieb for repeatedly attacking his foreman.[8] He was malarial and depressed from his long confinement, and Imbrie hoped to have him released soon on the basis of a mistrial. He often had Seymour accompany him on outings, including to the bazaar and the barbershop.

Shortly before 11:00 a.m. the men got in a hired carriage and rode to the Aqa Sheikh Hadi district near the bazaar. There a miraculous healing, of which there were several versions, was reputed to have occurred two weeks earlier. According to the reports, a man who had not made a free-will offering had been struck blind after drinking from one of many public fountains in the city. After repenting he had regained his sight. The fountain, or *sagah khartum*, had since attracted great attention as a holy place, with beggars and bureaucrats milling about discussing the miracle. Diseased people in tatters had tied rag ropes to the fountain railings as conductors of healing.[9] Given the hot, dry summer day, the fountain would have normally been crowded, but with the miracle, the numbers had burgeoned. Among the crowd were police, government agents, and foreign spies. Large donations from grandees and others had brought out preachers to rouse the faithful.

About twenty-five yards from the shrine a log barricaded the approach. Imbrie, Seymour, and Meshedi Mehmed swung out of their carriage and slipped under the barrier. Imbrie took the precaution of handing Seymour his cudgel. Seymour commented, "Well, we may have to use it, and if we do we will use it good." They walked about twenty-five or fifty feet when Seymour overheard two men talking about beating them up. "*Saresh bezan*," one man said. "Crack him on the head." Seymour repeated the words to Imbrie. "Let them try it," he responded, and he unpacked his camera and took a few pictures. A sayyid bellowed that they were taking pictures of Muslim women to sell in Europe.[10] Someone else yelled that they were Baha'is poisoning the well. The crowd began to converge on the two *farangis*, or foreigners. An Armenian and several Cossacks tried to curb the crowd, and a Turk, seeing the men in trouble, lifted the log so the carriage could pull forward. The driver, hanging out the side, waved them in. With no time to waste, they leapt aboard. Stones hailed down on the carriage. Another Cossack and a policeman futilely tried to intervene. The carriage lurched forward. The crowd lunged after it, again and again. Imbrie yelled for the driver to head for Khiabaan Lakezar, a broad commercial avenue lined with fashionable shops and Western banks. He ignored the instruction. As the carriage broke free, pushing through the congested streets with the crowd in pursuit, someone heaved a large stone. More stones were thrown, and rioters pulled alongside the carriage, reaching to restrain the horses, screaming, "*Englisee bee-den*" (Englishmen without religion).[11] By this time the carriage was careening toward the barracks of the Cossack Brigade, about a mile from the shrine. The Cossacks, the most important military detachment in Persia, were feared by the police.[12] The regiment commander was Reza Kahn.

A Chaldean servant of Dr. Packard, named Isaac Joseph, spotted the carriage and, running with the crowd, saw a motorcycle tear past and cut off the carriage near the parade grounds. With that, Imbrie stood up and pulled out his identification card, shouting to a police officer who he was. Someone struck him down. He pitched forward and landed hard on the ground, his leg momentarily caught in the carriage. As he pulled free, the carriage moved on, through the gate of the parade ground with Seymour still in it. There Seymour told a cavalry captain he was an American and wanted to be taken to the consulate. Instead, the officer struck him on the head with the hilt of his sword. Seymour got out of the carriage to argue and was again hit by the officer. The mob descended on him, and he lost consciousness.

Meanwhile Imbrie was on his own, facing a mob. In a car about thirty-five yards away, a clerk with the British consulate saw Cossacks waving sticks and Shaska swords and wondered at the tumult.[13] The police, but not the Cossacks, seemed to be trying to intervene in the melee. Thus far, no shot had been fired by either the police or Cossacks to stay the rioters.[14] Imbrie tried to defend himself, backing up against the wall of the police headquarters. There he was struck with a piece of metal, perhaps a sword.

At that point policemen broke through the crowd and retrieved first Imbrie and then Seymour, piled both into a Ford, and drove them to the police hospital a few hundred yards away. There they were carried through the rear entrance and placed in separate operating rooms. But Imbrie was not safe. As he lay helpless on an examining table, the mob gathered strength and, led by the sayyid from the fountain and accompanied by Cossacks with drawn swords, broke into the hospital, found Imbrie, and attacked him with whatever they had or could grab—sticks, stones, sabers, and floor tiles.

Meantime Isaac Joseph had raced off to find Dr. Harry Packard at his dispensary.[15] Packard rushed to the consulate in the hospital's Ford to be sure Katherine first heard the news from him and then the two hurried to the police compound, followed by Mrs. Packard and an Italian official, arriving, at Packard's estimate, about thirty minutes after a blow that had sliced into Imbrie's face and scalp. The two Americans eluded policemen guarding the hospital, going to the back entrance and cutting through courtyards. Inside they found Imbrie in a blood-spattered room, with windows, chairs, and cabinets smashed and tiles ripped up. Katherine was appalled at the sight. Small details filled her vision—her husband's right hand was a jellied mess; his silk suit lay piled on the floor saturated with his blood.[16] Imbrie told Packard to "take care of Katherine" and then turned to her and said, "Go with the Packards and do whatever Dr. Packard thinks best for you."[17] He asked for water. Packard began working on him. Imbrie's breathing was very shallow; his pulse was 140 and respiration 50; his condition, "extremely grave." "Profound" hemorrhaging issued from over 138 wounds, so numerous and extensive that they ran into each other, making an accurate count impossible.

Over the next hour Packard cleaned and closed the wounds, without anesthetic so as not to add to the shock. He had never seen such a brutal attack. Yet Imbrie remained conscious, talking to Packard, thanking him for coming, and repeatedly asking for water.

Imbrie's face had ten lacerations and contusions, his lower left jaw was fractured, and four teeth had been knocked out. His scalp bore twenty wounds, many reaching his skull. Among them was a clean cut made by a sharp instrument in the right front-parietal region, three and a half inches long, and four other shorter wounds with clean edges on other parts of the scalp.[18] On the left arm and hand were at least twenty-five severe contusions, one of them lacerated; on the right arm were more than twenty contusions, some of them lacerated. On the back of his right hand were two cleanly incised wounds, one about three and a half inches long, the other, two inches long. On the front of his torso were at least twelve contusions, some lacerated. There was swelling, and one or more ribs were fractured. His scrotum was bruised. His legs had at least thirty contusions, and his back at least fifteen extensive contusions, some lacerated.

When Packard finished treating Imbrie, he moved him from the operating room to a newly made bed, and because of her own physical condition, Katherine left the hospital. She seemed to be reacting emotionally and physically to the trauma, but something else could have been affecting her, as later revealed. Mrs. Packard and the Italian chargé d'affaires, Count Montefiore, accompanied her to the consulate. Once there, Katherine called the hospital, only to learn her husband's condition was rapidly deteriorating. She and Mrs. Packard hurriedly drove back, but they were too late. Robert Whitney Imbrie had died. The cause was excessive hemorrhaging leading to shock. The man who had weathered the battlefields of France and the Balkans, the Russian Revolution and civil war, and the Turkish War of Independence had succumbed to mob violence. His exuberance for life had breathed its last. An attorney, adventurer, foreign service officer, writer, photographer, friend, husband, and in his words a he-man, Imbrie was gone. As Mrs. Packard wrote, "He died as he had lived, nobly and unselfishly."[19]

The next morning at the postmortem, Packard found subcutaneous hemorrhages in the chest, extending to the sternum. The left fifth and sixth ribs had been fractured two inches from the left edge of the sternum. There was intense congestion at the base of the left lung and a little free blood in the left pleura. Inside the skull Packard found extensive hemorrhages. The whole of the scalp was infiltrated with coagulated blood. In addition, there was congestion of the vessels of the pia mater. When the brain was removed, about two ounces of free blood was found in the cranial vault. Once attacked, Imbrie hadn't had a chance.[20]

The injuries inflicted on Seymour were also extensive, but he survived because when the mob rushed the hospital, they ignored Seymour, perhaps thinking he was dead.[21] Nevertheless, he had been badly mauled. When Soper arrived at the hospital shortly after Imbrie's death, he thought Seymour looked like "a piece of raw meat."[22] The roustabout's injuries were grave. He had twelve contusions and lacerations on the face, eight lacerations on the scalp, both ears severely wounded, hands and arms with twenty-five lacerations and contusions, torso bruised front and back, hips severely bruised, legs and feet with thirty or more contusions and lacerations, and one eye badly damaged. A month later the eye still had not healed, his equilibrium remained disturbed, he was sore and stiff, and five of his wounds were infected.[23] He was lucky to survive.

Back at the consulate, Katherine tried to contact the legation, telephoning the police and the Persian Minister of Foreign Affairs, Mohammed Ali Foroughi, to convey her message. Katherine also sent a note to Murray, but it took the messenger an hour, even with good horses, to reach his house in the country. Murray, however, was away playing tennis, which unreasonably but understandably distressed Katherine, as if he were blithely ignoring a tragedy. As hours passed, she took it upon herself to telegram the secretary of state. Her telegram was blunt: "Imbrie killed today. Wire instructions concerning consular office."[24] A jolting two-sentence telegram, three words announcing a death, and five asking for bureaucratic follow-up. Yet the telegram was carefully written: Katherine wanted the consulate protected and in continuous operation. Her telegram landed on the desk of Joseph Grew, serving as acting secretary of state while Charles Hughes was out of the country. Grew later wrote with a heavy dose of irony that the death of Imbrie "disturbed the peacefulness of [his] çhargéship."[25]

By the time Murray and Kornfeld met with Katherine at 6:00 p.m., she had already instructed Packard and Dr. Samuel Jordan, president of the American College of Teheran, to handle the details of her husband's burial scheduled for the next day, including the selection of a casket. She told Kornfeld that she did not need his help, the implication being that he should work on the investigation. Instead, Kornfeld went up country to his summer residence, and Murray went to a card party, although at some time that evening, the two men argued over what to tell the State Department. That night both Packards stayed with Katherine, after which Mrs. Packard stayed for over a week. Katherine then moved to the Packards' home.

Although Kornfeld took the first depositions the next day, Katherine resented the delay. Eventually she accused Kornfeld of disloyalty and even treason, and Murray of "grossly mishandling" the case.[26] Katherine expected too much of Kornfeld, an amateur diplomat who had submitted his resignation months earlier and was ready to return home. He was not disloyal, but he failed to rise to the occasion. Murray, a commendable foreign officer, did not deserve her censure, although he made at least one grievous error, as will be seen. A vice consul who later worked under Murray, Henry S. Villard, described him as "tough, incisive, extremely able, shrewd, astute, [a man who] never spared his men in any way, extremely hard working, . . . a person from whom one could learn an enormous amount."[27] Villard, who was posted to Teheran in 1929, recalled that when he arrived, "people were still talking about the Imbrie case. It was not a very encouraging start to living in Persia."

Kornfeld was deeply distressed by the murder when he notified the State Department of the event: "Vice Consul Imbrie died at three p.m. today of shock following murderous assault by Persian mob which practically cut and beat him to death."[28] Unfortunately he followed this introduction with a confused account of the murder. As the first extended report that Washington received, it colored others. In it Kornfeld stated that during the previous ten days there had been anti-Baha'i demonstrations. On the morning of July 18 at 11 a.m., Imbrie and Seymour had stopped at one of these demonstrations and allegedly taken pictures. The mob rushed him, crying that he was a Baha'i, dragged him from the carriage, and attacked him, despite Dr. Packard's servant clearly proclaiming that he was the American consul. Kornfeld noted that Teheran's streets were always crowded with police and military and that two policemen had been slightly injured in delivering Imbrie and Seymour to the hospital. He concluded, "I have viewed body of Imbrie. Took deposition from carriage driver. Seymour's condition grave and he could make no statement. Department's instruction urgently requested."

Kornfeld's statement that civil peace had been disrupted during the past ten days was wrong. Peace had held from July 12 until July 18. His error is baffling. Other errors are more understandable given the early stage of the investigation. When attacked, Imbrie was not photographing an anti-Baha'i demonstration, but an Islamic site. Contrary to Kornfeld's report, Imbrie's attack was in three stages—by the fountain, by the police headquarters, and in the hospital. Packard's servant was not present at the first stage. There is no mention of the attack in the hospital. However, Kornfeld does mention one detail omitted in all the other reports, an extremely important point in understanding the murder: that Teheran's streets were "always crowded with police and military." The negligence of the police became a major issue in the investigation.

None of the errors or omissions, however, detracts from Kornfeld's initial efforts. The scene must have been chaotic as sympathizers crowded the embassy and consulate with their condolences, and fear took hold. The death of one foreign official frightened all the legations and, as news spread, all foreigners in Teheran. Count Montefiore volunteered to provide a written statement of the incident but did not do so, Kornfeld surmised out of fear.[29] In his next telegram Kornfeld stated that a military officer had delivered the fatal sword thrust, and he called for "very drastic action on the part of [the U.S.] government."[30] If the military were involved, the death was no mere "act of fanaticism."[31] Kornfeld's denunciation of the military officer was virtually ignored during the subsequent trial.

Grew telegrammed Kornfeld to exert extreme caution in proceeding, counseling him on his next steps. And then he asked whether Imbrie had been "rash or negligent."[32] That is, was Imbrie responsible for the attack in any way? Grew seemed not to be questioning Imbrie's behavior in general, but only on the day of the murder. Had Imbrie failed to exercise sufficient caution? Had he been reckless? Or was the attack an unprovoked assault on a U.S. foreign officer? He seemed reassured of Imbrie's innocence by the time he sent condolences to Katherine, praising Imbrie as "a capable and loyal official of the Government."[33] From then on the State Department viewed the incident as a wanton assault on a foreign service officer. Some others did not.

When Millspaugh heard of Imbrie's death, he was dining in the garden of the Iran Club at Gulehek, north of the city. Without hesitation, he blamed Imbrie for indiscretion. He wrote that given the "tense emotionalism, even fanaticism, manifested at such an exceptional place . . . a foreigner, although feeling perfect security in general, should have realized the extreme danger [at the fountain]."[34] Yet Imbrie, who had been in wars and revolutions, would not have regarded a visit to a shrine as extremely dangerous. Further, he could not have anticipated, any more than Millspaugh could, the assassination of an American official. Millspaugh was grievously wrong about the reality of "perfect security." He wrote, "Previous to the Imbrie affair, no foreigner in Persia, as far as I could know or guess, felt any apprehension regarding his safety."[35] His caveat—"as far as I know or guess"—exudes false confidence in himself as an authority. He ignored or implausibly did not know of the threats and attacks on the American Baha'is. He believed that "had Major Imbrie had been ordinarily discreet, he would not have been the incitement or the object of a mob attack. . . . [He] went under provocative appearances into a place and into conditions which had the elements of danger."[36] The "provocative appearances" seemingly refers to carrying a camera. Perhaps, though, Millspaugh was deflecting attention, sensing that he had played an unwitting role in the tragedy. The day before Imbrie's death, he had given Reza Khan an ultimatum, threatening to restrict the funding for the army.[37] It is possible and even likely that Millspaugh's demand doomed Imbrie, moving up the date of the assassination by two weeks and even targeting a foreign officer to heighten its impact. Despite placing blame on Imbrie, Millspaugh encouraged the State Department to insist on a high indemnity from the Persian government, ultimately placing blame on it and not on Imbrie.

Unlike Millspaugh, who claimed to feel safe, Murray did not. He requested permission from the State Department to ask for increased protection,[38] and the next spring Millspaugh himself was assigned a guard. Ironically Millspaugh's mission, which became increasingly at odds with the Persian government over military funding, was probably temporarily extended by Imbrie's death. The Persian government could not chance further damage to U.S.-Persian relations by dissolving the mission in the wake of Imbrie's death. Nevertheless, in 1927, when the new contract for the American mission came before the Majlis, the conditions were such that Millspaugh rejected them and returned to America. His role as administrator general was temporarily assumed by none other than Reza Khan, who, in doing so, was able to grab the purse strings and dissolve the mission promoted by a Persian Baha'i.[39]

The issue of Imbrie's photography threaded itself through the investigation, but Imbrie's long experience in photographing foreign peoples and the increased use of cameras at the time exonerate him. For example, three American filmmakers had arrived at Imbrie's office in late June after spending forty-five days filming the migration of a Persian tribe from winter quarters to summer pastures, five thousand people with fifty thousand animals. Two of the filmmakers stayed with Imbrie while they were in the city, and he notarized their work.[40] The film, titled *Grass*, was released in 1925. Near the end appears Imbrie's notarization and signature: "Sworn to me by Amir Jang, Prince of the Barklyariat Teheran this 28th day of June, 1924. Robert W. Imbrie, Vice Consul of the United States." This documentary kept Imbrie's name literally in front of the American people for several years. It also illustrates the wide use of photography at this time, including in Persia. Nasar al-Di (1831–96), the longest reigning shah of the Qajar dynasty, was a great patron of photography in Persia.[41]

Nevertheless, newspapers picked up on the topic of Imbrie's photography. The *Washington Star* reported that according to one account, the assailants thought Imbrie's camera was spraying "suffocating gas." It stated that Muslims believed that picture taking was "injurious to their chances of salvation" by reproducing their images, that they even objected to pictures being taken of Christian monuments and historical sites. The *Star* article concluded, however, that given Major Imbrie's wide experience in the Near East, there had to be some other cause of his death than "the mere use of a camera."[42]

Stories such as the *Washington Star*'s may have prompted friends to defend Imbrie. Lewis K. Davis, a friend in Turkey, wrote that Imbrie, having had vast experience, "was not a man who would go counter to the customs of the Country, as he was always most particular," and in Davis's own experience, he had found people in the Near East enjoyed having their pictures taken. They regarded it an "honor."[43]

At the heart of the attacks was the integrity of the travel reporter and, although the term was not in use, the photojournalist. John Oliver La Gorce, vice president of the National Geographic Society, defended Imbrie, writing that he had been publishing Imbrie's photographs for several years, and it was doubtful Imbrie would have offended his hosts.[44] He recollected a conversation in which Imbrie described some of his experiences: "I have a very healthy respect for the religious beliefs of the Oriental and feel that he is in every way entitled to the practice of his own religious convictions, and I have always kept out of mosques and holy places where the intrusion of Christians was objectionable; and, further, I do not feel it is proper to make photographs of religious ceremonies or what they construe as shrines or holy places where there is any evidence of a feeling of trespass in such action."[45] When Imbrie's article about Turkey was published in the October 1924 issue of the *National Geographic* magazine, the editors prefaced it with this acclamation: "[Imbrie] was an American gentleman—honorable, considerate, and brave. He served his country gallantly on the field of battle and in important diplomatic missions." His death "was a great loss to the Foreign Service of the United States."

Assistant Secretary of State Wilbur Carr responded to La Gorce, stating how shocked members of the State Department were at Imbrie's death and attested to his "considerable experience" in Muslim countries.[46]

Imbrie had lived abroad for the better part of the previous eight years. He was not naive. Further, as Katherine later noted, he was a fellow in the Royal Geographic Society of Great Britain, a prestigious professional organization.[47]

Soper, too, defended Imbrie, saying Imbrie would not abuse his position in Persia, that he knew Muslim ways, that Americans were well liked by the Persians, and that Imbrie had no enemies. Further, Soper wrote, Imbrie "had a beautiful collection of photographs which he had taken in various parts of the world and it was his habit to carry his camera when it was convenient for him to do so; on this particular day he had his camera. However, there was nothing unusual in this for I myself took pictures from the midst of the great 10th Moharrum demonstrations in 1922 and even got spattered with the blood of the fanatics. At that time [the Persians] seemed to enjoy having their pictures taken and some of the gory faithful even posed for me."[48]

George Gregg Fuller, the American vice consul posted in Bushire, Persia, described his own experience with a camera, at Abadeh, equally nonthreatening. He wrote: "We spent an hour at lunch . . . surrounded by three hundred curious natives, including many religious fanatics and dervishes. The General and his escort motored ahead, leaving me with my servant surrounded by a crowd of 150 men, pushing about the car and clamoring for money, but though we walked in this mob for a quarter of an hour quite alone, they were always good natured and showed no resentment at our having eaten and taken photographs within the Imamzadeh."[49] Although he did not explicitly relate his experience to Imbrie's, his report supports Imbrie.

The concern over photography deserves consideration because it runs through the commentary, including contemporary ones. One recent historian concluded, "Despite much evidence that Iranians loved to be photographed, the collective memory of Americans in Teheran held that Imbrie was killed because he photographed a religious event."[50] He noted, "In the 1950s the American Embassy [in Teheran] routinely warned Americans not to photograph religious events, citing the Imbrie murder as evidence of what might happen." But this warning could simply be evidence of institutional memory at work, an unquestioning acceptance of a party line that passes into policy. Further, not long after Imbrie's death, a Pathé crew filmed one of the sites where Imbrie was attacked.[51] A Pathé crew had also filmed Imbrie himself twice in Turkey. The verdict must be that Imbrie, the photographer, did not incite the mob to the extent of its attacking with such ferocity, duration, and reach. The responsibility for the incident had to lie elsewhere. Disturbing was the shoot-from-the-hip inclination to blame Imbrie in a situation that oozed imbalance between cause and effect, even before an adequate investigation had occurred.

Murray, newly named chargé d'affaires of the consulate in the wake of the murder, led the investigation. Significantly, he disregarded Imbrie's photography. After providing funding for Katherine until her return home, hiring an automobile to expedite the inquiry, and having his telegraph allowance increased, he cleared his desk of all else.[52]

The day after the murder Reza Kahn called on the American embassy to convey his condolences, and the Persian Foreign Office sent a note of apology and explanation, which Kornfeld found "entirely inadequate." When a Persian official in Washington stated that Imbrie was wearing a Persian cap at the time of the attack, making him look like a Baha'i, Grew bristled.[53] To mollify him, the Persian embassy gave him the translations of two cablegrams from its Foreign Office. They stated that a "great religious revival" had occurred "unexpectedly" in the few days before Imbrie's death and alluded to "happenings" at one of the fountains in the city. The reference to the anti-Baha'i riots as a "revival" is disingenuous. Also, the report erroneously claimed that several policemen were wounded, "three of them seriously," and that one soldier had died from his injuries." The telegram then blamed Imbrie for being "careless" in going to the fountain. This cable is the first mention in the investigation of miracles at the fateful *sagah khartum*. Ominously, the Persian cable noted that in light of the murder Reza Khan had declared martial law on July 19.[54] This act changed the course of Persian history. Grew forwarded the translations to President Coolidge.

In two cablegrams, Kornfeld quickly corrected the Persian Foreign Office account: only one policeman and one soldier were injured in aiding Imbrie, another policeman was slightly injured but never admitted to the hospital, and the soldier who had died was unconnected with Imbrie's death.[55] Only Imbrie had died in the assault.

But then another life was lost. On July 22 Katherine Imbrie and the Packards planned an outing to Shah abdul Azim, a shrine south of the city where coincidentally Reza Khan had consulted mullahs before deciding that Persia was not ready to be a republic. On the way out of town they stopped for a friend, and as she settled in the car, a boy of ten or twelve jumped on the running board. Dr. Packard reached for him. The youth leapt back, flailing, grabbing at Katherine's veil. The veil, pinned between her and the seat, slid from his hand, briefly dangled from the car, and was recovered by Katherine. As they drove on, another boy threw dirt at the car. A clod landed in Katherine's lap. She felt personally threatened. Although a policeman was nearby, Packard thought it safer to leave the scene quickly. This brief incident was not particularly noteworthy, except in light of Imbrie's murder. The next day Packard reported it to Kornfeld and Murray, who notified the Persian police. The culprits were never found. Then, some days later, Katherine experienced hemorrhaging. Packard could not determine if it were a delayed menstruation or a miscarriage. Katherine had no doubt. She had lost a child, attributable to the trauma of her husband's murder.[56]

Katherine's report on the incident was the first mention of her pregnancy, and this additional loss of life became part of the legal wrangling between her and the U.S. government that continued until 1950. In the coming days there were other attacks on foreigners—on a British foreign officer, a British physician, a French woman, and an Italian attaché, but none resulted in serious injury, and all were deemed common criminal acts, such as pickpocketing.[57] However, after Katherine's attack, the Persian government advised foreigners to avoid the bazaar. In covering Katherine's incident, the *Times* (London) complained that the Persian government permitted the publication of an incendiary article, "The Lion and the Unicorn," which accused the British of arranging for Imbrie's death in order to sow discord between the United States and Persia and prevent the confirmation of the North Persian Oil Concession.[58]

The attack on Katherine may have prompted the United States to speed up the investigation. The State Department issued five demands to the Persian government: adequate reparation and prompt punishment for Imbrie's killers and for those who allowed the attacks to proceed, publication of the punishments to deter further attacks, immediate protection for Americans in Persia with guards placed at the embassy and consulate, payment for the expense of bringing home Imbrie's remains, and due honors awarded for Imbrie, including a guard to accompany the body to the port of departure. Any further communication between the United States and Persia depended on the actions of the Persian government. These demands, approved by President Coolidge, were to be made public on July 28.[59] In sum, the U.S. government was pressing Persia to adhere to international law requiring the protection of foreign officials in a host country.

Moving ahead in the investigation, Murray informed the State Department that Imbrie's death had "political aspects," which he could not communicate for lack of a code,[60] but that he had questioned Seymour and was confident an assailant had been identified, a mullah who had led the Cossacks to Imbrie. Arrests quickly followed, including those of Sayyid Hossein and Private Morteza, who was arrested for inciting the mob but who confessed under questioning to striking Imbrie. Katherine Imbrie recognized the mullah as the same man who had held religious meetings in a district next to the consulate and who had seen Imbrie on several occasions.[61] This detail supported a conspiracy theory, that the murder was not a spontaneous act of fanaticism, echoing Kornfeld's earlier conclusion. But how would Sayyid Hossein have known that Imbrie would be at the fountain at a certain time? Speculation suggests that he either learned of Imbrie's plans or tailed him. Further, he would have known that if he were arrested after the assault, he would be exempt from the death penalty as a descendant of Mohammed. And if the conspiracy was revealed to have been authorized at a high level, he might avoid prosecution altogether.

The foreign delegations debated whether Imbrie's death was a spontaneous act by fanatics or a part of a conspiracy. When the Russian legation accused the British of their own conspiracy, the British demanded a retraction. The Russians refused.[62] In addition, eighteen Persian newspapers claimed that Imbrie's murder was part of a British conspiracy to gain control of all of Persia's oil concessions.[63] The newspaper *Iran,* a government organ, wrote that Imbrie's death was part of a plot to block the Sinclair Oil Company concession.[64] These stories were not dismissed out of hand by the Americans. Murray was convinced that the secretary of APOC was offering bribes to members of the Majlis to defeat the Sinclair bill, but he also knew that the Russians were underwriting some of the Persian newspapers pinning Imbrie's death on the British. One rumor contended that instead of Imbrie, Roger Soper, Sinclair's representative, was the intended victim.[65]

Soper must have taken the rumor to heart. It had begun on the day Imbrie died.[66] When Soper visited Reza Khan and accused the military of involvement, Reza Khan flew into a rage.[67] Soper informed the Persian government that further negotiations depended on its handling of the Imbrie case. He left for Moscow on July 28.[68] His threat was hollow. When the three years of negotiations between Sinclair and Moscow fizzled, Soper did not blame Persia for the failure; rather, he accused the State Department of making negotiations too difficult for American companies in Persia, contrasting it to Whitehall's active role in supporting British commerce.[69]

Despite the swirling accusations, the foreign legations met to marshal a response to Imbrie's murder. In the first meeting, there was an effort to attribute the death to religious fanaticism orchestrated to lend support to Reza Kahn and deal a blow to the opposition. That meeting ended in a stalemate. In the second meeting, the corps refused to discuss the demands that the American government had sent to the Persian government and walked out in a body. Murray suspected that the posturing was designed to protect their commercial interests.[70] Finally, at a third meeting, the legations formulated a note expressing the need for urgency in dealing with the murder and in providing security for foreigners and religious minorities. The signers included Afghanistan, Belgium, France, Germany, Great Britain, Italy, and Turkey.[71] Russia did not sign.

The simplest explanation of the crime, the one the Persians would have preferred, was that the murder was unplanned. The sequence of events, however, makes that impossible. The reports, which conflict in some areas, agree that the first attack occurred at 11:00 near the fountain. Imbrie died at 3:00.[72] Four hours elapsed between the start of the mob action and Imbrie's death. The first two hours can be broken into two segments. Most likely forty-five minutes passed while Imbrie fled from the fountain to the Cossack Barracks a mile away, was attacked there, and was transported to the police hospital by car, a few hundred yards away. In the next hour and fifteen minutes, there was a pause in the attacks, and then the final attack, the flight of the attackers, the positioning of guards at the hospital entrances, the arrival of a Persian doctor, and the arrival of Dr. Packard and Katherine Imbrie at the hospital at 1:00. Based on this scenario, it is unlikely that such ferocious and sustained attacks covering multiple sites would have been spontaneous, pointing to Imbrie's death being planned. Who planned it and why, and whether such could even be determined, did not yield a ready answer, and Katherine left Persia without it on August 14.

To aid with the investigation, Maj. Sherman Miles was sent from Constantinople to Teheran via Beirut, Damascus, and Baghdad, arriving on August 12. Miles, who had been a military attaché to Admiral Bristol since 1922, was a West Point graduate, an impressive six feet two inches tall, and the same age as Imbrie. Katherine was greatly relieved when he arrived, having known him in Turkey. Mrs. Packard wrote, "Things have been made inexcusably hard for her by the inefficiency of our U.S. minster; and our hearts have burned at the unnecessary suffering she had to endure. We were very thankful when Major Miles came to help with the investigations."[73] With his own departure imminent, Kornfeld hoped

Miles would hold the Persian government to its promise and secure justice.[74] Miles was also to oversee the return of Imbrie's remains to America. As a military officer, he knew the protocol for dealing with Reza Khan and the Persian chief of staff, and his help was welcome. One senses Katherine's relief at learning of his assignment. Although she showed little faith in either Kornfeld or Murray, she never found fault with Miles. When Miles returned to Turkey, George Fuller came from Bushire to Teheran to help Murray, aware that if Imbrie had not replaced Gotlieb, he would have been the temporary consul and likely the murder victim.[75]

Meanwhile condolences and expressions of concern reached Katherine in quick succession, including telegrams about the attack on her. Messages came from President Coolidge, Herbert Hengstler, and Joseph Grew, from foreign service officers in the field, from the Fishbaughs in Washington DC, from Katherine's family in Massachusetts, and from others. One telegram from the Athens legation reads: "For Mrs. Imbrie is Bob safe worried."[76] The legation also received condolences. One letter from an export agent in Meched, Persia, dated July 30 and received August 11, exuded florid prose and may have implied concern over trade relations, although the legation took it at face value: "With utmost horror and consternation I have heard of the sad death of your late Vice Consul and his companion resulting from the injuries received by a Persian mob. I offer my heartfelt condolences to you and the bereaved families and pray to the Almighty to give His peace to the soul of the deceased and patience to their families to bear this hard trial calmly. . . . As an Asiatic myself I hang my head in shame for this atrocious act."[77] The letter was acknowledged on October 14, 1924, with an apology for tardiness in responding; it was not a perfunctory response but heartfelt in its own way.[78]

In the days after Imbrie's Persian funeral, Katherine worked on the arrangements to return his body to the United States. In contrast to the transportation of Alexander Griboyedov's body in 1829, which was carried on an oxcart from Teheran to Tiflis, Georgia, this was a complicated task, particularly the transportation from Teheran to the Persian Gulf. Arrangements involved the British in Iraq, the United States Department of the Navy, the Persian government, the Mesopotamian Railroads in Baghdad, the Teheran Motor and Trading Company, the Mesopotamia Trading and Agency Company (Australia) Ltd. at Baghdad, and the U.S. consuls along the route, including those at Baghdad, Villefrance, and Gibraltar.

The plan for the first leg of the journey was for the entourage to leave Teheran in a motorcade through Qazvin, Hamadan, and Kermanshah. After crossing the border into Iraq, they would board a train for Baghdad, where they would connect to a train for Basrah. At Basrah they would board a steamer to Bushire, where the USS *Trenton* would meet them for the last leg home. At first the navy refused to allow Katherine to travel on a warship, as it was against navy regulations, but when she pointed out that she had been sailing on U.S. warships for five years as a relief worker, the secretary of the navy, within hours, approved her passage.[79]

The *Trenton,* a light cruiser commissioned in April, was on its twenty-five-thousand-mile test cruise. Under the command of Captain Edward C. Kalbfus, it had left the Brooklyn Navy Yard on May 24 and headed to Durban, South Africa, to celebrate the centennial of its first English settlement.[80] The cruiser had then moved up the east coast of Africa to Egypt when it was ordered to Bushire to claim the body of Robert Imbrie.

Prior to her departure from Teheran, Katherine packed her belongings along with her husband's, including a photograph of their first home—the railroad car in Angora—and two volumes of *Arabia Deserta* and a copy of *Hadji,* bound in pieces of Bohara rug. The former book was a travel narrative by Charles Montagu Doughty published in 1888; the latter, a satire of Persian manners and morals, was written by James Morier in 1824 and translated into Persian by an opponent of the Qajar regime. Neither book depicted contemporary Persia, but both were very popular among Westerners. Missing from the belongings was Imbrie's ring; it was later said to be in the possession of a Persian army officer.[81]

On August 17 all attention to the investigation was put aside as Imbrie's body was disinterred from the Protestant Cemetery and readied for its last journey. At 7:00 a.m. the official mourners and a Persian guard, with black mourning bands on their left sleeves, rendezvoused at the American School. Eight members of the Persian Honor Guard flanked the hearse, walking four on each side as the cortege left for the Maidan Mashgh, the parade grounds, winding its way through guarded streets cleared of citizenry. In front of and behind the column of mourners was the Cavalry Guard. Cabinet ministers, members of Majlis, and members of the various diplomatic corps waited at the parade grounds, sheltered by a tent.[82] The entire garrison was drawn up. Upon arrival, the hearse circled the grounds with the troops presenting arms and a band playing until it came to rest facing the main gate where Imbrie had been assaulted. Although the Persian Army chief of staff had contested hosting the ceremony on the parade grounds, so as not to implicate the army in the murder, the Americans had held firm for this symbolic site.

As the music ended, the troops were brought to order, and Kornfeld, Murray, Miles, and their staff left the stands, along with Persian officials, and lined up on one side of the hearse. Troops again presented arms, "The Stars and Stripes" was played, and a cannon salute of eleven guns was fired, at which point Kornfeld and Mohammed Ali Foroughi, the minister of foreign affairs, and their staffs assembled behind the hearse as the band played Beethoven's "Funeral March."[83] The hearse then pulled out of the gate, officials got into the cars, and the cortege proceeded to the consulate for Katherine. There are several possible explanations as to why Katherine did not attend the ceremonies at the parade grounds: she was registering a protest, she felt ill, or as a woman she was unwelcome, or just the first two. At the consulate the motorcade thinned to include only those driving to Iraq. There were three cars and two "vanets." The first car carried Katherine with an attendant and a Persian officer; the second carried the coffin and a guard, and the others conveyed guards and baggage. An advance car of guards preceded the convoy by two kilometers. The drive through the street was eerily quiet. The convoy reached the Qazvin Gate and passed out of Teheran. Ahead lay the 470-mile trip to the border of Iraq in heat and gusting winds. Among the party were Maj. Sherman Miles, Major Rutholiak, the Persian representative designated to accompany the body to Washington, and Maj. Ruhollah Khan, a translator.[84]

At the border on August 21 an honor guard of Iraqi gendarmerie and British officers met the convoy while British military planes flew overhead. The Persian general had requested that the ceremonial exchange be conducted well before dusk so his battery could avoid brigands on its return trip. Murray scoffed at the demand. The party transferred to rail, and the next leg of the journey began.

In Baghdad a contingent of officials met the party, including the British high commissioner, the British air commander-in-chief and his aides-de-camp, and the ranking officer assigned to British defense, as well as the French and American consuls, the Persian consul general, and the police inspector general. There was also a large honor guard from the Iraqi army. The director of railways gave Katherine the use of his private car; Persian and Iraqi guards attended the coffin in another car. When the party arrived in Basrah, it boarded the HRM *Vita* for the journey to Bushire, accompanied by a guard of British Royal Air Force officers.[85] All along the route to Basrah, troops and town officials turned out, rendering "satisfactory" and even "profuse" honors.[86]

Behind the scenes of the transferal, myriad details demanded attention—motor passes to avoid road tolls; permission for Persian guards to be on Iraqi soil; the Persian payment of $4,872.80 for the Suez Canal toll; and the right-of-way for the *Trenton* to clear the canal.[87]

On August 24 the party reached Bushire. Fuller and Persian army and navy officials met the *Vita*. Fuller drove Katherine to the consulate, although unfortunately on the way a boy threw a rock, hitting the car door a few inches from Katherine. Fuller reported the incident, which he said was a common occurrence, and Katherine made no note of it, further underscoring the importance she gave the incident on July 22.[88] Imbrie's remains were taken by gunboat to be received by a military band and Persian officials wearing black military in the hot sun.[89] Hundreds of leading citizens dressed in mourning met the party. American, British, and French officials gathered as "The Stars and Stripes" was played and the remains placed in a military truck covered with pine branches and escorted through police lines. Thousands of Persians lined the road to a military barracks. The room housing the coffin for the night was decorated with Persian rugs.[90]

The *Trenton* arrived the next day, the first American warship ever to enter Persian waters.[91] Fifty of its officers and sailors in crisp white uniforms, with flags and a band, met the funeral party at 11:00 a.m. The procession from the barracks to the wharf consisted of the *Trenton*'s captain, a Persian general, a lieutenant governor, other high officials, including the consul general of Britain, the French consul, and six British officers, a band, and a Persian rear guard as well as other Americans. The heat was intense, reportedly at least 120 degrees, and the humidity high.

At the wharf a British mine-sweeping sloop, the HMS *Crocus*, half-masted its colors and fired eleven-minute guns while the coffin was lowered onto the *Trenton*'s launch.[92] The Americans then returned the salute as planes from the *Trenton* circled the harbor until the casket was placed amidships. The Persian battery fired a national salute of twenty-one guns as well as an additional, unscripted salute of eleven-minute guns in recognition of Imbrie's being the American consul at the time of his death.[93] The British launch and the *Trenton* answered the Persian salutes, gun for gun. Fuller then left the *Trenton*; at 6:00 p.m. the man-of-war began its long journey home, and the Persian guard removed their mourning bands.[94]

The *Trenton* reached Villefrance on September 9. As salutes were exchanged with shore batteries, the "shrill and plaintive notes from French bugles [sounded] the last post to honor the memory . . . of an American citizen who by his undoubted bravery [during the war] achieved the highest decoration of any Frenchman's ambition, obtained only by a few, the Legion of Honor, the Croix de Guerre, and the Medaille Militaire."[95] A church service in Imbrie's honor was held that Sunday, attended by Katherine and officers and sailors from the *Trenton*.[96]

On September 28 the battleship *Wisconsin* met the *Trenton* as it entered the Virginia Capes and escorted it up the bay. At Piney Point, situated at the juncture of the Chesapeake Bay and the Potomac River, Paul Fishbaugh, John Oliver La Gorce, and Herbert Hengstler came aboard to keep vigil as the ship proceeded to the Washington Navy Yard.[97] The next day—a rainy, chilly day—the honorary pallbearers met at the University Club at 15 and I Streets NW, where Imbrie held membership, and proceeded to the Washington Navy Yard, arriving at 1:30. They were Wilbur J. Carr, Evan E. Young, Allen W. Dulles, Herbert C. Hengstler, J. B. Ford Jr., Otis Gates, John Oliver La Gorce, Howard McCormick, Charles Howe, and Felix H. Smith.[98] Paul Fishbaugh chose the last six as Imbrie's "most intimate friends available."[99] Together the pallbearers formed a montage of Imbrie's life.

As noncommissioned officers carried the casket down the ramp to the waiting hearse, just as boxy as Imbrie's Great War ambulance, eleven-minute guns signaled the end of the navy's task. The attendants stood quietly in navy uniforms or top coats and fedoras.

The 2:00 p.m. funeral was held at the New York Avenue Presbyterian Church, where Imbrie's father and uncle had been so active, where Imbrie himself had once served as pallbearer, the same church that had provided the eulogist for Abraham Lincoln's state funeral. Outside a small crowd had gathered in the now-driving rain to see the cortege. Inside a large number of friends filled the pews alongside Imbrie's family members. In attendance were President and Mrs. Coolidge, Secretary of State and Mrs. Charles Evans Hughes, high officials of the War and Navy Department, a delegation from the Washington Assembly of Baha'is, and the Persian chargé d'affaires, Bagher M. Kazemi, as well as representatives from the British and French governments and other government officials.[100] President and Mrs. Coolidge took their place in the pew where Abraham Lincoln had once sat. Rev. Wallace Radcliffe, pastor emeritus, prayed for "the brotherhood of all men, in the promotion of peace and good fellowship in international relations."[101] Rev. Joseph R. Sizoo, pastor, gave the sermon. An organist and quartet provided the music. Among the memorials was an enneagram of red roses, its banner reading, "In Memory of Major Robert Imbrie from the Baha'is of Persia and America."[102]

A plot with two graves at Arlington National Cemetery was at the ready.[103] Soper called it "a beautiful spot in Arlington, which is as it should be."[104] It is on a rise in the southern section of the cemetery, today near the tomb of Adm. George Dewey. At the grave Kazemi placed a wreath on the coffin, his legation at 1720 Sixteenth Street NW having set its flag at half-staff for the day, and the services ended. In Teheran the American mission closed at noon and also set its flags at half-staff, paying last honors to their colleague who had been "an inspiration to many . . . a vivid and arresting spirit."[105]

The next day life moved on, in Persia with the continuing investigation into Imbrie's murder and in Washington with Katherine seeking justice for her husband's death. In November the *American Foreign Service Journal* published a poem she had written:

DIPLOMACY

My heart can weep in silence,
E'en while I smile or laugh in mockery of glee;
And this I hold the first sad lesson learned,
The first stern page of life's diplomacy,
That I now know to smile, with lips and eyes,
While all my heart is weeping silently.

The poem, sentimental and even maudlin, did not capture the outspoken nature of Katherine Imbrie. She would hardly stay silent.

TEN

The Pursuit of Adequate Justice

August 14, 1924, was seven years to the day that Imbrie had applied to the State Department's Consular Service. In Teheran the trial of his accused murderers was underway. That night, a shadow gradually spread over the full moon, the Blood Moon. It left the city in threatening darkness. It was a very long eclipse.

After Imbrie's murder Reza Khan had declared martial law, ordered the arrests of influential mullahs and opposition leaders, and banned preaching from the pulpit on political matters. He also began moving people into positions that would support him in the investigation. One was Gen. Morteza Khan of the Pahlavi Regiment, whom he had named governor of Teheran.[1] For ten days Prime Minister Reza Khan had denied that any military were involved in the murder, and the Majlis had voted to exclude references to the military in the trial and lay blame on religious fanaticism, a move meant to find favor with the prime minister.[2] Only after pressure from the American legation did Reza Khan reverse his position and offer a thorough investigation, claiming to have formed an investigative commission the day of the murder. Heading that investigation were Col. Hassan Asha Ismaili, commander of the Pahlavi Regiment,[3] and Capt. Fatholla Kahn

Bahman, chief of police, both of whom were implicated in the crime. He also placed Lt. Col. Saifollah Jahanbani in charge of the military court, although according to Persian military law he had no authority over military senior officers.[4] The court martial consisted of seven officers, one from army headquarters, one from each of the four brigades at Teheran, and two from police headquarters. Maj. Sherman Miles and Chargé d'affaires Wallace Murray met with Saifollah Jahanbani to clarify the role of the court. It could call witnesses and instigate charges; it could sentence; it could not order an execution. Over both the investigation and the court martial was Gen. Morteza Khan.[5] He alone had the power to order an execution. It was a cozy setup, as if defense attorneys were doubling as jurors.

When the court martial convened, Murray was unimpressed. To him it was obvious that the government was "attempting to whitewash [the] military."[6] Witnesses were not even required to take an oath. Miles agreed with Murray, concluding that the government was shielding its army and other officials.[7] Ambassador Kornfeld, too, was disgusted: "The Prime Minister is a dictator whose power rests on his army."[8] However, from Washington, far from the action, Secretary of State Charles Hughes cautioned against making impossible demands on the Persian government and estranging the two countries.[9] This caution played into Reza Khan's hands.[10]

Dr. Samuel Jordan, president of the American College of Teheran, warned Murray that reliable witnesses would be scarce. One of his former students, now a Persian officer, had reported that when martial law was declared, officers were told that if any military personnel "wagged his tongue," it would be cut off. Kornfeld heard that witnesses feared being killed.[11] Murray knew punishment would be delivered to placate the Americans, but he doubted it would be "*adequate* punishment."[12] He seemed to mean that some or all of the responsible persons would escape punishment. Miles, too, was doubtful that justice would be done. He wrote that the "system of investigation and trial . . . precluded any possibility of attaching responsibility to those who [had] failed to do their duty." He bemoaned that the two men responsible for maintaining law and order the day of Imbrie's murder were in charge of the investigation and that "no single person in authority . . . was removed from command." The Persians were "shielding their Army."[13]

Between August 12 and August 14 Miles and Murray had met with the principals overseeing the trials. The interview with the chief of police had elicited "nothing of importance," and the military governor was most interested in convincing the Americans that "superhuman efforts" had been expended on the case and that the guilty, all civilians, had already been tried and sentenced. He sidestepped Miles's question as to whether all the guards on duty on July 18 had been interrogated. The two officials gave conflicting stories, one saying the army was not complicit in the crime, and the other saying he wanted all guilty officers and soldiers brought to justice, including those charged with neglect of duty. Miles told Reza Khan that both officials should have been removed from office, but Reza Khan tried to exonerate the police and military, saying that orders had been given for the police and military not to use arms during the holy month of Murraham. The point was irrelevant. Murraham had not begun until August 2. Further, the military governor said no such order had been given. When Miles pressed Reza Khan on his men's failure to provide protection, he responded that he could not always rely on his officers to act on their own initiative—"the machinery of the Persian Government was imperfect"—and the officer of the day had not been removed because the government had been distracted in catching the actual murderers. Miles stressed that those in authority needed to be punished. He recoiled when Reza Khan cozied up to him in the guise of a fellow officer to complain about the difficulty of controlling subordinates.

On August 21 Melvin Seymour was sufficiently recovered from his injuries—Katherine Imbrie had paid for a private nurse—to appear before the seven-man tribunal.[14] In recounting his experience, he accused the officer of the day, 2nd Lt. Jehan Bash Khan, of being his assailant;[15] however, he was unable to point him out because the lieutenant was not in the courtroom. It appeared that the military was hiding him.[16]

To support Seymour's testimony Murray appealed to 1st Lt. Sultan Mahmoud Khan, who told him that Jehan Bash Khan had admitted his part in the attack. However, shortly after midnight on August 21, Murray was startled from sleep by someone pounding on his door. It was Sultan Mahmoud Khan, so frantic he was unintelligible. He appeared to have been threatened, and on August 23 when he was called to the stand, he failed to testify against his fellow officer. Jehan Bash Khan was subsequently found guilty only of neglect of duty and given a dishonorable discharge.

Sultan Mahmoud Khan had also fingered Second Lieutenant Habibollah for not protecting Imbrie, but the court merely reprimanded him for not using his sword or pistol in Imbrie's defense and then, astoundingly, commended him for his service with the army. Capt. Fatholla Kahn Bahman, the chief of police, likewise defended himself, saying that when faced with soldiers from the garrison, he was unable to command respect, perhaps a true statement as the police feared the eight thousand or so Cossacks housed in the city.

In contrast to the foregoing witnesses was police lieutenant Nematullah Khan. His report of the incident, placing blame on police and military officers, infuriated Reza Khan. Consequently, although there were no legitimate charges against him, he was brought to trial. Murray feared he would be executed. His fear was warranted. Nematullah Khan was found guilty of trumped-up charges, flogged, tortured, and sentenced to banishment. Banishment was a euphemism for death. Katherine Imbrie and Miles came upon one of Nematullah Khan's beatings when they were driving outside the city walls. On October 3 he disappeared, said to have died in an attempted escape.[17]

In the end, ten military, five police, and ten civilians were convicted, with eight civilians and one policeman acquitted. Among those convicted was a Cossack who failed to use his sword, another who failed to dispatch the cavalry, a major who left the scene to attend his sick mother, and a police officer who failed to dispatch his subordinates. Among the civilians was a beggar sentenced to hard labor for being among the assailants, a twelve-year-old with a cleft lip given fifty stripes for being in the mob and two months' hard labor, and an apprentice fruit seller, given four months' hard labor. Three men—one soldier and two civilians—were condemned to death. They were Private Morteza for attacking Imbrie, Ali Reshti, a camel driver, for striking Imbrie on the head with a rock, and Sayyid Hossein for leading the mob and assaulting Imbrie but not for murdering Imbrie, although when he left the hospital, he reportedly was heard shouting, "We have killed them."[18] Only the three men sentenced to death and two army porters were convicted for participating in the crime. All the others were convicted for negative actions, that is, for not helping when they should have.[19] No person in a position of authority was convicted for engineering the death or allowing it to occur. The highest-ranking military official to be punished was Col. Hassan Agha Ismaili, commander of the Pahlavi Regiment, who was relieved of duty after the trials ended. He had led the investigation.

The State Department doubted that the three executions would be carried out. It was generally accepted that the executions could not occur during Muharram, the tenth day of which commemorates the martyrdom of Mohammed's grandson, Hussein, with its traditional demonstrations that Kornfeld described as "fanatical" and potentially "dangerous."[20] Further Shi'a law also forbade executions during the following month of Safar, also sacred, pushing the earliest date to the end of September. Then as that date approached, Reza Khan announced that according to Shi'a law only one person could be executed for any one death and, as a descendant of Mohammed, a sayyid could not be executed. His defiance of the court's decision seemed opportunistic rather than pietistic, meant to ingratiate himself with the mullahs.

History also conspired against justice in the Imbrie case. On

March 9, 1904, Rev. Benjamin Woods Labaree, a Presbyterian minister, had been murdered by a band of Kurds near Urmia, the first murder in the mission's seventy-year history. The motive was either religious or racial hatred, combined with robbery.[21] The American minister to Persia, Richmond Pearson, had demanded that the murderers be promptly caught and punished and an indemnity paid. Yet two months later only the leader, Sayyid Gaffar, had been apprehended. When Pearson demanded the sayyid's execution, the shah claimed that executing him would be a sacrilege and could result in reprisals against Christians. The shah instead proposed life imprisonment for him and execution for the accomplices. The latter were seized in February 1905, although they escaped in October. Some later died in skirmishes; the others fled to Turkey. The sayyid died in prison in 1907, and the case officially closed in March 1908, despite the State Department's dissatisfaction. In 1924 the State Department did not want a repeat of this earlier travesty in which the "Persian Government continually offered effusive protestations of friendship and good faith and promised repeatedly to meet [American] demands, [but was insincere in] its entire actions and correspondence."[22]

The United States was, however, concerned about the age of Ali Reshti, prompting a delay in the execution so Dr. Packard could examine him. When Packard concluded that Ali was past puberty, probably sixteen or seventeen, Murray seemed satisfied, though coldhearted, concluding that "an oriental at the age of 16 is much more mature than an occidental of the same age and he reaches legal maturity in Persia at the age of 15."[23] Unfortunately, delaying the execution for the examination had the unintended consequence of encouraging Reza Khan to procrastinate all the more.

Before the executions took place, Kornfeld and his family left Teheran. He did not resign from his post because of the murder, having announced his plan to resign as early as January and having tendered his resignation in June so that when Imbrie arrived, Kornfeld was no longer vested in his post.[24] The posting had been a difficult one, even before Imbrie's death. He had been in near constant conflict with the British mission, the Persian government, and the American Financial Mission.[25] Dulles had found him "indifferent" in providing information to the State Department.[26] He was considered "untrustworthy for having argued too strongly and sentimentally for more American aid to the Armenian refugees in [Persia]," and his resignation had been happily accepted.[27] On August 27 he requested two weeks' leave and left Teheran on September 1, reporting to Washington on October 22, almost a month after Imbrie's stateside funeral. Kornfeld no doubt hoped that the Imbrie case was behind him, but it was not.

Meanwhile, the State Department kept President Coolidge informed about the case with occasional updates. He was, though, at the time suffering from the worst tragedy of his life, a child's death. His favored son and namesake had developed blood poisoning after a blister formed during a tennis match. After an agonizing week, the youth died on July 7, just short of his sixteenth birthday. Imbrie's death came eleven days after this family tragedy. Some historians surmise that the boy's death sank Coolidge into a depression from which he never recovered. His grief removed him from much involvement in the Imbrie case, and one wonders what he might have done had he compared the age of the camel driver, Ali Reshti, with that of his own son. In early 1925, when Katherine Imbrie visited Coolidge, she seemed unaware of the president's deep grief, as did most Americans.

When the sacred month of Safar ended, Murray inquired again about the execution dates. He was repulsed. Reza Khan persisted in saying that "it was contrary to law to execute three persons for the murder of one."[28] Only Private Morteza was to be executed. Why then, posed Murray, had the tribunal handed down three death sentences? While Murray pursued the contradiction, Morteza's execution was set for October 2.

On that day, at 7:30 a.m., Murray and George Fuller, vice consul to Bashra, met with the chief of police, several generals, and other officers in the garden of the Eshratabad Barracks, about a half mile outside the city; tea was served.[29] With about twelve thousand troops assembled, Gen. Morteza Khan showed the Americans a color-coded sketch of where each unit was located in the yard and suggested that the Americans not be observed at the execution. Fuller was unclear whether that was because of the army's anti-foreign or anticlerical sentiment. The officers then went to the drill ground with an American legation translator, Allah Yar Khan Saleh. Fuller heard strains from the military band. The order of execution was read, explained to the troops, and translated for Fuller. Although Morteza was arrested for inciting the mob, he was executed for insubordination and attacking Imbrie but not for murder. The charges read to Fuller seem a gross sham. Incensed, Fuller concluded that the verdict had nothing to do with the "rights of foreigners, the duty to protect non-moslems [*sic*] or the necessity of maintaining [civil] order." To Murray, the execution was merely a tool to foster discipline in the army and would not deter similar acts; Morteza's involvement in Imbrie's death was "incidental" to the sentence.[30]

Flanked by two soldiers with bayonets, Morteza was brought into the yard. He asked to drink from a brook, a poignant request, coming from a man whose last moments were seeping away and whose crime was at a fountain, but a man still alive and with human, physical needs.[31] He was allowed his drink and then blindfolded. The fifteen-man firing squad fell into place, seven kneeling and eight standing. Morteza cried out that he was innocent. At 8:20 a.m. the officer gave the signal, a volley was fired, and Morteza fell; two more volleys were delivered, a medical officer pronounced him dead, and his body was carried off the field on a stretcher. When Dulles learned of the execution, he considered it a "sop," but he also regarded life imprisonment a "farce," given the likelihood of commutation or "escape," in this case leading to freedom.[32]

In the coming days, Murray pursued the execution of the other condemned men, but delays persisted. On October 27 Murray met with Reza Khan and threatened him with a "rupture or curtailment of [U.S.] relations with Persia."[33] Reza Khan continued to stall, marshalling a string of reasons, as if a mere listing would overwhelm American protests. He said that "he would rather that his Government fall than that he should be obliged to order the executions, . . . the Court Martial in pronouncing three death sentences did not mean that all three persons must be executed; it intended that two of them at least should be saved by the appeal for clemency," that religious law disallowed the executions, and that the military did not have legal jurisdiction over these two civilians since the death occurred before martial law was declared, and, finally, that all countries did not resort to execution.[34] At the time there were two courts in Persia, military and Shi'a, but not civilian, which left no avenue for a civil appeal.[35] Exasperated, Murray cut short his interview with Reza Khan and left in high dudgeon. Reza Khan, seeing his intransigence backfire, conferred with his minister of foreign affairs and telephoned Murray to placate him, saying his views just expressed were unofficial. In mid-afternoon, he sent an emissary to the consulate with a last plea for clemency. Murray, though, wanted justice, as he saw it. The prime minster relented and ordered the executions to "wipe out [the] shame."[36] To comply with Shi'a law, one man was to be executed for the murder, and two men were to be executed for disobeying orders. To this day, which of the three was executed for murder remains unclear.

Murray's persistence had trumped Reza Khan's resistance. On November 2 at 6:40 a.m. on the grounds of the Bagh-i-Shah Barracks, Ali Reshti and Sayyid Hossein were executed.[37] Murray had interpreted Morteza's courage at his death as evidence that he believed himself a martyr—he had been protecting a sacred shrine—and that his reward would be Paradise. In contrast, he found Ali Reshti and Sayyid Hossein pitiable in their protestations of innocence as they were led into the yard by policemen. They threw themselves on the ground and kissed their guards' boots, pleading for mercy. As the first rays of the sun called for prayer, Ali Reshti recited the traditional morning prayer, made poignant under the circumstances, "We have awoken and all of creation has woken. . . . I ask you for the best the day has to offer." Afterward Sayyid Hossein removed his turban and sash, symbols of his lineage from Mohammed. The two men were led to the wall and blindfolded. A firing squad of thirty soldiers of the Pahlavi Regiment marched onto the grounds and took their position. Then Sayyid Hossein bolted, four volleys erupted, and both prisoners collapsed. A final shot was dealt to the head of Sayyid Hossein, perhaps, according to Murray, as a statement of the military's anticlericalism, all the more evident in their executing a mullah.[38] And so, as Fuller described, "two simple men and [a] boy" were executed; in Miles's words, "poor ignorant creatures who were caught in the net of chance."[39] Justice, however, had not been achieved. Reza Khan had promised "drastic punishment" to those convicted, and the U.S. government assumed that police and military officers would be among those "drastically" punished, yet the only soldier punished had had a "relatively minor" role in the incident.[40]

Murray was especially sympathetic regarding Morteza and Ali Reshti, who he believed were "by no means criminally inclined." They were perhaps caught up in a murderous moment, inspired by the Islamic belief associated with jihad, or suffered "an elemental outburst of nature which comes without warning, spreads destruction in its path, and disappears leaving no explanation as to its origin."[41]

Even while the investigation, trials, and executions in Persia were taking place, there was another matter under negotiation, the indemnity for Imbrie's murder. It became a long, drawn-out affair. At first Arthur Millspaugh and Col. Daniel W. MacCormick, director of internal revenue in the Finance Mission, warned against "mistaken moderation."[42] Disregarding that he had earlier blamed Imbrie for indiscretion, Millspaugh thought the least amount to demand was $100,000; others in his mission thought $250,000, that less would be "totally inadequate,"[43] a sign of American weakness that could jeopardize their mission. Fuller reported a grandee saying, "When we heard a Consul had been killed in Teheran we were terrified for fear that it might have been the British or Russian Consul, but when we heard it was only the American Consul, we knew it would be all right." Although the Persian treasury was strained, Reza Khan was dismissive of even greater amounts: "What is five hundred thousand to Persia? It is nothing," he said to Millspaugh. However, when Millspaugh planned to draw the indemnity from the War Ministry's budget, he baulked.

The State Department chose to be less demanding than Millspaugh and the Finance Mission. Looking to the future, they feared setting the precedent of a high indemnity when the United States might be at fault.[44] Practicality overrode principle. Before Imbrie's body left Persia, the State Department set the indemnity at $60,000, and on August 23 the Persian government accepted. When Katherine learned of the agreement, she fired off an angry response from aboard the USS *Trenton* at Port Said, asking why the question of indemnity could not have waited.[45] She had not been consulted.

In contrast to the American demand was Britain's response to the murder of one of its officials shortly after Imbrie's death. In Egypt on November 19, 1924, just four months after Imbrie's murder, Sir Lee Stack was cut down in broad daylight as he was chauffeured through the streets of Cairo. When his open-air car stopped to allow a streetcar to pass, seven men had opened fire. The chauffeur, slightly injured, careened off to the British compound, but Stack died the next day of hemorrhage and shock, much as Imbrie had.[46]

Stack had spent most of his career in northern Africa, dating from 1899. He had held high positions, including commander-in-chief of the British-controlled Egyptian Army and governor-general of Sudan, but the rise of nationalism in Egypt and Sudan and the local disaffection with British rule led to his death. The British government reacted strongly and immediately to his murder, putting the British Mediterranean Fleet on standby at Malta as well as nearby battalions of the British army. The British high commissioner of Egypt, Field Marshall Viscount Henry Allenby, presented a twenty-four-hour ultimatum to the Egyptian government, including an indemnity of £500,000.[47] The Egyptian prime minister resigned, the indemnity was paid, and a secret society was unearthed and dismantled.[48] The guilty parties were convicted, largely on the basis of ballistic evidence, and all but one of the eight were executed eight months after the murder.[49] In contrast, in the Imbrie case the investigation was flawed, no forensic evidence was offered, and the indemnity was minimal.

Stack's death, including the staggering amount of the indemnity, was widely publicized in U.S. newspapers, which Katherine Imbrie could well have seen before her visit with President Coolidge. The news coverage may have given her false hope. It may have even incensed her. Two facts, however, help explain the different responses to Imbrie's and Stack's murders. British troops were occupying Egypt when Stack was murdered, whereas no American troops were in Persia at the time of Imbrie's death, although some Americans, with a poor sense of geography, proposed sending battleships to bomb Teheran. Also, Britain had a history of oppression in Egypt, whereas the United States did not in Persia; in fact, quite the opposite.[50] There was no question that Britain was to be feared. The United States, on the other hand, had not been tested in the Middle East. Finally, Stack was a high-ranking individual; Imbrie was not.

For her part Katherine began a one-woman crusade. She marshaled all she could on her and her husband's behalf. While in France, on her way home, she informed a correspondent that she planned to tell the story of the assassination "providing secrecy does not force her to silence."[51] Even before the *Trenton* reached Quantico, she began a letter-writing campaign that Dulles referred to as a "deluge."[52] She hoped to sound reasonable and fearless in her letters. She noted that she had been on her own in embattled Trebizond while her husband was in Constantinople and that she had fared well.[53] She wanted credibility. She was, however, concerned that her communications with and about Kornfeld had made her sound "hysterical or flighty." Dulles collected the letters in preparation for her visit the Monday after the funeral—the paper trail that did not benefit her cause.

In one letter she had written that "[Kornfeld] has never forgotten the fact that he was born in the Ghetto, and that he belongs to it; and, primarily and essentially, the Jews are his first consideration."[54] In another she had written that "it was an open secret in the Diplomatic Corps that Kornfeld was an absolute washout and that no efforts were being made to bring Imbrie's murderers to justice."[55] She tried commiserating with the State Department, stating that Kornfeld was "a political legacy and it would [have been] very difficult to remove him," even though the department had "ample grounds for his recall." She wrote that several American advisers wanted to cable Washington and demand Kornfeld's removal, but she had objected, thinking it best that in the circumstances he work with Murray, although she felt that "such a man could not represent the United States well." She referred to Kornfeld as kowtowing to the British, consulting them on everything, and dragging the United States through the mud. Her rancor was not solely directed at Kornfeld, however. She maligned Murray as well as "not a very strong man," easily "muddled" but "not dishonest," saved from travesty only by the appearance of Major Miles.[56] The letter writing regarding the indemnity also did Katherine no favors and could account in part for the runaround the State Department gave her.

Six days after Imbrie's American funeral Katherine brought the inventories from the consulates at Tabriz and Teheran to Dulles. Consuls often used personal money in the course of their jobs and reconciled accounts later. Imbrie's Persian account had been reconciled two weeks before his death; however, he still had outstanding accounts from Russia and Turkey. Dulles arranged for her to meet with William McNeir, chief of the Bureau of Accounts, but McNeir handed her off to Victor Loftus, a clerk. When she received two statements from the Office of the Comptroller, both had errors. She returned to Loftus, and the two went to the Office of the Comptroller, which sent them to the Department of State, where there was no resolution.

On October 16, when Katherine returned to the Office of the Comptroller, she was again directed to the State Department, but there she was asked to return the following day. That night she collapsed and was rushed to the hospital. She underwent surgery, apparently related to her miscarriage in July, and spent most of the rest of the year recovering. In early November Dulles visited her in the hospital, and on November 21 she received the indemnity check without the adjustments she wanted. Katherine remained dissatisfied, harkening back to the indemnity's being negotiated without her knowledge or involvement.

Persia had paid out the $60,000 indemnity the day before Private Morteza was executed. The United States had settled on that amount based on a review of other cases, notably that of the missionary Benjamin Labaree. When the shah had offered to pay a $9,000 indemnity to Labaree's widow, who had two young children, American minister Pearson countered with a demand for $50,000. Mrs. Labaree entered into the negotiations by pointing out that the amount would be perceived as "blood money," not an indemnity, and most likely would come from a levy imposed on the poor. She requested $16,000, which Pearson considered inadequate. In a compromise, he asked for $30,000 in cash, which Mrs. Labaree accepted on the condition that no special tax be levied. To assure that the shah kept his word about the tax, Pearson insisted that an additional $20,000 would be paid if the original terms were not met.

In writing to the State Department, Pearson wryly noted that "the indemnity is still three times greater than the maximum ever heretofore paid by the Persian government for the murder of a private person [and] it is the first instance in a recorded history of twenty-six hundred years in which the Persian government has agreed to pay more than the injured party was willing to accept."[57] He noted that the widow could use the additional money as she wished, distributing it to the poor or, ironically, even returning it to the "sorely depleted" Persian treasury, strapped by demands such as a cholera epidemic. In 1924 Reza Khan was told that, on the basis of the Labaree case, the United States government would not consider less than $50,000 and felt that the offer should be considerably more as an American official was in a different category than a civilian.[58] In this way the offer of $60,000 was reached, a mere $10,000 more for a U.S. representative.

Melvin Seymour, an American citizen but not a U.S. official, received $3,000 for his injuries, which were serious but not permanent.[59] As historian Marjorie Whiteman wrote in assessing indemnities, "The measure of damages may be influenced to a considerable degree by the official or business status of the injured person. . . . The effect of official status . . . is perhaps nowhere more aptly illustrated than in the cases of Robert M. [*sic*] Imbrie and Melvin Seymour."[60] Negotiations about Seymour's indemnity included testimony from two key figures. Seymour's mother informed the State Department that he was her only son and sole support, and Dr. Harry Packard testified that Seymour's injuries were severe enough to keep him from working full time for three or four months.[61] The State Department demanded an indemnity of $2,500, plus $500 for medical and hospital expenses incurred by the legation. In all, Seymour received $2,583.67, including unused money intended for medical expenses.[62]

In pressing for the indemnity, the American government never placed blame on Imbrie or Seymour. The fault was Persia's for not providing adequate protection for foreigners: it was absurd for Persia to contend that because of religious tensions, the police and military could not protect ordinary citizens and foreigners. Persia should pay. After reviewing damage cases, Whiteman concluded, "One outstanding characteristic revealed by the cases [she studied] is the glaring lack of uniformity in the decisions."[63] She noted that when a case was settled through diplomatic channels rather than through arbitration, the average settlement was usually larger. Her tables also revealed that when a case was settled through diplomatic channels for a widow without children, the amount awarded was higher than that awarded a widow with children. Likewise, the average amount awarded minor children for the death of their parents was less than the amount awarded older children.[64] Such seemingly odd variables skewed the settlements.[65]

Although Katherine thought the indemnity unfair, in twenty-six cases where the average amount claimed was $63,131.52, the average award was $18,131.05. In five cases where an average of $89,120 was claimed through diplomatic channels, $26,250 was awarded.[66] In Whiteman's review of cases, Katherine was the only person who received more than the initial amount claimed, $50,000; she received $60,000. Of all the cases, Katherine was only the widow of a foreign service officer. Further, precedence did not suggest her award would be great. U.S. consul William E. Chapman, who was permanently disabled when shot through the chest during a robbery attempt in Mexico, received only $15,000.[67]

Although Katherine was free to cash the indemnity check written by the U.S. Treasury, she haggled throughout 1925, disputing the government's proposed settlement by appealing to the president and to Congress. On January 9, 1925, while she was under a nurse's care and visiting family in Rhode Island, Assistant Secretary of State J. Bell Wright wrote her demanding $136.49 to reconcile her husband's accounts. He had worked with Imbrie in Russia and admired him, but Katherine tried his patience. When Dulles asked her to come to his office to sign papers, she demurred as needing a clearer statement of the accounts. Dulles eventually described her husband's accounts as a "tangled mess" and accused her of not cooperating in straightening them out. It is no wonder she sought out an executive order.

On January 17, 1925, Katherine met with President Coolidge about her husband's case. He assured her he would review her case, but she must have felt dismissed. The *New York Times* quoted her as saying that she might sue the Persian government if she did not get satisfaction, and in what seems a veiled threat, she promised not to interfere with the settlement until after the November presidential elections.[68] She followed up her visit to Coolidge with a letter, stating that when her husband was killed, he was "on the verge of a brilliant career," and $60,000 was not enough to provide an income for her, even equivalent to the salary he was drawing at the time of his death, which was a "meager sum."[69] As proof she alluded to the purchasing power of income from $50,000 in 1904—what Mrs. Labaree had been offered—and claimed rightly that it would take an investment of at least $124,000 to yield an equivalent return in 1925. On the basis of being "the direct sufferer from the murder of Major Imbrie," she appealed to Coolidge for some of the $110,000 expense money that Persia had paid to the U.S. government for the use of the *Trenton*. She proposed an executive order on her behalf and, failing that, support for a bill of relief.

On February 2 she left materials for Coolidge with his secretary, who forwarded them to the State Department. She claimed "that the Imbrie case shows too clearly that Riza [*sic*] Khan was correct in thinking that the cheapest and least troublesome foreigner to murder in Persia was an American; also because they have proof of the disloyalty and treason of our minister, they 'tarred us all with the same brush.'" She wrote that if she were mercenary, she would have made more of the attack on herself and would have allowed the Turkish ambassador and the British chargé to handle her case as they had offered to do. She noted that Dr. Packard was on his way to the United States, implying he would back her story.[70] Eventually she and Packard met with Dulles; presumably they also spoke about her miscarriage, but there is no record.[71]

Curiously Imbrie's nemesis from Turkey, journalist William T. Ellis, also visited with Packard, in support of the Imbries, and reported that the two men discussed the conduct of Kornfeld and Gotlieb and cleared up some of the "whispered reflections" about Imbrie. He suggested another meeting between Packard and the State Department, and although Dulles agreed to it, none seems to have occurred.[72]

On July 2, 1925, Katherine filed a copy of Robert Imbrie's will for probate in the District of Columbia. Included was a petition naming his wife executrix and itemizing his estate, which came to just under $10,000 and included a house at 1545 Columbia Street

NW, valued at $3,272, a half interest in a lot valued at $325, and personal property valued at $6,145, including $1,905.29 cash. The petition stipulated that Katherine file a bond conditioned upon, among other things, "payment of all debts and just claims against the testator." This bond was in the amount of $1,000. Her filing made her personally liable for her husband's debts and resulted in a six-year tussle with the government.

Failing to secure an executive order, Katherine laid out her claim for a bill of relief based on the contention that an attack in Teheran had caused her to miscarry, ending her baby's life and compromising her health, and that Persia had failed to meet the demands of the U.S. government as stipulated on July 26, 1924.[73]

The first point on which Katherine built her case was her pregnancy. It appeared in the record abruptly. Prior to the receipt of the $60,000, she surprisingly did not mention her loss in writing. Katherine married late, this was her first pregnancy, as far as we know, and from the doctors' prognosis, it would be her last. But there is no explicit mention of it until after her return to the United States. Dr. Packard believed she might have been pregnant, but he did not know for certain, and he confused matters by waffling on the issue, at one point saying he had no recollection of her being pregnant. He was firm in saying if she were pregnant, she could not have been more than two months along.

Katherine's second point was Persia's failure to meet U.S. demands. One of the five demands originally placed on the Persian government was to cover the cost of transporting Imbrie's remains home, $110,000, which on July 29, 1924, the Persian government agreed to pay. On November 2 Murray made an ill-advised suggestion to Secretary of State Hughes: establish a trust fund with the $110,000 for Persian students to study in America. He reasoned that it would be an "effective antidote" to anti-American feelings that could threaten trade agreements between the two countries.[74] Murray's altruistic gesture cloaked national self-interest.

On November 9, with Hughes's approval, Murray sent the proposal to the Persian government, stating that its goal was to promote "closer relations and a better understanding between the peoples of the two countries."[75] It seemed like an amicable gesture, but it made America appear weak when it needed to stand strong, as two incidents indicate.

A few days after Imbrie's death a contingent of Persian military marched into the Finance Mission offices, demanding money supposedly owed to the War Department. The incident was peacefully defused, and Reza Khan promised Millspaugh there would be no recurrence. But on November 4 there was. Murray suspected that the British had orchestrated both intrusions to discredit Millspaugh, and in the face of "such unsportsmanlike maneuvers," he encouraged a prompt announcement of the scholarship fund.[76] Persia paid the money in four installments between December 24, 1924, and March 29, 1925; in effect, they were funneling money to the U.S. Treasury to educate their youth. In addition, Murray was using the money to help Millspaugh save face and to restrain the Persian military's expansion.

The use of an indemnity for educational advancement was not new and was much in the air at the time. It might have prompted Murray to make his suggestion. In 1900 in northern China a radical movement opposed to Western influence incited a tremendous slaughter. Between June and August, rebels, called Boxers for their martial arts rituals, murdered tens of thousands of Chinese converts to Christianity, often horrifically. Additionally, in the port city of Tientsin 200 foreigners were murdered or wounded; in the hinterland 200 missionaries and their families were killed; in Peking nearly 900 foreigners were besieged in the diplomatic quarter, and in nearby Peitang Cathedral 400 persons died, mostly converts, including 166 children. The number of Boxers who died in the siege is unknown.[77]

When the Boxer Rebellion ended, the foreign legations demanded an indemnity; in U.S. dollars, it amounted to $335 million. The American portion was $25 million, which was excessive, and after all the claims were allocated, Congress decided to remit the surplus with the proviso that it be used to educate Chinese students.[78] As before, the scholarship program concealed self-interest: a modernized society would yield, among other benefits, improved commercial ties. Following an act of Congress in 1924, the first transfer of funds to China was made in July 1925, authorized by President Coolidge.[79] To Katherine, however, assigning the *Trenton* money to a scholarship program broke the original agreement. Worse, it devalued her husband's death.

In the fall of 1925, when Katherine met with Dulles, he told her it would probably take an act of Congress to change the distribution. By then Katherine was already exploring this path, as Dulles well knew. Katherine continued to seek compensatory, not punitive damages, by finding fault with Persia's compliance with U.S. demands. Some were minor, including the deference paid to Imbrie's body in Persia and the number of honorary shots fired—in her memory ten in Teheran, not twenty-one as agreed upon. But her strongest objections were the failure of the Persian government to convict anyone in authority for the murder of her husband and the legitimacy of Murray's proposed use of what came to be called the Trenton Fund.

The former objection is detailed in the previous chapter. That it remained raw to Katherine is suggested by her reaction to a story in the *Dearborn Independent* in September 1925. On the way home on leave, Murray and his wife met news correspondent Cameron Wilkie aboard the *Sphinx*. The resulting article lauded Murray for his actions in handling the "difficult situation" stemming from Imbrie's murder and proceeded to give an account of the murder. Both Murray and Katherine responded to the story. Carried on the *Independent*'s front page, Murray asserted that he had not discussed the incident with Wilkie except to comment on "the spirit of moderation and the firmness of purpose" that the Department of State maintained "in effecting a satisfactory settlement." Katherine's ire was prompted by Wilkie's statement that a military officer with the rank of major had been executed for the crime. She wrote to the State Department to upbraid Murray, holding him accountable for the errors.[80]

On December 24, three days after her contentious meeting with Dulles, Senator C. Bascom Slemp of Virginia asked the State Department for details of the case. In April Martin B. Madden, chairman of the House Committee on Appropriations, also asked for materials. His request was followed by another from Charles Gifford, representative from Massachusetts, Katherine's home state. Assistant Secretary of State Frank Kellogg wrote in a conciliatory tone to Madden as well as to Massachusetts Senator Frederick H. Gillett that the department had "the deepest sympathy for Mrs. Imbrie and has in the past endeavored to render her every assistance consistent with the law."[81] The statement is weaselly. He also wrote in the same vein to the chairman of the Committee on Claims, Charles L. Underhill, and to Massachusetts senator William M. Butler.

To bolster its case the Department of State wrote the U.S. legation in Persia for its records, only to learn that the account of the attack on Katherine was missing from the files and that most Persians attributed Imbrie's death to political causes designed to destroy the opposition, establish military law, and ensure the ascendency of the current government. The reply did not warm hearts in the State Department. The year 1925 ended unsatisfactorily for all parties. The matter simply folded over to the next year and the next.

In March 1927 Kornfeld reappeared on the scene, jeopardizing Katherine's case with the help of Dulles. Kornfeld wrote to the State Department that Katherine had accused him and his son of being un-American. He argued that he had heretofore exercised "forbearance," but he accused her of "seeking to discredit" him and his son, who was preparing for an examination for the foreign service. He did not want to create an "unfavorable impression" by instituting a civil case, which he had considered doing, suggesting that the press might favor the widow, but at the same time he felt that the State Department needed to advise her "that her charges [were] entirely unwarranted and her conduct most reprehensible." Without needing to do so, Dulles showed the letter "informally" to Representative Theodore E. Burton of Ohio, a keen supporter of Coolidge, perhaps with the intent of his passing it on to the president.

By April the House committee was "hopelessly divided" on the case, one side accusing the State Department of assuming congressional authority in assigning the Trenton Fund as it had and the other maintaining that a portion be given to Katherine. The committee felt that if the Bill of Relief, HR 2858, reached the floor of the House, a "great deal of unfortunate discussion" would ensue, suggesting that information would come out that had better not be made public. Dulles prepared to testify and sought Ralph Soper's permission to use his account of the murder, which supported Katherine but also attested that the murder was apolitical.

Katherine won a round when Joint Resolution 112 was brought forth in the House of Representatives in impassioned rhetoric on her behalf, regarding "the most atrocious assault upon an official of the United States Government in the history of the Republic."[82] Its purpose was to provide relief for her—$30,000 to supplement the $60,000 indemnity. At issue were three considerations—when Katherine had learned of her settlement of $60,000, whether she had had any part in the negotiations, and whether the original amount took into account the miscarriage. Cooper Henry Allen of Wisconsin concluded that "she ought to have received the whole $110,000" of the Trenton Fund. Thomas Blanton of Texas noted that "this is not an ordinary private bill. . . . This bill is one in which the whole people of the United States are interested, because it affects one of our diplomatic officers in a foreign country and his heirs." However, when Edith N. Rogers of Massachusetts introduced Katherine's miscarriage for consideration, Eugene Black of Texas brought up a procedural point—the bill had been sent to the Committee on Foreign Affairs but should have gone to the Committee on Claims. Black's abrupt segue sounds as if a miscarriage was too delicate a topic for congressional ears. John Linthicum, who had known Imbrie from his early days in Maryland, seized the reins from Black and recited the claim's history. Shortly thereafter the bill passed, a victory for Katherine, but it did not overtly address the miscarriage. According to *Damages in International Law*, awards for the loss of a minor child settled through diplomatic channels averaged $2,500. There was no figure concerning a miscarriage, and this case did not set a precedent.

For fear of weakening their case, neither Katherine nor the State Department wanted to give an inch. On March 4, 1927, the U.S. Treasury prepared a check for $30,000 for Katherine, but with the proviso that it be accepted in full settlement of all claims for injuries she incurred and for the death of her husband. She did not cash the check, objecting to the U.S. Treasury's claims against her husband's estate, one for $91.01 and another for $1,366.11. These claims came from several disallowances in Imbrie's expense accounts, chiefly transportation expenses, salary while on leave, and subsistence expenses exceeding the maximum allowance. On September 5, 1930, the U.S. attorney at Washington DC wrote the solicitor of the U.S. Treasury, suggesting the two claims be paid from funds held in Katherine's name by the Treasury and a copy of the decision be mailed to her, as well as a check for $28,674.14, on the basis that, as the United States was both creditor and debtor, indebtedness could be set off against credit. On December 5, 1930, the U.S. district attorney for the District of Columbia agreed on the deduction. On January 24, 1931, Katherine asked for the opinion of the Office of the Comptroller General in this regard. Their decision came on March 24, 1931, backing the district attorney. Katherine cashed the check for $28,674.14. Despite the condition of finality in the Bill of Relief settlement, Katherine retained hope for more compensation, including part or all of the Trenton Fund. Nineteen years passed without her giving way.

Katherine's claim to the Trenton Fund lay on the legitimacy of the distribution. This claim was challenged on September 19, 1950, when Senator J. William Fulbright of Arkansas brought forth a bill "to discharge a fiduciary obligation to Iran," that is, to discharge the Trenton money.[83] Fulbright was a former Rhodes Scholar, university president, and champion of a 1946 bill to enact an educational exchange program, inspired by the Boxer indemnity scholarships.[84] The Cold War had created an atmosphere of suspicion, fear, and insularity. Soviet Russia was extending its tentacled influence throughout Europe and in 1949 had tested a nuclear weapon. The Red Scare was living up to its name. Fulbright thought that an exchange program instilling American values in Iranians could serve as a small but significant bulwark to communism.

Another, more immediate inducement for Fulbright's bill had a familiar refrain. In 1947 a treaty was pending between Iran and the Soviet Union regarding a fifty-year oil concession in northern Iran.[85] Rumors cast the United States as opposing the Soviet concession because it wanted the oil for itself. Despite U.S. denials, the rumors persisted. Great Britain found itself siding with Russia to safeguard its own oil assets in southern Iran from nationalization. The United States protested that its sole interest was in assuring that Iran was not being coerced by foreign interests. In 1948 Acting Secretary of State Robert Lovett telegrammed the embassy in Teheran regarding U.S. aid to Iran, specifically arms for the purpose of internal stability.[86] Referring to the implementation of the Fulbright Bill, he wrote that the passage and availability of the "Imbrie funds," an interesting attribution, would contribute to achieving U.S. objectives in Iran.[87] As with the Murray and Hughes initiative, altruism overlay self-interest.

In 1948 Comptroller General Lindsay Warren, prompted by a letter, addressed whether Murray's proposal to the Persian government in 1924 had established a trust fund or was instead a gratuitous offer and therefore nonbinding.[88] He concluded it was the latter, thereby favoring Katherine's cause. Although he conceded that the State Department had the latitude to negotiate an agreement like that of July 1924, his concern was with the terms of this particular agreement. He concluded that the Persian government had "unconditionally" accepted the U.S. demands on July 29, 1924: that action constituted a binding agreement. Because the Persian government "clearly" committed itself to paying whatever the expense of the *Trenton* turned out to be, the subsequent offer by the United States was gratuitous, neither binding nor obligatory.

Further, Warren noted, the executive and legislative branches of the government recognized the need for statutory authority at the time they received the payments from Persia. Consequently on February 19, 1925, President Coolidge had sent a letter to Congress from Secretary of State Hughes requesting legislation to authorize the use of the funds for educating Persian students. As a result a joint resolution was passed in the House on March 2, 1925, but no action was taken by the Senate before it adjourned two days later. The next year Secretary of State Kellogg had asked the president to resubmit the matter to Congress, which he did on January 6, 1926, but again the bill never became law. The subsequent lapse of time implied to Warren that the State Department itself thought the proposal gratuitous, requiring an act of Congress to authorize it. He therefore denied the request to "establish a trust fund on the books of the Treasury."[89]

Unfortunately Katherine had no reason to celebrate. Fulbright virtually ignored Warren's decision. Instead he appealed to the political realities of the day, asserting that "particularly at this time" it would behoove the United States to enact the scholarship. Also, it was a moral imperative: "It ought to be done," said Fulbright. According to the senator, the fund had fallen into neglect because of the "diplomatic and political history of the intervening years," a position Warren had rejected. Fulbright addressed his fellow senators (there were six in chambers when he began), calling attention to the long hiatus and stating that it had languished perhaps because it was such a small amount, but also because "the widow of Mr. Imbrie has gone from one Member of Congress to another and persuaded them this [fund] is a dastardly thing." Mrs. Imbrie's persistence was "the sole reason why this case had not been settled in the past," he said, apparently ignoring his earlier assertion that the delay was for diplomatic and political reasons.

Fulbright's description of Katherine prompted Joseph O'Mahoney of Wyoming to leap to her defense, saying that he wished the senators could hear the testimony from the 1924 congressional debate.[90] He stated that in the twenty years he had been helping Mrs. Imbrie with her appeal, she had never once suggested she wanted any part of the money, whereupon Fulbright pulled out her letter dated August 2, 1949, which concluded, "It is my request that I be given a hearing and present my claim for the Trenton Fund." Fulbright said that the letter was just one piece of evidence as to her intentions and that there was "an enormous file in this matter." Fulbright also felt that the $90,000 she had already received was adequate and stated that the U.S. government itself had "never given that much [when it had] caused a death." He noted that the previous year the cap was $25,000 and prior to that it had been $10,000.

Fulbright completely sidestepped Katherine's key complaint that those most responsible for her husband's death had gone unpunished, stating "it is rather difficult to say who is responsible when there is a mob." Fulbright's position rested solely on the exchange of notes in November 1924 between the State Department and Persia. He regarded this exchange as establishing a fiduciary relationship.

The Senate discussion illustrates the thin grasp on the Imbrie incident in 1950. O'Mahoney detailed the service that Imbrie had given his country, stating Imbrie had "contributed very largely to the westernization of Turkey and the establishment of a much more democratic attitude among the people of Turkey. . . . He was a friend of the Finns, and he had made a great struggle to be of aid and assistance to them. . . . [T]here is every reason to believe that he was assassinated in Tehran in a riot which was caused by the Bolsheviks, whom he had offended by his actions as a representative of the United States."

O'Mahoney then reached back to Imbrie's days in Petrograd by reading from Edgar Sisson's *One Hundred Red Days*. Sisson's memoir related how Imbrie had become an

> intelligence officer, and continued in that capacity after the Americans left Russia going then to the border city of Viborg, in Finland. His work, as far as I know, never had received public credit, and certainly not its desserts. Nor have I felt that his death . . . was free from mystery. . . . Tehran at that time was a center for a Bolshevik group plotting Asiatic turmoil. . . . I was protected from the Bolsheviks by the publication of my report [detailing a German-Bolshevik conspiracy]. To have harmed me afterward would have been a silly form of confession. Imbrie, however, never had that protection. He remained on distant service.[91]

Putting aside Sisson's book, O'Mahoney concluded that "it seems to be impossible to conceive that we should take that money and use it for a trust fund for foreign students." He repeatedly asserted that no one had been punished for Imbrie's death and therefore the conditions of the trust were never executed. O'Mahoney's blaming the Bolsheviks for Imbrie's death reflects the American attitude to Soviet Russia at the time. Unfortunately he did not press the more important part of his case: Persia's failure to punish those most responsible for Imbrie's death.

Fulbright countered Mahoney. He argued that the State Department had proposed the trust fund. The issue was whether the United States and Persia had entered into an agreement to establish it before any of the money was paid out and after Imbrie's body was brought home and after the execution of three men. It had complied on all counts. To Fulbright, when the proposal for the trust fund was accepted by Persia in 1924, it became a legal trust. The offer was not a gratuitous act.

O'Mahoney persisted: "The fact remains that a great mystery has surrounded this case from the very beginning until the end." He objected to spending money on the citizenry of the country that produced the assassins. When O'Mahoney asked that the bill be returned to committee, Thomas Connelly of Texas noted that the bill had passed by a very large majority of the House and had been reported unanimously to the Senate from its Committee on Foreign Affairs. Allen Ellender of Louisiana asserted that returning it to committee would kill it. With that last remark, a vote was called—there were now sixty members in attendance—and the motion to recommit the bill to committee was rejected. The bill was read a third time, and it passed. Katherine would not be awarded any money from the Trenton Fund. Most of the senators voting had not been present for the argument.

For Katherine, her later years did not bring much peace. She had left the mill town of her youth, seen a good deal of the wide world, given her energies to the cause of orphans, found a midlife love, and been widowed within two years of her marriage. She had lost her only child. Her husband's death changed the entire trajectory of the second half of her life, much of it devoted to battling the president, Congress, the Department of State, and the U.S. Treasury, but she also constructed a parallel life. In the first twenty years of her widowhood she hosted social events; one of her teas was covered in the *Washington Post* directly below an event of Mrs. Coolidge's.[92] She continued in her support of the Near East Relief.[93] She took trips to visit family and friends and toured Europe. She dined occasionally with a U.S. senator, who lived as she did in the Wardman Park Arms Hotel, and she was active in her church. But she seemed not to have risen far above her grievances.

Katherine was eagle-eyed in looking for slights to her husband's memory and her case. In 1941 *There Shall Be No Night* by Robert Sherwood won the Pulitzer Prize for drama. Katherine wrote to Sherwood objecting to the play—on what grounds is unclear. He responded by sending her a copy of the book inscribed, "For Katherine Imbrie, who, starting with birth in New Bedford, Mass., has seen and suffered much the same kind of tragedy that comes to Miranda Valkonen in this play—with all hope for a better world—Robert Sherwood. January 1, 1941." Set in Finland during the Winter War of 1939–40, when Finland fought a Russian invasion, the play presents the struggles of a family, consisting of Kaarlo and Miranda Valkonen and their son, Erik. By the end of the play the major characters are dead or dying, and only Erik's pregnant fiancé escapes to America, where the child will provide "one little link with the future," although it may only be an "illusion of survival." Katherine may have thought the play alluded to her husband falsely, as helping organize an anti-Bolshevik attack from Finland and scheming to capture Petrograd and Moscow.[94] That contention casts Imbrie as a maverick or, worse, a warmonger and is unsupported by documentary evidence. Unfortunately Katherine was not exaggerating her concern. In a 2013 history of the State Department, Imbrie is cast in just that role but, again, without documentary evidence.

Sherwood had served in the Great War and had been gassed at Vimy Ridge. After the war he became a vocal pacifist, although by the end of the 1930s he had concluded that totalitarianism could only be defeated militarily. *There Shall Be No Night* was a call to action. In the play's preface he outlined his move away from pacifism: "There is no more dangerous error of foreign policy than for the government to say, 'We are not concerned with the internal affairs of other nations.'"[95] The message-driven play was successful. Two luminaries, Alfred Lunt and Lynn Fontanne, starred in it both on Broadway and on the road until its closing on December 13, 1941, when Finland allied with Germany.[96]

The play subsequently resurfaced after the war. When in 1950 the *U.S. Steel Hour* planned to televise the play, Katherine wrote to Benjamin Fairless, president of U.S. Steel, protesting the performance because of legal proceedings concerning what she called "The Imbrie Incident." She received a phone call from a U.S. Steel representative who asked if he could contact her attorney. She told him her attorney, William J. Walsh Jr., would be more demanding than she was. A few days later a union attorney visited her, who, although "a bit arrogant" in Katherine's opinion, agreed there was "something" to her protest. In a letter to Walsh she noted her objection "that as a ghost writer for F D R [Sherwood] had access to the State Dept files which neither I, Members of Congress nor the Attorneys acting for me while my husband's accounts were in litigation [had]."[97] Katherine is referring to Sherwood's positions in the Roosevelt administration from 1940 to 1945 as a speechwriter, special assistant to the secretary of war and secretary of the navy, and director of the overseas branch of the Office of War Information. Regardless of her efforts, the play was broadcast in September 1950. What Robert Sherwood might have seen in State Department files is unknown. A 1957 Hallmark Hall of Fame version updated the play to the Hungarian revolution, starring Katherine Cornell in a rare video appearance.

When Katherine Imbrie died on November 18, 1968, she was buried in Arlington Cemetery beside her husband. In a detailed will she bequeathed money to Catholic causes, family members, and her husband's namesake, the son of Felix Harold Schmitt, who had been Robert's law school classmate, travel companion, correspondent, pallbearer, and dear friend. She left some of Robert's books and other possessions to Georgetown University, the Pittsburgh Carnegie Library, the Smithsonian, and individuals. Included were his passport, a Navajo rug purchased in 1906, and the camera, typewriter, and portable desk he had used on his postings. She directed that her husband's diary, covering the years 1906 to his death, be burned.

ELEVEN

What Was Manifest

In July 1924, from Nagasaki to Calcutta, from Switzerland to Halifax to Lahore, from Sacramento to New York City, newspapers spread the word of Robert Imbrie's death. Rumors abounded that that the murder was not spontaneous but planned. Chargé d'affaires Wallace Murray suspected from the beginning that the murder was political, grounding his suspicion in its "viciousness and savagery."[1] To Murray the crime was "all the more remarkable" in that even in the revolution of Persia in 1906, foreigners were protected. Why not in 1924? Dr. Henry Packard, too, thought Imbrie's death was politically motivated—Reza Khan wanted to enact martial law. When Imbrie was killed, Packard had been in charge of the American Hospital in Teheran for eighteen years.[2] By 1925 he had supervised the care of 250,000 patients in Persia and performed 5,000 major operations. He knew Persia well, and his perception carried weight. Ambassador Joseph Kornfeld's first thoughts, too, were of a sinister plot.

When the Imbrie files were ready to be released by the Department of State in 1950, the Iranian government objected. In a headnote to volume 2 of the *Foreign Relations of the United States*, Persia, 1924, the State Department explained that it

> had hoped to print . . . the full record of the case concerning the killing of Vice Consul Robert W. Imbrie at Teheran, Persia, on July 18, 1924. However, when certain documents in the case were, in accordance with established practice, submitted to the Iranian Government . . . , that Government requested that the documents in question be not published at this time. In view of the importance of the Imbrie case in regard to international law, the Department considered that it would be undesirable to publish only a part of the record since such publication would detract from a proper understanding of the case. In the circumstance, the Department reluctantly reached the conclusion that it would be best to defer publication until such time as the Iranian Government was in a position to give its consent to the publication of the above-mentioned document, and at that time to publish the entire record.[3]

As of 2019, the State Department has found it too expensive to publish the documents, even without the consent of the Iranian government, but has released all documents to the National Archives. These documents provide essential information about the Imbrie case, but they do not answer the question: Who killed Robert Imbrie?

Without a doubt, Imbrie died for political reasons, and the guilty parties were never brought to justice. However, informed guesses can be made as to the culprit or culprits. Possible suspects include Armenians or Greeks objecting to Imbrie's support of Turkish nationalism, Standard Oil opposed to Sinclair's overtures in Persia, Islamic fundamentalists resisting foreign influence, and opium smugglers, but three other suspects stand out as more likely: two countries and one man.

First, though, a brief stage setting. In 1919, in the midst of its civil war, Russia appeared conciliatory toward Persia, abrogating the tsar's Persian treaties, claims on debt, and concessions, except for one, the Caspian Sea fisheries.[4] In return, Persia recognized Russia and established diplomatic relations. Soviet Russia's first minister arrived in April 1921, Theodore Rothstein. He immediately started spreading Bolshevik ideas through newspapers, trade unions, and agents. When Imbrie arrived, Rothstein's successor was in place, Boris Shumyatsky, a slight man with a toothbrush mustache, whose later work in Soviet films showed his talent for propaganda. By 1924 Russia believed that the Qajar dynasty was at an end, but that a communist state was impossible, at least for the time.

The British were also eyeing Persia. In 1919 Foreign Secretary Lord Curzon proposed a treaty that would make Persia a virtual protectorate. It contrasted sharply with the more conciliatory Russian gestures and prompted a public outcry in Teheran. By early 1921 Herman Norman, British minister to Persia, knew that its ratification was impossible. After the coup of February 1921, which brought Reza Khan to power, Norman was recalled, as were Brigadier W. E. R. Dickson, head of the British military commission, and Reginald Bridgeman, counsellor of legation. All three had been critical of Curzon's policy toward Persia, and all were retired on pensions. Bridgeman was only thirty-nine years old.[5] Replacing Noman was Percy Loraine. It was his first ministerial post; his career depended on his success. His policy was nonintervention, and he earned a reputation as a "brilliant manager of British interests" in Persia.[6] The embassy's counsellor was Edmund Ovey, who had married an American. Years earlier, when Turkey aligned with Germany during the Great War, he was too ill from typhoid to leave Constantinople, and the American embassy had taken him in, probably saving his life. Following Imbrie's death, he had these personal reasons for encouraging friendship with America. He also had professional reasons. Eight days before Imbrie died, Britain approached the U.S. State Department with an appeal to help control the opium trade between the Persian Gulf and the Far East. Ovey was the British point man in presenting this alliance to Kornfeld and Murray.[7] Britain needed the United States.

With Britain and Russia in a stalemate over oil, Reza Khan foresaw his rise to power. It was as if Persia were suddenly subject to a Samson pushing the pillars of Britain and Russia asunder. On

October 28, 1923, Reza Khan was named prime minister without surrendering the office of minister of war. Except for the shah, who could dismiss him at any time, his power was supreme. If, however, Persia were a republic, he as president would be virtually inviolable. This seemed to be his goal in early 1924. By summer, however, in the face of growing opposition from the mullahs, he had traded the idea of a republic for a dictatorship. Meanwhile Russia and Great Britain were watching Persia's transformation in the weeks before Imbrie's death. It is therefore these suspects—Russia, Great Britain, and Reza Khan—that deserve a closer look.

Russia

In 1924 Secretary of State Charles Hughes was no friend of Soviet Russia. He thought the Bolsheviks had plunged Russia into medievalism, and his long list of grievances against them included the seizure of American property without indemnification, the abnegation of debts, their "ruthless despotism," and their threats of world revolution intent on destroying the American way of life.[8] He pointed a finger at Trotsky's forecast that a "long, protracted, cruel, and sanguinary" revolution was coming to Europe and America "with gnashing of teeth."[9] Despite pressure from American socialists, humanitarians, and businesses to normalize relations between the two countries, Hughes steadfastly refused to recognize the Soviet government as the legitimate will of the Russian people. Although by 1920 Washington had lifted most of its trade restrictions and in 1924 Congress had reopened its discussion to normalize relations with Russia, Hughes could find no ground for mutual respect between the two governments, although he acknowledged the long friendship between the two peoples.[10]

Meanwhile the Bolsheviks were laying the groundwork of a massive industrial state. Russia had suffered terribly in both the Great War and its civil war. In 1921, in the face of economic disaster, Lenin had announced a new economic policy—"a much-expanded domestic market system, a return of private enterprise, and a broadening of the Soviet commitment to foreign trade and

[to] selling concessions."[11] Hughes recognized that Lenin was making accommodations necessary to promote trade with capitalist countries and alleviate suffering in Russia, but he also knew that these concessions could easily be canceled. He did not trust the Bolsheviks.

Given the relationship between the two governments, did Imbrie fall victim to their mutual hostility? If so, what could have incited Russia to have Imbrie murdered on July 18, 1924?

As soon as Imbrie arrived in Persia, he turned his attention to an area of Russian-Persian conflict, the south Caspian Seas fisheries. In May Arthur Millspaugh, director of the Financial Mission in Persia, had ordered their seizure from the Soviets, who were operating them in violation of the 1921 Russo-Persian Treaty.[12] The Caspian Sea is the primary source for beluga sturgeon, which yields the most valued caviar in the world. The Russians responded to the threat against their "black gold" with force, landing troops from a warship. After a protest from the Persian government, the warship left, although a contingent of troops remained. Imbrie wrote a report in June on this conflict.[13]

After Imbrie's death, in October 1924 Persian officials met with the Soviet minister to sign a fisheries concession. Uninvited, Millspaugh interrupted the meeting, supposedly by happenstance. He vigorously objected to the concession on several grounds, chief being that the Russians would pay the Persians very little for their harvest and sell it on the world market for a great deal. Millspaugh was justifiably incensed. His job was to protect Persian resources and the treasury. Further, the contract would give Russia a "foothold in northern Persia," opening the way to bringing in more troops on the pretext of protecting the fisheries. Millspaugh feared that sooner or later Russia would control all the ports along the Caspian's south shore.[14]

Despite Millspaugh's strong protest, Reza Khan began pressuring him to accept the concession. Then in November the Soviet manager of the fisheries presented Millspaugh with a check for 100,000 tomans for Reza Khan. Millspaugh was appalled. It appeared that the manager was paying for goods to which he had no right. Accepting the check would be tantamount to acknowledging that right. Further, the Persians were owed at least 950,000 tomans for use of the fisheries for the previous two years. The check could only be construed as a bribe. Millspaugh rejected it, but as soon as he was dismissed in 1927, Reza Khan signed the agreement. As one American official wrote, it was "payday; the ghost walked at the palace."[15]

The fisheries were valuable both in themselves and for what they might bring in bribes. In 1932 the American minister to Persia, Charles Hart, wrote that the Soviets paid $850,000 in cash to Reza Khan's minister of court to thwart an American company's interest in the fisheries.[16] The Russians no doubt resented an American's control over Persian finances, but Millspaugh's conflicts with Reza Khan and his 1927 dismissal show that Russia could bend Persia's will without resorting to a dramatic assassination.

Nevertheless, American newspapers were quick to connect Imbrie's death to Russia. The *New York Times* carried such an accusation on July 21, but it is garbled and hyperbolic, moving the incident of Imbrie's raising the flag over the U.S. consulate in Petrograd to an American Relief Administration warehouse in Riga, as well as stating that Imbrie was in constant danger in Constantinople and asserting that a Bolshevik mob had killed him.

Unsolicited letters also arrived at the State Department blaming Russia, some of them bizarre. Emily V. Lorraine, an actress whose most famous role came in a film adaptation of Edna Ferber's short story "A Gay Old Dog" (1919), wrote a six-page testament of Imbrie, "this brave, fearless friend of the Russian Christian people,"[17] and then proceeded to cast the plot in anti-Semitic terms. She concluded that Imbrie, this "fearless American," was murdered by Jewish Soviets of Moscow, unprotected by the Persian government as he would have been if the U.S. ambassador had been a Christian.

Most letters implicating the Russians in Imbrie's death were more measured such as that from Lewis K. Davis, who described himself as an "intimate friend" of Imbrie. Davis felt it would have been very easy for the Russians to have had Imbrie killed and recalled a conversation in which Imbrie had told him of a price on his head: "The Soviets will get me if there is any possible way of doing so." Davis felt that if Imbrie was murdered by the Soviets, it should be publicized.[18]

It is true that Russia had cause for wanting Imbrie dead—particularly for his anti-Bolshevism and his intelligence activities. However, Russia had condemned him to death five years earlier. They had issued a bounty. He had been in easy reach of assassins in Petrograd, Viborg, Constantinople, and Angora—and myriad other places, including Estonia, Bulgaria, Thrace, Samsun, Trebizond, and Konia. He had survived in all these places. Had the Russians honed in on Imbrie in Persia because he was the State Department's Russian expert? The United States wanted to keep Persia from Russian control and hoped that Reza Khan would resist Russian expansion and develop a Western-style democracy and economy.[19] Yet neither the State Department nor the American legation in Persia blamed Russia for Imbrie's death despite the bounty. When Imbrie died, Russia was still holding onto the possibility of a contract with Sinclair Oil. At home Americans were agitating for the normalization of relations with Russia. When Reza Khan's accession to the throne was announced, the Russian acknowledgment was diplomatic, although pointedly brief and bland.[20] Further they gained nothing from Imbrie's death; trade between Russia and America was more important than revenge on a vice consul, a lucrative fishing agreement with Persia, or a Sinclair loan to the Persian government.

A recent book suggests how far afield Imbrie's story could veer from fact in blaming the Russians. In the *Dictionary of Iran*, the Imbrie entry relates that prior to his death, the Russians spread rumors that the Americans were poisoning well water with oil. When Imbrie photographed a procession of flagellants commemorating the death of Mohammed's grandson, Hossein, flagellants fell upon him, chanting, "How can we drink cool water when Hossein's throat burns with thirst?" According to legend, Hossein and his entourage were under siege within sight of water when Hossein, near death from thirst, was shot in the throat by an arrow. Consequently, the crowd held Imbrie spread-eagle and poured "boiling water laced with crude [oil] . . . down his throat," a victim of the Russians.[21] Russians may have wanted Imbrie dead, but not in the summer of 1924.

Great Britain

After Imbrie's death, a spotlight also shone on Great Britain. Was it to blame? Some Persian newspapers, reportedly bribed by the Russians, accused the British of Imbrie's death and were silenced only when Reza Khan threatened them with "drastic punishment."[22] American vice consul George Fuller heard from a British citizen that the British held proof of Reza Khan's own guilt, which they had leveraged to quash the stories. But was the British citizen planting a lie he knew Fuller would report, thereby smearing Reza Khan?

Similarly a story in an Italian newspaper, *Il Mattino,* attributed Imbrie's death to the British Secret Service, although a U.S. official in Rome thought the story a Russian plant.[23] The Italian newspaper noted that the Reuters Agency had described Imbrie's death in detail but had not explained why soldiers and police did not protect him. It noted that the British Secret Service had recently "overstepped its national duties [and was] in large part in the service of the English petroleum companies" so that while the British government was not implicated in Imbrie's death, "It is known how England wishes to develop alone enormous Persian oil fields . . . and how she is, for this reason, in bitter conflict with the United States." According to the paper, "Imbrie was engaged in combatting the monopoly of the English companies." The Italian newspaper drew parallels between Imbrie's death and the murder of the anti-fascist Giacomo Matteotti on June 10, just weeks before Imbrie was killed, blaming both deaths on the blood-bath created by the competition for petroleum and ignoring Matteotti's opposition to Mussolini, for which he was surely killed.

An item from the Soviet organ *Pravda*, titled "Dark Intrigues," also insinuated a plot but without naming the British: "It is learned from authoritative sources that the murder of the Consul was the result of a political scheme planned beforehand, the object of which was to cause the [Persian] Cabinet to resign and undermine the question of American oil concessions and an American loan. . . . The leaders of the mob received on the eve of the murder a large sum of money from a certain person occupying a high position and standing close to the circles of opposition of the Cabinet."[24] The story described Imbrie as having lived a long time in the Near East studying religious cults, making one wonder if the Russians had intercepted Imbrie's July report on religion.

Fuller wrote that many people blamed the British:

> At first this seemed to be the unreasonable habit of blaming every disaster on the British, but afterwards it became more logical. They argued that the British, by financially supporting the religious enthusiasm as the sacred month of Muharram approached, created a situation which could not but result in disorder, and the possible assaulting of Baha'is or foreigners. This would discredit the government in the eyes of American investors, just as the [Sinclair] loan was to be concluded. It would probably result in martial law and greater security, but American confidence would already have been shaken and the resulting increase in the authority of the Sardar Sepah [Reza Khan] would also be to their interests, as he was becoming more and more a tool of their government. The merchant class, who had been hoping for American friendship and cooperation, were especially bitter at this so-called British intrigue. They felt that their bitterest enemy had again proved too clever for them, and that if the result was alienation of American friendship, there was no future for their country.[25]

With the merchant class favoring American interests, but with American confidence in the viability of commercial ventures in Persia shaken by Imbrie's murder, Britain would tie a string to

Reza Khan's rise and make Persia its marionette. Descriptions of this scenario wafted through the streets of Teheran.

Another scenario blamed British and American Zionists. A story in the Paris edition of the *New York Herald*, titled "Friend of Imbrie Says Death Due to Oil War," asserted that according to a source "Major Robert Imbrie . . . was the victim of a mob organized at the instigation of Jewish financiers in the United States and England who believed his influence might serve to swing the valuable Persian oil fields . . . to an American syndicate in which the Sinclair oil interests were largely represented."[26] The article concluded that this "amazing statement . . . may result in a State Department inquiry." The source of the story was Harold Spencer, who had attended the U.S. Naval Academy, class of 1913, but had left before graduation to join the British Secret Service prior to the Great War. Spencer claimed that "Major's Imbrie's assassination [was] engineered by the crowd that is trying to hold Persia's oil resources as the financial backbone of the great Jewish empire which will, if it succeeds, have Jerusalem as its religious capital." He went on to claim that an assassination plot was developed several days before Imbrie's death. William Van der Heggen, he wrote, was "a Dutch representative of the Sinclair oil interest in Persia" and was with Imbrie when he died. He was now on the way to Washington to report on Imbrie's death. According to Spencer, Van der Heggen was married to a Persian princess and feared for his life at the hands "of the financiers who are behind the movement for a Zionist empire."

Piqued, Murray dismissed Spencer's theories of Zionists' plotting outright but took the time to describe with some relish Van der Heggen: "The Legation is only too well informed as to the antecedent and character of Van der Haggen, who, it may be remarked incidentally, left Teheran more than a year before the killing of Imbrie."[27] A Sinclair representative, Lester Thompson, had hired him as his secretary. Subsequently Thompson gave Van der Heggen $1,800, an enormous amount, smacking of a bribe, to cover his expenses returning to America, which he spent "to the last penny on riotous living in Teheran." Van der Heggen thereupon appealed to the American colony to pay his way to Paris. The "Persian heiress" referred to was an Armenian woman "of exceedingly questionable character." Murray concluded that Van der Heggen was "a charlatan of the first water," whom Murray believed was "mentally unbalanced."

Norman Armour, Assistant to the Undersecretary of State, wrote an extended report from Rome on Spencer,[28] who had called at the embassy in Rome on July 29. In investigating Spencer, Armour learned from a British foreign official that he had been attached to their Adriatic Mission during the war, obtained a commission, and eventually arrived in Rome where he had served as secretary to two British ambassadors. His source stated that "Spencer is erratic to the extent at times of being mentally unbalanced, [but] his statements usually contain an element of truth although apt to be considerably exaggerated." The source consequently believed that Spencer's theory represented "the view of the officials in London." In other words, the British were blaming the Russians, but were they deflecting their own guilt?

Gen. Habibolleh Khan Cheybani, chief of the Persian mission in Paris, overseeing some fifty Persian officers at the École de Guerre, spoke about Imbrie with Chargé d'affaires Sheldon Whitehouse at the U.S. embassy in Paris. Habibolleh did not think that the British were involved in something so "crude" as a murder; however, he believed the death to be a "byproduct" of British efforts "to influence Persian sentiment of every kind—commercial, political, and religious—in hope that this popular hatred would be sufficiently violent to prevent the Persian government from ratifying the agreement with the Sinclair Oil Company." British oil interests were backed "at every turn by the British Government and all of its official and unofficial agencies in Persia." He said that the British would "fight by every means any invasion" of what they regarded as rightfully theirs and that the British had driven the first American financial mission of 1911 out of Persia. They were now set on destroying American credibility in Persia. Although he did not believe the British directly responsible for Imbrie's death, he concluded that "any violent quarrel with America resulting in Major Imbrie's assassination would be what the British desired and had planned for."[29]

Ralph Soper took a similar tack, stating that he did not think the British directly responsible for Imbrie's murder. However, he did believe that they periodically paid bribes to Muslims to assault or murder religious minorities such as Jews or Christian Armenians. According to Soper, the foreign legations responsible for the demonstrations used them as evidence that the Persian government in power could not maintain order. Nevertheless, he did not think anyone in particular plotted against Imbrie, including Sinclair's archrivals, the British.[30]

When Imbrie died, the Sinclair concession was being finalized. The British had worked vigorously to defeat it, but it had been roundly approved in the Majlis, 68 to 50, and signed by Reza Khan and Ralph Soper on December 29, 1923.[31] Kornfeld had forwarded a translation of the contract on January 5, 1924, which the State Department received in mid-February.[32] In a desperation move after the signing, Standard Oil dragged out an old and invalid claim to the northern concession, its shared ownership with APOC of the Khostaria concession. This move only further weakened their position due to the strong anti-British feelings in the Persian government.[33] Meanwhile Sinclair moved ahead to secure a loan of $10 million for the Persian government, a contingent to the concession. In May an agreement was reached with Reza Shah, Millspaugh, and Sinclair to secure the loan with all of Persia's revenues. Britain strenuously objected, asserting a prior claim to the revenues based on Persia's war debts. The bill was to be reported out of the Majlis on July 20, but Imbrie was murdered on July 18, and by July 29 Soper had left Persia, the Sinclair concession all but dead, and Reza Khan was without his $10 million. Britain seemed to have won the day with its objections and delaying tactics.

It is doubtful, however, that the loan would have come through, even with the backing of Persian revenues. Sinclair had struggled to find a lender. American newspapers were casting Persia as unstable, "a country that God forgot."[34] Not even the venerable J. P. Morgan Company could swing the loan, although it offered to float half the loan as long as the British provided the other half, with APOC royalties as security, a specious offer.[35] Bringing Britain and APOC into the Sinclair agreement would violate the 1923 law requiring the north Persian concession be granted only to an independent American company.[36]

The unraveling of the Sinclair agreement accelerated. By January 1925 the Persian government's Oil Commission still had not met to approve it. On January 17 Soper, then in the United States, instructed his Persian secretary to unearth the government's intentions. Murray also could not account for the delay, although he thought that if Soper had remained in Teheran or returned after the Imbrie affair was settled, the concession might have passed the Majlis. Meanwhile the British legation continued to combat Sinclair's efforts "with all its energy."[37] In April Murray learned that allied independent oil interests were considering an offer regarding the concession, including a loan, but that one of the companies was an affiliate of Standard Oil, again a violation of the 1923 law.[38] By the end of 1925 Sinclair believed the logistics of laying pipeline and establishing a tanker service in the north were insurmountable.[39] The next month Reza Khan was named shah. Afterward any hope for the concession died, as Murray had predicted it would. In 1927 Standard Oil also withdrew its bid, leaving Britain the only foreign power in Persia with substantial control of oil interests, a situation that continued until after World War II.

At first it seems that Great Britain benefited enormously from Imbrie's death, so much so as to be implicated. Britain had facilitated Reza Khan's rapid rise to power to offset Bolshevik influences. At the time the move seemed an easy remedy to a difficult situation. Britain was facing a decline as a world power, lacking the "money to defeat the Soviets, suppress unrest in Iraq, occupy Iran, and subsidize the Tehran government."[40] The reality of postwar struggles at home—high unemployment, inflation, deflation, strikes, and overwhelming debt—were puncturing Britain's imperial status. It was thought that a strong central government in Persia would benefit Britain at little cost.

Ultimately, though, Reza Khan's rise did not aid Britain. As has been pointed out, "What Britain chiefly got from the coup was the reputation of having been behind it, and that idea was proof to [Persian] nationalists of England's perfidy."[41] In hoping to block Soviet intervention in Persia, Britain backed a man they could not control. They were left adopting an "attitude of watchful inaction."[42] In turn Reza Khan came to believe Britain would not interfere in internal politics.[43] As soon as the guilty parties in Imbrie's death were executed, he left Teheran with an army to extend his control.[44] Ironically for Britain, in doing so he destroyed the authority of the local tribes with long-established ties to Britain. By the end of 1927 the British in Teheran were reporting that the new shah, who had taken the name Reza Pahlavi, was "one thousand times worse than Ahmad Shah in his love of money and land."[45]

Like a low-lying fog, suspicions implicating Britain in Imbrie's death blurred the landscape of international affairs. These suspicions reappeared in the fall of 1929 when the U.S. Senate Subcommittee on Naval Affairs held hearings concerning the failed Geneva Naval Disarmament Conference of 1927. At the heart of the inquiry was a self-proclaimed expert in naval matters, William Shearer, a lobbyist on Capitol Hill. *Time* magazine described him as "a big thick-shouldered man in a tweed suit, a red necktie and yellow shoes," but a more sympathetic source noted that he was good looking, a careful dresser, and a bright and easy conversationalist.[46] Regardless, he was a bit of a charlatan. At the conference he had posed as a journalist while employed by the three largest shipbuilders in America, stirring up Anglo-American animosity by daily circulating anti-British communiqués.[47] Following the conference Shearer's role in Geneva became the target of a Senate investigation regarding the influence of big business on matters of national security.[48] The climax of the hearing was the appearance of Shearer himself. He insisted he had done nothing other than help the American cause. His great concern, he said, was to keep America from becoming Britain's industrial lackey, and he was not surprised that his patriotic efforts had made him an enemy of Britain, even leading to threats on his life.[49] He testified that *New York Times* correspondent Wythe Williams had warned him not to return home by way of the Suez Canal or any British territory, and more specifically, a Chinese delegate had warned him that if he traveled through British territory, "they would get [him], the same as they got Imbrie in Persia."[50] Shearer's testimony was picked up the next day by the *Times* (London).[51] No senator asked for a clarification regarding Imbrie, and their silence seemed to convey an unwillingness to pursue the accusation against an ally. When the hearings ended, Shearer's days as a lobbyist were virtually over. Although he was not responsible for the failed conference, his name continued to crop up throughout the 1930s during heated discussions that cast industrialists as warmongers.

It seems to have been convenient to blame Britain for Imbrie's death for any number of reasons, but especially for its desire to monopolize the Middle East. However, Imbrie's death did not advance that power and may actually have strained the relationship between Great Britain and Persia. It might be tempting to say that Great Britain had Imbrie killed but failed in the outcome of that venture, but supposing the British engineered a plot against an American official seems too farfetched, open to too great a fallout to justify. In addition, Britain had reason to maintain at least a veneer of good relations with the United States: Standard Oil was continuing to court a partnership with APOC, and the British wanted U.S. help in controlling the opium trade in Persia. There were also deep personal connections between the two legations. Murray was about to marry a British citizen, and British counsellor Ovey owed his life to the care Americans had given him in Turkey. Finally, British minster Percy Loraine, aloof and elitist, was not the cloak-and-dagger type.

Reza Khan / Reza Shah

Last of the three suspects is Reza Khan. In early 1924 he had watched his power seeping away month by month in the face of clerical opposition. Then an opportunity arose to stem the tide. On March 3, 1924, Turkey, now a republic, ended the caliphate, the position of universal spiritual leader, on the grounds that it was unable to defend Islam in lands beyond its border. In Persia this decision galvanized the clerical opposition to republicanism. In a bold move Reza Khan, who had envisioned himself as president of a new republic, tossed that dream aside and issued a joint statement with the ayatollahs of Qom that the Islamic faith forbade a republic.[52] He needed the clerics' support to maintain his power, and he used his submission to the clerics when dealing with Imbrie's murder.

After Imbrie's death Reza Khan claimed that he had issued verbal instructions—hence, there is no record—that both the police and military should not intervene in religious demonstrations, although this order goes unmentioned in the defense of the accused, and some of the accused were punished for not providing protection. He used the sanctity of calendar months to delay the executions of the condemned; he appealed to Muslim law to try to avoid two of the executions; and he allowed his cherished, anticlerical military to be punished.

Clerical support was not enough, though, to secure Reza Khan's position. The day before Imbrie's death, Millspaugh had delivered an ultimatum to Reza Khan to restrict the amount of revenue that he could spend on the army.[53] With the mullahs opposed to a republic and the Americans trying to trim his army, an intriguing scenario emerges, based on circumstantial evidence. To solidify his power, Reza Khan had used the mullahs to stir up trouble, about which Imbrie himself reported, writing in a dispatch, "At every teahouse a Mullah harranged [*sic*] the crowd. Mobs, fired by oratory and hashish, swarmed the streets, unhindered by the Police, crying against the Baha'iists."[54] Conceivably Reza Khan had an agitator recruited, Sayyid Hossein.

In executing Sayyid Hossein, Reza Khan reversed his submission to the clerics and asserted his domination.[55] He used Imbrie's death as the excuse to establish martial law and jail his opponents. Almost a year after the execution of Sayyid Hossein, the Majlis voted on October 31, 1925, to depose Ahmad Shah and change the constitution. By December Reza Khan held total power. His coronation as supreme ruler was held on April 25, 1926. Henceforth, he was Reza Shah, founder of the Pahlavi dynasty.

In the ensuing years Persia modernized. When Reza Shah came into power, Persia had only about 800 miles of road and 150 miles of railroad. By the end of his era there were 14,000 miles of roads, and the Trans-Iranian Railroad ran from the Caspian Sea to the Persian Gulf in a country about the size of Alaska but with a much denser population. In 1925 there were 600 cars in Persia; in 1942 there were 25,000. By the late 1930s all of its cities had electric power, and there were 6,000 miles of telephone lines. By 1941 there were seventeen times as many modern manufacturing plants in Persia as there had been in 1925. By 1935 the number of physicians had increased from 1 per 11,000 to 1 per 4,000.[56]

Educational opportunities also grew. In 1927, of a population of 10 million, there were only 56,000 children in primary school, 14,500 in secondary school, and only 600 in institutions of higher learning.[57] By 1941 the number of primary students had grown sixfold, the number of secondary students had doubled, and the number of those in institutions of higher learning had risen fivefold. The University of Tehran had been founded, and women were allowed to enroll. Thirty-six teachers' colleges and thirty-two vocational schools had also been established.[58]

True, under Reza Shah Persia modernized, but it was forced modernization. The achievements cannot mask the harm done to Persia under his autocratic rule. Reza Shah was energetic and strong-willed, but he had a host of shortcomings. His rapaciousness seemed to know no bounds. The British stole from Persia, but so did he. From 1927 to 1941, the Persian government had no control over or access to oil revenues. They were under the shah's control. According to a study of the U.S. Treasury and State Department records, of $155 million of oil royalty payments, at least $100 million was diverted to Reza Shah.[59]

Even as early as 1924, Chargé d'affaires Wallace Murray noted Reza Khan's greed, saying that while "he has robbed less than many would have done in his place . . . it is nevertheless a fact that in the last two years he has acquired great wealth at the expense of a bankrupt country."[60] Murray reported Reza Khan's "only desire now was to pile up an immense fortune, invest it in Europe, and get out when things got too hot." Later, when the shah instituted universal military service, Murray suspected he would use it to exact substantial bribes from those who wanted exemptions.

Hoffman Philip, the American minister in 1928, described Reza Shah's reign as a "despotic oriental monarchy," its chief strength being the army, which Reza Shah used to displace tribes and seize land.[61] One of his estates came from his seizure of seven thousand villages, hamlets, and pastures. He relocated tribes to open up lands to acquisition. By 1932 Reza Shah was the largest single landowner in Persia. The U.S. minister in Teheran in 1933 referred to Reza Shah's "maniacal personal avarice."[62] He reported that the shah had deposited more than a million pounds in a London bank and also had bank accounts in Switzerland and New York.[63] According to Millspaugh, Persia had all the essentials for a progressive state in place by 1926—political, economic, and social—but under Reza Shah it lost its "golden opportunity to win lasting freedom."[64]

Reza Shah's acquisitiveness was abetted by his brutality. The American legation reports in the 1920s and 1930s relate the disappearances, trials, exiles, imprisonments, and deaths of the shah's political opponents. Sayyid Hassan Modarres, Reza Shah's chief clerical opponent, did not last long with the new government. After Imbrie's death Murray met with Modarres, whom he called a man "without personal fear," but weak and old.[65] He told Murray that Reza Khan was behind the murder, prompted by the British, but Murray also concluded that if Modarres was the only alternative to Reza Khan, then "God help Persia."[66] Perhaps Modarres's downfall was inevitable: Reza Khan had him imprisoned at the time of the 1921 coup, and Hart reported that "more than any other [person, Modarres had] blocked Khan's 1924 republican movement, and although there was in 1925 an apparent reconciliation, in 1928 the Shah rigged the elections to defeat Modarres."[67] A year later Modarres was banished to a town near the Afghanistan border, although he had not been convicted of any crime. In December 1937 he was murdered at the age of eighty-five.

In 1923 Consul Bernard Gotlieb had described Reza Khan as a man of "uncontrolled passions."[68] He reported on incidents of outbursts and proscribed beatings at imagined slights. He feared that Reza Khan's lack of restraint would create "an incident with far-reaching results." An American reported to Kornfeld that a newspaper editor had been beaten by Reza Khan and his teeth knocked out. The Belgian minister reported that a Cossack officer had beaten him for not turning over 3,000 tomans on Reza Khan's order.[69] Legation reports from this period are full of such incidents, which, even if some were mere rumors, identify the widespread perception of Reza Khan's violence. On July 9 Imbrie had gone to the police station to report an attempted assault on two Americans. Had word spread to this violent man of this confrontational visit? When Imbrie died, he was preparing a report on Reza Khan himself, and as part of his investigation, he had interviewed Reza Khan's secretary, supposedly a friendly source, but perhaps not. Imbrie knew someone would be murdered as part of the plan. He knew he was dealing with viciousness.

When Charles Hart, the last American minister to Persia before it was renamed Iran, met Reza Shah in 1930, he thought him a man "only a few jumps from savagery," whose interest was "self-glorification and personal aggrandizement."[70] Having just come from a posting in Albania, Hart thought Persia would be more advanced but believed it a century behind Albania. Two years later he wrote that he had not changed his opinion, saying that "there is no end to the stories one hears of Reza Shah's personal cruelty,"[71] a cruelty that was indiscriminate, dealt to government ministers, sheiks, chauffeurs, butlers, and cooks alike.

In one 1934 dispatch American minister William Hornibrook listed the names of thirty-five individuals who had been tried in military courts and whose punishments had been published. Eight were to be executed and nineteen imprisoned; eight were acquitted. Hornibrook concluded that Reza Shah seemed intent on liquidating "any and every individual whom [he] conceives may stand directly or indirectly in the way of the maintenance of the Pahlavi dynasty. . . . Only the future can tell whether he has sown the seeds of dissolution of his own dynasty."[72] In 1938 an American journalist reported on the imprisonment of Majlis deputies and newspaper editors in what Hart called the "Persian Bastille."[73] While Reza Shah admired Mustafa Kemal and his modernization of Turkey, in his actions he was more like Mussolini. Doubtless the British bilking of Persia contributed to the country's sorry condition in the first half of the twentieth century, but British actions cannot excuse Reza Shah's perfidy. Of the three main suspects in Imbrie's murder, Reza Shah seems the most likely perpetrator, based on his political and personal agenda and the aftermath of Imbrie's death.

In a twist of fate, as events unfolded following Imbrie's death, the United States lost its position as the benign power to which Persia could turn in the face of British and Russian pressure.[74] And as the likelihood of a republic faded, the United States opted to support Reza Khan's militarism and autocracy rather than a theocracy and to acquiesce to Reza Khan's assessment that Persia was not ready to be a republic.[75]

In this episode the United States lost an arrow-slit opportunity to champion republicanism, if it had so chosen. The United States also lost an opportunity to become an early player in the oil fields of the Near East. By 1928 that opportunity was gone. By then the problem of the oil industry was overproduction, soon to be severely aggravated by the Great Depression.[76]

As the world spiraled toward another world war, American

influence in the region became negligible. The United States and Britain, which had competed for oil, now moved into a lopsided cooperation to keep Persia from Russia's clutches.[77] Reza Khan needed Russian markets, yet he feared its intrusion. His fear was justified. In 1926, when the dispute over fishing rights in the Caspian revived, Russia placed an embargo on Persian imports, creating great suffering in northern Persia.

Faced with the power of its northern neighbor and even as it courted Weimar Germany to increase trade, Persia needed Britain.[78] Britain's embassy in Teheran and extensive network of consuls and agents working with regional potentates and nomadic tribes created such a presence in the area—including Iraq, India, and the Persian Gulf—that while its association with Persia was not friendly, it was in each nation's interest to work together. Furthermore Britain owned one of the world's largest refineries on the Persian island of Abadan, creating a huge network of services directly or indirectly connected with the oil industry. In 1933 Persia and APOC signed an agreement providing for a concession valid for sixty years. It gave Persia a considerable increase in oil revenues, but it also gave Great Britain the right to cancel the contract with two years' notice. Persia received no similar right. As one historian points out, "the manner by which the concession was negotiated [confirmed] that the Anglo-Persian Oil Company was not a business concern but a representative of [a] foreign office assigned with the task of economic and political domination in Iran."[79]

Of the three suspects discussed, Reza Khan benefited the most and the most immediately from Imbrie's death. He came swiftly to power and wielded that power with the self-assuredness of an autocrat for seventeen years. He ultimately, however, was overwhelmed by the conflagration that was World War II. In what would have seemed an improbable alliance in 1924, and a great irony, Russia and Britain invaded Iran in August 1941, and Reza Shah was forced into exile. But before his fall, as the above account suggests, he orchestrated Imbrie's death and in doing so reaped almost twenty years of power, privilege, and personal prosperity—a vast return on the expenses associated with the indemnities and transport for Imbrie's body.

Taking Responsibility

And what about Imbrie? How much responsibility does he bear for his own death? In September 1923 Allen Dulles wrote, "In sending a man of Imbrie's rather impetuous disposition to far away countries we are taking a certain risk. The only question is as to whether the advantages to be gained would justify this risk. I am rather inclined to think they would."[80] A month later Dulles wrote that Imbrie "has done good work in the past and I think will do good work in the future, and personally I should be glad to see him at Tabriz."

Tredwell was more confident in recommending Imbrie for the post in Tabriz as "one of the ablest commercial and political reporting officers in the Service."[81] The Department of State was shocked at his death. However, Imbrie was also an adventurer, captivated by the "he-man" persona of the times. When he was in Turkey, he complained about being stuck in Constantinople and not doing field work: he wanted a "he-man" job.[82] On arriving in Persia, he wrote, "I began to feel when I saw men wearing knives that at last we were in he-country. We had poor luck not being held up or shot at, but aside from that we had a very good trip."[83] When the Great War broke out, his aunt, Mary Fishbaugh, described him as "restless": she wrote that he wanted to see "active service," he wanted to get to the front.[84] His bravado was also noted in a news story when he was awarded the Croix de Guerre. Imbrie's penchant for adventure characterized him. An associate of Imbrie's in Turkey, G. Howland Shaw, wrote that the person who enters the foreign service is "endowed with a dash of adventuresomeness and the more generous the dash the better," but he continued: "Adventuresomeness is not irresponsibility or vagabondage. . . . It is a zest for living and learning, a constructive discontent and restlessness, an impatient desire to grow." When he wrote those words in 1930, he may well have been writing Imbrie's eulogy.[85]

In a landmark essay on Ernest Hemingway, Robert Penn Warren identifies "the discipline of the soldier, the form of the athlete, the gameness of the sportsman" that give meaning, order, and even moral significance to characters who play out their lives in the "shadow of ruin,"[86] but whereas Hemingway's characters live in a bleak world, one without a center, Imbrie never lost his enthusiasm for life. The Hemingway hero is solipsistic; Imbrie was not. He was committed to a goal larger than himself. That is what gave him courage.

One question remains, however: had Imbrie grown overconfident after living in danger zones for seven years? Ironically, did his success at surviving contribute to his death? Perhaps. He was sent to Persia as an expert on oil and on Russia. It is unlikely that any other consular officer was as qualified as Imbrie for this posting. In accepting the assignment Imbrie took a chance. One feels Imbrie would not have wanted it any other way. And so, on a hot summer day Robert Whitney Imbrie set out to explore the unknown as he had in the American West, the jungles of Africa, the wartorn villages of France, the bazaars and mountains of Macedonia, the streets and countryside of Petrograd and Viborg, the alleys of Constantinople, and the plains of Anatolia, a day like many others. But somehow, this time, he stepped into history. After the murder the Persian prince regent sent a telegram about the murder to Ahmad Shah in Paris. In it he quoted a proverb, "What is manifest requires no explanation."[87] What was manifest to the prince regent was Reza Khan's guilt, but what required an explanation, despite the proverb, was how one particular American came to die in a far-off land, on distant service. That required understanding his life and times.

NOTES

Introduction

1. This spelling of Teheran is used throughout this book except when an alternate spelling is used in titles and direct quotations.

2. "Iran papers says [*sic*] to negotiate about 'assassination' not nuclear issue," BBC Monitoring Middle East—Political, July 16, 2012, source: *Javan Daily* (Teheran), in Persian, July 12, 2012.

3. The title "Foreign Service of the United States" dates to the Rogers Act of 1924, which combined the diplomatic and consular service. I use the term generically.

4. The second foreign service officer murdered was Victor F. W. Stanwood, killed in Madagascar in 1888 by a ship's captain suspected of gunrunning. The captain was never charged.

5. Information on the Benghazi attack and its aftermath draws from David D. Kirkpatrick, "A Deadly Mix in Benghazi," *New York Times*, December 28, 2013; Ethan Chorin, "Setting the Record Straight on Benghazi," *Foreign Affairs*, February 10, 2016; and various U.S. Senate and House committee reports.

1. In Search of an Orbit

1. B. Imbrie, Philbrook, and A. Imbrie, *Genealogy of the Imbrie Family*. Also, Federal Census 1860; Census Place: Big Beaver, Beaver County, Pennsylvania; Roll: M653_1071; Page: 20; Image: 24; Family History Library Film: 805071.

2. Federal Census 1900; Washington, District of Columbia; Roll: 160, 8B; Enumeration District: 0046; FHL microfilm: 1240160. Also, Federal Census 1910; Washington, District of Columbia; Roll: T624_153; Page: 1A; Enumeration District: 0141; FHL microfilm: 1374166. The Fishbaugh home currently serves as an office building.

3. "Heroism of Ambulance Drivers Wins Decorations," *Washington Times*, March 7, 1918, 1.

4. "Will Take His Degree," *Washington Times*, June 25, 1906, last ed., 6. The item mistakenly lists Georgetown for Imbrie's undergraduate degree.

5. H(enry) L. Rennick, "Imbrie, Acting, in Red Petrograd," *New York Times*, September 7, 1924, SM8. Rennick wrongly described Imbrie as being six feet tall.

6. B. Imbrie, Philbrook, and A. Imbrie, *Genealogy of the Imbrie Family*, 108.

7. Imbrie, "The Graduate Class," *Shingle* (Yale University, 1906), 70.

8. Letters from Robert Imbrie to Felix Harold Schmitt, November 26, 1906; April 20, 1907; June 19, 1907; August 6, 1907, June 22, 1909; hereafter FHS. The letters are the personal property of Robert Imbrie Smith Jr. and are used with his permission.

9. Imbrie, "Jurisdiction of the Federal Courts," viii.

10. Imbrie, "Jurisdiction of the Federal Courts," 38.

11. "Potomac Basin Spawning Bed," *Washington Post*, July 8, 1906, 4. Charles Fishbaugh was an avid bass fisherman, which probably contributed to Imbrie's love of the outdoors.

12. Interview on September 29, 2014, by phone with Tamara Smith, widow of Robert Imbrie Smith, who was Felix Schmitt's son and Robert's namesake, born 1931. At some time, the name Schmitt was changed to Smith. The Navajo rug was willed to Smith by Imbrie's widow. For information on Schmitt's son, see Gould, "Robert Imbrie Smith."

13. FHS, November 26, 1906.

14. FHS, November 26, 1906.

15. Robert Imbrie, Application for Appointment to the United States Consulate, Form 205a, August 14, 1917. Imbrie does not list the Nautical School in his application. His wife, Katherine, lists it in the biographical sketch of her husband provided when she donated materials to the Smithsonian Museum, Accession No. 98,532 (1927). The Nautical School is now the State University of New York's Maritime College.

16. FHS, January 7, 1907; February 8, 1907.

17. FHS, November 7, 1907.

18. FHS, August 6, 1907.

19. FHS, October 7, 1907; October 20, 1907.

20. FHS, October 31,1907.

21. Frederick Boyd Stevenson, "Where Lawyers Work without Fees," *Brooklyn Daily Eagle*, November 11, 1906, 19.

22. FHS, October 31, 1907.

23. FHS, November 15, 1907.

24. FHS, April 30, 1907; January 1, 1908.

25. FHS, December 2, 1907.

26. F. Stevenson, "Where Lawyers Work," 19.

27. *The Ucayali*, 164 F. 897 (EDNY 1908) Court Opinion 898. Robert W. Imbrie for libellant, Whitridge, Butler & Rice for claimant, November 17, 1908. Accessed on Bloomberg Law.

28. *Rose's Notes*, Book 12, 1085–86 (available online).

29. Fink, *Sweatshops at Sea*, 94.

30. Fink, *Sweatshops at Sea*, 219n3.

31. FHS, December 2, 1907.

32. FHS, August 4, 1908.

33. FHS, October 5, 1908; December 1, 1908.

34. Sharp letter in B. Imbrie, Philbrook and A. Imbrie, *Genealogy of the Imbrie Family*, 205.

35. Katherine Imbrie to Calvin Coolidge, letter and enclosures, January 24, 1925, National Archives, RG 59 (hereafter NA), 123 Im 1/419.

36. FHS, May 17, 1908; May 19, 1908; July 30, 1909.

37. FHS, September 21, 1909.

38. FHS, January 7, 1907.

39. "Carr to Be Chief Clerk . . . Herbert C. Hengstler Is Appointed to Former Old's Place—Both Are Natives of Ohio," *Washington Post*, May 9, 1907, 5.

40. FHS, February 8, 1907; September 9, 1910.

41. FHS, September 28, 1910.

42. FHS, September 28, 1910.

43. *Yale University Obituary Record of Graduates Deceased during the Year Ending July 1, 1925*, Bulletin of Yale University, 21st series, no. 22, August 1925, 1555–56. McCormick's career path suggests he may have wished to follow in his father's footsteps, but according to his World War I draft registration, he was blind in one eye. McCormick served as witness for Imbrie's passport application in 1915. McCormick eventually left the law for a long and distinguished career as an English professor at the U.S. Naval Academy.

44. "Slain U.S. Vice-Consul Had Lived in Baltimore," *Baltimore Sun*, July 20, 1924, 1.

45. "Democrat and Republican Lawyers against the Amendment," *Baltimore Sun*, October 26, 1909, 1.

46. Rennick, "Imbrie, Acting, in Red Petrograd," SM8.

47. FHS, April 8, 1909.

48. Roosevelt, *African Game Trails*, 468.

49. Rich, "Ida Vera Simonton's Imperial Masquerades," 323–24.

50. Unless otherwise noted, information on Garner comes from Rich, *Missing Links*.

51. Quoted in Rich, *Missing Links*, 15.

52. Rich, *Missing Links*, 4.

53. Rich, *Missing Links*, 16.

54. FHS, September 28, 1910.

55. "Chronicle of International Events," 473. Also see Rich, *Missing Links*, 47–48.

56. Garner letter, April 6, 1911, from the William Hornaday Papers (hereafter WHP), Box 47, Wildlife Conservation Society Library, New York. I am indebted to Jeremy Rich for copies of these letters. Elihu Root was a New York corporate lawyer, adviser to Theodore Roosevelt, and secretary of war, as well as secretary of state before becoming senator. He later served as an unofficial U.S. representative to the League of Nations.

57. FHS, May 2, 1911.

58. FHS, May 2, 1911.

59. FHS, August 3, 1911.

60. Garner letter, July 13, 1911, WHP, Box 47.

61. Garner letter, May 26, 1911, WHP, Box 47.

62. Garner letter, July 13, 1911, WHP, Box 47.

63. Garner letter, July 13, 1911, WHP, Box 47.

64. Garner letter, July 13, 1911, WHP, Box 47.

65. Garner letter, July 18, 1911, WHP, Box 47.

66. FHS, August 3, 1911. Imbrie arrived in New York on October 11, having sailed from Dover on the *Kroonland*.

67. W. Stevenson, *At the Front*, 78–79.

68. "Miss Lilian Howard Wiley Wed to F. Harold Schmitt," *Chicago Daily Tribune*, April 25, 1912, 8. A year after the wedding Imbrie was the godfather for Felix Harold Schmitt Jr., born February 11, 1913. FHS, April 23, 1913. Lilian died on October 15, 1918, of pneumonia brought on by the Spanish flu.

69. Linthicum later helped Imbrie's widow seek redress for her husband's death.

70. "R. W. Imbrie Wants Place," *Baltimore Sun*, April 5, 1913, 16.

2. Merry Hell and More

1. O'Brien, "American Press," 446.

2. Haller, *Battlefield Medicine*, 16.

3. Wartime demands for wheat led to disastrous agricultural practices in the American Midwest, the story of which is grippingly told in Egan, *Worst Hard Time*.

4. George Plimpton, preface to Hansen, *Gentlemen Volunteers*, xiv. Hansen's book is a major source for this chapter. At the start of the war, Russia's army had only two motorized ambulances. Sebestyan, *Lenin*, 238.

5. The American Field Service archives were not modernized until 2010. Although cards were kept on drivers in Paris, these cards are incomplete. Imbrie's is missing. The office in New York City where Imbrie interviewed was at 14 Wall Street.

6. This chapter relies heavily on Imbrie's book *Behind the Wheel of an Ambulance*. In some places Imbrie's recollections have been augmented by those of other drivers, which are noted. Also, at times Imbrie does not provide complete names, but where possible those persons have been identified and the sources noted. I have retained the spellings as Imbrie gave them.

7. Plimpton in Hansen, *Gentlemen Volunteers*, xvii.

8. Details of the trip come from recollections by Capt. Joseph R. Greenwood in the *Field Service Bulletin*, no. 87 (April 26, 1919).

9. The packing list comes from John P. Nelson, *Letters and Diaries of David T. Nelson, 1914–1919*. Nelson served with Imbrie in Section One of the AFS in early 1916 (79, 115).

10. Fenton, "Ambulance Drivers in France and Italy," 329–30.

11. Andrew, *Friends of France*, 118.

12. Livesey, *Historical Atlas of World War I*, 131.

13. In his memoir Imbrie refers to George as "Freddie." George Frederick Spaulding was at St. John's College when he volunteered. At least twenty-five Rhodes Scholars served with the AFS. Rhodes Scholar David T. Nelson recounted how thinly populated the colleges were in the war years following the exodus of young men for the front. One college had only twelve students in the fall of 1915. The students in attendance shared accommodations with wounded soldiers. Nelson, *Letters and Diaries*, 19, 67. Melissa Downing, archivist and record keeper, Rhodes Trust, Oxford, in an email on April 4, 2016, noted that the *Record of War Service of Rhodes Scholars from the Dominions beyond the Seas and the United States of America*, published in 1920, lists the record of war service for Rhodes Scholars, but the Rhodes Trust does not have a specific list of Rhodes Scholars serving with the AFS. The list provided does not name David T. Nelson, suggesting other American Rhodes Scholars may also be missing.

14. Barracks' details come from Nelson, *Letters and Diaries*, 81.

15. W. Stevenson, *From "Poilu" to "Yank."* The list may be resorting to hyperbolic humor but seems to be true.

16. When Imbrie died in 1924, his attending physician, Dr. Harry Packard, wrote to End detailing the circumstances. "Letter Tells How U.S. Consul Killed in Persia," *Reading (PA) Times*, August 27, 1924, 2.

17. Fenton, "Ambulance Drivers," 333–34.

18. W. Stevenson, *At the Front*, 117.

19. "War Honor to R. W. Imbrie," *Washington Post*, February 12, 1917, 3; also see Seymour, *History of the American Field Service*, 437; Clark and Clark, *Soldier Letters*. Imbrie was with Coleman Clark in Section Three in the Balkans. Both brothers were killed in France in 1918. For Imbrie's medals for work in France and the Balkans, see Clark and Clark, *Soldier Letters*, 65.

20. Morse, *Vanguard of American Volunteers*, 137. Hall was a 1915 Dartmouth graduate. His ambulance bore Dartmouth plates to recognize the funds raised by his college for the ambulance corps. He is buried in Moosch, France.

21. Imbrie's vehicle was donated by Cleveland H. Dodge, a New York philanthropist and adviser to President Wilson.

22. Franz, *Tinkering*, 9. In advertising for drivers the AFS stipulated, besides good health and a clean record, the ability to drive and repair automobiles. See plate 49, Haller, *Battlefield Medicines*, 139.

23. Haller, *Battlefield Medicines*, 171.

24. The term *ambulancier* originally applied to the personnel of a field hospital but came to be used for ambulance drivers.

25. Haller, *Battlefield Medicines*, 43.

26. Fenton, "Ambulance Drivers," 333.

27. Hansen, *Battlefield Medicines*, 111.

28. Once when a driver forgot the password, he drawled, "I don't remember exactly, but it seems to me it sounded something like 'Motor Boat.'" The guard let him pass. The word was "Montauban." W. Stevenson, *At the Front*, 140.

29. William H. Woolverton's papers are held in the Manuscripts and Archives Division, Sterling Memorial Library, Yale University, MS1748.

30. Two of Victor White's World War I paintings are in the Museum of the City of New York.

31. Gliddon, *Somme 1916*, 326–28.

32. Gliddon, *Somme 1916*, 121. Gliddon describes Cappy as suffering very little artillery damage during the war. Imbrie describes the village as "devastated by days and months of bombardment" (57).

33. The address of the AFS headquarters was 21 Rue Raynouard.

34. Olson, "Evolution," 79.

35. FHS, May 10, 1916.

36. The description of *repos* is taken from the recollections of P. Rice, *An American Crusader at Verdun*, 81–89.

37. FHS, May 10, 1916.

38. FHS, December 31, 1918.

39. FHS, December 31, 1918.

40. FHS, May 10, 1916.

41. Imbrie, *Behind the Wheel*, 69.

42. W. Stevenson, *At the Front*, 63.

43. Seymour, *Memorial Volume of the American Field Service in France*, 19.

44. FHS, May 10, 1916.

45. W. Stevenson, *At the Front*, 65–66.

46. FHS, May 10, 1916.

47. W. Stevenson, *At the Front*, 69–70.

48. Hansen, *Gentlemen Volunteers*, 108–9.

49. Gliddon, *Somme 1916*, 10–15.

50. Gliddon, *Somme 1916*, 16.

51. FHS, May 10, 1916.

52. Stevenson, *At the Front*, 82.

53. Stevenson, *At the Front*, 86–87.

54. Stevenson, *At the Front*, 104.

55. Philpot, *Three Armies on the Somme*, 120–21.

56. Stevenson, *At the Front*, 103–4.

57. Keegan, *Illustrated History*, 267.

58. Olson, "Evolution," 104.

59. Keegan, *First World War*, 282.

60. Keegan, *Illustrated History*, 259–60.

61. Quoted in W. Stevenson, *At the Front*, 125.

62. Seymour, *History of the American Field Service*, 272.

63. A. Piatt Andrew, quoted in Morse, *Vanguard of the American Volunteers*, 131. Imbrie's service was noted in the *Field Service Bulletin*, no. 9 (September 1, 1917).

64. W. Stevenson, *At the Front*, 131.

65. W. Rice and Brown, "With the Ambulance Service," 288.

66. W. Rice and Brown, "With the Ambulance Service," 288n10.

67. *Field Service Bulletin*, no. 9 (September 1, 1917) notes his receiving the Croix de Guerre. For a list of Imbrie's wartime awards, see "State Department Begins Inquiry," *New York Times*, July 20, 1924, 1.

68. Imbrie, *Behind the Wheel*, 125.

69. Seymour, *History of the American Field Service*, 469.

70. Stevenson, *At the Front*, 225.

71. Stevenson, *At the Front*, 229.

72. Section One was designated Section 625 when folded into the U.S. Army. During its tenure in both the French and U.S. armies, four members died. In addition, six men were slightly wounded and six badly gassed. Its members received one Legion of Honor, one Medaille Militaire, seventy Croix de Guerre, and three Commendation Letters from General Pershing. The section served for more than four years. Stevenson, who was in the

United States when it entered the war, wanted to be a pilot but had poor eyesight. Instead he returned to France in April to serve as an *ambulancier* for the duration. W. Stevenson, *From "Poilu" to "Yank,"* 369. In 1922 Stevenson died of pneumonia.

3. All There Is of Terrible

1. Much of the information on Imbrie in this chapter is taken from his book *Behind the Wheel of an Ambulance* and his articles "Across Albania in an Ambulance" and "Polyglot Salonica." In some places Imbrie's recollections have been augmented by those of other drivers, which are noted. Also, at times Imbrie does not provide complete names, but where possible those persons have been identified and the sources noted. I have retained the spellings as Imbrie gave them.

2. Winant, "Soldier's Manuscript."

3. Winant, "Soldier's Manuscript," n.p.

4. Winant, "Soldier's Manuscript," n.p.

5. Palmer, *Gardeners of Salonika,* 32–33.

6. Palmer, *Gardeners of Salonika,* 81–82.

7. In "Polyglot Salonica," Imbrie puts quotation marks around "cot right next to mine," perhaps alluding to Kipling's poem "Danny Deever." The only other AFS *ambulancier* to die in the Balkans was Henry Suckley, who was wounded in an air attack at Zemlak, Albania, on March 18, 1917, and died the next day in Coritza, where he is buried. Imbrie was stationed in Coritza for two weeks in January 1917.

8. The dangerous driving conditions prompted one *ambulancier* to return to France. Ruffino and Chizari, *Where the Border Stands,* n.p.

9. Wakefield and Moody, *Under the Devil's Eye,* 60.

10. Service, "The Land God Forgot," 13.

11. Wakefield, and Moody, *Under the Devil's Eye,* 19.

12. In *Behind the Wheel,* Imbrie calls Winant "Vive."

13. Winant, "Soldier's Manuscript," n.p.

14. "American Ambulance near Monastir Cited for Valor," *Chicago Daily Tribune,* February 12, 1917, 5.

15. Winant, "Soldier's Manuscript," n.p.

16. FHS, May 10, 1916.

17. Giles Franklyn and George End left Macedonia on May 14. See Clark and Clark, *Soldier Letters,* 85. When Frank Baylies returned to Paris, he joined the Lafayette Escadrille. He died in an air battle in June 1918. The last *ambulancier* in the Orient Section arrived in Paris in August 1917.

18. In her husband's vita, Katherine Imbrie lists his rank as major, U.S. Army Officer Reserve Corps, but underneath his name and rank on his gravestone in Arlington Cemetery is written "French Army." Katherine Imbrie to Calvin Coolidge, letter and enclosures, January 24, 1925, NA, 123 Im 1/419.

19. Katherine Imbrie to Calvin Coolidge, letter and enclosures, January 24, 1925, NA, 123 Im 1/419. The American Legion Post in Paris was established on December 13, 1919.

20. The description of the voyage comes from Nelson, *Letters and Diaries*. Nelson returned to the United States in late April 1917, relinquishing his Rhodes Scholarship to enlist in the U.S. Army. He had served with Imbrie in Section One of the AFS in early 1916 (146–51).

21. *Booklist*, 258.

22. Seymour, *History of the American Field Service*, 553.

23. Jenkins, *Worlds to Explore*, 95.

24. Imbrie, *Behind the Wheel*, xxi. Imbrie's memoir went through three editions. When the *New York Times* issued its biannual review of books in October 1918, it included Imbrie's book, noting that since its spring issue nearly five hundred books relating to the war had been published, evidence of American interest in the topic. See "Growing Literature of the War," *New York Times*, October 20, 1918, 65.

25. A passage from Imbrie, *Behind the Wheel*, was included in *First World War Centenary Prose Collection*, vol. 2 (LibriVox, 2014, https://librivox.org/ww1-prose-vol-i/).

26. Irwin, *Making of a Reporter*, 244. Irwin was a classmate of Herbert Hoover at Stanford University and in 1914 urged Hoover to oversee the Commission for Relief in Belgium. After the war Hoover headed the United States Food Relief program, which played a significant role in Imbrie's story.

27. Irwin, *Making of a Reporter*, 245.

28. Irwin, *Making of a Reporter*, 246.

29. Macleod, "Ellis Ashmead-Bartlett," 31–48.

30. John Dos Passos's *Three Soldiers* (1921), about disillusioned ambulance drivers, was much resented by the AFS and scornfully reviewed in its bulletin.

31. Hansen, *Gentlemen Volunteers*. According to Hansen (159–60), Hemingway saw active duty with the American Red Cross from June 4 to July 8, 1918, half of which was spent in the ambulance corps, operating near Vicenza, Italy. His section was relatively inactive, and it is likely that he only drove an ambulance once or twice, at the most. He earned his medals as a canteen runner, riding a bicycle to the front line with cigarettes and chocolate. It was in the role of runner that he was wounded. See also James McGrath Morris, "Hemingway's World War I Savior Is Anonymous No More," *Washington Post*, Outlook section, B8, January 18, 2019.

32. P. Rice, *American Crusader at Verdun*, 56.

33. Olson, "Evolution," 18.

34. Quoted in Hansen, *Gentlemen Volunteers*, 131.

35. Imbrie, *Behind the Wheel*, 99. The 1908 poem "The Ship of Fools" by Sir John Lucas alludes to Francis Drake's circumnavigation of the globe.

4. Imbrie, Acting

1. Two sources are especially helpful in detailing Imbrie's activities in Petrograd: Imbrie, "Report on the Petrograd Consulate, April 5 to September 1, 1918," enclosed in Imbrie to Basil Miles, December 18, 1918, NA, 123.813/7-1/2; and Rennick, "Imbrie, Acting, in Red Petrograd," SM8. For the background to Imbrie's report, see Langbart, "Five Months in Petrograd," web supplement. The Imbrie report is attached to this article.

2. Consul North Winship, Petrograd, to Secretary of State, March 20, 1917, NA, 861.00/330, no 274/Foreign Relations of the United States (FRUS)/Russia: Chapter 1/1918, 7–11.

3. Crosley, *Intimate Letters from Petrograd*, 87.

4. Crosley, *Intimate Letters from Petrograd*, 107. The Crosleys were among a party that left Petrograd on February 24, 1918. Captain Crosley was awarded the Naval Cross for providing the group safe conduct to Sweden. For an account of this harrowing journey, see 277–96.

5. Quoted in Barnes, *Standing on a Volcano*, 243, from J. Butler Wright's diaries held at Princeton University. There is nothing about Imbrie in Wright's diaries, according to an email to this author, May 15, 2015, by Lorraine Lees, coeditor of DeWitt Clinton Poole's memoirs of Bolshevik Russia.

6. Barnes, *Standing on a Volcano*, 183.

7. Quoted in Foglesong, *America's Secret War*, 111.

8. Summers joined the consular service in 1899 and had served in various European and South American posts before being posted to Russia (Poole, *American Diplomat*, xx).

9. The State Department did not formally approve Summers's request for additional consuls until February 1918 (Foglesong, *America's Secret War*, 111–12; Poole, *American Diplomat*, 94n113).

10. Barnes, *Standing on a Volcano*, 189.

11. The building today is also known as the House of Books.

12. Tredwell, "Bolsheviki Days," 9.

13. Tredwell, "Bolsheviki Days," 9.

14. Imbrie, *Behind the Wheel*, 160.

15. FHS, May 6, 1918.

16. Imbrie, "Report on the Petrograd Consulate."

17. Kesaris, *Confidential U.S. Diplomatic Post Records*.

18. Dennis, *Russia in Revolution and Its Lesson to America*. When Dennis returned home, he became the director of Northwestern University's School of Oratory.

19. Some of the information on William Lancaster Jenkins, who rotated between Vologda and Moscow, came from documents on Ancestry.com, such as his passport applications, his World War I draft registration, and passenger lists. Jenkins was not reimbursed by the U.S. Treasury for his lost belongings until 1937. He was in Calcutta with the consular service at the time of Imbrie's final posting, to Persia. Today Trebizond is known as Trabson.

20. Bacino, *Reconstructing Russia*, 56–57.

21. Information on both men's official duties prior to the war comes from their passports.

22. Imbrie, "Report on the Petrograd Consulate"; Langbart, "Five Months in Petrograd," note 8.

23. Imbrie, "Report on the Petrograd Consulate."

24. John W. Davis (London) to the Secretary of State (Charles E. Hughes), March 1, 1921, enclosure: "Confidential Memorandum on British Counter-Revolutionary Activities in Russia" by Z. M. Kennedy, submitted February 21, 1921, RG 165, Entry A1 65, MIS Correspondence, Box 2192, Folder 9771-245.

25. Cheka stood for the All-Russia Extraordinary Commission for Combating Counter-Revolution and Sabotage, abbreviated to Extraordinary Commission—the Ch-K, or Cheka in Russian. The commission was a forerunner of the KGB.

26. The description of Smolny is adapted from chapter 4 of Bryant, *Six Months in Red Russia*.

27. Imbrie, "Report on the Petrograd Consulate." Leon Trotsky was the alias of Lev Davidovich Bronstein.

28. Applebaum, *Gulag*, 9. Vladimir Lenin was the alias of Vladimir Ilyich Ulyanov.

29. Quoted in Rennick, "Imbrie, Acting, in Red Petrograd," SM8.

30. Imbrie, "Report on the Petrograd Consulate."

31. FHS, May 6, 1918.

32. Quoted in Rennick, "Imbrie, Acting, in Red Petrograd," SM8.

33. Imbrie, "Memorandum Regarding the 'Information Service' Established in the Petrograd," December 3, 1918. Attached as Document II in Langbart, "Five Months in Petrograd." A notation on the report indicated that the department sent a copy to Military Intelligence Division on January 15, 1919. A note dated October 3, 1919, by Basil Miles to C. Poole reads, "I have kept this out of the file for the time. It is real romance but highly important to keep quiet until Imbrie gets out of range." By January Imbrie had left Russia. See Langbart, "Five Months in Petrograd," note 38.

34. Undated letter from John Perts to Earl Packer, Earl Packer Papers, Columbia University Libraries Bakhmeteff Archives. John Perts and Earl Packer developed a lifelong friendship. Michael Perts died in Riga in March 1932. When Russia threatened to take over the Baltic states in October 1939, John left Riga and moved permanently to the United States. Imbrie spelled the name Perts, as did John; the Russian name was Akimov-Peretz. FindaGrave.com.

35. Kennan, "Sisson Documents," 130–54.

36. Imbrie, "Report on the Petrograd Consulate."

37. Quoted in Kennan, *Decision to Intervene*, 180.

38. Kennan, *Decision to Intervene*, 180, 228. Kennan dedicated this book to Poole and Summers.

39. Summers's stress was compounded by his wife's family, which hounded him for help. Poole recalled that he had no premonition of Summers's death. Poole, *American Diplomat*, xx, 6.

40. When Francis left Russia, he had to be carried aboard ship on a stretcher. Upon arrival in London, he underwent prostate surgery.

41. Imbrie, "Report on the Petrograd Consulate"; FHS, May 6, 1918.

42. Rennick, "Imbrie, Acting, in Red Petrograd," SM8.

43. Imbrie to Younger, June 7, 1918, Petrograd files, RG 84. Langbart, "Five Months in Petrograd," note 31.

44. Quoted in Langbart, "Five Months in Petrograd," 3. Despite the maverick nature of the story, it was not the first such use of the flag. In mid-August 1914, after the destruction of the German embassy in Petrograd, Chargé d'affaires Charles Wilson, fearing that the Austrian embassy would be ransacked, asked and received permission to raise the American flag to protect lives and property. See West, *Department of State*, 136.

45. Rennick, "Imbrie, Acting, in Red Petrograd," SM8.

46. Quoted in Barnes, *Standing on a Volcano*, 334. David Francis to Imbrie, May 25, 1918, held in the Francis archives at the Missouri Historical Society.

47. Barnes, *Standing on a Volcano*, 336–38.

48. Asgarov, "Reporting from the Frontlines," 59.

49. Barnes, *Standing on a Volcano*, 339. See also Foglesong, *America's Secret War*, 100–103.

50. FHS, September 26, 1918.

51. Imbrie, "Report on the Petrograd Consulate"; FHS, September 26, 1918.

52. Rennick, "Imbrie, Acting, in Red Petrograd," SM8.

53. "Petrograd Facing Winter Hardships," *Washington Star*, November 10, 1918, 10.

54. Rennick, "Imbrie, Acting, in Red Petrograd," SM8.

55. Barnes, *Standing on a Volcano*, 340–41.

56. Poole, *American Diplomat*, 109.

57. Lockhart, *Memoirs of a British Agent*, 299.

58. Imbrie, "Report on the Petrograd Consulate."

59. Quoted in Barnes, *Standing on a Volcano*, 342.

60. In his State of the Union address on January, 25, 1984, President Ronald Reagan said, "Tonight I want to speak to the people of the Soviet Union to tell them: It's true our governments have had serious differences, but our sons and daughters have never fought each other in war." The 1918 Archangel expedition contradicts Reagan's assertion.

61. Boot, *Savage Wars of Peace*, 210, 215, 225. A year later the Red Army numbered three million. The Americans withdrew from North Russia in June 1919; in September the British began withdrawing. On February 20, 1920, the Russian army entered Archangel and two days later took Murmansk.

62. Barnes, *Standing on a Volcano*, 346; Chicherin came from a noble family and had served in the tsarist diplomatic service.

63. Both the Vologda and Archangel provinces became sites of political concentration camps, made notorious by Stalin but dating to Lenin. See Applebaum, *Gulag*, xxxiii.

64. Imbrie, "Report on the Petrograd Consulate."

65. Rennick, "Imbrie, Acting, in Red Petrograd," SM8.

66. Imbrie, "Report on the Petrograd Consulate."

67. Langbart, "Five Months in Petrograd," note 28.

68. See Imbrie to Taylor, June 5, 1918, Petrograd files, RG 84, quoted in Langbart, "Five Months in Petrograd," note 11.

69. Imbrie, "Report on the Petrograd Consulate." The French took a much more active role than the British or Americans in funding anti-Bolshevik activities and providing explosives to destroy rail installations. The French had the most to lose if German troops were released to the Western Front. Poole, *American Diplomat*, 118n24, 138, in Carley, *Revolution and Intervention*.

70. Imbrie, "Report on the Petrograd Consulate."

71. See, for example, "Declaration of War Is Made by Russia against US, Is Report," *Albuquerque Morning Journal*, city ed., 1; "Reds Declare War on America," *New York Times*, August 23, 1918, 3. Three weeks passed between Lenin's speech and its news coverage in America, illustrating the great difficulties in communication.

72. Hengstler to Carr, November 13, 1920, NA, 123 AL 51/162, Box 1207.

73. FHS, May 6, 1918.

74. Imbrie, "Report on the Petrograd Consulate"; FHS, August 15, 1918.

75. Foglesong, *America's Secret War*, 117.

76. Imbrie, "Report on the Petrograd Consulate."

77. Imbrie, "Report on the Petrograd Consulate."

78. DeWitt Clinton Poole to Wilson, September 18, 1918, NA, 861.00/2743, quoted in Asgarov, "Reporting from the Frontlines," 70.

79. Imbrie, "Report on the Petrograd Consulate." The story of these records in recounted in Langley, "Hunt for American Archives," 265–75. See Langbart, "No Little Historic Value," for an elaboration on what happened to the U.S. diplomatic and consular records in Russia after the severance of diplomatic relations.

80. Langley, "Hunt for American Archives," 275.

81. Michael Zirinsky states that Imbrie was expelled from Russia, but the details of his last days there suggest that he escaped to avoid arrest. Zirinsky, "Blood, Power, and Hypocrisy," 277.

82. Imbrie, "Report on the Petrograd Consulate." The primary sources on Cromie are Bainton, *Honoured by Strangers*; Occleshaw, *Dances in Deep Shadows*.

83. Imbrie, "Report on the Petrograd Consulate"; "The Petrograd Terror: Evil Days in Petrograd: How Captain Cromie Died," *Times* (London), October 24, 1918, 6.

84. The much-reduced Norwegian legation left Petrograd in December 1918. Among its members was military attaché Vidkum Quisling, whose name became synonymous with "collaborator." He was executed by the Norwegians after World War II for high treason. Dahl, *Quisling*, 30, 34. As military attaché, he might have transported Imbrie to the train station.

85. Hill, *Go Spy the Land*, 241. It could have happened on August 31.

86. Lockhart, *Memoirs of a British Agent*, ch. 9. Marguerite Harrison, an American journalist with the Associated Press and the *Baltimore Sun*, was imprisoned in Lubyenka in 1920–21. Imbrie met her in Teheran, shortly before his death.

87. Lockhart, *Memoirs of a British Agent*, ch. 10.

88. Hill, *Go Spy the Land*, 228, 230.

89. Asgarov, "Reporting from the Frontlines," 73–74; Barnes, *Standing on a Volcano*, 364. Poole later returned to Russia to relieve David Francis in Archangel, leaving Russia for a final time in June 1919. Poole, *American Diplomat*, xvi.

90. FHS, August 15, 1918.

5. Living with Banquo's Ghost

1. Dukes, *Red Dusk*, 12.

2. Imbrie to the Secretary of State, "Establishment of Consular Office at Viborg, Finland," March 21, 1919, NA, 125.972/1. Much of the information on Imbrie in Finland is taken from this report. Other sources are noted as appropriate. Imbrie left for Finland December 30, 1918. He arrived two months later in Viborg. It is unknown what he did in these two months, though he may have visited London and Paris, where he had friends, including State Department appointees.

3. J. Robert Moskin claims that Imbrie "bizarrely organized an anti-Bolshevik attack from Finland and even schemed to capture Petrograd and Moscow." Moskin, *American Statecraft*, 319, citing Foglesong, *America's Secret War*, 252. This claim seems an overstatement of the evidence. Imbrie, like Ambassador Francis and others in the State Department,

believed that Bolshevism could only be defeated with external force, but Imbrie himself was an observer, not an active conspirator or organizer of an armed attack on Red Russia. See NA, 125.972, 1–3, 20 (Imbrie's telegrams and dispatches from Viborg) and dispatch 3, March 29, 1919, NA, 861.00.8852, cited in Zirinsky, "Blood, Power, and Hypocrisy," 288n11.

4. Foglesong, *America's Secret War*, 124.

5. Imbrie, "Establishment and Operation," NA, 125.972/2.

6. A detailed account of the offensive is given in Brüggemann, "Defending National Sovereignty," 22–51. See also Kukk, "Failure of Iudenich's Northwestern Army," 362–83, for the translation of a letter written by a supply officer in the White Army in 1919. The letter, dated December 4, 1919, is held at the Hoover Institution, Stanford University.

7. See Imbrie, NA, FRUS/Russia/1919, 670–749.

8. Imbrie to Acting Secretary of State (Polk), March 2, 1919, NA, 861.00/4005, telegram, FRUS/Russia/1919, 670–71.

9. Best, "Food Relief," 80–81.

10. Acting Secretary of State (Polk) to Imbrie, March 8, 1919, NA, 861.00/4005, telegram, FRUS/Russia/1919, 673.

11. Acting Secretary of State to Ambassador in France (Sharp), March 18, 1919, NA, 8 61.00/40861/2, FRUS/Russia/1919, 674.

12. Imbrie to the Acting Secretary of State, July 11, 1919, NA, 861.00/4996, FRUS/Russia /1919, 687–91.

13. Imbrie file, NA, notation regarding telegraph, March 21, 1919.

14. Imbrie to Secretary of State, "Political and Economic Situation in Soviet Russia," March 29, 1919, NA, 861.00.8852.

15. Imbrie report of March 4, 1919, included in NA, 861.00/4020, March 11, 1919, from Acting Secretary of State Polk to the Commission to Negotiate Peace regarding the proposal of Dr. Fridtjof Nansen for Relief of Russia under Supervision of Northern Neutrals, FRUS/Russia/1919, 98.

16. Grose, *Gentleman Spy*, 49.

17. Hoover, *Memoirs of Herbert Hoover*, 416.

18. Grose, *Memoirs of Herbert Hoover*, 56.

19. Thompson, *Russia, Bolshevism*, 231.

20. Applebaum, *Red Famine*, 62–63.

21. Tredwell, "Bolsheviki Days," 9. Frederick M. Bailey's memoirs as a British operative contain an account of Tredwell's stay in Tashkent but have some errors such as Tredwell's official position there. See Bailey, *Mission to Tashkent*.

22. DeWitt Clinton Poole to Secretary of State, September 25, 1918, NA, 861.00.2799, FRUS/Russia/1918, 673.

23. "Tredwell was arrested twice in October 1918; he was released within hours the first time but was detained on the second occasion and was not released until May 1919." Poole, *American Diplomat*, 97n119.

24. "Predicts Russia Will Be Reclaimed," *New York Times*, July 26, 1919, 5.

25. In 1922, while Imbrie was stationed in Turkey, Tredwell became the U.S. consul general-at-large for Central Asia and Africa, essentially Imbrie's boss.

26. Imbrie to the Acting Secretary of State, July 11, 1919, NA, 861.00/4996, FRUS/Russia /1919, 690.

27. The Chairman of the American Relief Administration (Hoover) to the Secretary of State, undated, received August 7, 1919, NA, 861.48/918, FRUS/Russia/1919, 698–99.

28. Imbrie to the Acting Secretary of State, July 22, 1919, NA, 861.24/160, telegram, FRUS/Russia/1919, 692.

29. Imbrie to Secretary of State, August 28, 1919, NA, 125.9723.1-2. He was gone from August 30 to September 15, leaving a man named Rarogaiwisz in charge of the Vyborg office. Imbrie to Secretary of State, August 30, 1919, NA, 125.973/4.

30. Brüggemann, "Defending National Sovereignty," 40.

31. Imbrie to Secretary of State, October 22, 1919, NA, 861.00/5454, telegram, FRUS/ Russia/1919, 726.

32. Acting Secretary of State to Vice Consul at Viborg (Imbrie), October 17, 1919, NA, 861.00/5414c, telegram, FRUS/Russia/1919, 725.

33. Acting Secretary of State to the Commission to Negotiate Peace, October 25, 1919, NA, 861.48/982, telegram, FRUS/Russia/1919, 733.

34. Imbrie to the Secretary of State, October 18, 1919, NA, 861.00/5420, telegram; Imbrie to Secretary of State, October 22, 1919, NA, 861.00/5454, telegram, FRUS/Russia/1919, 725–26.

35. The Commission to Negotiate Peace to the Acting Secretary of State, October 23, 1919, NA, 861.48/982, telegram, FRUS/Russia/1919, 729.

36. Imbrie to Acting Secretary of State, October 25, 1919, NA, 861.00/5175, telegram, FRUS/Russia/1919, 732.

37. Imbrie to the Secretary of State, December 15, 1919, NA, 861.43/1050, telegram; Secretary of State to the Commissioner at Riga (Gade), December 15, 1919, NA, 861.48/1035, telegram; Imbrie to the Secretary of State, December 19, 1919, NA, 861.48/1050, telegram; Secretary of State to the Commissioner at Riga, December 31, 1919, NA, 861.48/106, telegram, FRUS/Russia/1919, 748–49.

38. Brüggemann, "Defending National Sovereignty," 45.

39. Kenez, *Civil War in South Russia*, 214–15.

40. See Langbart, "No Little Historic Value." See telegram 69 from Consulate Viborg, July 25, 1919, NA, 124.61/54; dispatch 16 from Consulate Viborg, September 6, 1919, NA, 124.61/59.

41. The following is taken from John W. Davis (London) to the Secretary of State, March 1, 1921, enclosure: "Confidential Memorandum on British Counter-Revolutionary Activities in Russia" by Z. M. Kennedy, submitted February 21, 1921, RG 165, Entry A1 65, MIS Correspondence, Box 2192, Folder 9771-245.

42. The exploits of Sidney Reilly have often been recounted. See, for example, Cook, *Ace of Spies*. Fleming denied that Reilly was the inspiration for Bond.

43. Rustam-Bek, *Aerial Russia*, 4–9.

44. For an account of the British naval attempt to rescue Dukes, see Ferguson, *Operation Kronstadt*. Also see Agar, *Baltic Episode*.

45. Note in Imbrie file, NA, 125.9723/8 regarding 361.1123k38/ Tel. from Viborg, November 29, 1919, #155.

46. Imbrie to Secretary of State, January 1, 1920, NA, 125.9723/9.

47. Felix Cole to Herbert C. Hengstler, February 2, 1920, NA, 125.9723/11.

48. William Thornwell Haynes to Secretary of State, February 20, 1920, NA, 125.9723/12 and 125.9723/13.

49. Asgarov, "Reporting from the Frontlines," 108–9.

50. Imbrie to Secretary of State, June 5, 1920, NA, 125.9723/27; Wilbur J. Carr to Imbrie, October 15, 1920, NA, 125.9723/27. Note the long delay in response to Imbrie's June dispatch. For exceptions to the rules about awards following World War I, see Plischke, *U.S. Department of State*, 341.

51. Dr. Zeidler had been a well-regarded physician in St. Petersburg. When the former prime minister Pyotr Stolypin was shot, Zeidler was called to his deathbed. In 1917 Zeidler returned to Viborg, his birthplace, where he became head of the Special Committee on Russian Affairs in Finland. He was able to raise money for refugees in Paris, based on his reputation. He died in 1940 in Finland.

52. George A. Simons, letter to Roger C. Tredwell, Chief Personnel Branch, Consular Service, October 27, 1920, Imbrie Personnel Corresponds file. Simons probably first met Imbrie in Petrograd, where he had been stationed as a missionary since 1907. Foglesong, "Redeeming Russia," 356.

53. Willett, *Russian Sideshow*, 252.

54. Willett, *Russian Sideshow*, 255–26. See also Miller, *Wild Children of the Urals*. As a personal aside, my mother, Fannie D. Gleeson, helped with the research on this book in her capacity as director of public relations for the St. Louis Bi-State Chapter of the American National Red Cross.

55. Robinson Smith to Roger C. Tredwell, October 20, 1920, attachment to Hengstler to (Wilbur) Carr, November 13, 1920, NA, 123 AL 51/162, Box 1207.

56. Smith to Tredwell, October 20, 1920; also Ebertha Roelofs to Roger C. Tredwell, October 19, 1920, Imbrie Personnel Corresponds file.

57. Robinson Smith farewell address at Viborg, May 7, 1920, Imbrie Personnel Corresponds file.

58. B. Ivanitsky to the United States Ambassador to France, Myron T. Herrick, July 26, 1924, NA, 123 Im 1/170. My translation from the French.

59. Ebertha Roelofs Papers, 1906–1920, Immigration History Research Center Archives, University of Minnesota. Among Roelofs's papers are photographs, which she annotated, depicting the life the Americans led in Finland (IHRC2275). See also "From the Report of Ebertha Roelofs and Gladys Cline."

60. Heath, "Needs of Finland and Esthonia," 11.

61. Hendricks, *Report of the Overseas Committee of the War Work Council*, 92–94.

62. Ebertha Roelofs to Roger Tredwell, October 19, 1920, Imbrie Personnel Corresponds file.

63. Ebertha Roelofs Papers, 1906–1920, IHM document 164-65. Four reports from Roelofs and Cline are in the YWCA records, Sophia Smith Collection, Smith College, Box 708, Folder 2, dated October 1919 to March 1920. Only one concerns her work with Imbrie.

64. Imbrie to Secretary of State, March 15, 1920, NA, 125.9723/14.

65. Imbrie's recommendation of Harold Barlow Quarton as his replacement was approved. "Soviet Russia Fights to Forestall Famine," *Washington Times*, October 6, 1920, 17. In 1922 Quarton was appointed consul at Riga.

66. Wilbur Carr to Imbrie, April 29, 1920, NA, 125.9723/14. See also Imbrie to Secretary of State, May 12, 1920, NA, 125.9723/16. Zirinsky wrote that Imbrie left Finland after "his cover was blown," but he stayed for six months after he learned of his death sentence. See Zirinsky, "Blood, Power, and Hypocrisy," 277.

67. Mary O. Fishbaugh, quoted in "State Department Begins Inquiry," *New York Times*, July 20, 1924, 1.

6. Roaming the Black Sea

1. "Of Maps and Mapmakers," 3.

2. Passenger Lists of Vessels Arriving at New York, New York, 1820–1897, Microfilm Publication M237, 675 rolls; Records of the U.S. Customs Service, NA, RG 36, 1920; Arrival: New York, Microfilm Serial: T715, 1897–1957, Microfilm Roll: Roll 2805, Line: 17, Page Number: 123, Ancestry.com.

3. William Randolph Hearst, "Why Was Root Asked Proper Course as to League of Nations?" *Washington Times*, November 10, 1920, final edition, 1. Three of the four candidates in the 1919 campaign eventually became president—Harding, Calvin Coolidge, and Franklin Delano Roosevelt, their presidencies spanning much of the first half of the twentieth century.

4. Grew, *Turbulent Era*, 406.

5. Roger Tredwell to Herbert Hengstler, September 27, 1920, Imbrie Personnel Corresponds file.

6. Van S. Merle Smith to Newton A. McCully, Rear Admiral, U.S.N., Special Agent of the Department of State, October 15, 1920, Box 1448, NA, 123 Im 1/1a.

7. Charles Allen to Secretary of State, December 6, 1920, Box 1448, NA, 123 Im 1/4. Before leaving Crimea, McCully, although a bachelor, adopted six Russian orphans and brought them to America along with a nanny, also an orphan. See Weeks, *American Naval Diplomat*.

8. Moose, "Russians of Saloniki," 176.

9. Brownell and Billings, *So Close to Greatness*, 140.

10. Bristol had arrived in January 1919 as senior officer of the U.S. naval detachment in Turkish waters. In May he was appointed chief political officer and in August high commissioner. As soon as the political situation in Turkey sorted itself out, the State Department intended to post a diplomatic (as opposed to naval) representative to Turkey, either as minister or ambassador. Bristol stayed until 1927. See also Shenk, *America's Black Sea Fleet*, 42.

11. DeNovo, "Movement," 856.

12. Allen Dulles, quoted in Srodes, *Allen Dulles*, 131.

13. Srodes, *Allen Dulles*, 121.

14. According to one story, oft-repeated by Dulles in later years, when Lenin tried to contact the U.S. embassy in Bern, Dulles, who had scheduled a tennis game, dodged him. The next day Lenin took a train to Petrograd and to revolution. Srodes, *Allen Dulles*, 80–81. Merridale repeats this story in *Lenin on the Train*, 144.

15. Grose, *Gentleman Spy*, 84.

16. Grose, *Gentleman Spy*, 84.

17. Srodes, *Allen Dulles*, 131.

18. Trask, *United States Response*, 29.

19. Srodes, *Allen Dulles*, 126.

20. Imbrie had a running dispute over his salary in Turkey as he had agreed to the posting at a salary of $3,000 with an additional $1,500 for expenses, including a translator. When the posting at Sebastopol fell through due to Wrangel's defeat, Imbrie wanted to retain the $1,500 for expenses in information gathering and was stonewalled by the State Department.

21. Thomas J. Carolan Jr., "History of the Former Consulate Building: Palazzo Corpi," American Foreign Service Association, 2002, c.

22. Solano, "Constantinople Today," 660–61.

23. Shenk, *America's Black Sea Fleet*, 70, 75–76.

24. Mark Bristol to Department of State, December 20, 1921, NA, 123 Im 1/7.

25. The Immigration Act of 1921 is discussed in Hassell, "Russian Refugees"; and Lehtinen, "America Would Lose Its Soul." From 1910 to 1919, 1.1 million Russians emigrated to the United States, compared to 2,463 from 1930 to 1939, a decline of more than 99 percent. Anderson, *Immigration*, 10.

26. Imbrie, quoted in Allen Dulles to Secretary of State, December 10, 1920, NA, 123 Im 1/6.

27. Mark Bristol to the Secretary of State, December 20, 1920, NA, 123 Im 1/7, telegram.

28. Frank C. Lee to Herbert Hengstler, March 7, 1921, detailing December 29, 1920, telegram from Department of State to Mark Bristol, NA, 123 Im 1/13.

29. The letter was written during Prohibition.

30. Imbrie breezily describes his visits to the Russian embassy, even though Gen. Anton Deníkin's aide Romanovsky was assassinated in its lobby in April 1920.

31. The references are to Herbert C. Hengstler, chief of Consular Bureau, and Frank C. Lee, Office of Consular Personnel. During the war Lee had been detailed to Petrograd, Moscow, Stockholm, and Archangel.

32. Constanza was a port on the Black Sea, shipping significant amounts of petroleum products.

33. Robert Imbrie to Roger Tredwell, February 1, 1921, NA, 123 Im 1/12. Imbrie knew Tredwell well enough that he mentioned owing a letter to his mother but was so "unsettled and disturbed" that he hadn't written anyone else. He also referred to receiving a long personal letter from Felix Cole, who had been a vice-consul in Petrograd from 1916 to 1917. Wrangel stayed in Constantinople until 1924 and resettled in Belgium. He died in 1924, perhaps having been poisoned.

34. Moukhanoff, *Nelka*, 964. The marriage date comes from *Social Register* (Social Register Association, 1919), 340.

35. Located at 1801 Massachusetts Ave. N.W. on Embassy Row, the mansion now houses the Sulgrave Club. Nelka often stayed there for the social seasons during 1902–11. Martha Wadsworth prided herself in besting Theodore Roosevelt in a cross-country horse race.

36. Berthlesen, *Tin Can Man*, 123. The destroyers were called "tin cans" because their plates were so thin.

37. Ch. K. Papastathis and E. A. Hekimoglou, "The Great Fire of Thessaloniki (1917)," http://www.academia.edu/2306858/The_Great_Fire_of_Thessaloniki_1917_.

38. Berthelsen does not mention Imbrie being on board for this trip; however, Imbrie wrote that he was at Batum when it fell. The *Smith Thompson* was the only U.S. ship he could have been on. The USS *J. D. Edwards* met the *Smith Thompson* at Batum, and after the two ships parted, it picked up Nelka from an Italian ship. Upon hearing of the fall of Batum, Nelka had left Constantinople to search for Max. By elimination that left the *Smith Thomson* as carrying Imbrie.

39. Berthelsen, *Tin Can Man*, 117.

40. Imbrie to Alexander Munro Barton, April 20, 1921, held in the Alexander Munro Barton files, 92107–10, V, Hoover Institution Archives, Stanford University. Barton hoped Imbrie might find him a job in Turkey when the Chester Concession went through. Charles J. Petherick (d. 1929) was a British citizen who worked for the U.S. State Department for sixty years.

41. After leaving Turkey, Imbrie submitted a voucher for expenses of $517.70, which the government did not pay, as they considered him on leave, but which helps track his movements.

42. *Bulletin of the American Field Service Association*, no. 6 (November 1921), http://www.ourstory.info/library/3-FF/Bulletins/htmls/afsab06.html. At the time End was in business at 3 rue Taitbout. End tried a variety of careers, including farmer and entrepreneur. His last business was as owner of the Rattlesnake Cannery and Emporium in Florida. He died of a rattlesnake bite in 1944.

43. Ancestry.com passenger lists.

44. Wilbur Carr to C. J. Petherick, Deputy United States Despatch Agent, London, England, October 22, 1921, NA, 123 Im 1/24a. At one time Imbrie's collection of daggers, knives, swords, scimitars, and other such weapons hung in Paul Fishbaugh's house in Washington DC, along with Imbrie's service medals, ten in all.

45. "Washington Society," *Chicago Daily Tribune*, December 22, 1921, 15.

46. W. R. (Warren D. Robbins) to Robert Bliss, November 8, 1921, NA, 123 Im 1/43a. Robert Bliss had served in the U.S. embassy in St. Petersburg from 1904 to 1907 and was living in Paris when the war broke out. He and his wife donated an entire section of twenty-three ambulances and three staff cars to the war effort. They also opened and equipped a depot for the distribution of medical and surgical supplies and clothing in Paris. Bliss was third assistant secretary of state from 1921 to 1923. Robbins was acting chief of the Division of Near Eastern Affairs beginning June 14, 1920. He was named chief on December 20, 1921.

47. Henry P. Fletcher to Robert Imbrie, February 9, 1922, NA, 123 Im/26a. Fletcher had been one of Theodore Roosevelt's Rough Riders. He was undersecretary of state at the time of this letter.

48. Imbrie to Alexander Munro Barton, February 13, 1922, Barton files.

49. Mango, *Ataturk*, 310, 327–28. Semyon Ivanovich Aralov used his diplomatic cover in Angora for information gathering. He eventually became Russia's ambassador to the United States.

50. When the house burned down, killing a pet bear, the ambassador variously accused Prime Minister Raouf Bey and a French officer, Colonel Mongin, of arson. Mango, *Ataturk*, 328.

51. The word "genocide" was not coined until 1943, but the phrase "human rights" came out of this tragedy, coined by Woodrow Wilson. Henry Morgenthau, former ambassador to Turkey, used the term "race extermination." For a recent estimate of the number of Armenians killed between 1894 and 1924, see Morris and Ze'Evi, *Thirty-Year Genocide,* 486.

52. Mark Bristol to James L. Barton, chairman of Near East Relief, March 28, 1921, Bristol Papers, General Correspondence, Container 34, Library of Congress. Under Barton's leadership Near East Relief raised over $110 million and saved over one million lives, including those of many Armenians.

53. R. Cook, "United States," 309.

54. Secretary of State to President Harding, May 20, 1922, NA, 867.4016/498, FRUS/Turkey/1922, 921–22.

55. "America to Join European Powers in Turkish Inquiry," *New York Times,* June 4, 1922, 1.

56. Secretary of State to President Harding, May 20, 1922.

57. Imbrie to Secretary of State, June 25, 1922, NA, 123 Im 1/39.

58. Isaac F. Marcosson, "Kemal Pasha: Conflict in Turkey," *Saturday Evening Post,* October 20, 1923, 8–9, 141–42, 144–46, 149, http://www.saturdayeveningpost.com/2012/09/05/archives/kemal-pasha.html.

59. Imbrie, "Crossing Asia Minor," 464. This article is also excerpted in Jenkins, *Worlds to Explore,* 95–101.

60. Imbrie to Fletcher, February 9, 1922, NA, 123 Im/26a.

61. Marcosson, "Kemal Pasha," 8.

62. *American Consular Bulletin* article of September 1923 excerpted in Newberry, *Foreign Service Reader,* 55.

63. The following account on Mustapha Kemal relies on Mango, *Ataturk,* xvi, 182, 194–96, 201, 209, 212–14, 220.

7. Netting Oil

1. Imbrie to Secretary of State, June 25, 1922, NA, 123 Im 1/39. I retained Imbrie's spellings of the ministers' names.

2. Allen Dulles to Undersecretary of State William Phillips, July 26, 1922, NA, Imbrie, Box 1448, no identifying file number.

3. The region attracted mystery men and adventurers, one of whom was Henry Mason Day. Day convinced Bristol and his commercial attaché Julian Gillespie (no relation to Imbrie's wife) that he had been appointed trustee for the Union of Azerbaijan, Georgia, and Armenia and had in addition been given the oil rights, lumber concession, licorice root, and tobacco monopolies for the Caucasus. As trustee, he claimed to be in sole charge of disposing of all the stocks of raw materials in the Caucasus and to be the purchasing agent for these countries. Bristol sent Gillespie's enthusiastic report about Day to the secretary of state, who recommended caution. Later Day appeared in Persia as an agent for Sinclair Oil, and later still he was tried for attempting to rig a jury during the Teapot Dome trials. He received a four-month sentence and a $1,000 fine. Imbrie became involved in the Sinclair Oil efforts to secure Persia's northern oil concessions. See Bristol to Secretary of State, August 30, 1921, NA, 661.115/346 regarding the report on Day as trustee.

4. DeNovo, *American Interests,* 58; FRUS/Russia/1921, 778–84.

5. Mark Malkasian, "Disintegration," 365n100.

6. Bryson, "Admiral Mark L. Bristol," 464.

7. DeNovo, *American Interests*, 217.

8. Kermit Roosevelt was the father of "Kim" Roosevelt, who as a senior officer in the CIA's Middle East Division was involved in the 1953 overthrow of the Mossadegh government in Iran after its parliament voted to nationalize the oil industry. See Kinzer, *All the Shah's Men*.

9. Imbrie to Secretary of State, December 7, 1922, NA, 867.602 Ot 81/239, FRUS/Turkey/1922, 981–83.

10. Prior to the Great War people used business cards and personal cards when traveling to foreign countries, so Kennedy is behind the times, perhaps for his own reasons. Passports and visas came into more universal use with the war.

11. Acting Secretary of State to Mark Bristol, September 17, 1923, NA, 867.602 Ot 81/393, FRUS/Turkey/1922, 1241–43.

12. Imbrie, "Crossing Asia Minor," 445–72.

13. The catastrophic burning of Smyrna is a blot on Turkey's modern history. The story is beyond the province of this book, and there are many good historical accounts of the incident, including Dobkin, *Smyrna*. Reportedly, one of the escapees from the conflagration was a young Aristotle Onassis, future husband of John F. Kennedy's widow. Not all scholars agree that the Turks burned the city. See, for example, Naimark, *Fires of Hatred*.

14. Morris and Ze'Evi, *Thirty-Year Genocide*, 365.

15. Jastrow, *War and the Baghdad Rail Way*, 160.

16. Imbrie, "Crossing Asia Minor," 450.

17. Morris and Ze'Evi, *Thirty-Year Genocide*, 223.

18. Mango, *Atatürk*, 339.

19. Quoted in Morris and Ze'Evi, *Thirty-Year Genocide*, 222.

20. Morris and Ze'Evi, *Thirty-Year Genocide*, 187, 189–90.

21. Morris and Ze'Evi, *Thirty-Year Genocide*, 457–58.

22. Information on Katherine Gillespie's early life comes from federal census and passport records as well as NER's *Team Work*, 1924, https://neareastmuseum.com/archives/page/3/?search_query&tax_collections=relief-workers (click on Katherine's picture). Information on New Bedford's mill industry comes from Pease, *History of New Bedford*; Brian Morris, "New Bedford's Textile Mills: Relics of an Industry That Flourished . . . Then Faded into History," WCAI, NPR Radio, Woods Hole MA, September 23, 2014, http://capeandislands.org/post/new-bedfords-textile-mills-relics-industry-flourishedthen-faded-history#stream/0; Mindy Todd, "New Bedford Textile Mills, Then and Now," WCAI, NPR Radio, Woods Hole MA, September 25, 2014, http://capeandislands.org/post/new-bedford-textile-mills-then-and-now#stream/0.

23. Gillespie left New York on the SS *New Amsterdam* on March 25, 1922. Information accessed on Ancestry.com.

24. The marriage certificate in the U.S. Consular Reports of Marriages identifies the church as the Cathedral of Saint Esprit with Fr. MacGuiness CF presiding. The certificate lists G. Bie Ravndal as witness, Katherine as age twenty-nine, and Imbrie as thirty-eight. In fact, Katherine was a half year older than Robert, and her correct age is on the ship's

manifest when they returned home from Turkey. There seems to be no intent of deception on her part.

25. Mark Bristol to Robert Imbrie, March 7, 1923. See also "Wedded in Constantinople: Miss Gillespie Relief Worker, Bride of Robert Imbrie of Baltimore," *New York Times*, December 31, 1922, 2.

26. FHS, March 15, 1923.

27. Mark Bristol, War Diary, January 5, 1923, Mark L. Bristol Papers, Diaries, Library of Congress, Manuscript Division.

28. "A Box Car," *Time*, May 28, 1923.

29. FHS, March 15, 1923.

30. Lowry, "Diplomatic and Social Life."

31. Mark Bristol to Secretary of State, August 24, 1922, NA, 123 Im 1/41. Also see Bristol to Secretary of State, September 22, 1922, NA, 123 Im 1/43; Charles Hughes to Mark Bristol, October 3, 1922, NA, 123 Im 1/46a.

32. Hughes to Bristol, October 3, 1922.

33. Charles Hughes to Mark Bristol, March 9, 1923, NA, 711.672/14, FRUS/Turkey/1923, 1046–47. Bristol's response follows, 1047–49.

34. Bristol, War Diary, March 13, 1923.

35. Bristol, War Diary, February 26, 1923.

36. "U.S. Consul Detained in Anatolia," *Washington Post*, April 25, 1923, 2.

37. Bristol, War Diary, May 5, 1923.

38. Imbrie to the Secretary of State, December 7, 1922, NA, 867.602 Ot 81/239, FRUS/Turkey/1922, 981–83.

39. Mark Bristol to Charles Hughes, April 16, 1923, NA, 867.602 Ot 81/264, FRUS/Turkey/1923, 1202–4.

40. Bristol, War Diary, May 7, 1923.

41. Mark Bristol to Charles Hughes, May 2, 1923, NA, 867.602 Ot 81/294, FRUS/Turkey/1923, 1209.

42. Robert Imbrie to Charles Hughes, February 20, 1923, quoted in DeNovo, *American Interests*, 225.

43. Rear Admiral C. M. Chester, USN (Ret.) to the Secretary of State, July 22, 1924, NA, 123 Im 1/121.

44. Carter was the temporary minister in charge of the embassy at Constantinople, not the U.S. ambassador. Chester is referring to their association in 1911.

45. "Imbrie on Bolsheviki Death List," *New York Times*, July 22, 1924, 5. See also Emily V. Lorraine to Acting Secretary of State, July 29, 1924, NA, 123 Im/134; Maynard Barnes to Wilbur Carr, June 23, 1923, NA, 123 Im 1/82.

46. Mark Bristol to Secretary of State, June 3, 1923, NA, 123 Im 1/63.

47. Blake had school expenses for two children living in Italy with his first wife; he had hoped to bring his second wife and infant to Angora but found the housing situation impossible. Bristol had hoped that Blake would "realize what an opportunity he had to go to Angora and make a place for himself under conditions that have never existed before under like conditions." Bristol, War Diary, June 22, 1923.

48. Heinrichs, *American Ambassador*, 63.

49. Grew, *Turbulent Era*, 354.

50. Grew, *Turbulent Era*, 355.

51. Georgii Chicherin was replaced for the second session by Vatslav Varovski, thus escaping assassination. On May 10, 1923, Varovski was murdered by Maurice Conradi, a former officer in the Russian army, avenging his father's death at the hands of the Bolsheviks.

52. Heinrichs, *American Ambassador*, 486.

53. Grew, *Turbulent Era*, 554.

54. Heinrichs, *American Ambassador*, 79.

55. Grew, *Turbulent Era*, 572.

56. Quoted in Shenk, *America's Black Sea Fleet*, 45, 50.

57. Grew, *Turbulent Era*, 578.

58. While in Petrograd, Ellis criticized American opposition toward the Bolsheviks. Kennan, *Russia Leaves the War*, 386; Poole, *American Diplomat*, 238n88; William T. Ellis to Charles E. Hughes, June 11, 1923, NA, 123 Im 1/66.

59. Ellis to Hughes, June 11, 1923.

60. "What to Do for Armenia," *Literary Digest*, June 26, 1920, 22–23; Hibben, "How Can We Help Armenia?," 37.

61. Maxwell Blake to Wilbur Carr, June 23, 1923, NA, 123 Im 1/82. Blake was assigned to Angora from April until November 1923. He was then detailed to Melbourne, Australia.

62. Bristol, War Diary, July 24, 1924. Bristol's comments were made to Raymond S. Fredrick of the *Chicago Daily Tribune*.

63. Consul General Ravndal to Charles E. Hughes, June 25, 1923, NA, 123 Im 1/68.

64. "Angora Notes," Anonymous Report, Admiral Mark L. Bristol Papers, Box 61, document MLB164-25, Library of Congress, Manuscript Division. This box is of undated material, but from internal evidence, this particular report is probably from 1923, after Imbrie left Angora. It casts Mustapha Kemal as a dictator, his government as run by a "gang of toughs," and the reform movement as doomed.

65. Ravndal to Hughes, June 25, 1923. Today Bokhara is a region of Uzbekistan.

66. Bryant is sympathetically portrayed by Diane Keaton in the 1981 movie *Reds*.

67. Bristol, War Diary, June 28, 1923.

68. Louise Bryant to Charles Hughes, Secretary of State, July 17, 1923, NA, 123 Im 1/70.

69. Etkind, *Roads Not Taken*, 71.

70. Reed, "Turkey and Her Nationalist Leaders," 86. Also, see Hemingway, *Dateline, Toronto*. Shenk makes the point that Hemingway never got to the interior of Turkey, penning his reports that appear to be eyewitness accounts based on a few days in Constantinople, "some bar conversation, and a few military press conferences, at least one of which, significantly, had been given by Bristol himself." Shenk, *America's Black Sea Fleet*, 253. Shenk also makes the point that Hemingway was sick during much of his stay in Turkey and when not sick "ran with the British."

71. Dearborn, *Queen of Bohemia*, 172–73, 182.

72. Quoted in Reed, "Turkey and Her Nationalist Leaders," 94.

73. Louise Bryant, unpublished Turkey Journal, Louise Bryant Papers, MS 1840, Box 16, Folder 108, Journals and Notebooks, Turkey 1923, Manuscripts and Archives, Sterling Memorial Library, Yale University. This diary was discovered among papers donated by Anne Moen Bullitt, her daughter, to Yale University in 2004. Hemingway filed reports from Constantinople from September to November 1922 and then went to Lausanne, where he filed reports in January and February 1923. Imbrie and Hemingway could have met in Turkey, but there is no evidence of their paths crossing.

74. Bryant, unpublished Turkey Journal, n.p.

75. *American Consular Bulletin* article of September 1923 excerpted in Newberry, *Foreign Service Reader*, 55.

76. Zirinsky claims that Imbrie was recalled to Washington to answer charges, "most notably that he had endangered the life of Louise Bryant." Zirinsky, "Blood, Power, and Hypocrisy," 277. In writing this article Zirinsky did not have access to Bryant's diary.

77. Commendation for Imbrie's work at Angora, June 25, 1923, NA, 123 Im 1/68. See also Bristol, War Diary, May 7, 1923, for another commendation of Imbrie.

78. Bristol, War Diary, June 25, 1923.

79. Secretary of State Charles E. Hughes to William T. Ellis, June 11, 1923, NA, 123 Im 1/66.

80. Venn, "Oleaginous Diplomacy," 424. Also see Hughes to American Mission, Lausanne, December 16, 1922, NA, 890G.6363T84/67, M722/24.

81. Secretary of State Frank B. Kellogg to Senator William E. Borah, Committee on Foreign Relations, December 29, 1926, FRUS 1926, vol. 2, 968–90.

82. Demirici, "Lausanne Conference," 162.

83. William T. Ellis to Charles E. Hughes, April 25, 1923, NA, 123 Im 1/66. Ellis left London on August 4. Ancestry.com passenger lists. Ironically Katherine was on the same ship as Ellis; Robert Imbrie sailed separately, probably to return quickly to address State Department concerns. According to Mary O. Fishbaugh, Imbrie arrived home in July 1923. "State Department Begins Inquiry," *New York Times*, July 20, 1924, 1.

84. Allen Dulles to William Phillips, September 18, 1923, NA, 123 Imbrie 1/263, memorandum.

85. Imbrie to Secretary of State, August 25, 1925, NA, 123 Im 1/72.

86. Imbrie to Secretary of State, August 25, 1923.

87. One of the journalists was Isaac R. Marcosson of the *Saturday Evening Post*, whose interview with Mustafa Kemal occurred on Friday, June 13. His article on his trip to Angora appeared in the magazine's October 20, 1923, issue. Others were Frazier Hunt, European manager of Hearst's International; Edward George Lowery, editor-in-chief of the *Philadelphia Public Ledger*; Larry Rue of the *Chicago Tribune*; and Clarence Streit, Constantinople manager of the *Philadelphia Public Ledger*. Marcosson had visited Bristol before going to Angora and was told he should plan on staying at least three weeks to understand the situation properly. Bristol felt that American newspapers were printing anti-Turkish propaganda and needed to know that the future of the Near East depended on solving economic problems. Bristol, War Diary, June 15, 1923.

88. Halsey, *Admiral Halsey's Story*, x, 44.

89. HGD (Harry G. Dwight) to Herbert C. Hengstler, August 21, 1923, Imbrie Personnel Corresponds file.

90. "Says Ellis Was Agitator," *New York Times*, June 27, 1919, 7.

91. Bristol to Secretary of State, September 24, 1923, NA, 123 Im 1/74.

92. A. Cook, *Ace of Spies*, 312.

93. Imbrie to Herbert C. Hengstler, August 11, 1923, NA, 123 Im 1/69, appended note by Hughes.

94. Morgenthau, *Ambassador Morgenthau's Story*, 275.

95. William T. Ellis, "Transformations Make Turkey Wonder of the Modern World," *Sunday Star* (Washington DC), July 31, 1938. Photocopy filed in Imbrie Personnel Corresponds file, sent by Katherine Imbrie to Gardiner Howland Shaw at the State Department. Shaw served as Bristol's translator.

96. William Ellis to Richard Southgate, Chief, Near East Division, June 8, 1925, NA, 123 Im 1/460.

97. Imbrie to Wilbur Carr, October 26, 1923, NA, 123 Im 1/75.

98. "State Department Begins Inquiry," *New York Times*, July 20, 1924, 1; Allen Dulles to William Phillips, October 23, 1923, Imbrie Personnel Corresponds file.

99. Imbrie to Wilbur Carr, January 2, 1924, NA, 123 Im 1/79a.

100. Supreme Court of the District of Columbia: Last Will and Testament of Robert Whitney Imbrie written on October 31, 1923, and filed on September 30, 1924. He left his estate to his wife and named her executer. Imbrie to Wilbur Carr, January 26, 1924, NA, 123 Im 1/79. Imbrie hoped to get away in mid-February but was delayed. See Ancestry.com for passenger list.

8. Before the Last Picnic

1. Kelly, *Diplomacy and Murder*, 159. Griboyedov was double-crossed in his assignment to repatriate the defectors, who were massacred by Russian authorities on returning home, foreshadowing Stalin's slaughter of returned prisoners of war in 1945.

2. Kelly, *Diplomacy and Murder*, 197.

3. Griboyedov's murder was referred to by news media in the aftermath of the murder of Andrey Karlov, ambassador to Turkey, in Ankara on December 19, 2016.

4. Bernstein, "American Hero in Iran," 23–25. See also Shuster, *Strangling of Persia*, xli.

5. Yerkin, *Prize*, 113.

6. Yerkin, *Prize*, 115.

7. Yerkin, *Prize*, 129.

8. DeNovo, *American Interests*, 284.

9. Yerkin, *Prize*, 119, 121.

10. For a full account of Anglo-Persian's formation, see Yerkin, *Prize*, ch. 8.

11. "Sinclair Oil Gets Persian Oil Grant," *Wall Street Journal*, December 28, 1923, 9.

12. Yerkin, *Prize*, 94.

13. DeNovo, *American Interests*, 284.

14. Yerkin, *Prize*, 196.

15. Yerkin, *Prize*, 194.

16. Yerkin, *Prize*, 196.

17. DeNovo, "Movement," 856.

18. Leonard M. Fanning, "Petroleum," *Encyclopedia Britannica*, 1922. One barrel equates to forty-two U.S. gallons.

19. DeNovo, "Movement," 865; Yerkin, *Prize*, 117.

20. DeNovo, "Movement," 865.

21. DeNovo, "Movement," 857.

22. DeNovo, "Movement," 867–68.

23. DeNovo, "Movement," 868–69.

24. Imbrie to American Legation, Teheran, March 25, 1924, NA, 123 Im 1/80c, telegram. Also see Consul W. Wilbur Keblinger to Secretary of State, July 25, 1924, NA, 123 Im 1/200, with clippings from Indian newspapers.

25. *Earthly Powers* by Anthony Burgess provides some of the travel details in this paragraph. On board Imbrie's ship to London was Consul Leland Morris and his family, headed to Cologne. Morris in 1945 became the first U.S. ambassador to Iran.

26. Rinehart, *Nomad's Land*, 127.

27. Rinehart, *Nomad's Land*, 135.

28. Rinehart, *Nomad's Land*, 159.

29. Rinehart, *Nomad's Land*, 159–60.

30. Details for this part of the Imbries' journey are based on Reginald Teague-Jones's trip taken in 1925 as he drove a Ford from Baghdad through Persia to India. See Teague-Jones, *Adventures in Persia*, 55–111.

31. Imbrie to Felix Harold Smith, February 8, 1907.

32. Wilbur Carr to Imbrie, January 2, 1924, NA, 123 Im 1/79a.

33. Herbert C. Hengstler to Imbrie, January 21, 1924, NA, 123 Im 1/75b; Imbrie to Secretary of State, May 12, 1924, NA, 123 Im 1/84; passenger lists on Ancesry.com. After Imbrie's death Gotlieb came to Washington DC from his home in New York to confer with the State Department. When the *Washington Post* tracked him to the Capitol Park Hotel, he refused to discuss the case. "Persia to Send Imbrie Body to United States," *Washington Post*, August 3, 1924, 3.

34. Persia had had an earlier American adviser, William Morgan Shuster, from December 1910 to December 1911, when he was removed at the instigation of the Russians. He was highly regarded by the Persians but was unavailable for another Persian mission in 1922.

35. Millspaugh, *American Task in Persia*, 92.

36. Ambassador Henry S. Villard, Oral History Interview by Dimitri Villard, Association for Diplomatic Studies and Training, Foreign Affairs Oral History Project, initial interview July 18, 1991, copyright 1998, accessed January 7, 2015, http://lcweb2.loc.gov/service/mss/mfdip/2004/2004vil01/2004vil01.pdf.

37. Millspaugh, *American Task in Persia*, 161.

38. Millspaugh, *American Task in Persia*, 213.

39. Millspaugh, *American Task in Persia*, 189.

40. Zirinsky, "Blood, Power, and Hypocrisy," 281.

41. Ferrier and Bamberg, *History of the British Petroleum Company*.

42. DeNovo, *American Interests*, 284.

43. David Starr Jordon to the Secretary of State, July 18, 1925, NA, 123 Im 1/462.

44. For an in-depth treatment of the Standard Oil–Sinclair rivalry, see Rubin, "Stumbling through the 'Open Door,'" 203–29.

45. Ghani, *Iran and the Rise*, 277.

46. DeNovo, *American Interests*, 285.

47. David Starr Jordon to Secretary of State, July 18, 1925, NA, 123 Im 1/462. Soper's account was dated Moscow, March 31, 1925. Dulles requested permission to use it in the congressional hearings of 1926 regarding the Trenton Fund, described in a later chapter. Soper visited the State Department on October 7, 1924; see Kellogg to Jordan, July 30, 1925, NA, 123 Im 1/462.

48. Imbrie report, June 11, 1924, NA, 891.6363-SO/370, quoted in Majd, *Oil and the Killing*, 233–37.

49. Ghani, *Iran and the Rise*, 21–22.

50. Ghani, *Iran and the Rise*, 53.

51. Ghani, *Iran and the Rise*, 105.

52. Ghani, *Iran and the Rise*, 53–54.

53. Imbrie report, June 11, 1924, NA, 891.6363-SO/370, quoted in Majd, *Oil and the Killing*, 236–37.

54. Imbrie report, June 11, 1924, NA, 891.6363-SO/370, quoted in Majd, *Oil and the Killing*, 237.

55. Ghani, *Iran and the Rise*, 17.

56. Amanat, *Iran*, 413.

57. Ghani, *Iran and the Rise*, 56.

58. Wilber, *Riza Shah Pahlavi*, 12. Zirinsky identifies this biography as "the only full-scale biography" of Reza Khan, but "uncritical" and "Pro-Pahlavi," written "with the support of the Pahlavi family" (Zirinsky, "Riza Shah's Abrogation," 97; Zirinsky, "Rise of Reza Khan," 44).

59. Wilber, *Riza Shah Pahlavi*, 6–12.

50. Wilber, *Riza Shah Pahlavi*, 41, 47n4.

61. Wilber, *Riza Shah Pahlavi*, 11.

62. Ghani, *Iran and the Rise*, 151–52.

63. Ghani, *Iran and the Rise*, 215–16.

64. Wilber, *Riza Shah Pahlavi*, 54.

65. Atabaki and Zurcher, *Men of Order*, 10.

66. Fischel, "Jews of Persia," 119. For a discussion of the Jewish population in Persia at the start of the twentieth century, see Tsadik, *Between Foreigners and Shi'is*, 6–8.

67. Tsadik, *Between Foreigners and Shi'is*, 178.

68. Zirinsky, "Rise of Reza Khan," 282.

69. It may be recalled that Imbrie belonged to a prominent Presbyterian church in Washington DC.

70. Moore, *From Moscow*, 228–29.

71. Imbrie report, July 14, 1924, NA, 891.00/1297, quoted in Majd, *Oil and the Killing*, 241–43.

72. The number of mourners was estimated at 30,000 in a city of 150,000. Imbrie report, July 14, 1924, NA, 891.00/1297, quoted in Majd, *Oil and the Killing*, 241–43.

73. Wallace Smith Murray to State Department, January 8, 1925, NA, 834.891.404/1, dispatch, quoted in Majd, *Oil and the Killing*, 277.

74. Murray to State Department, January 8, 1925.

75. Imbrie report, July 14, 1924, NA, 891.00/1297, quoted in Majd, *Oil and the Killing*, 241–43.

76. Katherine Imbrie to Charles Hughes, Secretary of State, August 14, 1924, NA, 123 Im 1/255.

77. See Dinnerstein, *Antisemitism in America*, for more on anti-Semitism at the time.

78. Murray succeeded Allen Dulles as chief of what by then was the Near East and African Affairs Department and served as ambassador to Iran at the start of the Cold War, 1945–46.

79. Frances Packard to F. H. Smith, August 24, 1924.

80. Katherine Imbrie to Calvin Coolidge, letter and enclosures, January 24, 1925, NA, 123 Im 1/419.

81. Katherine Imbrie to Calvin Coolidge, letter and enclosures, January 24, 1925, NA, 123 Im 1/419.

82. Packard to Smith, August 24, 1924.

9. Death on Distant Service

1. The following information is taken from Baedeker, *Russia with Tehran*, and from the 11th edition of the *Encyclopedia Britannica*.

2. Soper's account came as an enclosure from David Starr Jordan to Secretary of State, July 12, 1925, NA, 123 Im 1/462. The account was dated Moscow, March 31, 1925.

3. "Imbrie Murder Laid to Religious Hate," *New York Times*, July 24, 1924, 2.

4. In a significant deviation from other accounts, my account relies on the court testimony of Melvin Seymour more than the depositions taken by Kornfeld on July 18 and July 22 from the chauffeur and legation guard, which seem self-serving and questionable. Further, Kornfeld did not press these men in places that would have clarified their roles. Both men told Kornfeld that they had stayed for a time with Imbrie before running off. The guard claimed that his American insignia was torn off his coat, including his buttons, allowing him to meld into the crowd and escape. That seems rather too neat. According to Seymour, when Imbrie's party arrived at the fountain, Imbrie, Seymour, and the consulate guard exited the carriage, leaving behind only the driver, yet Seymour says a carriage with two men picked them up in their flight. He implies they were unknown to him. Kornfeld to Secretary of State, July 27, 1924, NA, 123 Im 1/201, depositions of Habibullah, Teki eh Dabag Kaneh, and Aga Ala-ed-Din, witnessed by Kornfeld, Murray, and Lieutenant Nematullah.

5. Katherine Imbrie to Charles Hughes, Secretary of State, August 14, 1924, NA, 123 Im 1/255.

6. A *New York Times* article quoted Imbrie's aunt stating that Imbrie was on a *National Geographic* assignment when he was killed. The *National Geographic* magazine had devoted its April 1921 issue to Persia, and it is doubtful that they would do another story so soon. The next story on Persia/Iran did not occur until 1933. Imbrie may, however, have been

taking pictures for a National Geographic Society lecture similar to the one he had delivered on Turkey during his home stay. "State Department Begins Inquiry," *New York Times*, July 20, 1924, 1. The color of Imbrie's camera could refer to a shellac finish.

7. In his passport picture after Imbrie's death, Seymour looks forlorn, far from pugnacious.

8. Zirinsky, "Blood, Power, and Hypocrisy," 275. About sixteen months after Imbrie's murder, Seymour applied for a passport at the U.S. consulate in Teheran, which Dr. Packard witnessed, and on February 24, 1925, he arrived in San Francisco, having left Hong Kong on January 31. He settled in California to continue his life as an oil worker and died in 1959. He was described in one newspaper as Imbrie's secretary. See the *Lincoln (NE) Evening Journal*, March 7, 1925, 2.

9. Katouzian, "Miracles at the *Saqqa-khanih*," 299.

10. Joseph Saul Kornfeld, dispatch, July 27, 1924, depositions, NA, 123 Im 1/201.

11. Joseph Saul Kornfeld, dispatch, July 27, 1924, depositions.

12. Zirinksy, "Blood, Power, and Hypocrisy," 275.

13. Joseph Saul Kornfeld to Secretary of State, July 27, 1924, deposition of Mirza Mohammed, munshi (secretary) of the British Consulate.

14. Joseph Saul Kornfeld, dispatch, July 27, 1924, depositions. One witness, a prominent Italian, said that one shot was fired in the forty-five-minute attack. Kornfeld, telegram 65, July 26, 1924, NA, 123 Im 1/113.

15. Frances Packard to F. H. Smith, August 24, 1924.

16. Joseph Saul Kornfeld to Secretary of State, telegram 61, July 24, 1924, 5:00 p.m., NA, 123 Im 1/106.

17. Packard to Smith, August 24, 1924.

18. These five wounds would be of major importance in the investigation.

19. Packard to Smith, August 24, 1924.

20. The details of Imbrie's injuries are taken from Packard's postmortem performed the next day with Arthur Richard Neligan, physician to the British legation. Kornfeld to Secretary of State, July 27, 1924; the enclosures included the Post Mortem Report signed July 20, 1924. Neligan had been in Persia since 1906 and founded the first pathology laboratory in Teheran.

21. Katherine Imbrie thought the crowd mistook him for a Muslim because he was circumcised.

22. David Starr Jordan to the Secretary of State, July 12, 1925, NA, 123 Im 1/462. Enclosure written by Soper, dated Moscow, March 31, 1925.

23. Whiteman, *Damages in International Law*, 566n142. See also NA, 391.1113 Seymour/Melvin/11 enclosures, quoted in Whiteman.

24. Katherine Imbrie to Secretary of State, July 18, 1924, NA, 123 Im 1/86, telegram.

25. Grew, *Turbulent Era*, 658n6. Hughes was in Europe attending an international law conference. Grew's composure served him well. He was the U.S. ambassador to Japan when Pearl Harbor was bombed. He and his staff were confined to the U.S. embassy compound in Tokyo until June 1942, when they were traded for Japanese diplomats.

26. Katherine Imbrie to Calvin Coolidge, letter and enclosures, January 24, 1925, NA, 123 Im 1/419.

27. Villard, Oral History Interview, July 18, 1991.

28. Kornfeld, telegram 52, July 18, 1924, 6:00 p.m., NA, 123 Im 1/87.

29. Joseph Saul Kornfeld to Secretary of State, July 26, 1924, NA, 123 Im 1/113, telegram.

30. Kornfeld to Secretary of State, July 19, 1924, NA, 123 Im 1/88, telegram.

31. Kornfeld to Secretary of State, July 20, 1924, 5:00 p.m., NA, 123 Im 1/90, telegram. Moharem (Muharram) is the first month of the year in the Islamic calendar and is considered sacred.

32. Joseph C. Grew to American Legation, Persia, July 19, 1924, 1:30 p.m., NA, 123 Im 1/101d, telegram.

33. Grew to American Legation, Persia, July 19, 1924, NA, 123 Im 1/101c, telegram.

34. Millspaugh, *American Task in Persia*, 215.

35. Millspaugh, *American Task in Persia*, 223.

36. Millspaugh, *American Task in Persia*, 223.

37. Zirinsky, "Blood, Power, and Hypocrisy," 282.

38. Wallace Smith Murray to Secretary of State, August 5, 1924, NA, 123 Im 1/145.

39. Turlington, "Financial Independence of Persia," 658–67.

40. Naficy, "Lured by the East," 124, 127, 133. The film was first shown in Iran after Reza Shah's overthrow in 1941 in a forty-minute sound version featuring Nicolay Rimsky-Korsakov's *Scheherazade* as the soundtrack and a Persian-language voice-over narration. The film was popular with Iranians, some of whom recognized themselves in the film as children. Naficy, "Lured by the East," 135.

41. *Grass* is considered one of the best films of 1925, a year that also saw the release of John Ford's *The Iron Horse* and Charlie Chaplin's *The Gold Rush*, and is regarded by some historians as a "classic" of documentary cinema, second only to Robert Flaherty's *Nanook of the North*. Two of the cinematographers went on to make the 1933 epic *King Kong*. Imbrie's notarization appears at 1:09:58 of the film. Naficy, "Lured by the East," 133–34.

42. "Maj. Imbrie Beaten and Cut to Death by Fanatical Mob," *Washington Star*, July 20, 1924, 1.

43. Lewis K. Davis to Charles Hughes, July 24, 1924, NA, 123 Im 1/112.

44. "Denies Imbrie Offended," *New York Times*, August 4, 1924.

45. "Denies Imbrie Offended," 15.

46. Wilbur Carr to John Oliver La Gorce, July 28, 1924, NA, 123 Im 1/150a.

47. "Biographical Sketch," *Relief of Katherine Imbrie*, Serial Set ID: 8690 H.rp., February 10, 1927, 4 pages.

48. David Starr Jordan to Charles Hughes, letter and enclosure, July 18, 1924, NA, 123 Im 1/462. Memoirs of the period frequently refer to cameras; the number of photographs from this period also attests to the common use of cameras.

49. George Gregg Fuller, "Persian Foreign Sentiment as Shown during Journey," October 19, 1924, 3, Correspondence American Consulate, Teheran, NA, C 8-5.17 1924, part 2.

50. Zirinsky, "Blood, Power, and Hypocrisy," 288n2.

51. Four reels of cuts exist for the documentary *Lure of the East*, which traces an expedition by car from Leeds to India in 1924. Reel 4 of cuts opens with intertitles: "The Barracks, built somewhat on Russian lines, in front of which the fatal attack on Major Imbrie took

place—The Authorities here were most nervous for our safety and insisted on an armed escort accompanying us anywhere we went." "Lure of the East Cuts, Reel 4, 1924," British Pathé, http://www.britishpathe.com/video/lure-of-the-east-cuts-reel-4/query/Imbrie.

52. Wallace Smith Murray to Secretary of State, July 23, 1924, appended unsigned note, probably Grew, NA, 123 Im 1/101.

53. "Promises Death for Slayers," *New York Times*, July 21, 1924, 1. See also H. S. Tavshanjian to Secretary of State, September 30, 1924, enclosure sent by Charles Jefferson, company representative, NA, 123 Im 1/277. While on reconnaissance, Imbrie often wore native headgear, but on the day he died, he wore a pith helmet.

54. Imperial Legation of Persia, Washington DC, to Grew, Acting Secretary of State, enclosure, July 21, 1924, NA, 123 Im 1/97.

55. Joseph Saul Kornfeld to Secretary of State, telegram 70, July 29, 4:00 p.m., NA, 123 Im 1/122.

56. Dr. Packard to Hoffman Philip, February 8, 1926, enclosure in Hoffman Philip to Secretary of State, February 11, 1926, NA, 123 Im 1/497. The attack was widely reported in newspapers, although Packard's eyewitness account seems the most reliable. See, for example, "Persian Youth Hurls Stones at Imbrie's Widow and the Tehran Police Take No Action," *New York Times*, July 25, 1924, 1.

57. Park, "Robert Imbrie Case," 50.

58. "Mrs. Imbrie Insulted in Teheran: Persian Xenophobia," *Times* (London), July 26, 1924, 12.

59. Joseph C. Grew to American Legation, July 25, 1924, NA, 123 Im 1/127c, quoted in Majd, *Oil and the Killing*, 286.

60. Wallace Smith Murray to Secretary of State, July 26, 1924, 12:00 p.m., NA, 123 Im 1/110.

61. Katherine Imbrie to Charles Hughes, August 14, 1924, NA, 123 Im 1/255.

62. Wallace Smith Murray to Secretary of State, July 28, 1924, 4:00 p.m., NA, 123 Im 1/117, telegram.

63. Lenczowski, *Middle East in World Affairs*, 131.

64. Lenczowski, *Middle East in World Affairs*, 131.

65. This rumor reemerged after Reza Khan ascended the throne. Junius Ward, "New Shah Blamed in Imbrie Murder: Rezi Khan Accused of Starting Riots in Which Consul Lost His Life," cable to the *Washington Star* and *Chicago Daily News*, Teheran, December 18, 1925, NA, 123 Im 1/496.

66. Katherine Imbrie to Calvin Coolidge, letter and enclosures, January 24, 1925, NA, 123 Im 1/419.

67. Wallace Smith Murray to Secretary of State, August 10, 1924, 123 Im 1/298.

68. Wallace Smith Murray to Secretary of State, July 24, 1924, NA, 891.51/351, telegram, FRUS/Persia/1924, 547.

69. Wallace Smith Murray to Secretary of State, September 19, 1924, NA, 891.51/361 No. 647, FRUS/Persia/1924, 548; Dulles memorandum, September 18, 1924, NA, 891.6363-SO/382, FRUS/Persia/1924: October 17, number 153.

70. Wallace Smith Murray to Secretary of State, July 29, 1924, 10:00 a.m., NA, 123 Im 1/118, telegram.

71. Park, "Robert Imbrie Case," 49–50.

72. Joseph Saul Kornfeld to Secretary of State, enclosures, August 6, 1925, NA, 123 Im 1/248.

73. Frances Packard to F. H. Smith, August 24, 1924.

74. Sherman Miles to Assistant Chief of Staff, G-2, August 31, 1924, NA, 123 Im 1/290.

75. State Department to Joseph Saul Kornfeld, March 10, 1924, NA, 123 Im 1/81, telegram.

76. Correspondence, American Consulate, Teheran, NA, C 8-5.17 1924, part 2.

77. Mr. G. S. Arora, Correspondence, American Consulate, Teheran, NA, C 8-5.17 1924, part 2.

78. George Gregg Fuller to G. S. Arora, Correspondence, American Consulate, Teheran, NA, C 8-5.17 1924, part 2.

79. Joseph C. Grew to American Legation, Teheran, August 7, 1924, NA, 123 Im 1/154. See Katherine Imbrie to Charles Hughes, August 7, 1924, NA, 123 Im 1/154.

80. "U.S.S. Trenton Leaves Tomorrow," *Brooklyn Daily Eagle*, May 23, 1924, 3.

81. Katherine Imbrie to Allen Dulles, December 9, 1925, NA, 123 Im 1/474; Dulles to Katherine Imbrie, December 17, 1925, NA, 123 Im 1/474.

82. "High Honors for Imbrie," *New York Times*, August 18, 1924, 13.

83. Miles noted that the cannon fire at the parade ground and later at the border between Persia and Iraq was irregular, but he concluded it was probably the best salute possible, given the muzzle-loaders. Miles report, August 31, 1924, NA, 123 Im 1/290.

84. Wallace Smith Murray, dispatch 651, September 22, 1924, NA, 123 Im 1/315. Ruhollah Khan served as Miles's translator during the investigation.

85. Constantine Brown, "Memory of Imbrie Honored by Official French Salute," *Scranton Republic*, September 15, 1924, 11; John Randolph to Secretary of State, August 22, 1924, NA, 123 Im 1/204; Randolph to Secretary of State, April 4, 1925, NA, 123 Im 1/452.

86. Joseph Saul Kornfeld to Secretary of State, August 24, 1924, NA, 123 Im 1/209.

87. John Bouchal to Secretary of State, August 14, 1924, NA, 123 Im 1/234. It was important to get the *Trenton* through the canal without delay because its propellers projected twelve feet from either side, and if it were moored in the canal, a wind could force the ship to brush against the bank and snap the blades. Bouchal to Secretary of State, August 24, 1924, NA, 123 Im 1/210.

88. George Gregg Fuller to Secretary of State, August 31, 1924, NA, 123 Im 1/224.

89. Launches could touch the shore at Bushire; steamers needed a minimum distance from shore of six miles, and a man-of-war needed twelve miles.

90. When the chief of staff objected to firing salutes in Teheran and Bushire, Murray reminded him of the murder of Griboyedov in 1829 and the resulting retribution and recompense. The chief of staff said no more. Miles report, August 31, 1924, NA, 123 Im 1/290.

91. George Gregg Fuller, dispatch 51, August 30, 1924, NA, 123 Im 1/279. The first U.S. warship entered the Persian Gulf in 1879, the *Ticonderoga*, which was on a round-the-world cruise meant to spread American ideals and ideas and to exhibit American strength. It was a sloop and not a battleship, nor was it there as part of an international incident. Hence, the validity of Fuller's claim in his dispatch.

92. Details on the HMS *Crocus* come from "Imbrie's Body Leaves Persia amid Salutes," *Washington Post*, August 27, 1924, 2.

93. Later Katherine contested this detail, claiming ten guns were fired, not twenty-one. The detail became part of her case in her attempt to claim the money in the Trenton Fund, discussed in the next chapter.

94. George Gregg Fuller to Secretary of State, August 30, 1924, NA, 123 Im 1/279; see also Whiteman, *Damages in International Law*, 138. Also, Miles report, August 31, 1924, NA, 123 Im 1/290.

95. Brown, "Memory of Imbrie Honored," 11.

96. "Service for Imbrie in Nice," *New York Times*, September 16, 1924, 23.

97. Paul Fishbaugh to Katherine Imbrie, September 25, 1924, NA, 123 Im 1/335; "Imbrie Body Reaches Quantico," *New York Times*, September 29, 1924, 17; "Coolidge Attends Imbrie's Funeral," *New York Times*, September 30, 1924, 12.

98. Wilbur J. Carr, assistant secretary of state; Evan E. Young, chief of the Division of Eastern European Affairs; Allen W. Dulles, chief of the Division of Near Eastern Affairs; Herbert C. Hengstler, chief of the Foreign Service, Division of Foreign Service Administration; John Oliver La Gorce, vice president of the National Geographic Society and an editor of the *National Geographic* magazine; Otis H. Gate, an attorney with the Office of the Solicitor, U.S. Department of Agriculture; and Charles E. Howe, treasurer, American Security and Trust Company of Washington DC; J. B. Ford Jr. remains unidentified in regard to Imbrie.

99. Allen Dulles, memo, "Honorary Pallbearers at Imbrie Funeral," September 27, 1924, NA, 123 Im 1/272.

100. Charles Hughes to American Legation, Teheran, September 30, 1924, NA, 123 Im 1/275a, telegram. Also, *Obituary Record of Yale Graduates, 1924–1925*, Bulletin of Yale University, 21st series, no. 22, August 1, 1925, http://mssa.library.yale.edu/obituary_record/1859_1924/1924-25.pdf.

101. "Coolidge Attends Imbrie's Funeral," 12. This source says that Major Miles was with Katherine on the *Trenton*.

102. Charles Mason Remey, Imbrie memorial, *Star of the West* 15, no. 9 (December 1924): 250, http://bahai.works/Star_of_the_West/Volume_15/Issue_9, 250.

103. R. K. Cravens, Adjutant General's Office, War Department to Division of Near Eastern Affairs, September 25, 1924, NA, 123 Im 1/268. The Imbrie grave is off Pershing Drive in section 4, grave 2903. Katherine Imbrie was told that two plots (for her and her husband) adjacent to her husband's father were not available, but J. Rankin Imbrie is buried at Glenwood Cemetery, Washington DC, not at Arlington.

104. Soper's words. David Starr Jordan to the Secretary of State, July 12, 1925, NA, 123 Im 1/462. Enclosure written by Soper, dated Moscow, March 31, 1925.

105. Hughes to American Legation, Teheran, September 26, 1924, NA, 123 Im 1/268a. To get a sense of the importance that the government assigned to Imbrie's death, when Arthur S. Cheney and his wife were killed in the collapse of the consulate in the 1908 earthquake in Messina in Sicily, the only representative of the federal government to attend their funeral was Herbert Hengstler, chief of the Consular Bureau. "Late Consul and His Wife Buried," *Marion (OH) Star*, January 30, 1909, 3; "Robert W. Imbrie," *American Foreign Service Journal*, November 1924, 1.

10. Pursuit of Adequate Justice

1. Sherman Miles report, August 31, 1924, NA, 123 Im 1/290.

2. Wallace Smith Murray to Secretary of State, telegram 16, July 29, 1924, NA, 123 Im 1/118.

3. Miles refers to the officer as Col. Hassan Agha. Miles report.

4. Miles identifies the officer as Lt. Col. Saifollah Mirza. Miles report.

5. Miles report.

6. Wallace Smith Murray to Secretary of State, telegram 16, August 13, 1924, NA, 123 Im 1/173.

7. Sherman Miles to Assistant Chief of Staff, G-2, August 31, 1924, NA, 123 Im 1/290.

8. Joseph Saul Kornfeld, telegram 96, August 13, 1924, NA, 123 Im 1/183.

9. Charles Hughes to Joseph Saul Kornfeld, instruction 69, August 16, 1924, NA, 123 Im 1/183.

10. Zirinsky, "Blood, Power, and Hypocrisy," 283.

11. Wallace Smith Murray to Secretary of State, telegram 3, July 24, 1924, NA, 23 Im 1/104.

12. Wallace Smith Murray to Secretary of State, September 16, 1924, NA, 123 Im 1/313, Murray's emphasis.

13. Sherman Miles to Assistant Chief of Staff, G-2, August 31, 1924, NA, 123 Im 1/290.

14. The summary of action to secure justice for Imbrie's murder comes from the following: Wallace Smith Murray, telegram 645, August 31, 1924, NA, 123 Im 1/229; Murray, telegram 118, September 13, 1924, NA, 123 Im 1/249; Murray to Secretary of State, dispatch 645, September 16, 1924, NA, 123 Im 1/313.

15. Sworn statement by Melvin Seymour, July 25, 1924, NA, 123 Im 1/218; Persians referred to this position as orderly officer. See also Miles report.

16. Wallace Smith Murray to Secretary of State, dispatch 645, September 16, 1924.

17. Park, "Robert Imbrie Case," 41.

18. Allen Dulles to Secretary of State, October 18, 1924, NA, 123 Im 1/397.

19. Park, "Robert Imbrie Case," 45.

20. Dulles quoting Joseph Saul Kornfeld, telegram 89 of October 10, 1924, to Secretary of State, October 18, 1924, NA, 123 Im 1/397.

21. Whiteman, *Damages in International Law*, 725–28. See also Allen Dulles to Secretary of State, October 18, 1924, NA, 123 Im 1/397, Memorandum on the Labaree Case by George Wadsworth, Near Eastern Division, October 14, 1924.

22. Allen Dulles to Secretary of State, October 18, 1924; "We Had to Threaten Persia," *New York Times*, April 21, 1905, 5.

23. Joseph Saul Kornfeld, telegram 101, August 18, 1924, 123 Im 1/189; Wallace Smith Murray, telegram 110, September 1, 1924, NA, 123 Im 1/226.

24. "Rabbi J. S. Kornfeld—A Former U.S. Envoy to Persia—Dies in Toronto Temple," *New York Times*, June 24, 1943, 21. Also see Kornfeld to President Coolidge, June 12, 1924, NA, 123 K 841/39.

25. The occasion of Kornfeld's resignation resulted in a historic moment. The first time a consul was nominated to the post of minister (thereby crossing from consular to diplomatic service) was in September 1924 when Carr recommended Robert Skinner, consul general in London and the highest-ranking official in the consular service, to replace Korn-

feld. Grew turned down the nomination, thereby damaging consular morale. Schulzinger, *Making of the Diplomatic Mind*, 119–20.

26. Allen Dulles, memo, April 23, 1923, NA, 124.916/44.

27. Schulzinger, *Making of the Diplomatic Mind*, 119. See William R. Castle to Jay Pierrepont Moffatt, January 20, 1925, Moffatt Papers, Harvard University.

28. Wallace Smith Murray, dispatch 668, October 4, 1924, NA, 123 Im 1/339.

29. George Gregg Fuller, dispatch, October 19, 1924, Correspondence, American Consulate, Teheran, NA, C 8-5.17 1924, part 2, 71.

30. George Gregg Fuller, dispatch 51, October 19, 1924, NA, 123 Im 1/363.

31. In 1931 in the essay "A Hanging," George Orwell described a similar scene in Burma, to which I allude here.

32. Allen Dulles to Secretary of State, October 18, 1924, NA, 123 Im 1/397.

33. Wallace Smith Murray, dispatch 710, October 27, 1924, NA, 123 Im 1/377.

34. Wallace Smith Murray to Secretary of State, January 22, 1925, NA, 123 Im 1/433.

35. Joseph Saul Kornfeld, telegram 96, August 13, 1924, NA, 123 Im 1/183.

36. Wallace Smith Murray, dispatch 716, October 30, 1924, NA, 123 Im 1/374.

37. On November 3, 1924, the newspaper *Iran* identified the two men as Sayyid Hossein, son of Sayyid Mousa, and Ali, son of Abou Taleb. John Randolph, American Consul, Baghdad, to George Gregg Fuller, enclosure, November 12, 1924.

38. Wallace Smith Murray, dispatch 717, November 2, 1924, NA, 123 Im 1/374.

39. Park, "Robert Imbrie Case," 42; Sherman Miles to Assistant Chief of Staff, G-2, August 31, 1924, NA, 123 Im 1/290.

40. Allen Dulles to Secretary of State, October 18, 1924, NA, 123 Im 1/397.

41. Wallace Smith Murray, dispatch 723, November 5, 1924, NA, 123 Im 1/374.

42. Wallace Smith Murray to Secretary of State, telegram 151, October 16, 1924, NA, 123 Im 1/299.

43. Wallace Smith Murray to Secretary of State, No. 694, October 19, 1924, NA, 123 Im 1/357.

44. Murray to Secretary of State, October 19, 1924.

45. Katherine Imbrie to Secretary of State, September 4, 1924, NA, 123 Im 1/490 and 502.

46. "British Army Ruler Shot by Egyptians in Streets of Cairo," *New York Times*, November 20, 1924, 1.

47. The 1924 exchange rate per British pound was $4.42.

48. Daly, "Stack, Sir Lee Oliver Fitzmaurice."

49. The use of ballistic evidence was in its infancy, but pathologist Sydney Smith, working in Egypt, had been experimenting with it for five years when Stack was murdered. With this case he was able at last to put his findings to work. Smith, *Mostly Murder*, 99–101.

50. When Joseph Grew was serving in Egypt as the U.S. consul general's private secretary, a favorite sport of the British and Americans was shooting wild pigeons, resented by the natives whose domestic pigeons were shot as well. When Denshawi villagers mobbed a shooting party and a British captain was killed and two others injured, the reprisal was grim, even sadistic. The punishment was dealt out on June 29, 1906. One man was hanged

first and left hanging while two others were flogged, another hanged, two more flogged, two more hanged, and the final two whipped. Grew, *Turbulent Era*, 25n5.

51. Constantine Brown, "Memory of Imbrie Honored by Official French Salute," *Scranton Republic*, September 15, 1924, 11.

52. Allen Dulles to Wilbur J. Carr, September 23, 1924, NA, 123 Im 1/328.

53. Katherine Imbrie to Charles Hughes, September 8, 1924, NA, 123 Im 1/328.

54. Katherine Imbrie to Charles Hughes, August 14, 1924, NA, 123 Im 1/255.

55. Katherine Imbrie to Charles Hughes, September 12, 1924, 123 Im 1/226.

56. K. Imbrie to Hughes, September 12, 1924.

57. Whiteman, *Damages in International Law*, 728.

58. Whiteman, *Damages in International Law*, 733.

59. Whiteman, *Damages in International Law*, 138.

60. Whiteman, *Damages in International Law*, 136.

61. Quoted in Whiteman, *Damages in International Law*, 566–67.

62. The U.S. government chose not to return the difference to the Persian government but to give it to Seymour.

63. Whiteman, *Damages in International Law*, 794.

64. Whiteman, *Damages in International Law*, 794–95.

65. Whiteman explains the apparent injustice to children. On average, an older child received more money than a younger child because it was easier to prove that more had been contributed to his or her care. Also, an older child may have reached a level of education that could be used to estimate the probability of continued future expenses. Whitman, *Damages in International Law*, 796.

66. Whiteman, *Damages in International Law*, 798.

67. Whiteman, *Damages in International Law*, 592.

68. "Mrs. Imbrie Sees Coolidge," *New York Times*, January 18, 1925, 21.

69. Katherine Imbrie to Calvin Coolidge, letter and enclosures, January 24, 1925, NA, 123 Im 1/419.

70. Katherine Imbrie to Calvin Coolidge, letter and enclosures, January 24, 1925, NA, 123 Im 1/419.

71. Edgar Turlington to William T. Ellis, July 17, 1925, NA, 123 Im 1/461. Turlington reports on the meeting of Allen Dulles, Dr. Packard, and Katherine Imbrie. No other record of it has been found.

72. William T. Ellis to Richard Southgate, June 8, 1925, NA, 123 Im 1/460.

73. "Biographical Sketch," *Relief of Katherine Imbrie*, Serial Set ID: 8690 H.rp., February 10, 1927, 4 pages.

74. Wallace Smith Murray to Secretary of State, November 2, 1924, NA, 123 Im 1/333.

75. "Wants Imbrie Fund Used for Students," *New York Times*, November 11, 1924, 13.

76. Wallace Smith Murray to Secretary of State, November 5, 1924, NA, 123 Im 1/381.

77. Among the defenders of Tientsin was a young couple, future U.S. president Herbert Hoover and his wife, Lou.

78. The debt, with principle and interest, totaled $46 million by the time the last installment was paid in 1939.

79. Preston, *Boxer Rebellion*, ix–xiv, 318, 397; King, "Boxer Indemnity," 678–79. See also Hunt, "American Remission," 539–59.

80. Cameron Wilkie, "Another Indemnity—This Time Persia," *Dearborn (MI) Independent*, September 9, 1925, 6. Murray, Letter to the Editor, *Dearborn Independent*, written October 6, 1925, published November 14, 1925, 1.

81. Assistant Secretary of State Frank Kellogg to Martin B. Madden and Senator Frederick H. Gillett, February 2, 1926, NA, 123 Im 1/491.

82. 68 Cong. Rec. 4720–4724 (1927).

83. 96 Cong. Rec. 15,080–15,088 (1950). HR 5731 and an identical bill, S 2342.

84. Bishop, *History of Cornell*, 403.

85. See NA, FRUS/The Near East and Africa/1947/Iran, 890–998, beginning with 891.6363/1-1147, Ambassador (George) Allen to Secretary of State, January 1, 1947, telegram.

86. See Majd, "Purchase of Armaments," 285–303.

87. Acting Secretary of State Robert Lovett to the Embassy in Iran: "Concern of the United States with the Hostile Attitude of the Soviet Union towards Iran; Political Support of Iran by the United States; The Question of Military and Economic Aid to Iran," January 3, 1948, NA, 891.24/12-947, telegram, FRUS/The Near East, South Asia, and Africa/Iran/1948, 88–90.

88. The writer and date of the letter are unidentified.

89. B-75005, April 16, 1948, 27 Comptroller General 641; Lindsay Warren, an attorney, was the third comptroller general of the United States, a former long-serving congressional representative from North Carolina with close ties to Franklin D. Roosevelt and Harry S Truman. At one time he served as House majority leader. Like Fulbright, Warren was a Democrat.

90. O'Mahoney, a Democrat, was appointed to the Senate in 1933 to fill a vacated position. He was elected for a full term in 1934 and served until 1952.

91. 96 Cong. Rec. 15,086.

92. Typical are postings such as the following: "Mrs. Robert Imbrie Plans Two Parties," *Washington Post*, February 4, 1934, Society Section, 1: "Mrs. Harlan Fiske Stone will be the guest of honor at a luncheon to be given at the Carlton Hotel February 13. Next Tuesday Mrs. Imbrie will be hostess to a bon voyage luncheon for Madame Prochnik, who will leave soon for a visit to Austria." "Mrs. Imbrie Will Entertain," *Washington Post*, October 20, 1944, Society Section, 1: "Mrs. Robert Whitney Imbrie will entertain at a 'Near East' tea Thursday, November 2, after 6 p.m. Guests of honor will be Rear Admiral and Mrs. A. Stanton Merril." In a 1955 news item, she was described as a "wealthy widow" when she entertained the new Turkish ambassador, Haydar Gork, and his wife with a "lavish luncheon." The luncheon's décor suggests that it was indeed a lavish affair. *Independent* (Helena MT), 12. The photograph accompanying the story was taken by the Washington DC studio of Harris & Ewing, known as the Photographers of National Notables.

93. Barton, *Story of Near East Relief*, 459.

94. Moskin, *American Statecraft*, 319, citing Foglesong, *America's Secret War*. Foglesong, however, does not depict Imbrie in this light, concluding only that Imbrie was enthusiastic about the possibility of the Whites overthrowing the Reds.

95. Sherwood, *There Shall Be No Night*, xxiv.

96. "Robert Sherwood Stops Finland War Play: 'There Shall Be No Night' to Close on Thursday, Called Inappropriate Now," *New York Times*, December 15, 1941, 24.

97. This notation is in the flyleaf of a copy of Sherwood, *There Shall Be No Night*. Laid in the pages is a typed note from Katherine Imbrie to the president of U.S. Steel, which is quoted in this chapter.

11. What Was Manifest

1. Wallace Smith Murray to Secretary of State, July 26, 1924, 12:00 p.m., NA, 123 Im 1/110; Murray to Secretary of State, August 10, 1924, NA, 123 Im 1/298.

2. "Tells of Imbrie's Death," *New York Times*, September 18, 1926, 34; "Henry P. Packard Tells of Near East Relief in Persia," *Canonsburg (PA) Daily Notes*, March 30, 1925, 4.

3. NA, FRUS/1924/volume 2/Persia, 1539.

4. Kazemzadeh, "Iranian Relations with Russia," 314–49; Greaves, "Relations with Britain and British India," 374–425; Hambley, "Pahlavi Autocracy," 213–43; Zirinsky, "Rise of Reza Khan," 44–77.

5. Zirinsky, "Blood, Power, and Hypocrisy," 280–81.

6. Zirinsky, "Rise of Reza Khan," 60.

7. Esme Howard, British Ambassador to the United States, to the Secretary of State, July 19, 1924, NA, 891.114 Narcotics/13 #624, FRUS/Persia/1924, 582–83.

8. "Continued Refusal by the United States to Recognize the Soviet Regime in Russia," press release issued by the Department of State, March 21, 1923, FRUS/Russia/1923, 758.

9. "Continued Refusal by the United States," 758.

10. See Wilson, *Ideology and Economics*.

11. Yerkin, *Prize*, 222.

12. Majd, *Great Britain*, 118.

13. Robert Imbrie, dispatch 42, June 14, 1924, NA, 891.628/6. See Majd, *Great Britain*, 119.

14. Millspaugh memorandum, "The Proposed Fishery Agreement with the Russians," October 23, 1924.

15. Charles C. Hart, dispatch of February 17, 1931, transcribed in Majd, *Great Britain*, 126.

16. Hart, dispatch 1158, NA, 891.44, transcribed in Majd, *Great Britain*, 124–25.

17. Emily V. Lorraine to Acting Secretary of State, July 29, 1924, NA, 123 Im 1/134.

18. Lewis K. Davis to Charles M. Hughes, July 24, 1924, NA, 123 Im 1/112.

19. Zirinsky, "Blood, Power, and Hypocrisy," 285.

20. Junius Ward, "New Shah Blamed in Imbrie Murder: Rezi Khan Accused of Starting Riots in Which Consul Lost His Life," cable to the *Washington Star* and *Chicago Daily News*, Teheran, December 18, 1925, NA, 123 Im 1/496.

21. Bradley, *Dictionary of Iran*, 1–2, 327. As has been noted, Imbrie's death predated the start of Muharram.

22. Quoted in Park, "Robert Imbrie Case," 57.

23. Norman Armour was writing on behalf of the U.S. ambassador to Italy, Henry P. Fletcher. *Il Mattino* (Naples) published the story on August 2, 1924. The translation is appended to Armour's letter, August 5, 1924, NA, 123 Im 1/191. Armour and Imbrie were

in Russia at the same time. Armour was arrested in Vologda and taken to Moscow. After he received permission to leave, he spent several tense days in Petrograd before the train was cleared for Finland, probably the same train that Imbrie used in his escape. In 1919 he married a Russian princess, whom he had helped to escape from Russia, and on April 23, 1924, he was appointed to the Rome legation.

24. Frederick Coleman to American Legation, Persia, "Murder of American Vice Consul Robert W. Imbrie," source: *Pravda* (Moscow), July 22, 1924, American Foreign Service report, July 24, 1924, NA, 123 Im 1/172.

25. George Gregg Fuller, dispatch 75, October 27, 1924, NA, 123 Im 1/392.

26. Wallace Smith Murray to Secretary of State, enclosure, October 18, 1924, NA, 123 Im 1/354; "Friend of Imbrie Says Death Due to Oil War," *New York Herald*, September 30, 1924, Paris ed.

27. Murray to Secretary of State, October 18, 1924.

28. Norman Armour to Secretary of State and Under Secretary, August 5, 1924, NA, 123 Im 1/191.

29. Sheldon Whitehouse to Secretary of State, August 21, 1924, NA, 123 Im 1/393. See also White House to Secretary of State, August 20, 1924, NA, 123 Im 1/236.

30. Ralph H. Soper, "The Imbrie Case in Tehran," March 31, 1925, sent to Secretary of State by David Starr Jordan, NA, 123 Im 1/461.

31. Bernard Gotlieb to Secretary of State, June 27, 1923, NA, 891.6363-SO/203, FRUS/Persia/1923, 713–15; Gotlieb to Secretary of State, December 20, 1923, NA, 891.6363-SO/3181/2, FRUS/Persia/1923, 720.

32. Joseph Saul Kornfeld to Secretary of State, January 5, 1924, NA, 891.6363-SO/327.

33. Dulles memorandum, January 24, 1924, NA, 891.6363-SO/328, FRUS/Persia/1924, 539. Also, Persian Minister (Alai Hosein) to the Secretary of State, February 21, 1924, NA, 891.6363-SO/347, FRUS/Persia/1924, 541.

34. Wallace Smith Murray, dispatch and enclosure, November 29, 1924, NA, 891.6363-SO/392.

35. Rubin, "Stumbling through the 'Open Door,'" 228.

36. Allen Dulles to Coffin, November 20, 1925, NA, 891.6363-SO/407.

37. Wallace Smith Murray, dispatch 953, March 8, 1925, NA, 891.6363-SO/399.

38. Wallace Smith Murray, dispatch 1045, May 4, 1925, NA, 891.6363-SO/403.

39. Dulles to Coffin, November 20, 1925.

40. Zirinsky, "Imperial Power and Dictatorship," 639–63, 664–65.

41. Zirinsky, "Imperial Power and Dictatorship," 647.

42. Zirinsky, "Blood, Power, and Hypocrisy," 292n68.

43. Zirinsky, "Imperial Power and Dictatorship," 655.

44. Zirinsky, "Blood, Power, and Hypocrisy," 284.

45. The name was probably chosen to evoke an ancient Persian dynasty that ruled for four hundred years. Amanat, *Iran*, 440. British sentiment, quoted in Zirinsky, "Imperial Power and Dictatorship," 657.

46. "Army & Navy: Lobbyist Shearer," *Time*, September 2, 1929, 15; Fanning, *Peace and Disarmament*, 66.

47. Fanning, *Peace and Disarmament*, 65–66.

48. Kitchens, *Shearer Scandal*, ix.

49. Kitchen, *Shearer Scandal*, 214.

50. U.S. Congress, Senate, Subcommittee of the Committee on Naval Affairs, Hearings: Alleged Activities of William B. Shearer in Behalf of Certain Shipbuilding Companies at the Geneva Conference and at Meetings of the Preparatory Commission, 71st Cong., 1st Sess., 1930, 544.

51. "U.S. Naval Inquiry: Mr. Shearer's Evidence," *The Times* (London), October 2, 1929, issue 45323, 14.

52. Zirinsky, "Imperial Power and Dictatorship," 648. These three grand ayatollahs had been deported by the British from Iraq. One of them became the teacher and mentor of the Ayatollah Khomeini, who became the founder of the Islamic Republic of Iran in 1979. Amanat, *Iran*, 433–34.

53. Zirinsky, "Blood, Power, and Hypocrisy," 282.

54. Quoted in Zirinksy, "Blood, Power, and Hypocrisy," 283.

55. Zirinsky, "Blood, Power, and Hypocrisy," 284.

56. Pollack, *Persian Puzzle*, 33.

57. Pollack, *Persian Puzzle*, 28–29.

58. See Ghani, *Iran and the Rise*.

59. Majd, *Great Britain*, 9.

60. Wallace Smith Murray, dispatch 663, September 28, 1924, NA, 891.00/1306.

61. Hoffman Philip, dispatch 543, February 21, 1928, NA, 891.00/1439.

62. Charles Hart, dispatch 1339, January 26, 1933, NA, 891.44/Teymourtache, Abdol H.K./4. Hart later became an oil executive and signed the treaty giving a north oil concession to an American oil company, Amiranian Oil, in 1936, which was relinquished in 1938 partly due to new oil discoveries in Saudi Arabia. DeNovo, *American Interests*, 315.

63. Majd, *Great Britain*, 10–11.

64. Millspaugh, *Americans in Persia*, 85.

65. Wallace Smith Murray to Secretary of State, October 16, 1924, NA, 123 Im 1/353.

66. Murray to Secretary of State, October 16, 1924.

67. Charles Hart, dispatch 947, November 7, 1931, NA, 891.00/1534.

68. Majd, *Great Britain*, 103–4.

69. Joseph Saul Kornfeld, dispatch 244, August 21, 1923, NA, 891.51A/115.

70. Charles Hart, dispatch 16, February 11, 1930, NA, 123 H 255/75.

71. Charles Hart, dispatch 1339, January 26, 1933, NA, 891.44, Teymourtache, Abdol H.K./4.

72. William Hornibrook, dispatch 275, November 28, 1931, NA, 891.00/1598; Hornibrook, dispatch 281, December 4, 1934, NA, 891.00/1599.

73. James Childs, dispatch 416, April 15, 1935, NA, 891.131/4, quoted in Majd, *Great Britain*, 199.

74. Zirinksy, "Blood, Power, and Hypocrisy," 286.

75. Zirinsky, "Blood, Power, and Hypocrisy," 286.

76. Yerkin, *Prize*, 247.

77. Lenczowski, *Middle East in World Affairs*, 183.

78. Lenczowski, *Middle East in World Affairs*, 185–86. See also Fatemi, *Oil Diplomacy*, 103.

79. Lenczowski, *Middle East in World Affairs*, 183.

80. Allen Dulles to William Phillips, October 23, 1923, NA, 123 Im 1/304.

81. State Department letter to Carr, September 21, 1923, Imbrie Personnel Corresponds file.

82. Imbrie to Alexander Munro Barton, April 20, 1921, held in the Alexander Munro Barton files, 92107-10, V, Hoover Institution Archives, Stanford University.

83. Quoted in "Our Consul Lynched in Persia," *Literary Digest*, August 9, 1924, 14.

84. "Heroism of Ambulance Drivers Win Decorations," *Washington Times*, March 17, 1918, 1.

85. Shaw, "Why Enter the Foreign Service?," in Newberry, *Foreign Service Reader*, 31–32. Newberry remarks that the spirit of adventuresomeness was still valued in 1997 when he compiled the essays for his book.

86. Warren, "Hemingway," 1–2.

87. Katouzian, *State and Society*, 290. The quotation alludes to the soldiers in the Pahlavi regiment responsible for killing Imbrie as being Armenian, but there is no other reference to an Armenian involvement in Imbrie's death in the documents, other than aid offered to Imbrie at the fountain. The prince regent seems to be scapegoating the Armenians for Imbrie's murder.

BIBLIOGRAPHY

Agar, Augustus. *Baltic Episode: A Classic of Secret Service in Russian Waters*. London: Hodder and Stoughton, 1963.

Amanat, Abbas. *Iran: A Modern History*. New Haven: Yale University Press, 2017.

Anderson, Stuart. *Immigration*. Santa Barbara CA: Greenwood, 2010.

Andrew, Abram Piatt. *Friends of France: The Field Service of the American Ambulance Described by Its Members*. New York: Houghton Mifflin, 1916.

Applebaum, Anne. *Gulag: A History*. New York: Doubleday, 2003.

———. *Red Famine: Stalin's War on Ukraine*. New York: Doubleday, 2017.

Asgarov, Asgar M. "Reporting from the Frontlines of the First Cold War: American Diplomatic Despatches about the Internal Conditions in the Soviet Union, 1917–1933." PhD diss., University of Maryland, 2007.

Atabaki, Touraj, and Erik J. Zurcher. *Men of Order: Authoritarian Modernization under Ataturk and Rezah Shah*. London: I. B. Tauris, 2004.

Avery, Peter, G. R. G. Hambly, and C. P. Melville, eds. *Cambridge History of Iran*. Vol. 7, *From Nadir Shah to the Islamic Republic*. Cambridge: Cambridge University Press, 1991.

Bacino, Leo J. *Reconstructing Russia: U.S. Policy in Revolutionary Russia, 1917–1922*. Kent OH: Kent State University Press, 2009.

Baedeker, Karl. *Russia with Tehran, Port Arthur, and Peking*. New York: Charles Scribner's Sons, 1914.

Bailey, Frederick M. *Mission to Tashkent*. Oxford: Oxford University Press, 1992.

Bainton, Roy. *Honoured by Strangers: The Life of Captain Francis Cromie*. Shrewsbury, England: Airlife, 2002.

Barnes, Harper. *Standing on a Volcano: The Life and Times of David Rowland Francis*. St. Louis: Missouri Historical Society, 2001.

Barton, James L. *Story of Near East Relief*. New York: Macmillan, 1930.

Bernstein, Mark F. "An American Hero in Iran." *Princeton Alumni Weekly* 107, no. 13 (2007): 23–25.

Berthlesen, Bert. *The Tin Can Man: Memoirs of Destroyer Duty after World War I*. New York: Exposition Press, 1963.

Best, Gary Dean. "Food Relief as Price Support: Hoover and American Pork, January–March 1919." *Agricultural History* 45, no. 2 (April 1971): 79–84. https://www.jstor.org/stable/3742071.

Bishop, Morris. *A History of Cornell*. Ithaca NY: Cornell University Press, 1962.

The Booklist: A Guide to the Best New Books. Vol. 15, *October 1918–July 1919*. Chicago: American Library Association Publishing Board, 1919.

Boot, Max. *The Savage Wars of Peace: Small Wars and the Rise of American Power*. Rev. ed. New York: Basic Books, 2014.

Bradley, D. [Duncan] L. [Lee]. *Dictionary of Iran: A Shorter Encyclopedia*. 2nd ed. Ruidoso NM: Khaneh-ye-Entesharha-ye-Navisandegan, 2015.

Brownell, Will, and Richard N. Billings. *So Close to Greatness: A Biography of William C. Bullitt*. New York: Macmillan, 1987.

Brüggemann, Karsten. "Defending National Sovereignty against Two Russias: Estonia in the Russian Civil War, 1918–1920." *Journal of Baltic Studies* 34, no. 1 (Spring 2003): 22–51.

Bryant, Louise. *Six Months in Red Russia*. New York: George H. Dorant, 1918. http://digital.library.upenn.edu/women/bryant/russia/russia-IV.html.

Bryson, Thomas A. "Admiral Mark L. Bristol, an Open-Door Diplomat in Turkey." *International Journal of Middle East Studies* 5, no. 4 (1974): 450–67.

Burgess, Anthony. *Earthly Powers*. New York: Simon and Schuster, 1980.

Carley, Michael Jabara. *Revolution and Intervention: The French Government and the Russian Civil War, 1917–1919*. Montreal: McGill-Queen's University Press, 1983.

"Chronicle of International Events." *American Journal of International Law* 3, no. 1 (1909).

Clark, Coleman Tileston, and Salter Storrs Clark Jr. *Soldier Letters*. Privately printed, 1919.

Cook, Andrew. *Ace of Spies: The True Story of Sidney Reilly*. 2nd ed. London: History Press, 2004.

Cook, Ralph E. "The United States and the Armenian Question, 1894–1924." PhD diss., Tufts University Fletcher School, 1957.

Cronin, Stephanie, ed. *The Making of Modern Iran: State and Society under Riza Shah, 1921–1941*. New York: RoutledgeCurzon, 2003.

Crosley, Pauline S. *Intimate Letters from Petrograd*. New York: E. P. Hutton, 1920. https://archive.org/details/intimateletters00crosgoog.

Currier, Richard C., ed. *Seaman's Branch of the Legal Aid Society*. 2nd ed. New York: Seaman's Branch of the Legal Aid Society, 1906.

Dahl, Hans Fredrik. *Quisling: A Study in Treachery*. Cambridge: Cambridge University Press, 1999.

Daly, M. W. "Stack, Sir Lee Oliver Fitzmaurice (1868–1924)." In *Oxford Dictionary of National Biography*, edited by H. C. G. Matthew and Brian Harrison. Oxford: Oxford University Press, 2004. Online ed., edited by Lawrence Goldman, 2011, https://www.oxforddnb.com/.

Davis, Louis K. "What to Do for Armenia." *Literary Digest* 65 (June 26, 1920): 22–23.

Dearborn, Mary V. *Queen of Bohemia: The Life of Louise Bryant*. Boston: Houghton Mifflin, 1996.

Demirici, Sevtap. "The Lausanne Conference: The Evolution of Turkish and British Diplomatic Strategies, 1922–1923." Diss., London School of Economics and Political Science, 1997. http://search.proquest.com/docview/301555981.

Dennis, Ralph Brownell. *Russia in Revolution and Its Lesson to America: An Address Delivered Before the Union League Club of Chicago, December 12, 1918*. Chicago: Union League Club of Chicago, 1919. Available at Google Books.

DeNovo, John A. *American Interests and Policies in the Middle East, 1900–1939*. Minneapolis: University of Minnesota Press, 1963.

———. "The Movement for an Aggressive American Oil Policy Abroad, 1918–1920." *American Historical Review* 61, no. 4 (1956): 854–76.

Dinnerstein, Leonard. *Antisemitism in America*. New York: Oxford University Press, 1995.

Dobkin, Marjorie Housepian. *Smyrna: The Destruction of a City*. Kent OH: Kent State University Press, 1988.

Dos Passos, John. *Three Soldiers*. New York: George H. Doran, 1921.

Dukes, Paul. *Red Dusk and the Morrow*, New York: Doubleday, Page, 1922.

Egan, Timothy. *The Worst Hard Time*. New York: Houghton Mifflin, 2005.

Etkind, Alexander. *Roads Not Taken: An Intellectual Biography of William Christian Bullitt*. Pittsburgh: University of Pittsburgh Press, 2017.

Fanning, Richard W. *Peace and Disarmament: Naval Rivalry and Arms Control, 1922–1933*. Lexington: University of Kentucky Press, 2015.

Fatemi, Nasrollah S. *Oil Diplomacy; Powderkeg in Iran*. New York: Whittier Books, 1954.

Fenton, Charles A. "Ambulance Drivers in France and Italy: 1914–1918." *American Quarterly* 3, no. 4 (1951): 326–43.

Ferguson, Harry. *Operation Kronstadt: The Greatest True Tale of Espionage to Come Out of the Early Years of MI6*. New York: Overlook Press, 2009.

Ferrier, Ronald W., and J. H. Bamberg. *The History of the British Petroleum Company*. Vol. 1, *The Developing Years, 1901–1932*. Cambridge: Cambridge University Press, 1982.

Fink, Leon. *Sweatshops at Sea: Merchant Seamen in the World's First Globalized Industry, from 1812 to the Present*. Chapel Hill: University of North Carolina Press, 2011.

Fischel, Walter J. "The Jews of Persia, 1795–1940." *Jewish Social Studies* 12, no. 2 (April 1950): 119–60.

Foglesong, David S. *America's Secret War against Bolshevism: U.S. Intervention in the Russian Civil War, 1917–1920*. Chapel Hill: University of North Carolina Press, 1995.

———. "Redeeming Russia: American Missionaries and Tsarist Russia, 1886–1917." *Religion, State & Society* 25, no. 4 (1997): 353–68.

Foran, John, ed. *A Century of Revolution: Social Movements in Iran*. Minneapolis: University of Minnesota Press, 1994.

Franz, Kathleen. *Tinkering: Consumers Reinvent the Early Automobile*. Philadelphia: University of Pennsylvania Press, 2011.

"From the Report of Ebertha Roelofs and Gladys Cline, Representatives for Russian Work in Finland, March 1 to April 15, 1920." *Association Monthly, Official Organ of the Young Women's Christian Association* 14, no. 7–12 (1920): 414–15. https://babel.hathitrust.org/cgi/pt?id=wu.89065731622;view=1up;seq=148.

Ghani, Cyrus. *Iran and the Rise of Reza Shah: From Qajar Collapse to Pahlavi Power*. London: I. B. Tauris, 1998.

Gliddon, Gerald. *Somme 1916: A Battlefield Companion*. Stroud, Gloucestershire: History Press, 2009.

Gould, John Wells. "Robert Imbrie Smith." *Proceedings of the American Philosophical Society* 155, no. 1 (March 2011): 109–14. https://www.questia.com/library/journal/1P3-2420669581/robert-imbrie-smith.

Greaves, Rose. "Relations with Britain and British India, 1798–1921." In Avery, Hambly, and Melville, *Cambridge History of Iran*, 374–425.

Grew, Joseph C. *Turbulent Era: A Diplomatic Record of Forty Years, 1904–1945*. Edited by Walter Johnson and assisted by Nancy Harvison Hooker. Boston: Houghton Mifflin, 1962.

Grose, Peter. *Gentleman Spy: The Life of Allen Dulles*. Boston: Houghton Mifflin, 1994.

Haller, John S., Jr. *Battlefield Medicine: A History of the Military Ambulance from the Napoleonic Wars through World War I*. 1992; rev. ed., Carbondale: Southern Illinois University Press, 2011.

Halsey, William Frederick, with Joseph Bryan. *Admiral Halsey's Story*. New York: Whittlesey House, 1947. https://archive.org/details/AdmiralHalseysStory.

Hambley, Gavin R. G. "The Pahlavi Autocracy: Reza Shah, 1921–1941." In Avery, Hambly, and Melville, *Cambridge History of Iran*, 213–43.

Hansen, Arlen J. *Gentlemen Volunteers: The Story of American Ambulance Drivers in the Great War, August 1914–September 1918*. New York: Arcade, 1996.

Hassell, James E. "Russian Refugees in France and the United States between the World Wars." *Transactions of the American Philosophical Society* 81, no. 7 (1991).

Heath, Maj. Ferry K. "Needs of Finland and Esthonia." *American Relief Administration Bulletin* (U.S. government) 14 (June 20, 1919).

Heinrichs, Waldo H., Jr. *American Ambassador: Joseph C. Grew and the Development of the United States Diplomatic Tradition*. Boston: Little, Brown, 1966.

Hemingway, Ernest. *Dateline, Toronto: The Complete Toronto Star Dispatches, 1920–1924*. Edited by William White. New York: Charles Scribner's Sons, 1985.

Hendricks, Helen, ed. *Report of the Overseas Committee of the War Work Council of the Young Women's Christian Association, 1917–1920*. New York: Publication Department, National Board, Young Women's Christian Association, 1921. https://iiif.lib.harvard.edu/manifests/view/drs:2580645$96i.

Hibben, Paxton. "How Can We Help Armenia? Weighing Armenia in the Balance." *Current Opinion* 69 (1920): 37.

Hill, George A. *Go Spy the Land*. London: Cassell, 1932.

Hoover, Herbert. *The Memoirs of Herbert Hoover*. Vol. 1, *Years of Adventure, 1874–1920*. New York: Macmillan, 1951.

Hunt, Michael H. "The American Remission of the Boxer Indemnity: A Reappraisal." *Journal of Asian Studies* 31, no. 3 (May 1972): 539–59. doi:10.2307/2052233.

Imbrie, Boyd Vincent, Mary E. Philbrook, and Addison Murray Imbrie. *Genealogy of the Imbrie Family of Western Pennsylvania: Descendants of James Imbrie, Pioneer Settler and His Wife Euphemia Smart*. Pittsburgh: D. H. Lucas, 1953.

Imbrie, Robert W. "Across Albania in an Ambulance." *Travel* 30, no. 6 (April 1918): 12–16, 37.

———. *Behind the Wheel of a War Ambulance*. New York: Robert M. McBride, 1918.

———. "Crossing Asia Minor, the Country of the New Turkish Republic." *National Geographic* 46 (1924): 444–72.

———. "The Jurisdiction of the Federal Courts in Admiralty." Master of Laws, Yale Law School, 1906.

———. "Polyglot Salonica: Being the Impressions of a Driver in the American Ambulance Field Service." *Travel* 32, no. 1 (November 1918): 1–15, 42.

Irwin, Will. *The Making of a Reporter*. New York: Putnam, 1942.

Jastrow, Morris. *The War and the Baghdad Rail Way: The Story of Asia Minor and Its Relation to the Present Conflict*. 1917; rev. ed., Philadelphia: J. B. Lippincott Company, 1918. https://archive.org/stream/warandthebagdadr001985mbp#page/n185/mode/2up/search/Adana.

Jenkins, Mark, ed. *Worlds to Explore: Classic Tales of Travel & Adventure from National Geographic*. Foreword by Simon Winchester. Washington DC: National Geographic Society, 2006.

Katouzian, Homa. "Miracles at the *Saqqa-khanih*: Power Struggles, Baha'i Pogrom and Murder of the American Envoy in Tehran." *British Journal of Middle Eastern Studies* 40, no. 3 (October 2013): 295–304.

——. *State and Society in Iran: The Eclipse of the Qajars and the Emergence of the Pahlavis*. London: I. B. Tauris, 2006.

Kazemzadeh, F. "Iranian Relations with Russia and the Soviet Union." In Avery, Hambly, and Melville, *Cambridge History of Iran*, 314–49.

Keegan, John. *The First World War*. New York: Alfred Knopf, 1999.

———. *An Illustrated History of the First World War*. New York: Alfred Knopf, 2001.

Kelly, Lawrence. *Diplomacy and Murder in Tehran: Alexander Griboyedov and Imperial Russia's Mission to the Shah of Persia*. London: I. B. Tauris, 2002.

Kenez, Peter. *Civil War in South Russia, 1919–1920: The Defeat of the Whites*. Berkeley: University of California Press, 1977.

Kennan, George F. *The Decision to Intervene*. Princeton NJ: Princeton University Press, 1958.

———. *Russia Leaves the War*. Princeton NJ: Princeton University Press, 1958.

———. "The Sisson Documents." *Journal of Modern History* 28, no. 2 (1956): 130–54.

Kesaris, Paul, ed. *Confidential U.S. Diplomatic Post Records: Russia and the Soviet Union; Part 1 From Czar to Commissars, 1914–1918*. Frederick MD: University Publications of America, 1982. Microfilm.

King, Frank H. H. "The Boxer Indemnity." *Modern Asia Studies* 40, no. 3 (July 2006): 663–89. http://www.jstor.org/stable/3876542.

Kinzer, Stephen. *All the Shah's Men*. New York: John Wiley & Sons, 2003.

Kitchens, Joseph H. "The Shearer Scandal and Its Origins: Big Navy Politics and Diplomacy in the 1920's." Diss., University of Georgia, 1968.

Koppes, Clayton R. "Captain Mahan, General Gordon, and the Origins of the Term 'Middle East.'" *Middle Eastern Studies* 12, no. 1 (1976): 95–98. http://www.jstor.org/stable/4282584.

Kukk, Hilja. "The Failure of Iudenich's Northwestern Army in 1919: A Dissenting White Russian View." *Journal of Baltic Studies* 12, no. 4 (Winter 1981): 362–83.

Langbart, David A. "Five Months in Petrograd in 1918: Robert W. Imbrie and the US Search for Information in Russia." *Studies in Intelligence: Journal of the American Intelligence Professional* 52, no. 1 (March 2008).

———. "'No Little Historic Value': The Records of Department of State Posts in Revolutionary Russia." *Prologue Magazine* 40, no. 1 (Spring 2008). http://www.archives.gov/publications/prologue/2008/spring/langbart.html.

Langley, Harold D. "The Hunt for American Archives in the Soviet Union." *American Archivist* 20 (April 1966): 265–75.

Lehtinen, Vilja. "'America Would Lose Its Soul': The Immigration Restriction Debate, 1920–1924." Master's thesis, University of Helsinki, 2002. https://helda.helsinki.fi/handle/10138/19601.

Lenczowski, George. *The Middle East in World Affairs*. Ithaca NY: Cornell University Press, 1962.

Livesey, Anthony. *The Historical Atlas of World War I*. New York: Henry Holt, 1994.

Lockhart, R. H. Bruce. *Memoirs of a British Agent*. New York: G. P. Putnam's Sons, 1933.

Lowry, Edward G. "Diplomatic and Social Life at Turkish Capital: Many Disillusions about Preconceived Notions of Ottoman Customs and Conventions." *Philadelphia Public Ledger*, April 27, 1923. Reprint, *American Consular Bulletin*, August 1923, 248–49.

Macleod, Jenny. "Ellis Ashmead-Bartlett, War Correspondence and the First World War." In *War, Journalism and History: War Correspondents in the Two World Wars*, edited by Yvonne T. McEwen and Fiona A. Fisken, 31–48. Oxford: Peter Lang, 2012.

Majd, Mohammad Gholi. *Great Britain and Reza Shah: The Plunder of Iran, 1921–1941*. Gainesville: University Press of Florida, 2001.

———. *Oil and the Killing of the American Consul in Tehran*. Lanham MD: University Press of America, 2006.

———. "The Purchase of Armaments, 1928–1941." In Majd, *Great Britain and Reza Shah*, 285–303.

Malkasian, Mark. "The Disintegration of the Armenian Cause in the United States, 1918–1927." *International Journal of Middle East Studies* 16, no. 3 (1984): 349–65.

Mango, Andrew. *Ataturk: The Biography of the Founder of Modern Turkey*. New York: Overlook Press/Peter Mayer, 1999.

Merridale, Catherine. *Lenin on the Train*. New York: Metropolitan Books, 2017.

Miller, Floyd. *The Wild Children of the Urals*. New York: E. P. Dutton, 1965.

Millspaugh, Arthur Chester. *The American Task in Persia*. New York: Century Club, 1925.

Moore, Benjamin Burges. *From Moscow to the Persian Gulf: Being the Journal of a Disenchanted Traveller in Turkestan and Persia*. New York: G. P. Putnam's Sons, 1915.

Moose, Eleanor Wood. "The Russians of Saloniki." In Newberry, *Foreign Service Reader*, 173–75.

Morgenthau, Henry. *Ambassador Morgenthau's Story: A Personal Account of the Armenian Genocide*. New York: Doubleday, Page, 1918.

Morris, Benny, and Dror Ze'Evi. *The Thirty-Year Genocide: Turkey's Destruction of Its Christian Minorities, 1894–1924*. Cambridge MA: Harvard University Press, 2019.

Morse, Edward. *The Vanguard of American Volunteers*. New York: Charles Scribner's Sons, 1918.

Moskin, J. Robert. *American Statecraft: The Story of the U.S. Foreign Service*. New York: St. Martin's Press, 2013.

Moukhanoff, Michael. *Nelka: Mrs. Helen De Smirnoff Moukhanoff, 1878–1963: A Biographical Sketch*. 1964. E-text prepared by John Young Le Bourgeois for Project Gutenberg, http://www.gutenberg.org/ebooks/22655?msg=welcome_stranger.

Naficy, Hamid. "Lured by the East: Ethnographic and Expedition Films about Nomadic Tribes—The Case of *Grass* (1925)." In *Virtual Voyages: Cinema and Travel*, edited by Jeffrey Ruoff, 117–38. Durham NC: Duke University Press, 2006.

Naimark, Norman M. *Fires of Hatred: Ethnic Cleansing in Twentieth-Century Europe*. Cambridge MA: Harvard University Press, 2002.

Nelson, John P., ed. *Letters and Diaries of David T. Nelson, 1914–1919*. Decorah IA: Anundsen, 1996.

Newberry, Daniel Oliver, comp. and ed. *The Foreign Service Reader: Selected Articles from 77 Years of the Foreign Service Journal*. Washington DC: American Foreign Service Association, 1997.

O'Brien, Phillips Payson. "The American Press, Public, and the Reaction to the Outbreak of the First World War." *Diplomatic History* 37, no. 3 (2013): 446–47.

Occleshaw, Michael. *Dances in Deep Shadows: The Clandestine War in Russia, 1917–1920*. New York: Carroll & Graf, 2006.

"Of Maps and Mapmakers." *New Near East* 6, no. 1 (October 1920): 3–6.

Olson, Russell G. "The Evolution of the American Field Service and Its Effect on American Engagement in WWI, 1914–1917." Master's thesis, California State University at Chico, 2014.

Palmer, Alan W. *The Gardeners of Salonika: The Macedonian Campaign, 1915–1918*. New York: Simon Shuster, 1965.

Park, Alan H. "The Robert Imbrie Case." Master's thesis in partial fulfillment of the requirements set forth by the Department of the Army and Princeton University for the Foreign Area Specialist Training Program, Princeton University, 1957.

Pease, Zeph W. *History of New Bedford*. New York: Lewis Historical, 1918.

Philpot, William. *Three Armies on the Somme: The First Battle of the Twentieth Century*. New York: Alfred Knopf, 2010.

Plischke, Elmer. *U.S. Department of State: A Reference History*. Westport CT: Greenwood Press, 1999.

Pollack, Kenneth M. *The Persian Puzzle: The Conflict between Iran and America*. New York: Random House, 2005.

Poole, DeWitt Clinton. *American Diplomat in Bolshevik Russia*. Edited by Lorraine M. Lees and William S. Rodner. Madison: University of Wisconsin Press, 2015.

Preston, Diana. *The Boxer Rebellion: The Dramatic Story of China's War on Foreigners That Shook the World in the Summer of 1900*. New York: Berkley Books, 2000.

Reed, Howard A. "Turkey and Her Nationalist Leaders as Seen in the 1923 Reports of Louise Bryant." In *Studies in Ataturk's Turkey: The American Dimension*, edited by George Sellers and Nur Bilge Criss, 83–95. Leiden, Netherlands: Koninklijke Brill NV, 2009.

Remey, Charles Mason. "Frontispiece." *Baha'i Magazine* 15, no. 9 (December 1924): 250. http://bahai.works/Star_of_the_West/Volume_15/Issue_9.

Rice, Philip Sidney. *An American Crusader at Verdun*. Princeton NJ: Self-published, 1918. Available at HathiTrust Digital Library.

Rice, William Gorham, Jr., and George C. Brown. "With the Ambulance Service in France: The Wartime Letters of William Gorham Rice, Jr." *Wisconsin Magazine of History* 64, no. 4 (Summer 1981): 278–93.

Rich, Jeremy. "Ida Vera Simonton's Imperial Masquerades: Intersections of Gender, Race and African Expertise in Progressive-Era America." *Gender & History* 22, no. 2 (2010): 322–40.

———. *Missing Links: The African and American Worlds of R. L. Garner, Primate Collector*. Athens: University of Georgia Press, 2012.

Rinehart, Mary Roberts. *Nomad's Land*. New York: George H. Doran, 1926.

"Robert W. Imbrie." *American Foreign Service Journal*, November 1924.

Roosevelt, Theodore. *African Game Trails: An Account of the African Wanderings of an American Hunter-Naturalist*. New York: Charles Scribner's Sons, 1910.

Rubin, Michael, A. "Stumbling through the 'Open Door': The U.S. in Persia and the Standard-Sinclair Oil Dispute, 1920–1925." *Iranian Studies* 28, no. 3/4 (Summer–Autumn, 1995): 203–29.

Ruffino, Roberta, and Stefania Chizari. *Where the Border Stands: From War Ambulances to Intercultural Exchanges*. Milan: Ulrico Hoepli Editore, 2014.

Rustam-Bek, Boris. *Aerial Russia: The Romance of the Giant Aeroplane*. New York: John Lane, 1916.

Schulzinger, Robert D. *The Making of the Diplomatic Mind: The Training, Outlook, and Style of United States Foreign Service Officers, 1908–1931*. Middletown CT: Wesleyan University Press, 1975.

Sebestyan, Victor. *Lenin: The Man, the Dictator, and the Master of Terror*. New York: Knopf Doubleday, 2017.

Service, Robert. "The Land God Forgot." In *The Spell of the Yukon and Other Poems*. Mineola NY: Dover, 2012.

Seymour, James W. D., ed. *History of the American Field Service Told by Its Members with Illustrations*. Vol. 3. Boston: Houghton Mifflin/Riverside Press, 1920.

———. *Memorial Volume of the American Field Service in France: "Friends of France."* Boston: American Field Service, 1921.

Shaw, G. Howland. "Why Enter the Foreign Service?" In Newberry, *Foreign Service Reader*, 31–32.

Shenk, Robert. *America's Black Sea Fleet: The U.S. Navy amidst War and Revolution, 1919–1923*. Annapolis MD: Naval Institute Press, 2012.

Sherwood, Robert E. *There Shall Be No Night*. New York: Charles Scriber's Sons, 1940.

Shuster, William Morgan. *The Strangling of Persia: A Personal Narrative*. New York: Century, 1912.

Smith, Sydney. *Mostly Murder*. New York: David McKay, 1960.

Solano, Solito. "Constantinople Today." *National Geographic* 41, no. 6 (June 1922): 647–80.

Srodes, James. *Allen Dulles: Master of Spies*. Washington DC: Regnery, 1999.

Stevenson, William Yorke. *At the Front in a Flivver*. New York: Houghton Mifflin, 1917.

———. *From "Poilu" to "Yank": Section No. 1, American Ambulance.* Boston: Houghton Mifflin, 1918.

Teague-Jones, Reginald (alias Ronald Sinclair). *Adventures in Persia: To India by the Back Door.* London: Victor Gollancz, 1990.

Thompson, John M. *Russia, Bolshevism, and the Versailles Peace.* Princeton NJ: Princeton University Press, 1966.

Trask, Roger R. *The United States Response to Turkish Nationalism and Reform, 1914–1939.* Minneapolis: University of Minnesota Press, 1971.

Tredwell, Roger C. "Bolsheviki Days." *American Consular Bulletin* 3, no. 9 (1921): 9–12.

Tsadik, Daniel. *Between Foreigners and Shi'is: Nineteenth-Century Iran and Its Jewish Minority.* Stanford CA: Stanford University Press, 2007.

Turlington, Edgar. "The Financial Independence of Persia." *Foreign Affairs* 6, no. 4 (July 1928): 658–67.

Venn, Fiona. "Oleaginous Diplomacy: Oil, Anglo-American Relations and the Lausanne Conference, 1922–1923." *Diplomacy and Statecraft* 20 (2009): 414–33.

Wakefield, Alan, and Simon Moody. *Under the Devil's Eye: The British Experience in Macedonia, 1915-1918.* Barnsley, South Yorkshire: Pen & Sword Military, 2010 (originally published by Sutton, 2004).

Warren, Robert Penn. "Hemingway." *Kenyon Review* 9, no. 1 (Winter 1947): 1–28.

Weeks, Charles J. *An American Naval Diplomat in Revolutionary Russia: The Life and Times of Admiral Newton A. McCully.* Annapolis MD: Naval Institute Press, 1993.

West, Rachel. *The Department of State on the Eve of the First World War.* Athens: University of Georgia Press, 1978.

Whiteman, Marjorie M. *Damages in International Law.* Vol. 1. Washington DC: U.S. Department of State, 1943.

Wilber, Donald N. *Riza Shah Pahlavi: The Resurrection and Reconstruction of Iran.* Hicksville NY: Exposition Press, 1975.

Willett, Robert L. *Russian Sideshow: America's Undeclared War, 1918–1920.* Washington DC: Potomac Books, 2003.

Williams, Joseph A. *Four Years before the Mast: A History of New York's Maritime College.* Bronx NY: Fort Schuyler Press, 2013.

Wilson, Joan Hoff. *Ideology and Economics: US Relations with the Soviet Union, 1918–1933.* Columbia: University of Missouri Press, 1974.

Winant, Cornelius. "A Soldier's Manuscript." Privately printed, 1919.

Yerkin, David. *The Prize: The Epic Quest for Oil, Money & Power with a New Epilogue.* New York: Free Press, 2009.

Zirinsky, Michael P. "Blood, Power, and Hypocrisy: The Murder of Robert Imbrie and American Relations with Pahlavi Iran, 1924." *International Journal of Middle East Studies* 18, no. 3 (1986): 275–92.

———. "Imperial Power and Dictatorship: Britain and the Rise of Reza Shah, 1921–1926." *International Journal of Middle East Studies* 24, no. 4 (1992): 639–63.

———. "The Rise of Reza Khan." In Foran, *A Century of Revolution*, 44–77.

———. "Riza Shah's Abrogation of Capitulations, 1927–1928." In Cronin, *The Making of Modern Iran*, 81–98.

INDEX

RI stands for Robert Whitney Imbrie.